THE CIVIL WAR IN HAMPSHIRE

Published by Rowanvale Books

Landford, Salisbury, Wiltshire, England

COPYRIGHT (c) 2000 by Tony MacLachlan

ISBN 0 9530785 3 1

All rights reserved. No part of this publication may be reproduced, stored in a retrieval system or transmitted in any form or by any means: electronic, mechanical, photocopying, recording or otherwise, without the prior written permission of the publishers.

Also by the same author

'The Civil War in Wiltshire'
Published in 1997 by Rowanvale Books
ISBN 0 9530785 0 7

Printed and bound by The Cromwell Press LTD, Trowbridge, England
Cover production and photos scanned by ColorTech, Southampton

THE CIVIL WAR IN HAMPSHIRE

Tony MacLachlan

Rowanvale Books

ACKNOWLEDGEMENTS

Several people have contributed in various ways to the production of this book and I would obviously wish to pay due credit to each of these. I am particularly grateful to my son, Tim, an I.T. expert, for converting my crude drawings into legible maps and conscientiously typesetting the final text.

I must also thank all those who read the text and offered advice and suggestions, most of which I accepted without any argument. I am particularly grateful to Alan Turton, the Site Manager of Basing House, for his extensive help during my visit to Basing and then reading my text. Thanks must also go to Richard Sawyer, an expert on the Battle of Cheriton and on the City of Winchester, for providing me with valuable information and advice and for allowing me access to his own extensive archives and written works. I would also wish to pay tribute to Stephen Ings, a local historian, whose profound knowledge of times past and meticulous eye for accuracy helped me to avoid some of the pitfalls into which I would probably have fallen, and to my daughter-in-law, Joanne, for reading the script.

It is fitting to pay some tribute to the Rev. George Nelson Godwin, author of the original 'The Civil War in Hampshire' whose 1904 publication provided the structure on which much of the present book is based.

I have also to acknowledge the assistance provided by the staff of the Local Studies Library in Winchester and the County Records Offices of Hampshire and the Isle of Wight, both of which organisations also kindly gave permission to re-produce some of the illustrations and texts used in the book.

Amongst other organisations that must be thanked are the Bodleian Library in Oxford and the British Library in London. Some of their manuscripts have provided me with valuable information and I am grateful to the staff of both libraries for their permission to use these texts. Perhaps I should also publicly thank the Chief Librarian of Poole Library for permission to re-produce a map of the town.

Lastly, I must pay some tribute to the combatants and their families, the men and women of the 17th Century, whose quarrels and actions have provided the material fabric of this book. If they had chosen not to argue, I would have been forced to write about something else instead.

Disclaimer: Every effort has been made to investigate where copyright exists, and lack of any acknowledgement in this text indicates that no evidence of copyright has been found.

ISLE OF WIGHT
COUNTY LIBRARY

Class	Acc. No.
942\ISL\2000	432717

INTRODUCTION

Hampshire played a significant role in this vicious war of principles. Situated along the route from the west that Cavalier armies chose to use in their efforts to strike towards London, the county became a major battleground and a venue for skirmishes and sieges. Here also lay England's premier naval port while much of the nation's trade flowed through Southampton's sheltered quays. Just across the narrow Solent lay the Isle of Wight, a backwater for much of the war, but eventually providing the gaol in which the fallen monarch was forced to reside. Here also lay Basing House, home of the Catholic Marquis of Winchester, faithful adherent to the King's cause, whose determined defence of his property provides the subject matter of so much of this book. Other slightly less eminent people played their parts too, lining up in support of both the arguing sides- their quarrels and actions fill the pages of this work.

The evidence, facts and attitudes of the times lie well recorded in the county's private homes and in the well-stocked libraries and archives of the county records office. Evidence is also revealed in the cratered walls of buildings, peppered by musket ball and grapeshot, and in the whispered secrets of centuries, which still pervade the county air.

The pain and sorrow of those who lived through these troubled times, wives deprived of husbands, children robbed of fathers and the one-legged veterans of countless battles, echo from the buildings or speak out to those that still want to hear. Modern Hampshire has kept relatively few of the relics of former times, but those that remain have not completely shaken off the reminders of those fear-filled years.

In setting out to re-create the events and traumas of the Civil War, I have visited many of the churches, farmhouses and manors where voices and swords were raised in anger. In more than thirty of these, mainly pubs today, Cromwell was reputed to have slept and in many of the barns his soldiers were billeted. The tarmac, concrete and artificial fertilizer that encases the county's surface is only superficial, and the vaporous world of the 17th Century flows out from the ground beneath.

LIST OF MAPS & CONTEMPORARY ILLUSTRATIONS

Hampshire in the Civil War	4	Battle of Cheriton (map 1)	225
Winchester in the time of the war	6	Battle of Cheriton (map 2)	230
Southampton in 1610	11	Report of the action at Cheriton	244
Proceedings of Col. Goring at Portsmouth	41	Report concerning fighting at	
Map of defences of Portsmouth	46	Warnborough	251
Taking of the castle of Portsmouth	51	Description of the siege of Basing	253
Isle of Wight in 17th century	57	Manoeuveres around Odiham and	
King's message to city of Winchester	74	Basing	255
Sir William Waller	82	2nd attack on Basing House	257
A plundering soldier	98	Map of Alton	267
Layout of Basing House	111	Relief of Basing House	288
1st Battle of Newbury (map 1)	124	Col. Henry Gage	291
1st Battle of Newbury (map 2)	129	The armies move to Newbury	307
Poole in the 17th century	134	2nd Battle of Newbury	310
Sir Ralph Hopton	140	Goring's winter campaign	326
1st attack on Basing House (map)	150	Winchester castle in the 17th	
1st attack on Basing House (plan)	154	century	362
Campaigns Nov-Dev 1643	159	Siege of Winchester	366
Attack on Alton	179	Marquis of Winchester	369
Narration of the great victory at Alton	183	Engraving of Basing House	378
Approaches to Cheriton	216	The storming of Basing House	382
		Carisbrooke Castle	410

CONTENTS

Chapter 1	Hampshire before the war	1
Chapter 2	The nation divides	17
Chapter 3	The sword replaces the pen	29
Chapter 4	Siege of Portsmouth and pacification of the Isle of Wight	36
Chapter 5	The war's first actions	61
Chapter 6	Sack of Winchester	69
Chapter 7	Winter campaigning 1642-43 and 1st Battle of Alton	85
Chapter 8	Battles of Lansdown and Roundway—and the 1st siege of Basing	100
Chapter 9	Siege of Gloucester and 1st Battle of Newbury	118
Chapter 10	Capture of Winchester, attack on Poole & unrest on Isle of Wight	131
Chapter 11	Renewed siege of Basing and contest for control of Hampshire	143
Chapter 12	2nd Battle of Alton and campaigning in the TestValley	172
Chapter 13	Fighting in S. Hampshire and the advance to Cheriton	198
Chapter 14	Battle of Cheriton.....and the aftermath	221
Chapter 15	2nd siege of Basing	246
Chapter 16	The relief of Basing House	277
Chapter 17	Siege of Basing renewed, Battles of Andover & 2nd Newbury	297
Chapter 18	Collapse of the siege of Basing and local skirmishes	314
Chapter 19	Arrival of the New Model Army and rise of the Clubmen	335
Chapter 20	Fall of Winchester and Basing House	356
Chapter 21	The final defeat and the King at Carisbrooke	387

BIBLIOGRAPHY

References to the war in Hampshire are scattered amongst a variety of primary documents, the news sheets of the time and the letters of those who marched with the armies and observed the clash of arms. Amongst these references, the following are the most informative and are frequently identified in the text:

Archer E. ' A True Relation of the marching of the Trained Bands' Thomason Tracts (T.T) E.40 and E.54
Birch J. 'Military Memoirs of Col. John Birch' written by his secretary, Camden Society 1873
Calendar of State Papers, Domestic (identified in test as C.S.P.D.)
Clarendon, Earl of 'The History of the Rebellion and Civil Wars in England' 1888 edition
Hopton R. 'De Bellum Civile' edited by Charles Healey 1902
Journals of the House of Commons
Journals of the House of Lords
Oglander J. ' The Commonplace Book of Sir John Oglander'
Peters H. 'The Fall and Last Relation of All Things concerning Basing House with divers other passages' 1647
Rushworth J. 'Historical Collections' 1680-1722
Sprigge J. 'Anglia Rediviva' 1647
Warburton E. 'Memoirs of Prince Rupert and the Cavaliers' 1849
Walker E. ' Historical Discources upon several occasions' 1705
Waller W. 'Recollections' and 'Vindications' various editions
Whitelocke, Bulstrode 'Memorials of the English Affairs' 1732
Vicars J. 'God on the Mount' or ' Jehovah-Jirah' 1646
And 'A Description of the Siege of Basing Castle kept by the Lord Marquis of Winchester for the service of his Majesty against the forces of the rebels under command of Col Norton' 1644 (reprinted in 1880 and possibly written by the Marquis himself)

Identified in text as the 'Siege Diary'

Amongst the most useful secondary sources are:

Adair J. 'Cheriton' Roundwood Press 1973
Burne A.' Battlefields of England' Methuen 1950
Firth, C. 'Cromwell's Army' Methuen 1912
Fortescue J. 'History of the British Army' Macmillan 1899
Gardiner S.R. 'History of the Great Civil War' Longmans 1911 edition
Godwin G.N. 'The Civil War in Hampshire' 1904 republished 1973 by Laurence Oxley
Money W. 'The First and Second Battles of Newbury' Simpkin, Marshall 1884
Wedgwood C. 'The Great Rebellion' Collins 1958

1

'The Sabbath like a market day is made'

JANE Harrison of Preston Candover was only nineteen when she gave birth to the 'devil's child.' Ugly and deformed, the tiny boy was snatched from her breast and hanged from a tree. At the other end of the county near Stockbridge, a Roundhead trooper stopped a merchant on the road and asked him a question to which there could be no safe answer: *'Are you for God or the King?'* Hesitating in his reply, the traveller was shot dead.

Events like these, although far from commonplace during the years of civil strife, were part of the sickly fabric of the 1640's. The humdrum daily routine of pre-war life would be savagely poisoned by politics and passion, and rocked from its foundations by the violence of the times. Enmity and distrust would stalk the nation's lanes, and the germs of suspicion would be implanted in everyone.

Hampshire was no less torn than any other county. Someone who knew the area well in the years before the war paints a landscape of near Arcadian charm and tranquility. *'The turf is of a short sweet grass, good for the sheep, and delightful to the eye, for its smoothness like a bowling green and pleasant to the traveller; who wants here only a variety of objects to make his journey less tedious, for here is ... not a tree, or rarely a bush to shelter one from a shower ... the innocent lives here of the shepherds do give us a resemblance of the golden age'.* [1]

He was describing the great belt of chalk land that sweeps through Hampshire and its neighbouring counties to east and west. Here was a landscape that had changed little in a thousand years. Scorched by the summer sun and iced by winter's chills, the area was inhabited only by hardened shepherds and the flocks that were in their charge. Hares and rabbits in profusion cropped the short grass, and birds of prey hung motionless overhead. Time was unimportant and only the march of the seasons dictated the pace of life.

In the valleys that crossed this open landscape, mixed farming, mainly subsistence, had been practised for centuries in the open fields that were the legacies of medieval times. And here, too, the more affluent lived, controlling the destinies of their estates from manorial homes and at the same time dictating the tenor of local politics.

The clays and sands of the Hampshire Basin presented a very different world. Wheat and barley were widely cultivated, mainly for the production of bread and beer. Where practical, mixed husbandry took place, root crops alternating with cereals to improve the fertility of the soil and to provide winter feed for cattle. Small tenant farms prevailed, edging the banks of the Avon, Test and Meon, and in this area a conservative society of farmers lived, treading contentedly in the paths of their fathers.

Yet this outward picture of rural stability disguised the enormous strains of the pre-war years. Agriculturally as well as socially, Hampshire was being forced to adapt to all the rigours of post-medieval life. The trauma of the Reformation had been followed by the rise of mercantilism and the market orientated economy, and the old close-knit system of subsistence and

---

1 Aubrey, John 'Antiquities of Wiltshire'

parochialism was being rapidly eroded. The lands of the monasteries had been sold to royal courtiers and favourites, and a host of newly imported men had begun to play a major role in the county's daily life.

Disposal of abbey lands at bargain prices had spurned a lively market and the chance to speculate. William Warham, Henry VII's Lord Chancellor, had been among the first, building Malshanger House and an adjacent church. William, 1st Lord Sandys, Henry VIII's Lord Chamberlain, was probably the next, constructing the Vyne near Basingstoke, a house still high on the list of the county's most imposing residences, and converting Mottisfont Priory into another comfortable home.

Thomas Wriothesley and Sir William Paulet did far better. Already the proud owner of scattered estates in every corner of Hampshire, Wriothesley, created 1st Earl of Southampton in 1547 for services to the Tudor crown, acquired Titchfield and Beaulieu Abbeys, together with Southwick Priory and a clutch of other ecclesiastical properties. Full of Reformation zeal, the Earl supervised the destruction of the shrine of St. Swithun in the priory of that name, working at night to avoid detection by those who might object. William Paulet, 1st Marquis of Winchester, was his equal in every way. Owning far-flung manors and inheriting the grand house of Basing, he later added the abbeys of Netley and the Itchen valley to his total.

Many of the later purchases of clerical land were the self-made men of England's burgeoning commerce, and soon the Hampshire countryside was studded with the proofs of their success. The Stawell family obtained the manor of Hinton Ampner, previously the property of the Almoner of St. Swithun's Priory in Winchester. The site of Wherwell Abbey was granted to Sir Thomas West, Lord de la Warr. The modest house they built has long since gone. The son of a London merchant, James Paget, built Grove Place near Southampton in the 1560's. Soon acquired by Sir Francis Knollys, *'a shining light in Queen Elizabeth's days'*, the house is

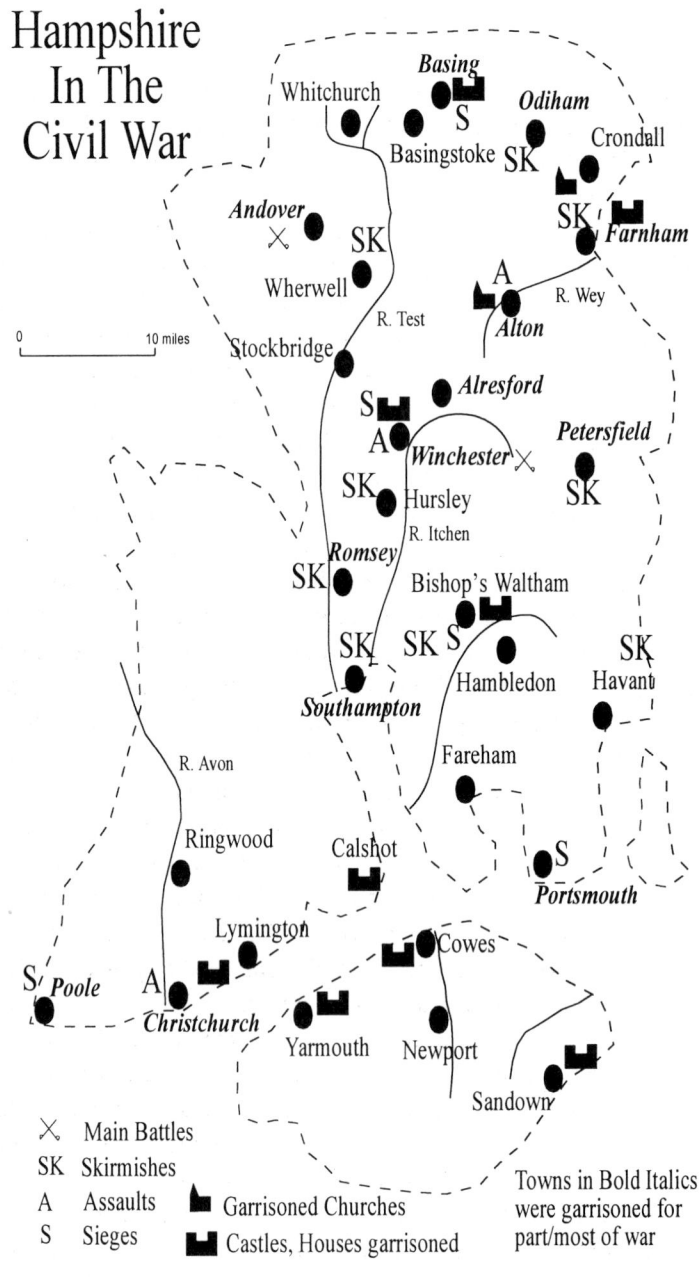

now a school. Breamore House rose two decades later, the creation of William Dodington. In 1600 he hurled himself to death from a London church, distressed, it seems, by a law suit in which he had become involved. Bramshill House, the home of Lord Zouche, appears in the reign of James I. And, at a lesser level, the Mille family, previously stewards of the Priory of St. Swithun, and families like the Nortons, Jervoises and Lisles were amongst the paler stars rising in the new social firmament. Soon in possession of ancient Hampshire manors, these new-made men, titled or otherwise, would provide the bulk of the county's MP's and future military leaders. For a while, little obvious change might have been noticeable; clerical lords had been replaced by secular, but the estates continued to operate on commercial grounds. Great houses had arisen from the monastic ruins and the age of materialism was born.

Yet the cohesive fabric that had so recently been stitched around this post- Reformation order was already beginning to unravel, tugged by even newer economic forces beyond the ability of any one man to control. Rapid demographic growth was partly to blame. The adult population in Hampshire in 1620 was about 60,000 and growing annually by nearly 1%. Land, the means for sustenance as well as social advance, was in short supply and a resulting rise in food prices became inevitable. A run of poor harvests made the situation still worse. Between 1626 and 1630 the price of wheat rose by 40%, and additional land for cultivation had to be reclaimed from the waste. Those forced to farm these more marginal lands were denied the right to self-sufficiency and so rapidly joined the ranks of the poor. Subdivision of holdings, the consequence of large families, commonly made farms uneconomic and rendered them vulnerable to purchase by the rich. Acres of chalk and clay were snatched from the common man and became the haunt of the imported gentry. Land, for some the golden path to greater wealth, became, for others, the thorny ground to ruin.

Worse was to follow. Aggravating this rural upheaval was the enclosure of the common field, the age-old system by which

'The Sabbath like a market day is made'

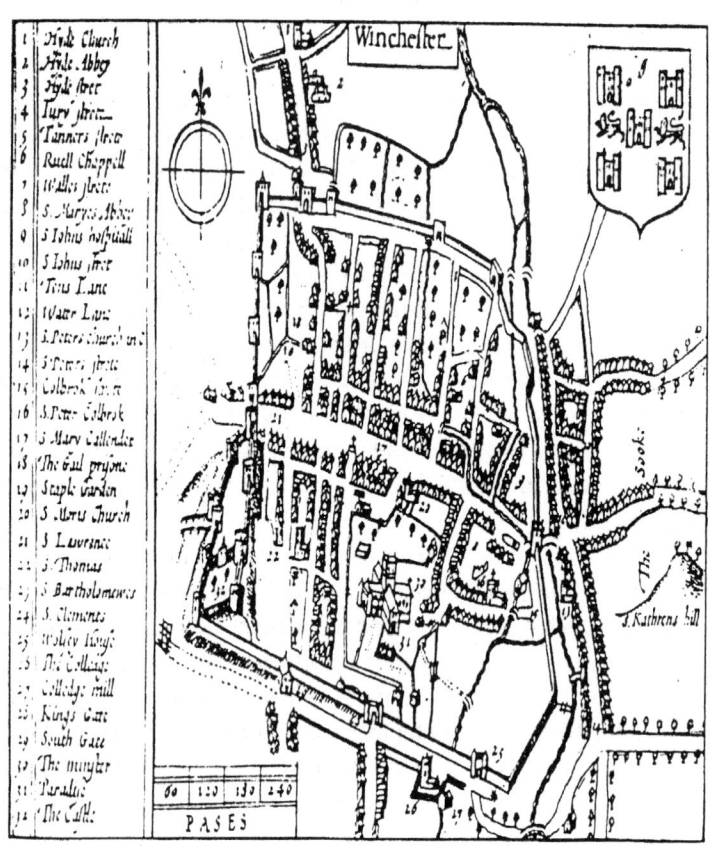

Winchester in the 17th century

medieval man had farmed the village lands. Plague and disease, never far distant, had caused a shortage of agricultural labour, forcing profit-minded landlords to seek alternative sources of wealth. Sheep runs required far less manpower than crop cultivation, and seemingly callous land owners, with no thoughts for their tenants, had been turning their rolling acres into vast pastures, displacing whole communities in their zeal to widen their source of profit. The evicted thronged the county's highways, and another cause of vagrancy was born. Other improvements in farming were attempted, too, aggravating the rural exodus that had continued unabated for more than a hundred years. A late 15th century document describes the agricultural upheaval that had affected the Isle of Wight: '*It is late decayed of people, by reason that many towns and villages have been let down and the fields dyked and made pastures for beasts and cattle, and also many dwelling places, farms and farmholds have of late time been used to be taken into one man's hold that of old time were wont to be in many several persons' holds and hands*'.[2] From Newport to Newbury, and Christchurch to Chichester, it was to be much the same: exploitation of the lower folk in the quest for financial gains.

Sometimes the dispossessed struck back. A spate of enclosures in the 1630's became too much for lowly men to bear. Levelling and destruction of hedges resulted, groups of villagers assembling in the pre-dawn light with axe and spade and then dispersing before the sun had risen. Some were more ostentatious, parading the fields with red feathers in their hair and banging drums to intimidate the landowner. Damage was extensive, but the campaigns were never co-ordinated and so remained largely ineffective.

Town life, too, was in a state of dislocation, fashioned by commerce and the uncertain demands of expanding industries. The clothing industry had long been dominant in most of Hampshire's towns, perhaps as many as one in five of the working population

---

2 V.C.H. Vol.5 p.422

engaged directly or indirectly in this widespread activity. Dependent on the flocks of sheep that roamed the chalky plains, this industry had transformed urban life since the Middle Ages, swelling small hamlets into the county's most noted towns. By 1300 New Alresford was numbered amongst the nation's ten leading markets for wool while Andover, Winchester, Whitchurch, Petersfield and Romsey all feature in sixteenth century accounts of the industry's growth. In these towns skilled weavers had settled from abroad: Huguenots from Flanders, Sicilians and Florentines - and some of these foreigners were amongst the later buyers of monastic estates. Associated trades had grown in tandem: dyeing and fulling, each drawing upon the clear waters of Hampshire's sparkling rivers.

But the days of prosperity were fading now and the shadows of decline had become painfully evident. John Trusell, twice mayor of Winchester, highlights the decline faced by his beloved city during the first three decades of the seventeenth century: *'Since which time this so ancient and goodly city hath every day more and more declined, trade therein for the most part being decayed, traffic in foreign parts altogether denied......clothing too little and poverty too much increasing, so that now the citizens may boast of their predecessors, and tell what they were, but few if any brag what themselves are'.*

The causes of decline are not hard to find: the loss of the English possessions in France at the end of the Hundred Years War, the virtual ending of the trade with Venetian merchants, who now took Spanish wool in preference, and the outbreak of all-embracing war on the Continent in 1618, which closed the remaining avenues for English exports. Hasty and unwarranted interference from London had also played a part. In 1614, James I granted Cockayne, a London alderman, the right to dye and finish cloth before its export to the Continent. Unwisely he supported this grant of a monopoly by actually banning the export of undyed cloth, the very product on which Hampshire's exporters largely depended. Unemployment was beginning to stalk the urban streets, a godsend for the recruiting sergeants. Many of those worst affected, the middle men of the clothing industry, would join the King's or Westminster's armies out of sheer financial necessity.

Other long-established industries, fed by expanding markets for their goods and less dependent upon the whims of trade, princes and politics, survived - and almost prospered. Honey making, charcoal burning and hurdle making were typical activities in the county's countryside, fish were landed in the Solent's bays, and Lymington's prosperity was partly based on the extraction of salt from the sea. Tanning, and the manufacture of shoes, gloves, saddles and delicate clay pipes were widespread activities in the more urban areas. Taking place in overcrowded towns where the stench of daily life would hang for ages in the open air, these industries sparked some of the earliest recorded environmental protests in the nation's annals, *'against those in trade who, do wash their skins in the common river, to the great nuisance of others'*. The Winchester town authority consequently restricted the practice, prohibiting those responsible from using river water after 6 a.m.

The proud skills of centuries were also threatened, this time by men with an eye for larger profit and exploitation of a growing market. In 1580, Winchester craftsmen complain of *'sundry abuses and enormities of late sprung up and suffered owing to divers persons setting up ... and using the trades, sciences and mysteries of shoemakers and cobblers without serving due apprenticeships, for wicked lucre and gain sake ... and selling to the people boots made of faulty, deceitful and evil tanned leather to the great hurt and deceit of the people'.* [3] Candles made of dripping instead of tallow were commonly sold; churchmen spoke of altar cloths damaged *'by means of the false wax, rosin and turpentine employed'.* Yet behind all this turmoil and uncertainty is a picture of hard work: laden packhorses on rutted roads, weekly fairs and industrious craftsmen, most impervious to the politics of the time.

Portsmouth, with nearly 5000 people, was the home of the

---

3 V.C.H. Vol.5 p.456

Stuart fleet. In the sheltered harbour rested the 'Prince Royal', with 55 guns the most powerful warship ever built. At her side nestled her smaller sisters, some of the thirteen 'Great Ships' upon which the nation's safety might depend. Conscious of this probability, Charles was in the process of building four more, paid for by the controversial Ship Money tax, one of the many causes of war. Men laboured in shore side huts to supply and service these wooden ships, like worker bees carrying sustenance to their insatiable queens, and beyond stretched the well fortified town. *'Portsmouth is a very good town, well built with stone and brick'*, wrote Celia Fiennes fifty years later. *'It's not a large town, there are walls and gates about it and at least eight bridges and gates without one another with ditches which secures it very strongly to the landward'* [4]

Southampton, with more than 4200 inhabitants, was Hampshire's second most populated town. An ordinance of 1320 had established the town as one of only seven ports nationally from which wool could be exported, and later measures had given the port a virtual monopoly on the import of sweet wines. But the high tide of commerce and trade no longer lapped as convincingly against the town's quays as it had in earlier times. *'This port is not frequented and haunted as it hath been with the repair of the carracks of Genoa and other great ships of Venice which within 20 years did lade and unlade their merchandise there'*, states a report of the 1590's while a poem about Southampton, written by John Speed, the city's mayor in 1681, mourns the town's commercial collapse:

> *'Hampton in the days of yore,*
> *The lawful pride of all the southern shore,*
> *With all the advantage of Nature graced,*
> *Betwixt the arms of fair Antonia placed;*
> *Guarded by forests, both on land and sea,*
> *From storms, and man, the ruder enemy.*
> *For age - who like a bloodhound glory traces,*
> *And destroys towns as well as handsome faces,*
> *Hath made thee poor*
> *And dull like other places.*

---

4   Fiennes, Celia ' Through England on a side saddle in the time of William and Mary'

'THE SABBATH LIKE A MARKET DAY IS MADE'

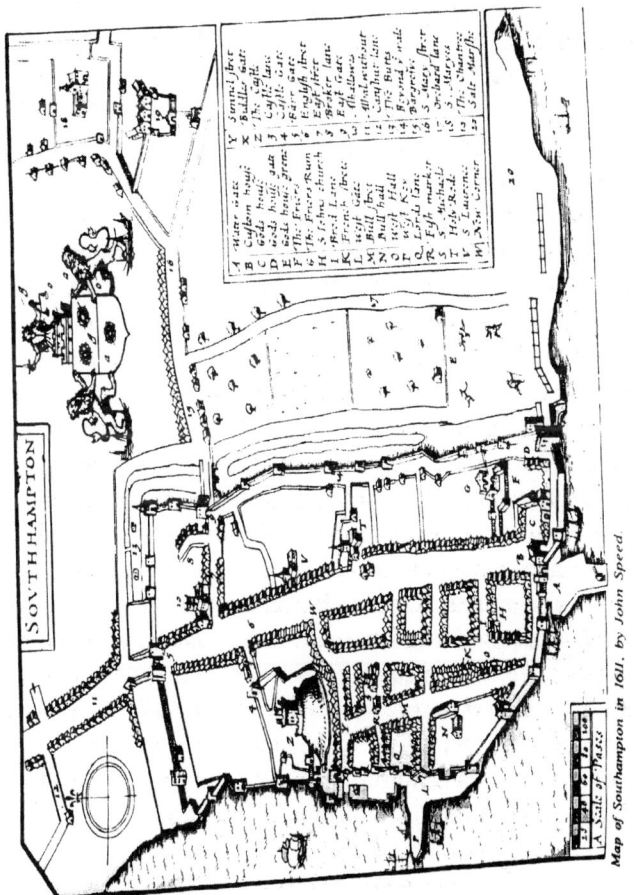

Southampton in 1610

'THE SABBATH LIKE A MARKET DAY IS MADE'

Winchester, with about 3000 people, ranked next. Here the workers of a dozen trades lived in close proximity. Cloth was stretched after fulling or was hung to dry in tiny yards behind the tenements. The horizons of these men seldom stretched beyond the outer edges of the city or the concerns of their particular trade. Working life was controlled and directed by the Guilds, who increasingly came to dominate the city's political life. This was a parochial world, as limited as the little village and just as unchanging. On market days animals from the grazing land that fringed the city would be driven through the streets and penned for sale. Monitoring the whole process, like a vigilant prefect, was the solid tower of the city's cathedral and the clerical world of the Close.

Andover, Basingstoke, and Petersfield, with between 2000 and 3000 inhabitants each, served as market centres, pulling in folk from the surrounding countryside. Weyhill fair, held near Andover annually at Michaelmas, was one of the nation's largest for hops, cheese and several other commodities '*and for sheep there is none so big*'.[5] But these towns were even more parochial than Winchester and just as susceptible to downturns in trade. A 1669 description of Basingstoke paints an uncomplimentary picture of apparent decay: '*The town, which is wretched, both in regard to the buildings the greater part of which are of wood, and the total absence of trade*'.

By the late 1630's, the political tremors excited by the King's controversial attempts to raise finance during the 11 years of personal rule, were about to assume the proportions of an earthquake -and the Stuart house of cards would eventually topple. 'Forced' loans, the fining of those owning land worth £40 p.a. who refused to pay for a knighthood, and a cluster of other extra-Parliamentary taxes, had been overshadowed, however, by the Ship Money tax, a demand on town and country to contribute financially to the construction and maintenance of the fleet. Imposed in 1634 and 1635, it was widely opposed as unconstitutional by those expected to pay. The tax ultimately sent many of those who might

---

5 Paul J. 'Andover -an Historical Portrait ' p.51

otherwise have served the King into Parliament's military camp. Hampshire's contribution was set at £6000, the figures levied on each town usefully giving an indication of these towns' abilities to pay. Southampton and Winchester are assessed at £200 each, Basingstoke £60, Andover £50 and Romsey £30. Portsmouth, less able to rely on industry and commerce, was assessed at only £70.

Religious discord had also left its mark, imprinting prejudice and intolerance in the minds of many. Controversy had been endemic in England since the Reformation; no one was immune to its consequences. The ideological debate might have been beyond the comprehension of many, but the changes in organisation that took place at parish level had affected the poor as much as the rich. The Elizabethan prayer book had instilled conformity in Sunday worship and helped to marginalise both Papism and Puritanism. Those who refused to attend church could be fined a shilling a week and might additionally suffer the disapproval of their God-fearing neighbours. For a while at least, something approaching religious uniformity returned and the muddy waters of spiritual upheaval began to calm.

But twenty years before the outbreak of war, it had begun again. In 1635 William Laud had been appointed as Canterbury's Archbishop - and a new bout of reform was unleashed.

Determined to elevate the image of the parish priest and deepen the mysticism of church worship, he had ordered the railing of altars in an attempt to separate the parson from his flock. Interpreted as a deliberate swing towards Catholicism, this ill-timed move caused the Puritans to rush to the barricades of religious defence - and one of the causes of war was slowly hatched. The licensing of Sunday sports, another of the age's religious innovations, was fiercely opposed in the more puritanical areas of the county.

Upheaval in town and countryside led to protest. But petition, not riot, was generally the chosen method. In 1620 unemployed cloth workers petitioned Whitehall for redress of their grievances, but spoke the language of moderation in their letter to the King: '*To starve is woeful, to steal ungodly and to beg unlawful*'.

Unemployment and social breakdown bred disorder - as another contemporary report complains: '... ... *lewd women with bastards clog the parish; and yet no man takes order for her punishment. The law ordained to curb licentiousness like straw lies trodden unregarded... ... The Sabbath like a market day is made'.*[6] Excessive drinking was blamed for much of the period's lawlessness. In 1630 Hampshire justices closed many of the ale houses, *'who are grown as doth manifestly appear to be a superfluous number',* and the pamphlets railed against the evils of the Godless times.

In such circumstances, the distant clouds of impending war were long ignored as an irrelevant and insignificant distraction. The effects of change, threatening the livelihood of local people, were of far greater concern. Only for the county's M.P.s and men of social significance did events in London have any meaning. Carried back from the capital by returning squires, the nation's bitter rows and squabbles would be eventually mimicked in regional versions within Hampshire's scattered towns, and laid on parlour tables for men to share. Inevitably the moods and opinions of those most involved would at last rub off on their tenants, and simpler folks might then take sides.

For this the social structure of the time was largely to blame. Pre-war society was hierarchical, glued by respect for superiors and knitted in unquestioned subservience. *'As it is a thing required by law and reason that children bear the honour and reverence to their natural parents which is commanded',* Thomas Beard, an influential writer, had written in 1597, *'so it is necessary... ...that all subjects perform that duty of honour and obedience to their Lords, Princes and Kings'.*

Yet that society had never been rigid. Wealth, not birth, provided the means and avenues for social advancement, and those with ambition could generally ascend. Hampshire's own experience in the preceding 100 years had amply demonstrated how rapidly the successful tradesman could acquire the styles and comforts of

---

6 Humble Remonstrance of the Dispossessed' Privately owned MSS

the upper classes- and even vie with the aristocracy for public office. Ownership of one's own coat of arms became the ultimate goal, enabling those who reached the highest pinnacles to distinguish themselves from those they left behind. Ennoblement might even follow, permitting the favoured to strut like lordly peacocks in the company of long-established aristocracy. Such men might then become obsessed with preserving their marks of status, complaining bitterly of anything that might blur their lofty stature. In 1621 a Hampshire M.P opposed legislation that obliged the families of gentry to wear broadcloth in winter. *'So little betwixt us and our servants'*, he moaned, ' *..a gentleman should not know his wife from his chambermaid'.*[7]

Social mobility could also be downward. The unlucky and imprudent could fall with a crash into the quagmire of pauperism, and become almost indistinguishable from the landless masses. This lowly sector of society, estimated at about 10% of the county's population, and expanding almost daily as a result of enclosure and industrial unemployment, was becoming increasingly costly to support. The Elizabethan Poor Law had made parishes responsible for the sustenance and relief of the poor, placing the burden on parish officials to find the means and methods. Faced by the rising cost and numbers on its lists, these officials normally refused to assist those who were unable to prove either birth or connection with the parish, and so even more people were found on the county's lanes.

Now those threatened routines of town and country were about to be savaged further by the arrival of this sudden war. For the victims of pre-war economic change, war would be a solution to unemployment and distress. Men joined the new armies for a variety of reasons: political, social and personal. But for many the motives would be less lofty: the chance to start afresh and fill their empty bellies. The lanes and highways of Hampshire would be suddenly almost clear of the casualties of progress, and unemployment nearly

---

[7] Carlton C. ' Going to the Wars'

disappeared.

But adverse effects would soon be felt. Fields were forsaken, workshops deserted and trade disrupted. A shortage of horses would make ploughing impossible. The bitter cry of widowed women would ring through Hampshire's hamlets and the lanes became filled with a new batch of paupers and the wounded men of other counties' battles. Human flocks would lose their spiritual shepherds too. The parsonage at Cholderton in Wiltshire would be typical of many throughout the nation. Abandoned by its war-going incumbent, it was made almost uninhabitable by neglect. And rectors would be forcibly ejected from parish pulpits for preaching a disfavoured creed. '*Whereas information was this day given to the House that Mr. Clarke, Vicar of Andover, doth obstinately refuse to obey the order of this House*', [8] began the Westminster order for the ejection of the cleric from his living. New men would then come to take charge of the spiritual flocks in countless villages, forcing new ways of worshipping that broke the trend of centuries. Yet life would not be permanently altered by the struggle. The seasons would continue to pass with immutable regularity, water wheels still turned, and countless ambitions would remain unfulfilled, much as they had done for centuries past. Memories of war would eventually fade and become interred beneath a new crop of spring grown corn. War, despite the upsets of the time, was to be little more than a hiccup on a landscape of solid resilience.

---

8 House of Commons Journals Vol.1 p.170

2

'The root and vice of all the plot'

'Every county has its civil war'[1] Lucy Hutchinson's comment is as valid in Hampshire as in any other of England's divided counties. In every region, with the possible exception of distant Cumbria and the more fortunate areas of East Anglia, the fabric of society was to be torn apart by political and religious issues beyond the comprehension of many and equally beyond the ability of any one man to solve.

Initially it seemed to be nothing more than the age-old squabble amongst the ruling classes. But when at last it seemed that only a military solution would be possible and the need for muscle became apparent, the arguing factions used their social status and powers of persuasion to call upon the lower orders for support. Ultimately the ploughman and the carpenter would be as much involved as the lord and his lady.

Soon this all-enveloping conflict would start to challenge society's existing norms and codes, throwing into question some of the established values of the time and creating less acceptable standards of behaviour. Faced by the horrors of war and largely

---

1 Hutchinson, Lucy 'The Life of Col. J.Hutchinson' p.121

concerned with self-survival and the protection of personal property, men would become more bestial and instinctive in their conduct. The quarrel would sadly pit brother against brother, father against son, and split the ordered society of pre-war England into two irreconcilable halves: *'Parents and children, brothers, kindred, I and dear friends have the seed of difference and division abundantly sowed in them.....I have heard foul language and desperate quarrelling even between old and entire friends, and how we can thus stand and not fall, certainly God must needs work a miracle'.*
[2] Henry Oxinden, a Kent landowner, wrote to a London friend in June 1642. His comments were as true in Hampshire as in any other troubled county.

The choice of which side to support was often a long and arduous process, and an encyclopedia of factors might have governed the eventual decision. Many of those who later fought beneath Parliament's banners saw little unpardonable fault in King Charles's arrogance and haughty manner. Believing that he had been led down paths of error by mischievous advisers, they sought only to extricate him from the clutches of men who had clearly set out to corrupt both church and State, a point that John Vicars, one of the most informative writers of the times confirms. *'Now the root and vice of all the plot was found to be a pernicious woven-knot of malignant active spirits combining and confederating together for the supplanting and utter subverting of the fundamental laws and principles of government, on which the religion and government of the kingdom were firmly established: And those actors and promoters were first and principally, Jesuited-Papists, whose teeth had long watered for, and whose eager appetites had long hungered after the subversion of our religion'.* [3]

Even before war had become inevitable, such men had begun their personal war of words, employing the Sunday pulpit and the eloquence of fiery preachers to purchase the hearts and minds

---

2 Gardiner D. 'The Oxinden and Peyton Letters' p.174

3 Vicars J. 'God in the Mount' p.16

of the masses. Puritanical speakers railed at their congregations for hours, instilling the virtues of Parliament's cause and reminding their listeners of their spiritual duty to resist God's enemies. Most favoured amongst the biblical texts employed to implant the seeds of insurrection in the slumbering masses were two apparent calls to arms, ingeniously misquoted but used with telling effect. One, from Proverbs, was selected to justify the removal from office, by force if necessary, all those who ill-advised the monarch. *'Take away the wicked from before the king, and his throne shall be established in righteousness'.* (Proverbs Ch. 25 v.5). The other attempted to infuse guilt into those who remained inactive: *'Curse ye bitterly the inhabitants thereof; because they came not to the help of the Lord, to the help of the Lord against the mighty'.* (Judges Ch.5, v.23)

Fed in large handfuls to the gullible and God fearing, these clarion calls were largely successful, but were promptly condemned by the other side, amongst them Lord Clarendon:

'these men.... infused seditious inclination into the hearts of men against the present government of the church, with many libellous invectives against the State too... they contained themselves with no bounds, and as freely and without control inveighed against the person of the King... to incense and stir up the people against their gracious sovereign'... and by this means the poorest and lowest of the people became informers against the richest and most substantial'. [4] Equally the King's men, arguing in support of God's anointed government, extolled the virtues of the rule of law and an ordered church where each man knew his place. A deep conviction in the sanctity of kingship, fear of social change and upheaval, and dread of Puritanism provided three powerful magnets to the regal cause.

Yet there were many in the King's ranks who did not adhere to all three and opposed the political excesses of Charles and his Archbishop. Sir Edmund Verney, a sincere and deeply religious man

---

4 Clarendon, Earl of 'The History of the Rebellion and Civil wars in England' Vol.11, Bk. VI, p.385

who later carried the royal standard at Edgehill, probably voiced the feelings of many: *'I do not like the quarrel, and do heartily wish that the King would yield and consent to what they desire. Yet I have eaten his bread, and served him near 30 years, and will not do so base a thing as to forsake him, and choose rather to lose my life'.*[5]

Killed during the fury of the fighting in the war's first major battle, Verney continued to clutch the standard in death as firmly as in life. To rescue the flag, Captain John Smith had to hack off the dead man's hand. Verney was just one of many martyrs for a cause in which they only partly believed. Similarly there were Episcopalians on Parliament's side, men who saw the rash excesses of Charles's rule as far more dangerous than Puritanism, and nowhere was social class the main determining factor in securing eventual allegiance.

A county's ultimate loyalty, therefore, was largely determined by the sympathies of its leaders and their powers to persuade. In East Anglia, a region strongly influenced by the puritanical zeal of the Netherlands, Parliament dominated the debate and support for the King was minimal. But in England's distant west, susceptible to the influence of Irish Catholicism, Royalism was the dominant hue. The counties in between, split almost equally between two rival philosophies, became fractious debating grounds - and ultimately the battle ground where the conflict would be settled militarily.

Hampshire was to be one of those areas of bitter division. When the sparks of conflict first threatened to set the county alight, the prominent men of town and countryside were quickly forced to declare their true allegiances. Neutrality was almost impossible, a stance mistrusted and interpreted by both sides as a secretly muttered declaration of support for the enemy. Lord John Paulet, the catholic Marquis of Winchester, a private man not much inclined to violence, was one of those who tried to distance himself from the passions of

---

5 Gardiner, S.R. 'History of the Great Civil War' Vol.1, p.4

'THE ROOT AND VICE OF ALL THE PLOT'

the arguing sides. *'The Marquis at first retired',* a contemporary article reported, *'hoping integrity and privacy might here have preserved his quiet, but the source of the time's villainy bearing down all before it, neither allowing neutrality, or permitting peace to any that desired to be less sinful than themselves, enforced him to stand upon his guard'.*[6]

His house at Basing was not permitted to remain neutral either. By August 1641, when peace loving Englishmen should still have been able to walk their lawns and corridors without disturbance, fingers of accusation began to point. A Mr. Sewer, possibly a servant of the marquis with a thirst for revenge, reported to the Commons that he had seen weapons in Basing, ' *enough to arm 1500 men'.* On November 4th, Westminster reacted to his report, ordering *'that the Lord Marquis of Winchester shall have liberty, by virtue of this order, to sell his arms to such tradesmen as will buy the same'.* [7] Lord John chose to refuse this kind offer and so prompted Parliament to attempt to rob the house of its armoury. Just before Christmas, the Marquis, with only six musketeers at his side, reputedly beat the intruders off. Angered by his mistreatment, he promptly declared for the King.

Two other high-status Aristocrats followed his example, openly asserting their Royalist credentials in the Spring of 1642. Thomas Wriothesley, the fourth Earl of Southampton, was praised by Clarendon for the honesty and depth of his commitment to the cause. Succeeding to the title in 1624 at the age of sixteen, the young earl gambled away some of his inheritance, but later *'sold and gave away all his race horses, intending to give over that sport'.* He was to serve as ambassador for the Court and as one of the King's most talented negotiators. He was consequently one of the first to be prescribed by Parliament for largely innocuous actions. Appearing in the Lords in August 1642 with messages from Charles, he clearly touched raw nerves amongst those who had decided to oppose the

---

6 Godwin G.N ' The Civil War in Hampshire'

7 Ibid.

8 Earl of Strafford's Letters Vol.1 p.225

crown. '*He as scarce sat down in his place when, with great passion, he was called upon to withdraw'.*[9]

Jerome Weston, the second Earl of Portland, had been Governor of the Isle of Wight since 1634 and now also served as the Lord Lieutenant of Hampshire. Openly sympathetic to Papism, he was detested by the Puritans, who also complained of the '*waste of powder, all the waste of wine, in the drinking of healths and other acts of jollity, whenever he had been at his government from the first hour of his entering upon it.*'[10] In November 1641 the Commons, suspicious of his loyalties, resolved to deprive him of his governorship. But protesting, '*his resolution to live and die a protestant, as his father did*', he was allowed to continue in office. Both his mother and father in reality were declared followers of Rome, a fact somehow forgotten during the discussion on an autumn evening. His brother, Nicholas, one of the M.P.s for Newton, was to compound the family's criminal record still further. Enthusiastically Royalist in his Spring time utterances, he was barred in August 1642 from sitting in the Commons, and Sir John Barrington was elected in his place. A few days later, when Portsmouth was threatened with siege, Nicholas Weston provided the defenders with £9000 and a flotilla of food and provisions. Only one of the family, Jerome's and Nicholas's younger brother, managed to climb out of the well of utter damnation. Elected in 1640 to serve as M.P for Dover, he declared for Parliament.

Sir William Ogle, representing Winchester in the Commons, unhesitatingly swung to the Royalist cause. One of the few Hampshire M.P.s with military experience, his future service on the field of battle was to be glorious and eventful. But the most colourful of all those that chose to serve the King was George Goring, a Portsmouth M.P. and governor of the town since 1639. The eldest son of the Earl of Norwich, this '*airy Bacchanalian*' had been wounded at the siege of Breda in 1637, and the constant pain in his

---

9 Clarendon Vol 1 Bk.1 p.86   10 ibid Vol. 11 Bk.V1 p.350

leg seems to have contributed to his infamous bad temper and his bouts of heavy drinking. Clarendon paints Goring in both black and white, recognising equally his strengths and failings. His behaviour was: *'devious, uncertain and unprincipled and shed disgrace upon the nobleness of his name, and upon the honourable profession of soldier.'* Yet he had a *'civility which shed itself over all his countenance... his courage was notorious and confessed; his wit equal to the best.... and his language and expression natural, sharp and flowing, adorned with a wonderful seeming modesty'* [11] In November 1641, alarmed by the presence of *'Papists and jovial clergymen'* in Portsmouth, the Commons summoned Goring to London to assess where his sympathies really lay. Already a closet Royalist and in secret liaison with the Earl of Portland, he successfully disguised his true sentiments during the lengthy interrogation that followed. Convinced of his sincerity, *'they would give no countenance to any information they received, from persons in whom they had great confidence, of anything to his prejudice'*, and so *'desired him again to repair to his government and to finish those works which were necessary for the safety of the place'.*[12] (Portsmouth) It was not until August 2nd that he threw off his mantle of deception and declared openly for the King.

Sir John Oglander, deputy governor of the Isle since 1624, was another of the region's unashamed Royalists. Serving as Hampshire's sheriff in 1637 and 1639, he had been given the task of collecting Ship money for the King, a duty which he performed without question: *'As you are a gentleman whom I love and respect, so I desire you not to force me to distrain your goods for his Majesty's ship moneys. I should be very loathe to do it to any, especially to yourself'*, [13] he had written in undisguised threat to one of the King's Hampshire subjects. In August 1642, when Goring and Portsmouth declared for King Charles, he and the two Weston brothers paraded 2000 men in arms for the King and took control of the island's

---

11 ibid. Vol.11 Bk. V p.438   12 ibid. Vol.11 Bk.V p. 440

13 Boucher Jones E. 'Letters Archaeological and Historical' and Oglander MSS.

strong points - the castles at Yarmouth, Cowes, Carisbrooke and Sandown. It was upon such men as these that the King would be forced to rely….and not one would let him down.

The lesser men of the county lined up on either side, joining the opposing causes for a variety of reasons: religious, political or purely opportunistic. The Sandys family of Mottisfont and the Tichbornes of West Tisted were Royalist, almost to a man. Sir Benjamin Tichborne fought long and hard for his king, finally going to ground after the Cavalier defeat at Cheriton. His nephew, Sir Henry, a veteran of the Irish campaign, was equally zealous. Only Sir Robert, a more distant kinsman, spoilt the family honour and sided with Parliament. One of those who signed the King's death warrant and later Lord Mayor of London, he was to be personally rewarded by Cromwell with a seat in the Protector's Upper House. The Nortons of Southwick were similarly divided in their loyalties. Richard Norton, dubbed 'Idle Dick' by friend and foe, later served as colonel of a Roundhead regiment of horse. With him on the field of battle in the coming campaigns were Francis St. Barbe of Broadlands in Romsey and Richard Major of Hursley, the senior representatives of the county's new gentry.

Only four more of the county's twenty six sitting M.P.s followed Ogle's, Goring's lead in declaring for the King. John Meux, the constituency of Newton's second member, was a *'wild young man'*, and Goring's favoured drinking partner. Expelled from the Commons for early delinquency, he was replaced by John Bulkeley. For the rest of the war, the young man served in the King's Parliament and drank with Oxford councillors instead. Matthew Davies, one of the Christchurch members, never openly declared for the King, but his inactivity alone was sufficient to place him in the halls of the damned; choosing to absent himself from the Commons, he was finally expelled in March 1643. Richard Edwards, a Bedfordshire squire, was elected in his stead. Sir William Uvedale, the Petersfield member and previously Treasurer for the Army, was to remain far more active in the cause of the king. He attended

Charles in the weeks before the war's start and carried messages to London, a crime for which most would never be forgiven. For reasons still unexplained, he was allowed to retain his seat in the Commons, serving intermittently until 1648. Lucius Carey, the second Viscount Falkland, Newport's other member and wooed by both sides, was to serve as the King's Secretary of State. He was killed at the first Battle of Newbury, seeking death, some later claimed, out of despair for what England had become.

The two Shire M.P.s, Sir Henry Wallop and Richard Whitehead, had both declared unequivocally for Parliament before the war began. The former had frequently offended the King. Summoned before the Star Chamber in 1633 for 'eating meat on Fridays', he later ignored a request for a contribution to the Crown. He then compounded his error by opposing the Earl of Strafford's Irish policies. Without doubt, one of the wealthiest men in Hampshire, he supplied and armed a company of horsemen at his own expense. The latter, with military experience that equalled Goring, had also fallen foul of the king on several occasions. He would soon raise an entire regiment of foot at his own expense and seldom let his sword sleep in his hand.

Sir Richard Jervoise and his son, Sir Thomas, the M.P.s for Whitchurch, were 'paper' Parliamentarians, active at Westminster, but seldom in the field. Along with William Jephson, M.P. for Stockbridge, the two Jervoises were inappropriately labelled by Clarendon as *'the greatest rebels in the county'*. John Lisle, Winchester's Roundhead M.P., found himself in endless conflict with eloquent Sir William Ogle, and the city was divided as a result. Robert Wallop, one of the members for Andover and the son of the shire M.P, already served as a colonel in the county's militia and was later to be listed among the regicides. But the undoubted 'lion' in the Parliamentary pride was Sir William Waller, the other member for Andover and the father-in-law of Ogle. Elected in a highly controversial by-election in April 1641 on the death of the previous M.P, Henry Rainsford,* he would soon rank as one of Westminster's three greatest generals. In June 1642, when asked by Westminster for money and horses, Sir William provided *'four bay horses with stars on their foreheads, their riders, armed with carabineers, pistols, buffcoats and swords, each horse and arms valued one with another at £26 a piece'*. According to Clarendon, Sir William's reasons for throwing in his lot with those opposed to royalty were narrow and dishonourable, moulded by a personal dispute with one of those who stood closest to the King. Quarrelling audibly outside Westminster Hall, the M.P. struck the courtier with his fist. Waller, however, fluently provides his reasons to stand firm with those who declared against the monarch. *'All the ends I had in the carrying out of that service were but to bring things to a fair and peaceable issue; that God might have had his fear; the King his honour; the Houses of Parliament their privileges; the people of the kingdom their liberties and properties'* [14]

Southampton's early allegiance to the Parliamentary cause was clearly assisted by the steadfastness of the city's two M.P.s, George Gollop and Edward Exton,, influential and vociferous in their attempts to convert the doubtful. And solidly behind them were the merchants of town and harbour, who governed the cosmopolitan town.

Allegiance of the county's M.P.s

For the King: Matthew Davies (Christchurch)
                 George Goring (Portsmouth)
                 John Meux (Newton)
                 William Ogle (Winchester)
                 Nicholas Weston (Newton)
                 William Ulvedale (Petersfield)
                 Lucius Carey, (Newport)

---

14 'Vindications of the Character and Conduct of Sir William Waller' p.303

'THE ROOT AND VICE OF ALL THE PLOT'

For the Parliament:　　John Button (Lymington)
　　　　　　　　　　　Henry Campion (Lymington)
　　　　　　　　　　　Edward Douse (Portsmouth)
　　　　　　　　　　　Edward Exton (Southampton)
　　　　　　　　　　　George Gollop (Southampton)
　　　　　　　　　　　William Heveningham (Stockbridge)
　　　　　　　　　　　William Jephson (Stockbridge)
　　　　　　　　　　　Sir Richard Jervoise (Whitchurch)
　　　　　　　　　　　Sir Thomas Jervoise (Whitchurch)
　　　　　　　　　　　Sir William Lewis (Petersfield)
　　　　　　　　　　　Sir John Leigh (Yarmouth)
　　　　　　　　　　　Philip, Lord Lisle (Yarmouth)
　　　　　　　　　　　John Lisle (Winchester)
　　　　　　　　　　　Henry Tulse (Christchurch)
　　　　　　　　　　　Sir William Waller (Andover)
　　　　　　　　　　　Sir Henry Worsley (Newport)
　　　　　　　　　　　Sir Henry Wallop (Shire)
　　　　　　　　　　　Robert Wallop (Andover)
　　　　　　　　　　　Richard Whitehead (Shire)

　　Men from outside the county would increasingly play a part. Philip, fourth Earl of Pembroke and Montgomery, was hoisted by Parliament into a position of some importance in the summer of 1642. For most of Charles's reign, he had served as the King's Lord Chamberlain. During his tenure of that office, he had displayed rare skills of self-survival and a cocktail of resilience and affability that had earned the respect of many of his contemporaries. In July 1641, however, he had fallen from grace and, from that moment on, Pembroke walked in Parliament's camp.

---

*In the poll following the death of Rainsford, the 18 burgesses of Andover split their votes equally between Waller and Henry Vernon. Three other voters, one a known supporter of Waller, were disqualified. Waller promptly petitioned the Commons and in May 1642 the Commons, by the narrow margin of 107 to 102, decided in favour of Waller.

'The Root And Vice Of All The Plot'

For a while at least, like condemned men waking on the morning of their execution, the factions would have time to reflect on their deeds and shudder in the dawn of expected war. In the Spring of that fateful year, the leading men of neighbouring Wiltshire petitioned Westminster *'for redress of grievances for those whose throats were exposed to the sword of the savage and barbarous foe'*. Fear of change and the upheavals that war would bring became paramount in the minds of thinking men. The Earl of Pembroke was just one of many to anticipate the destruction of the traditional order. *'We hear every fellow say in the streets as we pass by in our coaches, that they hope to see us on foot shortly....and be as good men as the Lords, and I think they will... if we take this course'*.[15]

Others were equally ashen about the likely loss of comfort. Those about to fight would be obliged to give up soft beds for the damp soil of a windy hillside. Those left behind to manage their estates were concerned about the absence of tenants and the non-payment of rates. And pamphleteers were in no doubt about the probable consequences of war. One is particularly full of foreboding:

> *'And let thy tears run down,*
> *To see the rent,*
> *Between the robes and Crown,*
> *War like a serpent, has its head got in,*
> *And will not end as soon as it did begin.'* [16]

But then the eloquence, oratory and self-pity had to stop. In April Sir John Hotham refused to allow the King to enter Hull. The physical dispute over ownership of the nation's fabric was about to commence. The sword would now replace both the mouth and the pen.

---

15 Sidney R, Earl of Leicester ,Sydney Papers (1825) p.xxl
16 Warburton E. 'Memoirs of Prince Rupert and the Cavaliers (1849) Vol.1 p.226

3

'A great blemish and disadvantage to the King's service'

THE leading men of the county would now become the recruiting sergeants by which men would be found to fill the ranks of the opposing armies. The problem was to find legal methods of procuring the required numbers, of somehow compelling men to join the ranks without resorting to impressment.

The most concrete source of soldiers was the Trained Band, the local defence force based upon the Saxon fyrd. Since those distant times, all the able bodied men of the county had been obliged to attend musters, officially four times a year in the summer months only, at assembly points chosen by the Lords Lieutenants and their deputies, and there drill and train for the defence of their home county. Those called were usually expected to provide equipment and weapons, a harsh demand on people often unable to provide even the most essential requirements of life. Theoretically a county muster of the bands could produce impressive numbers: a Hampshire muster role of 1639 includes nearly 8000 names! Both sides, anxious to raise troops quickly, consequently jockeyed to secure the allegiance of the Lords Lieutenants, the only men officially able to assemble the force. Throughout the 1630's, the college at Winchester obeyed more promptly than most of the other communities in Hampshire, sending two men to the musters; each received two shillings from the Bursar for his attendance.

Nationally, Westminster won the race to secure the militia. In Spring 1642, M.P.s hurried through a Militia Ordinance, snatching control of the militia from the King and appointing their own Lords Lieutenants and deputies in place of the King's earlier nominees. On June 21st, Hampshire's Parliamentary officials openly declared for Parliament and called the county's Trained Band to arms.

But these locally raised forces were impressive on paper only. Such forces could not be compelled to serve outside their county's boundaries, and the activity on the village green was often little more than a showy pantomime. Discipline was frequently poor and military skills absent, even amongst the officers. A contemporary report gives an idea of what sometimes happened: *'Officers love their bellies so well as that they are loath to take too much pains about disciplining their soldiers.... after a little careless hurrying over of their postures... they make them charge their muskets, and so prepare to give their captains a brave volley of shot at his entrance to the inn'.*[1] Payment to the men was seldom made. A letter to Hampshire J.P.s in February 1642 spells out the danger of a failure to pay: ' *'if a speedy course be not taken* (to get the money) *we suppose for want of pay the soldiers will hardly be kept from mutinying, and ourselves shall receive much prejudice, not only in the money we have already disbursed for the impress, but likewise in our own particular credit, having engaged ourselves for the costs, but most especially it will be a great blemish and disadvantage to the King's service'.* [2] Clearly incapable of providing a policing action within their home county's borders, such men could hardly be relied upon to win a war. More effective methods of raising forces and providing equipment would have to be found.

1 Carlton C 'Going to the Wars' *2Hampshire Magazine Sept. 1884*

'A Great Blemish and Disadvantage To The King's Service'

In late July, Westminster pre-empted any latent Cavalier attempt to secure weapons. Dated July 22nd, a wordy instruction was addressed to the county's J.P.s, constables and mayors to seize certain items that would have materially assisted the King. *'Whereas information has been given to the Parliament that divers ill-affected persons to the true Protestant Religion and the Peace of the Kingdom, have endeavoured to prepare horses, and store of arms, ammunition, and money with divers other provisions, in some parts of this kingdom, for the assisting and encouragement of those that intend war against the Parliament; And whereas it is probable that the said horses, arms or ammunition may be brought through some part of the County of Southampton, the Lords and Commons..do hereby require the High Sheriff of the County of Southampton, and all Justices of Peace, Mayors, Constables, and all other his Majesty's Officers, within the said county to be aiding and assisting in the execution of this order; and do hereby authorise the Deputy Lieutenants of the said county.....to make stay of all horses, arms, ammunition, money, or other provisions whatsoever, which they, or any of them, shall suspect to be preparing or carrying for the making of war against the Parliament as aforesaid'.*[3]

Orders were then sent to remove *'six field pieces, with double carriages, from Winchester and take them to Southampton or 'some convenient place of the said county as the deputy lieutenants...shall nominate or appoint'*. On 11th August, the county's first real skirmish took place as a result. Eighty partisans of Parliament set out from Southampton, intending to round up the last of the county's militia. They were attacked at Hounsdown by 170 leaderless Royalists, and an hour's fighting followed. At the end, 20 men lay dead or wounded, martyred during a tremor of excitement that vibrated throughout the south.

Both sides now sought to rely on the zeal of their supporters to raise and pay whole regiments of horse and foot. Invariably an influential member of the gentry would serve as recruiting agent by

---
3 Journals of the House of Commons Vol. 2 p.686

which men could be found to fill the ranks. Those summoned to his colours would find it difficult to refuse. With something of a semi-feudal hold over the masses, Hampshire's gentry were able to bring considerable pressure to bear upon their tenants. In an age when obedience and subservience formed the glue which held the social fabric in place, few men had the courage to resist their superiors' demands, and the threat of eviction from homes would generally persuade the most reluctant to conform.

But the raising of private armies was illegal; a lawful way of recruiting had first to be found. The King's chosen method was the Commission of Array, a medieval procedure with a document in Latin, which was impressed with the Great Seal. One was issued for each county or major town and contained the names of all the leading men who might be prepared to raise troops for the kingly cause. Heading the list in Hampshire were the Marquis of Winchester and the Earl of Southampton. Those addressed were summoned to a meeting at the home of one of those named, where the following instructions were read: *'Charles by the grace of God... To our trusted and well beloved... greeting. We do hereby constitute and appoint you to be* (Captain, colonel etc) *in the regiment of......You are forthwith to impress and retain of such as will willingly and voluntarily serve us for our pay, and for the defence of our Royal person, the two houses of parliament, the Protestant religion, the law of the land, the liberty and propriety of the subject......to bring them to our standard, and to cause them to be duly exercised in arms.* Armed with such authority, those commissioned could raise entire regiments, convinced that they had been called to action by God and His anointed one.

Parliament reacted swiftly, attempting to expose the unlawfulness of this move: *'Whereas several Commissions of Array have lately issued out under the Great Seal of England... It is ordered by the Lords and Commons assembled in Parliament, that the Judges and Justices of Assize... be required... openly to declare and publish... that the said Commissions of Array are against Law, and* against the Liberty and Property of the Subject: And that all those that are actors in putting the same in execution, shall be esteemed as disturbers of the peace'* [4].

Parliament then chose to rely upon an equally dubious procedure. Issuing commissions to individuals, it instructed them to raise companies or even whole regiments, or alternatively to accept the offers of others who might volunteer to recruit at their own expense. *'By virtue of an Ordinance authorising Philip, Earl of Pembroke and Montgomery to be Lieutenant of the County of Southampton... We do hereby appoint* (named individual) *to be Captain of a Company of Foot in the Regiment of........ As shall be delivered unto you by me by any one or more of my Deputy Lieutenants by my command. And I do further give warrant unto you hereby to train and pay a foot company at such days and in such places as by warrant from me or any one of them... And I do likewise give power to you to nominate sub-Lieutenants, ensigns and other officers under you as shall be necessary for the purpose....'*, the official summons began.[5] By the end of June 1642, 5000 men in Hampshire alone had been called to arms. Unlike the King, Westminster offered financial inducement; each commissioned captain was paid £1,100 'mounting money' for each troop of horse raised and slightly smaller amounts for units of foot.

Two complete regiments were raised by this method, producing the nucleus of an army well before the county's Royalist units had even begun to hatch in their nest. Working through the summer and autumn, 'Idle Dick' Norton produced a body of horsemen in time for the next summer's campaign. He was assisted in this mission by men such as Richard Major, who gave £20 and supplied 4 horses, *'completely armed with great saddles, pistols, carbines and buff coats valued with their furniture at twenty pounds apiece'*[5] Francis St. Barbe was equally generous, providing coats and guns for his chosen cause. Richard Whitehead raised the other early regiment, assembling 300 men by late summer, fully armed

---

4 ibid p.682   5 Cal. SP. Dom.1642-43 p.356

and with *'pennies in their pockets'*. William Waller would take far longer to raise his regiments of horse and foot. When the war broke out, he was at the head of just two or three troops of Andover men. Royalist field forces were not assembled until November. Townsmen, foreigners and ruffians formed the earliest garrison of Portsmouth where Goring was about to make his stand, hastily assembled in the hour of need. Broken when the town was taken, these rough-hewn troops chose mainly to return to their homes and few served in the winter campaign. On November 21st, William Villiers, Lord Grandison, reached Basing with an imported troop of horse. Here he began to requisition cloth and linen from sympathisers in the area. Retainers of the Marquis of Winchester dutifully responded to his call - and the first Royalist regiment in Hampshire was formed. Serving in Wiltshire in December, they returned to Hampshire in the new year and received additional scars of battle in actions near Winchester.

Many minor episodes of violence took place in the summer before the first real clash of arms. Appearing at the time as tests of strength, they were, in reality, probably more the settling of personal scores or criminal acts than any genuine gesture of partisan sympathy. Seven rough highwaymen, claiming to be in the service and pay of the King, attacked two travellers near Winchester, shooting their horses and robbing them of their load. They were cornered eventually in a tavern in Romsey and imprisoned briefly in Winchester's jail. Within days they were at liberty again to serve as captains in a Royalist regiment. A penniless Stockbridge farmer was impaled on a branch by his creditors for his *'dangerous tendencies'* and for *'uttering oaths out loud against the King'*, while a Papist priest who had refused to baptise an infant had his hair set alight by the child's outraged father. Roundhead soldiers were just as lawless, engaging in acts of brigandage that could never be politically justified: *'The truth is unless we were able to execute some exemplary punishment upon the principal malefactors, we have no hope to*

'A Great Blemish and Disadvantage To The King's Service'

redress this horrid enormity'. John Hampden, M.P., wrote to the Earl of Essex in September 1642, when the scale of the atrocities first reached Westminster. *'We beseech your Excellence to take this into your present and serious consideration, for if this go on awhile, the army will grow as odious to the country as the Cavaliers'.*[6] Men were choosing to confuse pettiness for principles, and blameless lives were put at risk. The solid framework of common law, developed over centuries past, was becoming little more than broken wreckage on a rocky coast.

---

6 Sanford 'Studies and Illustrations of the Great Rebellion' p.559

4

'Drink in his head...but no fire in his stomach'

GORING was to be the King's first champion and Portsmouth his first setback. On August 2nd, the Cavalier peer assembled the town's garrison on the bowling green and bribed them with promises of reward and regal favour. A contemporary account gives details: *'His Majesty....have commanded me to put in such a posture, that we may be able and ready, not only to maintain his Majesty's right in this place against any that shall dare to attempt the contrary, but also that this place may be fit for the guard and safety of his Majesty's person; and I trust I shall not need to urge many reasons to persuade or win you to a cheerful and willing obedience... And for you that are behind of your pay, although the parliament has made some promise to see you satisfied (re pay), yet such is the case and goodness of His Majesty towards you, that he has provided you money, which I have in my custody to distribute amongst you so soon as you have subscribed to some few words and conditions in writing'* [1]

An oath of loyalty was required and a declaration of undying

---

1 ' True News from Portsmouth, being Col. Goring his speech delivered to the Soldiers in Portsmouth' BM

support. Those who refused His Majesty's generous offer were to be free to depart. Only four, according to the report, chose to do so. Four hundred or more were purchased for the King.

The coffers were full enough. On June 30th, Westminster, still believing Goring to be a loyal servant, had voted £5030 for the payment of arrears to the garrison and for improvements to the defences. Weston's recent contribution had caused the chests to overflow, and the soldiers of the garrison ate and drunk well at night.

But little was actually spent on either the defences or on food. Clarendon criticises Goring for his failure to renew the fortifications of the city. He *'relied too much upon probable and casual assistance, and neglected to do that himself a vigilant officer would have done.'* [2] A small fort was built at Portsbridge to guard the island; from here twenty soldiers watched the narrow entrance to Portsea Island. In the harbour lay just one ship, the 'Henrietta Maria', a 6 gun pinnace and one of only six warships still flying the King's standard. The town's main battery had been left facing the sea while the bastions of the landward defences had been starved of weapons.

Yet Goring had grounds for optimism. Reports had filtered through of the imminent arrival of 5000 Frenchmen, while Lord Henry Jermyn, a favourite of the Queen, was busy recruiting in Rotterdam. Sitting in the hills of Portsdown to the north was Parliament's only field force, no more than 400 militia men of the county with less than 200 muskets at their disposal.

Food was freely obtained. Like homesteaders preparing for a violent storm, parties of horsemen rode out from Portsmouth into the surrounding countryside to collect supplies and provisions in order to survive the expected siege. Portsea Island was golden with ripening corn, and the harvest had not yet begun. Within a week, the fields were almost empty, but little of the produce lay in the owners' barns. A contemporary complains bitterly of Goring's

---

2 Clarendon Vol.11 Bk. VI p.2

savage treatment. *'He caused divers hundreds of cattle, sheep and swine, in the fruitful isle of Portsea to be brought into Portsmouth then, whether they were fat or lean, to be all killed and fatted up, and caused every house in that isle to be searched and all manner of provisions to be taken away from the owners, as corn, meat, flour, beef, bacon, bread, butter, cheese, eggs, and all their poultry and ducks, not leaving half loaves of bread, nor pieces of bread, nor pieces of meat'.* [3] Fruit trees and vegetable plots were plundered too, More than a thousand sheep in total were taken and penned *'within the town upon some ground below the moats that surround the town'*, the rightful owners forced to act as drovers and shepherds.

Some of the dispossessed joined the Roundhead ranks, which consequently began to grow. On 10th August, the militia units of Hampshire, Surrey and Sussex were joined by Sir William Waller and Colonel John Hurry, each at the head of a locally recruited troop of horse. Two days later, Sir John Merrick arrived with his regiment of foot - and Parliament's southern army was slowly born.

The King's men in Southern Hampshire tried to hinder its formation. At Havant a lone Cavalier and his servant were arrested when they attempted to persuade the townsmen to loot the Southwick home of Colonel Richard Norton. News of the detention prompted a larger group of Cavaliers to assemble at Southwick and stones were thrown at the colonel's windows. Norton, taking time to saddle his horse and collect his weapons, rode out at the head of a troop of horse and, although outnumbered, seemed intent on offering battle. His enemy, sensing easy victory, rode closer and accused Richard of cowardice, treachery and *'base dishonour'*. Norton's skull might have been broken in the minutes to follow and one of Parliament's future heroes might never have left his mark. One hundred well armed Parliamentary horsemen fortunately arrived in time and chased the colonel's baiters from the park. From that day onwards, Richard Norton remained active in the field and was to play his part

---

3 'Copy of a Letter... concerning divers passages at Portsmouth' Hampshire Records Office

in the ultimate victory.

The Parliamentary siege of Portsmouth had now begun. John Vicars claims that Waller's forces *'first showed themselves against Goring about Portsdown, way half mile from the Portsbridge'*[4] Goring, seeing their advance, withdrew his four guns from the tiny fort, abandoning one of the weapons when the carriage broke. He left a garrison of just eight men to hold the enemy advance.

But heavy rain delayed the assault for two days. Soon after 6 p.m. on the 12th, just twenty men moved towards the fort *'and beat the governor's troopers from the bridge, and the whole island, took a trooper prisoner, another's horse, the rider hardly escaping, having leapt from his horse'* [5] - and seven Royalist soldiers fled without a fight. Parliament had forced open the gate to Portsea and the route to Portsmouth's landward walls. *'I must tell you'*, states another contemporary report, *'the taking of this bridge is of greater moment than most think, for it possesses them of the island of Portsea'.*[6]

Goring was not the sort of man around whom legends are formed. No elevated principles guided this man of opportunities, and he would have willingly surrendered if that could be guaranteed to purchase his salvation and bring him personal gain. His decision to resist was prompted largely by expectations of financial reward and a chance to bask in the sunshine of King Charles' favour. On 13th August, seeing a chance for personal elevation and *'fain to leave that piece in the highway,* he and Thomas, Lord Wentworth, heir to the Earldom of Cleveland and now in Portsmouth with a message from the King, sortied from the town into Portsea Island with about sixty men to recapture the gun abandoned on the previous day.

The Parliamentarians did not see them arrive. Engrossed in the tedious routine of setting up camp, they had stacked their weapons in tidy lines. Soon, many of the men lay dead on the freshly

---

[4] Vicars J. 'Parliamentary Chronicles' p.157   [5] op.cit p.158   [6] 'The Taking of the Castle of Portsmouth' Letter by A. Clarke, Hants Records Office

turned earth and the Cavaliers had withdrawn, dragging back the unwheeled gun in their only triumph of the siege so far.

Parliament soon hit back. In the week following, Waller's horsemen tried vainly to seize the stolen livestock and return them to their owners. Intended clearly to buy the support of the dispossessed farmers, the raid secured nothing but the death of 30 animals and injury to soldiers.

Next the besiegers aimed for the stolen bags of flour that lay within the town's mills. Approaching well within the range of Royalist musketeers, the Roundheads laid skins on the ground upon which to drag away the heavy weights. Cavalier soldiers were soon at their throats and a schoolboy brawl ensued. The Parliamentarians were quick to withdraw, leaving a hat and sword in Royalist hands and patches of blood on the ground.

The besiegers guarding the northern approaches had difficult but less dangerous work to perform. They were to be the eyes and ears of the investing force. Royalist sympathisers were numerous: men, women and even children, who approached the lines in an attempt to smuggle messages, food and even weapons to those held within the town. Rumours of an imminent attack from the north and fanciful tales of Royalist intrigues reached them daily and every stranger on the highway was consequently transformed into the role of a plotter, spy or messenger of hope. Men, women and children, almost without exception, were stopped and searched - and almost everyone had a plausible reason to offer for their presence on that road: a return to a ravaged home on the island, a visit to a sick relative or a wife searching for a missing husband. A woman carrying a bundle claimed that it contained a baby. In fact, it turned out to be a covering of rags around a box full of letters. And an aged woman with an arched back was a Papist priest with robes concealed.

Goring and Wentworth galloped out again, this time at night with all their horse, two entire troops or 60 men in total. Close siege had fed their ambitions and sharpened their determinations. Goaded constantly by enemy taunts, they proposed now to strike at the heart

'DRINK IN HIS HEAD...BUT NO FIRE IN HIS STOMACH'

A TRVE RELATION

Of the severall passages and proceedings of Colonell *Goring* at *Portsmouth*, and how he is revolted from the Parliament, who imposed that trust in him, and keepes it for the King.

How he hath shut the Gates, and hath gotten a Garrison of above five hundred men with great store of money and Ammunition beside.

Also how the Parliament hath given Order to his excelency the E. of *Essex* to rayse Forces to demand *Portsmouth* and the Castle, and to apprehend Colonell *Goring* as guilty of high Treason.

With other severall matters of Note concerning *Portsmouth*, and *the Ile of* Wight.

Whereunto especially is added a catalogue of the names of the Lords, that subscribed to levy Horse to assist His Majesty in defence of his royall Person, the two Houses of Parliament, and the Protestant Religion, with the monies men and Horse, already subscribed unto by severall Counties of this Kingdom, and undertaken for His Majesties service, *August.* 6th. 1642.

LONDON,
Printed by *E. G.* for *Iohn Benson.*

of the Parliamentary camp, the rise in the ground where Waller had made his quarters. A townsman named Winters had volunteered to serve as their guide, offering to lead them through the gaps in the Roundhead picket line that he claimed to have identified. In the darkness of a perfect night, they almost reached their goal. Captives were taken by both sides, but hardly a soldier was felled. Winters was amongst the dozen or so taken by Parliament, the unfortunate man running into a fence in his attempt to keep out of the fighting. The Royalists took fewer, just 6 musketeers, one of whom had lost his weapon in a puddle. Five of the prisoners were forced to work at repairing Portsmouth's defences: the sixth refused and was rewarded with incarceration in a dark, damp cell with only a madman for company.

Winters, treated more hospitably, was held in the farmhouse that served as Waller's quarters. His son, permitted to carry fresh linen to his father, chose to serve also as a Royalist spy, carrying back to Goring any snippets of information or rumours that he happened to hear during his moments of eavesdropping in the enemy camp. Reports that the King himself was in Hampshire at the head of an army were dutifully carried back to Goring himself. The wily peer, hoping to steady his wavering troops, had the report broadcast throughout the town.

Waller and Merrick could now write the rules of play and even compose the rumours which they wished the besieged to hear. Goring's Royalists could merely react. Little of the war's true happenings ever reached the men in Portsmouth. Messengers from the King, carrying pledges of support and whispers of hope, were intercepted on the Down or chased for miles before their horses stumbled.

Portsmouth's seaward end was being sealed, too. Robert Rich, Earl of Warwick, appointed Lord High Admiral of the Fleet in March by Parliament, had secured the agreement of the captains of the larger vessels to serve under him, and now patrolled the south and east coasts of England with 11 men-of-war and several armed merchantmen. Hearing of Goring's obstinacy, he sent Captain Richard Swanley with the 44 gun *'Charles'* and 7 merchantmen to isolate the port.

The *'Henrietta Maria'* still remained at anchor, pitifully left to challenge the fleet's arrival. Swanley quickly made plans for her capture. On the night of the 15th, a moonless night without a breeze, the *'Martin'* was towed towards the harbour and positioned only yards from where the resting pinnace lay. Captain Brown Bushell, an opportunist adventurer and the sort of man about whom films are now made, took a handful of men and, faces blackened, boarded the Royalist vessel. An hour later, the King's crew in chains, the pinnace was in Parliament's hands and preparing to serve new masters.

With the arrival of the rest of the fleet on 18th August, the besiegers had little real need of this puny acquisition. Three of the captured ship's guns were placed in the Portsbridge fort, established behind strengthened works in a bastion that faced towards the north. Waller's forces were positioned nearby, 2000 or more men clumsily combining to fight for principles which they barely understood and for which they probably cared even less: adventurers from the towns with a longing for excitement, the soldiers of the trained Bands present in camp out of a legal obligation, and the men from the Portsea fields whose rural livelihoods had been cruelly destroyed.

By contrast, the Royalist garrison in Portsmouth was shrinking daily, reduced by desertion and a belated wish for survival. Filled bellies and flowing wine could never compensate for the expected punishment that would probably come to all those caught with the King's shilling in their hands when the town finally surrendered and the promises of the King turned to water. In the harbour were the masts and guns of 7 Parliamentary warships while the growing framework of Parliament's new fort at Gosport was marked out by the setting sun. Men left at night, scaling the walls in a sudden bid for faceless obscurity. One, a young man from Chichester, who had taken his father's best horse and ridden to Portsmouth to serve in

'DRINK IN HIS HEAD...BUT NO FIRE IN HIS STOMACH'

the garrison, hired a boat to make his escape. Others chose to swim. *'Sometimes 4, sometimes 6, at a time - sometimes more and sometimes less......and the most of his best gunners were gone from him* (Goring) *to the Parliamentary side, and such as were left of the garrison were even heartless, and did little, and that on compulsion'*, Vicars reports. [7]

Instead of being pulverised when the timbers first went up, the Gosport fort was allowed to grow. On August 18th, Goring's seaward batteries briefly tried to smash the distant structure. The main gun platform, however, was concealed behind a barn and the only casualty was a carpenter, who was unwisely standing on a beam with a lantern in his hand.

A trumpeter, sent by Waller to negotiate an exchange of prisoners, was far luckier. While standing below the town's defences and well within a musket's range, he was fired upon by several men. He was missed by all, although his instrument was holed. A few days later, a drunken soldier waged war single-handedly on Portsmouth's defenders. Passing through Parliament's front lines with a candle to light his path, he challenged the garrison to come out and fight. A single shot sent him on his way to Heaven.

In the week following Goring's timid attempt to smash the infant fort, the weapons of both sides lay strangely silent. It was as if the aggression and energy of both sides had flowed away like the harbour's tide, and only the ripples were left. The stolen animals were fed, repairs to defences took place in full view of the enemy, and soldiers breakfasted on the dewed grass above the trenches. The optimists might have been forgiven for believing that all the shadows and threats of war had flowed away too.

But, on August 22nd, the King raised his standard on Nottingham Castle's hill. *'At which time all the courtiers and spectators flung up their caps and whooped, crying 'God save King Charles and hang up the Roundheads'* [8] and the sense of impending

---

7 Vicars p.159

8 Hutchinson Lucy 'The Life of Col. J. Hutchinson'

catastrophe returned.

So, too, did the war in Portsmouth. On August 26th, the merchantman *'Santa Clara'*, sailing from the Continent with cochineal and silver, was forced into Southampton's port and stripped of its valuable load. Three wagons of silver were despatched to London. The Spanish ambassador naturally protested and the empty ship was eventually permitted to return to Spain. This legalised act of piracy created an earthquake of squabbles. Hampshire herring fishermen, for example, were amongst those who claimed a share of the booty, arguing that the merciless raids of the Dunkirk pirates over several decades entitled them to solid compensation.

The Gosport guns opened at last, smashing a bell in the tower of St. Thomas' Church in which Royalist lookouts had made their nest. Part of the structure went crashing to the ground. On the 27th, Waller again attempted to negotiate and was invited to dine in the town. At 10 a.m. the next morning, he entered with a small entourage while Wentworth went to dine at Parliament's headquarters.

But nothing came of such gentlemanly conduct - neither an offer to withdraw, nor an agreement to surrender. Letters of support and whispers of impending relief were still being intercepted and few ever reached the town. Goring, with everything to lose, but perhaps much to gain, politely refused Waller's gentle request, asking instead for permission to send a messenger to the King to ask for relief. If, after an interval of time, no such relief appeared, he would *'willingly give up his allegiance to the King, and hold the town for Parliament, as he had formerly done'*.[9] All the Royalist cavalry went out again that night, molesting the enemy lines as the besiegers cooked supper. But, passing too close, the bridles of the Royalist horses were seized and the riders brought crashing to the ground. One was despatched to another world with the knife that had just been used to cut up the mutton.

On the 29th, Royalist gunners opened at last on Gosport. Hardly a shot penetrated the fort, but the roofs of houses were

---
9 Godwin 'The Civil War in Hampshire' p.19

'Drink In His Head...But No Fire In His Stomach'

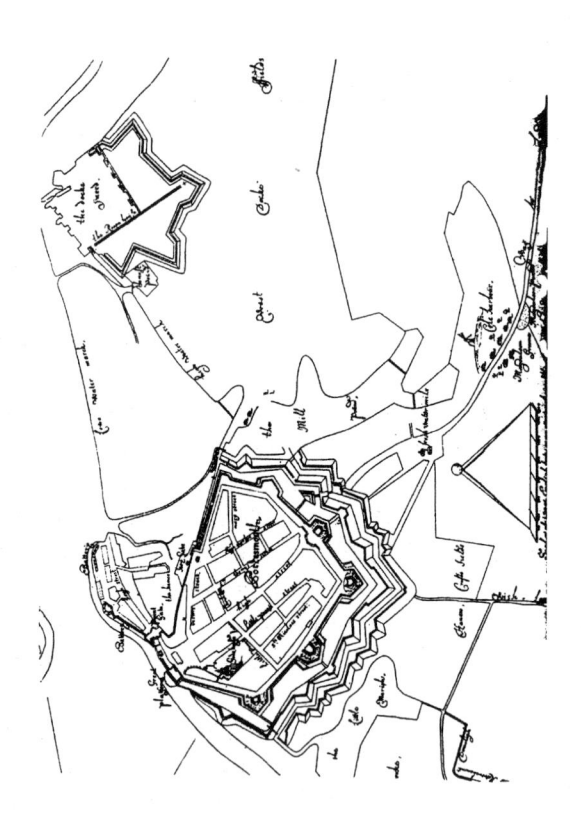

De Gomme's map of the defences of Portsmouth

'opened to the heavens'. Some of the inhabitants took revenge, hurrying up to the fort and offering to man the cannon that shot back in response.

On September 2nd, Waller tried again to gain by kindness what he seemed unable to win by force. Under a flag of truce, he presented Goring with a brace of bucks and fresh vegetables for the officers' tables. Goring sent his thanks but nothing more.

At 4 p.m., the Gosport battery opened in fury, targeting the church and the mill where the wheel still turned. A bullet passed through the miller's sheets and lodged in the empty bed. The occupant, fortunately, had risen early and none of his blood was spilled. *'We did more execution with our two pieces of ordnance than the governor had with the town ordnance in 14 or 16 days and so many nights, in which they shot at least 300 bullets and killed but one man in all that time, a most remarkable providence of the Lord'*,[10] the contemporary account maintains.

Waller now needed to find another form of persuasion. South of Portsmouth, still untested, was Southsea Castle, a fortress built by Henry VIII and described by a contemporary as *'the strongest castle in England for the bigness'*, and surrounded by a moat with walls 4 yards thick, *'with dainty chambers in it; fit to entertain a prince'*,[11] it would be an asset for which ever side could secure its help.

But Goring had underestimated its possible contribution to his cause; only a dozen men had been placed within its walls. Captain Challoner, heavy drinker, opportunist and no obvious leader of men, held the command, a replica in miniature of Goring himself. This man had done little to prepare the fortress against attack, apart from turning the 14 mounted guns to face landward instead of out to sea, and viewed his governorship in semi-feudal terms. Rarely in contact with his chief in Portsmouth, he imposed his own laws on the people of Southsea.

---

10 'True Relation of the Passages which happened at the town of Portsmouth' Hants. Records Office
11 'The Taking of the castle of Portsmouth' Letter by A. Clarke Hants Records Office

'DRINK IN HIS HEAD...BUT NO FIRE IN HIS STOMACH'

On Saturday, 3rd September (the 5th according to Vicars), the night chosen by Waller for his assault, Challoner was drinking as usual, and few of his tiny force were at their posts.

In the early hours of a moonless night, the parliamentarian sent 2 troops of horse and 400 foot under Browne Bushell, with scaling ladders and hooks into the narrow strip of land that lay between the fort and the sea. At 2 a.m., in disciplined silence, they lined up for attack and tested the depth of the moat.

Waller was as well acquainted with the arts of deceit as he was with the skills of war. To muffle the Southsea advance, he ordered a simultaneous feint against Portsmouth's main defences, hurling a force against the Landport in an effort to convince Goring that the dagger blow was aimed at the city's northern walls.

Browne Bushell waited until the feint had started. At 3 a.m., he led the storming party with their ladders through the shallow moat and personally hammered on the castle's door. Challoner, awakened from a drunken sleep, asked the visitors to return in the morning when his wits, no doubt, would be a little clearer. Displeased by his response, the Parliamentarians began to climb, scaling the virtually unmanned walls without a single casualty. Aroused again from his sleep to meet his new masters, the Southsea commander proposed a toast in their honour. He then calmly fired a gun at Portsmouth to inform Goring of Southsea's change of ownership.

Vicars, in his *'Chronicle'* uncharacteristically attempts to exonerate a Royalist, protecting Challoner from some of the mud of vilification that would later fly at all those who failed their King. *'They reported he had more drink in his head than was befitting such a time and service, and the Townsmen gave out that he had been bribed with money to yield up the castle, but 'twas false though the first may be true, yet was not that neither any furtherance to the taking of it'·*

Lord Goring had been only partially duped by the concurrent attack on the Landport. Forced to repel a lively attack on Portsmouth's walls, he still found time and energy to order his

'Drink In His Head...But No Fire In His Stomach'

Southsea Castle

southern wall batteries to fire on Southsea's new owners. The drawbridge of the fort was shot away and Parliament's colours were felled from a pole. *'Our captain was upon the bridge'*, Clarke reported in his account of this minor incident. '*.....and there came a piece close to him; and one thing is remarkable, when we came to the bridge, there was a great piece of timber and some ten men fell down behind it, for they saw the bullet coming, and it hit just on the log, and missed the men, we lost not a man'* [12.] But Waller had already placed 80 men to hold the fort; more soldiers, in fact, that now remained in Goring's Portsmouth garrison, and any Royalist dreams of re-capture would remain mere fancy.

Goring would also have to wake from his present dreams of grandeur and defiance to Westminster's local muscle. With only 50 men at his back, the Royalist peer could never hope to hold Portsmouth against such hopeless odds. Probably with some hidden sense of relief, he assembled his remaining officers on September 4th and discussed submission. At 8 a.m., his drummer went out to ask the enemy for their terms. At 10 a.m., the detailed negotiations began, and soldiers sat idly while the talking took place, like superfluous extras on an open-air film set when the rain sets in.

Waller and two officers entered the town that night, huddled under broad-rimmed hats for protection against the evening chill. For several hours, a candle burned in Goring's quarters, and enormous shadows were thrown against the internal walls by the talkers of both sides. For the two days following the talking went on, but hardly a soldier remained in Portsmouth's garrison to find out what surrender would entail. Some jumped the walls and crossed the fields, joining the Roundhead ranks in preference to a probable spell in captivity.

At 7 p.m. on the 7th, the terms of surrender finally emerged. Goring had held out to the end, threatening to detonate 1400 barrels of powder rather than accept conditions that would clothe him in dishonour. The conditions were consequently generous. Those that

---

12 A. Clarke's Letter

'Drink In His Head...But No Fire In His Stomach'

The Taking of the Castle of Portsmouth
Facsimile of the cover of the report

THE TAKING OF THE CASTLE OF PORTSMOVTH;

WITH THE CIRCUMSTANCES THEREOF:

Expreſt in a Letter Dated *Septemb.6.* from A *CLARKE* in the *LEAGUER.*

London Printed for *H. Blunden, Septemb. 9. 1642.*

remained at Goring's side were permitted to go wherever they pleased, but on the sole condition that they agreed never to take up arms against the Parliament. Goring, reluctant to face the scorn of his master and the wagging tongues of censors, took ship for Holland, throwing the keys to the defences into the harbour as he fled. But, within weeks, he returned to serve as Lieutenant-general of the Horse in the Royalist Army of the North before eventual promotion to the command of an army of his own.

The surrender of Portsmouth could not be as lightly overlooked. '*This blow struck the King to the very heart*',[13] Clarendon reports pithily, voicing the despair that followed the loss of the nation's premier port. The King's apologists were quick to justify the surrender, pointing out the reasons in a clearly worded document that appeared a week later. Titled ' A Declaration of all the passages at the taking of Portsmouth showing the reasons why it was surrendered', it lists the structural weakness of the town's defences, the lack of food and the low morale as the major reasons for capitulation. Vicars, by contrast, believed that God had led the Roundhead troops to victory: '*Thus it pleased the Lord most graciously to finish the great work of so high concernment to the Kingdom...And who now can be so dull-hearted and blind-sighted, as not to conceive and see plainly from all those last forementioned premises, especially these of this town of Portsmouth, and therewith all ingeniously confess and acknowledge the Lord Jehovah to be on the Mount of Mercies to us, and for his believing people's prosperity and welfare*'.[14]

The same tide of Royalist disaster flowed across the Isle of Wight. Alarmed by the possibility of a Cavalier domination of the Island, and the financial assistance provided by Nicholas Weston to the Royalists on the mainland, Parliamentary leaders in Hampshire felt forced to react. On August 4th, the Earl of Portland, absent in London to answer charges, was placed in the custody of the Sheriff

---

13 Clarendon Vol.11 Bk.VI   14 Vicars

of London, *'lest he should comply with Colonel Goring and command the Isle of Wight against the Parliament'*. Released on bail almost a year later, he remained in Oxford for the rest of the war. Two days later, in a gesture of political muscle-flexing, Westminster voted to rob Portland of the Captaincy of the Island. Philip Herbert, the Earl of Pembroke, was appointed in his place, an action which Clarendon acidly ridiculed: *'And when they were resolved no longer to trust the Isle of Wight in the hands of the Earl of Portland, who...had an absolute power over the affection of that people, they preferred the poor Earl of Pembroke ......, who kindly accepted it as a testimony of their favour and so got into actual rebellion, which he had never intended to do'*. [15]

The islanders promptly petitioned for Portland's reinstatement. Rejecting the charges of Papism laid at his feet by the Parliamentary high command, those who signed the petition spoke of his merits and loyalty to the Protestant church. *'For ourselves, we have a pregnant testimony amongst us of his pious affections and love to the reformed religion....We do therefore, at once, ...present our humble and grateful acknowledgement to this great and good assembly of the care taken of our weal and safety, which we conceive can no way be better advanced and continued upon us, than by your just approbation of the vigilance and fidelity of our prudent and able governor'*. [16]

Charles reacted immediately to news of the peer's dismissal, authorising Jerome Brett, Portland's official deputy, to serve as his Lieutenant-Governor on the island. *'You are to do your best to repel or kill or destroy them (*the enemy) *and we will command you and all the mayors, Justices of the Peace, Corporations and officers of the Trained Bands in the said isle..to be abiding and assisting to you'*. [17] On the 9th, the island's Cavalier gentry reacted, too, issuing a proclamation of loyalty to King, Parliament and the established religion *'that we will with our lives and estates be assistant to each*

---

15 Clarendon Vol.11 Bk.VI   16 Worsley R. 'History of the Isle of Wight' p.110
17 Newport Convocation Book

other in the defence of the true Protestant religion established in the Church of England (and) .....that we will unanimously join the uttermost of our endeavours for the peace of this island by protecting it by those forces already legally substituted amongst us and will admit no foreign power or forces or new government except his Majesty by advice of his Parliament upon occasions that may arise shall think it necessary to alter it in any particulars for the good and safety of the Kingdom'. [18]

Among those signing were influential Sir John Oglander of Nunwell and 3 of the island's 6 M.P.s: John Leigh, John Meux and Nicholas Weston. But no amount of ambivalence and semblance of neutrality could disguise the message's true meaning. Moses Read, Mayor of Newport, and a man on whom the Parliament could rely, sent a copy of this proclamation to London and asked for 30 barrels of powder with which to defend his town against probable Royalist attack. Days later, Nicholas Weston was expelled from the Commons, having committed *'ill service to the Parliament'*. Another newly declared Royalist on the Island, Sir Robert Dillington, was arrested at the head of a convoy of wagons. Halted by men from Newport, the carts were found to contain corn destined for Goring and the Royalists of Portsmouth.

But Parliamentary domination of the Island could never be secured until the Cavaliers had been flushed from Carisbrooke and Cowes. At Carisbrooke, Colonel Brett hosted the Countess of Portland, apparently keeping her in style and with a Papist priest and spaniel as her daily companions. Moses Read, a fanatical Puritan, railed incessantly against her presence and asked Westminster for the means with which to drive her out. The Island's Trained Bands, however, had almost ceased to exist, a fact which Sir John Dingley, Pembroke's deputy, revealed in his summer letter to the Earl....
'... as for the trained bands, which (next to the castles) is the strength of the Island, it is much weakened and decayed, ... if the enemy should

---

18 Newport Convocation Book

invade the country,' 'tis to be fear'd they would soon run away'.[19] Another Cavalier contingent under Captain Humphrey Turney held sway in Cowes Castle, and Newport's nervous Parliamentarians could never feel at ease.

The first shots of the island's short war were fired on August 12th. One of Swanley's ships, the merchantman 'Lion of Leith", lay at anchor off Cowes, ordered to detain any vessel that seemed destined for Portsmouth. Two low boats left the island that afternoon, and were instantly challenged by the patrolling ship's captain. Finding his call ignored, he fired a shot or two across the vessels' bows. Instantly a gun in Cowes Castle opened in response, fired, it is claimed, by Humphrey Turney himself *'in a furie, with his own hand'*. The boats were found to be carrying salt and money.

Open Papist activity in Carisbrooke and Jerome Brett's apparent support for the trapped Royalists in Portsmouth provided the spark that ignited the dry tinder of Roundhead resentment. But Brett was just as incensed by the incivility of the men of Newport and had begun to organise his crusade to free the town of the Puritans' evil influence.

He could never achieve this militarily - he had only 20 men. And Goring was asking for material support. On the 14th, a messenger arrived from the besieged town, appealing for men and supplies. Brett was unwilling to comply, pleading circumstances as his reason for refusal. *'For the present I cannot answer your desire for men, both by reason of the boatman's unwillingness to undertake the carrying of any, also, being Sunday, I could have no opportunity. Tomorrow I shall not fail to endeavour my uttermost'*.[20]

On the 15th, his men poured molten metal into the barrel of a brass cannon kept in Brading and then set out to bully the men of Newport. Accompanied by Captain Turney, Sir John Oglander and Sir Robert Dillington, he rode into the town to confront the Mayor. Jostled by the townspeople, he resorted to threats and warned his tormentors of the consequences of rebellion. Finding Read absent

---

19 Ibid. 20 Ibid.

and the mood growing uglier, he wisely retired to his nearby castle, complaining to the Mayor in a letter the following day about his reception in the town. *'Until you have put the town into a more civil posture.....I cannot compare your town to anything but a large Bedlam'.* [21]

Read and the corporation were angered by his hectoring and forceful demand to disarm the town's militia. *'As long as we neither hurt nor disturb any, give us leave within ourselves to do what we list for our own guard and security'*, he wrote in answer to Brett's complaints.

That very day, the 16th, the exasperated Royalists attempted to snatch Newport for the Crown. Details of the Cavalier strategy and the precise numbers of Royalists involved have been covered with time, and only a skeletal account of the midnight skirmish exists. Sir John Oglander and the island's scattered regal supporters must have assisted- for a force of more than 100 men is reported to have assembled. But Newport's defending force, 300 men or more, honed during the previous weeks to fighting sharpness by the vigilance and enthusiasm of a Captain Johnson, slept each night with their weapons by their beds. Alerted by the noise of the Cavalier horde, they sallied from the town and locked in clumsy combat. Muskets were fired, almost at random, pikes clashed in confusion and the toll of the wounded mounted. Men had not yet learned the intricacies of fighting, nor perfected the arts of courage. The Royalists were the first to break, fleeing under the cover of darkness in the direction of Cowes.

Cowes was hardly the place for refuge. A party of Parliament's sailors had come ashore on the 15th with a warrant for Captain Turney's arrest. The castle's gates, however, were locked, and a single musket shot was the Royalist's only response to Parliament's fragile demand. Retiring to an inn, the sailors waited for support to arrive.

An unplanned event was to bring the Royalist governor out.

---

21 Newport Convocation Book

'Drink In His Head...But No Fire In His Stomach'

Contemporary map of the Isle of Wight

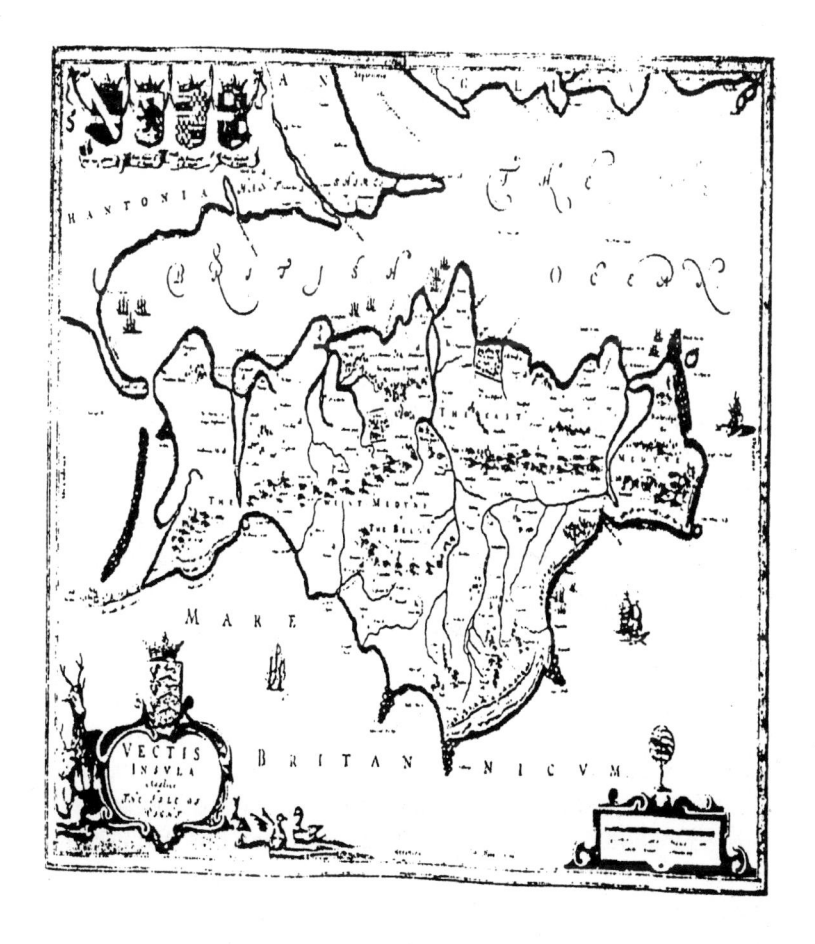

'DRINK IN HIS HEAD...BUT NO FIRE IN HIS STOMACH'

Two Cavalier gentlemen had been taken captive that afternoon and imprisoned in a house in Cowes. One, a man of considerable wealth, was carrying still undetected letters sealed within his clothes. Anxious to be rid of this incriminating evidence, he dropped them down a privy and into the sea. They were unfortunately found two days later by Parliamentary pickets on the beach, and later used in evidence against those named. Turney heard of the men's arrest. Vainly imagining himself a man of influence and persuasive power, he left the castle and demanded the prisoners' release. An hour later, he, too, was in custody on board a Roundhead ship.

The castle was manned by only two men. On the 17th it surrendered without a shot - and the first of the island's castles passed to Westminster's control. But John Burley, commanding at Yarmouth, was less co-operative, and a Parliamentary show of force seemed necessary. The *'Greyhound'* and *'Caesar'* trained their guns on the castle and called again for immediate surrender. Burley responded resolutely and was seen *'on the wall like a madman, having a barrel of powder at each corner of the castle with a linstock in his hands, saying that before he would lose his honour, he would die a thousand deaths'*. [22] The patient Swanley, witnessing the show from the decks of the *'Caesar'*, preferred to wear the man down., leaving the castle ringed by troops, he turned to confront the next of the coastal forts.

Sandown's tiny garrison, commanded by Brutus Bucke, was in a state of near-mutiny and so responded eagerly to Swanley's demands for unconditional surrender. The same day, the 18th, Hurst castle on the mainland opened its doors, threatened by only ten men. Yarmouth held for another 4 days; on the 22nd, the day that the King's standard was raised in Nottingham, Burley grudgingly agreed to capitulate.

Yet Carisbrooke, the largest fortification on the island, still held out. Inside were just 20 men, but with 60 barrels of powder and almost enough weapons to supply a small army.

---

[22] 'Letter from Capt. Swanley to the Earl of Northumberland' Private collection

Off the coast stood 11 Parliamentary ships, dutifully holding the seaward end of the Portsmouth lines of siege. Captain Swanley, now back in his flagship, the *'Charles'*, anchored in the Medina and sent messages of support to Read in Newport. On the 23rd, 400 sailors came ashore and spent the night in the streets of Cowes. Parliament now had the stomach, time and means to force Carisbrooke to surrender.

Brett was summoned that evening by 5 trumpeters outside the gate. Unimpressed, he refused their demands and dined instead on venison with the Countess and some friends. On Wednesday, 24th August, he was awakened early. Two hundred Newport men had joined the Parliamentary sailors and taken up a position on Mount Joy to the castle's east. There, at their front, audible from the parapets in the morning's near silence, was indomitable William Harby, the curate of Newport, distinguishing *'himself in spiriting up the besiegers against his lady and children, assigning for reason her being a Papist, and exhorting them, in the canting phraseology of the times, to be valiant, as they were about to fight the battle of the Lord'*. [23]

What followed was one of those rare but memorable episodes in war. Standing on the parapet with a lighted match in her hand, the countess threatened to fire the first cannon herself unless honourable terms were offered to her side. Hours of negotiation followed, Parliament's representatives split by argument while the countess watched. Read called for the punishment of Papists and the damnation of the wicked. The terms that ultimately emerged were just, more principled than some of those demanded or agreed in later years of the war. The countess was permitted to remain in residence and she watched as the victors marched in. In the courtyard, they found a cannon loaded with a charge of flints and musket shot, and a store of unused muskets. Nicholas Weston and Colonel Brett were given their liberty, but expressly forbidden to visit the mainland. Captain Browne Bushell was placed in command of a garrison of

---

23 Worsley R p.115 and MSS 'Memoirs of Sir John Oglander'

50 trusted men.

'*So now our whole island is at peace*', concluded a letter written by a Newport resident when this final Royalist garrison surrendered. And Charles, one day to be a prisoner in that very castle, was later heard to say '*that he had most confidence of the Isle of Wight, that they would have stood for him, than of any other parts of his Kingdom, but now by his experience he found few honest men there*'.

Those 'honest men' that remained chose to live in peace. There would be few incidents of violence or insurrection and, for most of the unfolding war, the island would lie undisturbed.

5

'Those birds were too old...to be caught with such chaff'

ON August 22nd King Charles raised his standard on Nottingham Castle hill, *'with little other ceremony than the sound of drum and trumpet'*. An eye witness has left an account of the event that marked the official birth of the war. *'His Majesty came into the castle yard, accompanied with the prince (Rupert) and Maurice his brother, the Duke of Richmond, and divers other courtiers and cavaliers, and finding out the highest pointed hill in the yard.....the standard was brought in there and erected'* [1].

At about the same moment, influential men in Hampshire were addressing their King in a last-ditch attempt to reconcile the monarch with his angry Parliament: *'Vouchsafe dread sovereign to regard your petitioners who are all with bleeding hearts prostrate at your Majesty's royal feet imploring your clemency to revive our withered and dying hopes, by affording to your Parliament the influence of your gracious favour, presence and happy concurrence; for we are most assured that there is not greater need of the bright*

---

[1] Lucy Hutchinson 'Life of Col. J. Hutchinson'

beams of the sun to ripen the corn and other fruits of the earth at this present, than of your Majesty's presence and assistance to perfect and bring to maturity this ardently desired harvest'.[2]

Full-scale war had been rocking Dorset and Somerset for several weeks already. On 4th August a skirmish had taken place at Marshall's Elm in Somerset, the first set piece action of any size in the south. Leading the Royalist forces in this early contest of strength was Ralph, Lord Hopton, one of the county's M.P.s, and William Seymour, Marquis of Hertford, a Wiltshire aristocrat with a proven pedigree. Reaching Poole in the middle of the month, Hertford called on the town's leaders to open the gates, reminding them *'that he was not only with being prime commissioner for the Array, but was by his Majesty made Lieutenant-General of all Wales, Dorsetshire, Somersetshire, Hampshire, Wiltshire etc. (styles enough to make a man break his shins, or else out of breath to run over them)'*[3] Promising that he would spend money in the town and improve the defences, he also spelt out the consequences if the townsmen resisted his summons.

Mayor and Council remained unimpressed *'for those birds were too old....to be caught with such chaff; for* (they) *sent him this answer; that their town was already very well fortified and provided with ordnance, horse and foot, to oppose any Malignant whatever'*.[4] Doors and gates remained firmly shut and the nobleman was forced to remain unsatisfied.

More sustained fighting took place a month later at Sherborne and Yeovil, this time by almost fully fledged armies that had grown like summer mushrooms on Somerset's damp levels. For a while, these Royalist gentlemen also held hopes of relieving Portsmouth and gaining Hampshire for the crown. But Parliament's success in the area of the Solent and a string of early setbacks for the King in Somerset shattered any hope of Cavalier ascendancy. On 19th September, Hertford, ' *having found just cause to*

---

2 Humble Petition of the Grand Jury attending Your Majesty' Service at the Assizes in the County of Southampton , Hants. Records Office' 15M8423/2   3 Vicars J. 'Parliamentary Chronicles' p.136   4 ibid p.137

discontinue the prosecution of such service, and being desirous to save the effusion of blood that must necessarily be spent',[5] agreed to surrender the castle at Sherborne to Parliament's waiting army. Three days later, permitted to leave with his force untouched, he divided his command at Watchet, withdrawing his infantry and guns across the Bristol Channel into Wales while Lord Hopton with 50 dragoons and 160 horse marched west to assist Cornwall's leaderless Cavaliers.

This retreat towards the more distant west enabled Hampshire's Parliamentarians to consolidate and plan. On September 8th, Sir William Lewis was appointed Governor of Portsmouth with authority over most of southern Hampshire. Later in the month, John Lisle personally carried the thanks of Westminster to all those involved in the taking of Portsmouth, acknowledging in the citation the splendid work of Captains Swanley and Browne Bushell in this enterprise. On October 3rd the Earl of Pembroke arrived on the Isle of Wight to take up his governorship. On the 19th he received additional responsibilities for Hampshire, Wiltshire, Dorset, Devon, Somerset and Cornwall. He was authorised to raise whatever forces he felt necessary *'for the suppression of rebellion and preventing insurrection'*, and even to seize the revenues or estates of those now fashionably branded as 'delinquents'. Militarily inept and with few qualities of real leadership, he had been mauled on his way to the island by an itinerant force of Cavaliers.

The lesser men of Hampshire would do far greater service for the Roundhead cause. The two Richards, Norton and Whitehead, had already started to raise their regiments, and money was arriving from within the county to equip these fighting units. A proclamation, issued nationally by both Houses of Parliament in June 1642 and presented in the Autumn, provided the colonels with tangible authority and support: *'They the said Lords and Commons do declare, that whosoever shall bring in any proportion of ready*

---

5 Propositions propounded by the marquis of Hertford to the Earl of Bedford' BM

money or plate, or shall underwrite to furnish and maintain any number of horse, horse men and arms, for the preservation of the public peace, and for the defence of the King and both houses of Parliament from force and violence, and to uphold the powers and privileges of Parliament, according to his Protestation, shall be held a good and acceptable service to the Commonwealth and a testimony of his good affection to the Protestant Religion, the laws, liberties and peace of this kingdom'. [6]

Nearly 3000 men were now in arms for Parliament in Hampshire, many from the county's units of militia, and others were being actively recruited. On October 27th, Sir Thomas Jervoise and Robert Wallop were sent down from Westminster to organise the forces that had emerged.

By then, the war's first major battle had been fought at Edgehill- and Hampshire men had participated. Since early September, when the King had started his recruitment in the midlands, and Robert Devereux, the Earl of Essex, had taken command of Parliament's growing army at Northampton, a major clash had been inevitable. Powick Bridge, a skirmish fought in meadows south of Worcester on September 23rd, had been a chance encounter, but an undoubted Royalist victory. Charles, fuelled by success at Powick, became anxious to reclaim his capital. And so the race for London began, two opposing armies moving in parallel lines in search of a strategy for success. News of the King's advance reached London, creating a whirlwind of panic in the city's streets. Chains were placed across the main thoroughfares, and the trained bands were on constant vigil. Royalist sympathisers, wearing red ribbons in their hats, were just as active, parading in the city's streets and preventing a mob from pulling down the organ in St. Paul's Cathedral. The dominant puritan hue of London and southern England seemed in danger of being washed away and replaced by the brighter colours of reviving Royalism.

---

6 'Proposition and Orders by the Lords and Commons in Parliament for the bringing in of money and plate' Vicars. p.91

The Battle of Edgehill on October 23rd was the result, an unplanned collision on an autumnal field. Nearly 30,000 men stood in arms that day, one of the largest engagements fought on English soil. For those who had seen service in the Continent's religious wars, the moments before battle were terrible, kindling fears of what might happen in the hours to come. Images of homes and families swum in tear filled eyes and lips trembled in anticipation. For those new to the military life, thoughts must have been more mixed, the fear of hurt or death somehow tempered by a sense of fascination and unreality. Like dreamers troubled in their sleep, they surveyed the opposing ranks, experiencing a transitory and artificial existence from which they would be bound to wake.

The King's army, each of its constituent regiments dressed in the fanciful colours of its colonel's choice, had occupied the ridge above Radway for most of that autumn morning. Essex's army, just as multi-coloured, lay a mile to the north-west, cautiously holding the lower ground near Kineton. The Parliamentary general was reluctant to strike the first blow, aware that this would be an unforgivable act of rebellion. But soon after 1 p.m., the Royalist army descended the ridge and minutes later the cavalry on both wings were thundering westwards in a furious assault on Parliament's unsure lines.

Essex's ranks melted in the heat of that steely charge. Within seconds, it seemed that Royalist arms had already triumphed: half the Roundhead army had left the field. But so too had much of the Royalist horse, intoxicated by success into wild pursuit of the fleeing enemy. The battle would be decided by those that remained; the entire Royalist infantry and seven shaky regiments of Parliamentary foot.

In the next few minutes, near defeat became near victory. For, finding themselves supported by thirteen troops of almost untouched cavalry that had remained detached at the edge of the field, the Roundhead lines were suddenly galvanised into a force of resistance by Thomas Ballard and John Meldrum, commanders of the foot. The Royalist euphoria, fed by their earlier success, was turned into panic by the unexpected Parliamentary advance that hit the infantry of the King's centre.

By 5 p.m. the field was smothered in darkness and the last sounds of battle slowly faded. Soon that tiny area of rural England would again be silent, the stillness of the night broken only by the calls of the wild and the cries of the wounded. The war's first battle had ended in stalemate.

Both sides, however, claimed near-victory. A Cavalier prayer penned soon after the fight generously conceded that God had played a part: *'We acknowledge with all the lowliness of mind that it was not our sword nor the multitude of our host that hath saved us but it was Thy hand alone that hath disposed of victory to Thy servant the King, that covered his head in the day of battle, and has kept his crown from being thrown to the ground'* [7]

Edgehill was a national affair: men from the kingdom's more distant shires fighting alongside those from nearer home. Slowly reports of that dreadful battle and its casualties would filter through to those far-off places, and the suspense and torment of loved ones would commence. The emotions of the battle's survivors and their families lie unrecorded, but their feelings are as ageless and tender as those caught up in the agonies of later wars.

Some accounts suggest that 5000 were killed or wounded that day. But such figures are unsupportable when measured against the total number of men engaged: a figure of 1000 dead and 2000 wounded is far more likely. Whatever the number, the blood at Edgehill confirmed that men were prepared to die for their convictions. From now on, people would rely upon the power of the sword and pike to resolve a dispute that fine rhetoric and reasoned argument had sadly failed to settle.

The opening days of November were probably the most favourable moments for the King in the entire war. A positive and

---

7 Vicars p.203

unhesitating move towards London might have gained him his capital and catapulted the Parliamentary leaders into headlong flight. In the event, Charles was to throw away his God-sent advantage; the opportunity of taking London was to never re-occur.

The Earl of Essex reached the capital first. Eight thousand of the city's trained band paraded in arms at Chelsea, and sections of the peer's army took up positions at Brentford. Denzil Holles's regiment of redcoats, about 700 men, guarded the road to Hounslow, whileLord Brooke's purple coats lay behind barricaded in the riverside town. On the morning of the 12th, in a heavy autumn mist, Prince Rupert, the King's nephew, attacked Parliament's Brentford lines. Within minutes, the lone regiment of redcoats had almost ceased to exist. It had been a brief fight, savagely intense and conducted, *'almost to handy-grips, and to the sword point, and to the butt end of our muskets'*[8].

Fragments of the regiment fell back to the barricades, buttressing the purple coats' defence of the town. But it was to be just as hopeless: a wave of whooping Royalist horsemen passed over the flimsy barriers, and many of the fleeing defenders were drowned as they tried to escape across the Thames. Washer women at the river's banks witnessed their plight. *'We lost many precious young saints, and brave resolute soldiers, who now wear their victorious palms in Heaven'*,[9] wrote John Vicars. Yet the most cautious accounts suggest that fewer than forty died, a happy contrast with the toll of Edgehill. Many lie in an unmarked grave in the grounds of the local church.

But delay at Brentford cost the King his victory. On Sunday 13th November, the day of the sack of Brentford, Sir James Ramsay with 3000 men hurried south to procure the bridge at Kingston, and the Earl left London to inspect his assembled troops on Turnham Green. Swelled by the arrival of the London trained bands, the Parliamentary army now numbered 24,000, nearly twice the size of

---

8 Lilburne J. 'State Trials'

9 Vicars p.209

the King's tired force. Slowly withdrawing his men from Brentford, Charles drew up his lines at Turnham Green to confront the enemy - but the mood of optimism had gone.

This might have been one of those stretched and suspended preludes to a great battle. Line upon line of muskets and fluttering colours faced each other across the broad expanse of Turnham Green, now part of the tarmac and concrete of London's western suburbs. The ground was unsuitable for cavalry action, the arm of warfare in which the King's army excelled, and his infantry were outnumbered by two to one. It had become a war of nerves, not tactics, and it was the King who gave way first. With hardly a gesture of defiance, the regal colours fell back to Hounslow during the night and a general retreat seemed about to begin.

The King's next move, therefore, was not anticipated and came as a response to sudden Parliamentary caution. Essex, although his Kingston detachment might have been used with effect against the King's southern flank, had ordered Ramsay to fall back to London Bridge. His motive might have been strategically sound, but his timing was flawed. Charles, instead of withdrawing west as expected, advanced on Kingston and set up his headquarters nearby. Believing that this signified an attempt by the King to link with his sympathisers in Kent before a march on London from the south, Essex hastily arranged for a bridge of boats to be constructed across the Thames at Putney to enable his forces to cross and deploy on the other side. The King had again been checked.

This was to be the nearest that Charles ever came to reaching his capital. He remained at Kingston for five days and his reluctance to advance or retreat is open to different interpretations. Indecision was the most likely reason. On the 19th, having gained almost nothing by this immobility, he fell back to Reading: the threat to London was at last removed. A few days later, Charles retired to Oxford, leaving Aston with two regiments of horse and six of foot to garrison the Berkshire town. With winter rapidly approaching, it seemed that the war and its players might be about to hibernate.

6

'Sweet cathedralists'

PORTSMOUTH'S fall was just the first in a chain of rapid events that shook Hampshire violently in the first full weeks of war. Most were probably unnoticed by the ordinary people, those folks of the villages and farms, for whom the passing seasons provided far greater challenges than the sweeping movements of rival armies. Royalist and Parliamentarian alike would be little more than sudden aberrations in a tiny world of limited horizons, and London politics would be almost as irrelevant as snowfall in China.

But for the serious minded men of war, Hampshire had now become a giant chessboard with untested strategies as the rules of play. Lords and commoners would become involved, each vying to be the foremost hero of the local war. Control of the county's towns and strong points was the route to success, and the contest for Portsmouth was the opening prize. Other towns were now to be the targets and territorial expansion would begin.

Southampton's allegiance to Parliament was never really in doubt, despite open Royalist sentiment in the early days. On November 4th 1642 Peter Seale, Southampton's Mayor, informed two commissioners sent by the Commons to assess the town's loyalties that *'all was quiet yet, but there are some ill affected'*.[1]

---
[1] Davies, J.S. 'History of Southampton' p.485

Strong Parliamentary sympathies flowed through the town's mercantilist veins and few of the community dared speak out openly for the King. A sudden show of force would probably mute them still more. Three hundred Parliamentary levies under Colonel Whitehead knocked at the town's gates on November 7th, asking for nothing more than use of the town's facilities. One hundred more arrived by sea from Portsmouth on the 13th, and these were personally greeted by Peter Seale at Southampton's Water gate.

Yet their presence merely helped to fuel the passions and rhetoric of the King's few champions, and the division within the Corporation became briefly more pronounced. Southampton, living as it did on its contacts with the wider world, would either break in two or turn its back on the narrow sphere of national politics.

The proximity of Swanley's fleet was probably the deciding factor. Anchored in the Solent's sheltered waters, it controlled the town's maritime trade and thus its ultimate commercial fate. On December 3rd, after a bullying bout of virtual piracy, the Parliamentary captain anchored the 'Charles' in the town's harbour and called by letter for an unequivocal declaration of support or, alternatively, to face the consequences: *'You well know in what distractions this Kingdom is in at this time......Your town is a considerable place of merchandise, and by reason thereof are men amongst you of very good fortune and estates, and to preserve their estates, and so in general through the whole kingdom with their religion and liberty, is the only aim of Parliament; and no question those that shall oppose either of these are unfit to enjoy either, but to be branded with baseness. There are divers reports in the country of your forwardness in opposing the Parliament herein.......To know the truth of this I have sent my letter unto you, as likewise whether you will submit yourselves obedient to the commands of Parliament, and so consequently to the directions and command of the Governor of Portsmouth;.......if no answer, I shall take it as a denial, and then if any unhappiness befall you, thank yourselves, for I shall to my uttermost endeavour use all my power to bring you thereunto'* [2]

For a moment the Corporation demurred, swayed unwisely

by the arguments of Royalists and clerics. But Netley, Calshot and the Solent forts were all in Parliament's hands, and the flagship's guns held the town's walls within their range. Seale's first reply to Swanley expressed surprise at the depth of the accusation. '*We cannot but marvel that reports of our disaffection to the Parliament should be spread of us, not knowing that we have done any act to deserve the same'.*[3] A message of defiance was prepared, but never sent. Sensible tongues eventually prevailed and the decision to send a deputation of submission to Portsmouth was made for '*it was thought that Swanley would have come up the river with his ships, and beat the town about our ears...and we hereby desire your assistance by furnishing us with some able and experienced men to direct us for the better defence of the town*'[4] Two days later, Major Peter Murford and a Parliamentary garrison entered the town, and another of Hampshire's centres had disclaimed its King.

Basingstoke was visited on November 21st, this time by Lord Grandison's two troops of horse on their way to make mischief in the neighbouring county of Wiltshire. Playing by the newly formulated rules of war, the cavaliers demanded linen and cloth, offering only 14 pennies a yard when the going price was considerably more. The merchants, of course, complained, and homes and shops were ransacked as a result. 500 yards of fashionable linen and 2000 yards of woollen cloth were carried away or left damaged in the dirt. One of the townsmen, writing about a neighbour who had gone to London and so been spared the torment of the day, comments on this man's lucky escape. '*He saved his purse in going away, but they made bold with his house; he may come down safely now and see what is done. Pray God send peace, or else I see what will come to this land quickly*'.[5] Part of Lord Paulet's Basing garrison rode off with Grandison into Wiltshire, and Basingstoke's citizens, free of their presence, could breathe again.

Heavy frosts and the silvered fields of early winter offered

---

2 ibid p.485   3 *Davies p.487*   4 Godwin p.7   5 ' Letter from Master Goates' Hants. Records Office

only a brief respite. The pens spat out, many of those involved attempting either to justify their actions or else lay claim to the moral high ground. King Charles, withdrawn to Oxford, which was to remain his capital throughout the war, sought to turn men's doubts to his advantage or offer forgiveness to those who had taken up arms against the Crown. On November 28th, he issued 'grace and pardon' to the citizens of Hampshire, specifically excluding from his offer Sir William Waller, Sir Thomas Jervoise and Richard Norton *'against all which we shall proceed according to the rules of law'*.[6] In early December, however, he adopted a more admonitory tone towards the inhabitants of Winchester, who had clearly offended him greatly: *'Whereas we in our princely care of you our subjects, gave command to our officers to draw to your said city with a small number of forces, for your defence, not destruction, to the end that you might be preserved from the violence of our, and your enemies, not expecting but to have received an answerable return of your loyalties toward us. But finding instead of friends you have openly declared yourselves enemies, and evil entreated those whom you had cause to entertain with all love and respect.........Therefore we have thought fit to declare, that we cannot but in justice to our own honour.....but give way to a vindication, for the satisfaction of all those that have been so betrayed'.*[7]

    The reply from the citizens was suitably respectful but defiant: *'May it please your majesty, we your loyal subjects, have seriously considered the sum of what is contained in your message.....We find no just cause of your Majesty's high displeasure against us, since what we have done, both the laws of God and Man authorize....we cannot be fully blamed for endeavouring to secure our lives, and to keep our wives and daughters from an inevitable destruction........We are infinitely sorry that we should be so engaged by our consciences, to disobey your command, but being as it is, we must be enforced to undergo the utmost*

---

6 'King's Proposition' Privately Owned MSS

7 The King's Majesty's Message to the Inhabitants of the City of Winchester, Local Studies Library, Winchester

event, trusting only in God's protection, by whose power we do not despair, but that at least your Majesty will plainly discern the truth of all things, and we shall at length appear your most loyal and obedient subjects. [8]

In messages to his more solid allies, the Church, his words were still silvered. Instead of threats and warnings of coming punishment, he appealed for money and support. Writing to the Dean and Chapter of Winchester Cathedral, he remained diplomatic and hopeful: '*It is well known to what straits we are put for moneys by reasons of the distractions and rebellious attempts against us, which have constrained us to make use of the good affections of our good subjects to enable us to raise and maintain forces for defence of our person, wherein as we doubt not but to find you forward and ready to contribute, so we have thought good by these our letters to authorize you by such good and speedy ways as you shall conceive best forthwith to collect such contributions towards our said great and extraordinary charge....*' [9]

Appeals like this became frequent, issued to clerics and laymen alike, anyone who seemed likely to uphold without question the sanctity of kingship. Both sides sought the favour of Winchester College, where opinion seemed equally divided. John Potynger, the headmaster, was a closet Roundhead, swayed by arguments of reason into support for Westminster. John Harris, the warden, inclined in the same direction. Ordered to preach to the Commons, he managed to excuse himself by claiming to have a weak voice. Most of the teaching body and students chose to be impartial, preferring the rigours of scholastic study to the strains of partisanship.

The period of military inactivity that had followed Edgehill was now over. A strong Parliamentary army was protecting London, and seemed to have taken root on the capital's south-western outskirts. Waller, however, had become active, and on 1st December, having selected the church in nearby Crondall to serve as barracks and stable for his assembled forces, he advanced on Farnham Castle,

---

[8] 'The Loyal Inhabitants' Reply' Local Studies Library   [9] 'Document relating to the History of the Cathedral Church of Winchester' Hampshire Record Society p.54

The Kings Majesties
MESSAGE
To the Inhabitants of the City of *Winchester*, concerning the late Battaile.

Also their Answer to the aforesaid Message.

Likewise a true relation of a famous Victory obtained by the Inhabitants of *Manchester*, against the Lord *Strange* forcing him to fly to *Westchester*, where they have besiedged him, and all his Forces, they having kil'd above a thousand of his men. *Decemb.* 13.

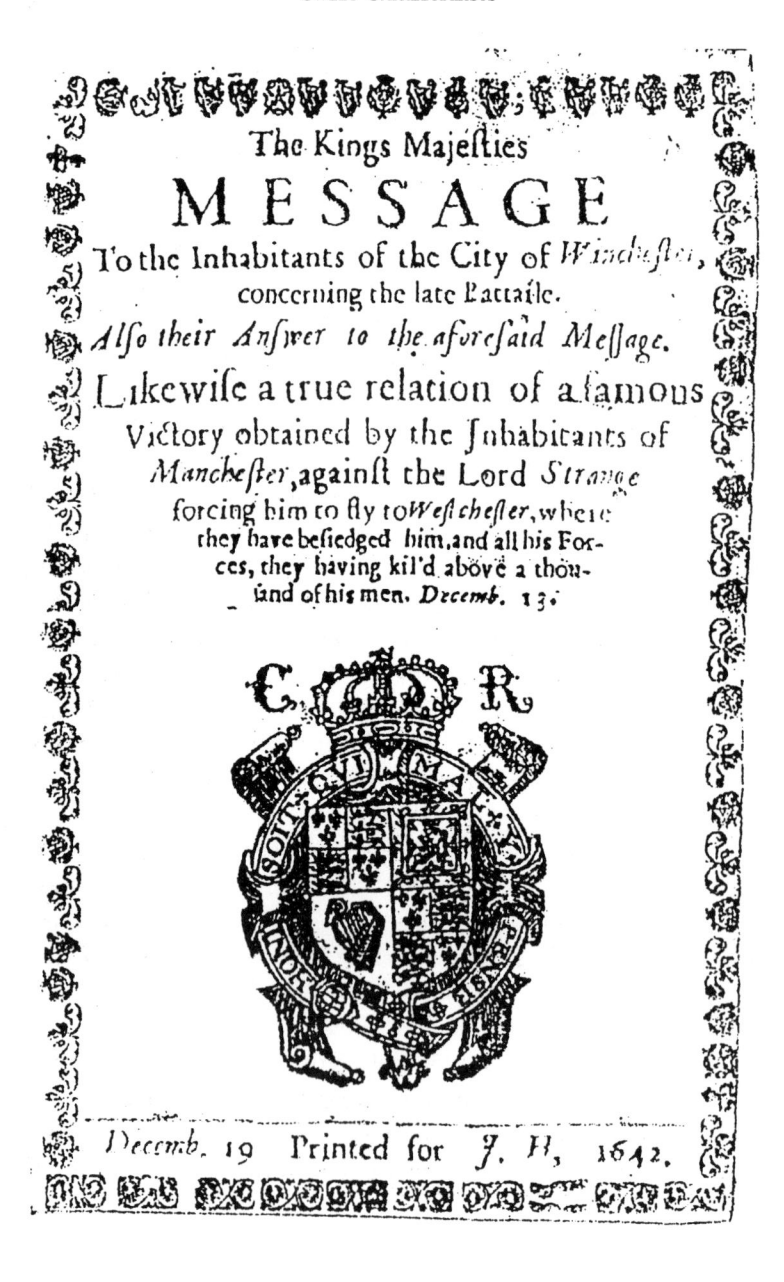

Decemb. 19 Printed for *J. H*, 1642.

held for the King since mid-October by Sir John Denham, Surrey's High Sheriff, and 100 men. Commanding the road from London to Southampton, its acquisition by Parliament would help to strengthen Westminster's fragile hold on the Hampshire coast, and perhaps far more.

With Hampshire regiments at his side, Sir William demanded the castle's surrender. Faced by the sort of stubbornness which became standard practice during the war, Waller prepared to steal by force what firm requests could not obtain. A petard was attached to the main gate and the door blown to pieces, the entire action watched by the enemy who made no attempt to interfere. But *'after the gate was shattered by the petard, yet they could not possibly enter, by reason they within had placed at the gate great piles of wood'*. [10] For well over an hour, the Parliamentarians struggled with the timbers, shoulders and brute strength taking the place of weapons. Eventually, the fortress was taken *'whereupon the Cavaliers within threw their arms over the wall, fell down upon their knees, crying for quarter...to depart like soldiers before the castle was entered'* [11] 100 oxen, 300 sheep and £40,000 in money and plate were found within - and Waller's soldiers were fed and paid. Only one man was killed that day - a Roundhead soldier shot through the cheek in an early exchange of fire.

Almost the entire garrison was housed for the night in St. Andrew's Church and was then taken by cart via Windsor to London to be there exhibited during a public bout of rejoicing. Almost immediately, however, they were released, some of the captured money given to them as compensation for their discomfort and humiliation.

Days later, December 5th, Marlborough, the Wiltshire town that stood on the direct route between Oxford and the nation's reservoir of Royalism in the south west, was stormed by Cavalier forces. Amongst the booty taken from the town was £200 worth of

---

10 Rushworth J. 'Historical Collections' Vol.11 p.92

11 Vicars p.223

The keep of Farnham Castle

cheese and several bales of cloth. Lord Grandison, whose regiment had participated in the ignoble slighting of the Wiltshire town, was reported to be returning into Hampshire with 4 troops of horse and 600 dragoons, his exact intentions unknown. Sir William Waller, now at the head of 2 regiments of dragoons and 4 regiments of horse, and the hero of the moment, was ordered in pursuit. John Middleton, colonel of one of these units of dragoons, was just 19 years old.

Waller's Hampshire army December 1642

Dragoons: John Middleton's Regiment
           Sir Richard Brown's Regiment
Horse: John Urrey (or Hurry's) Regiment
           Arthur Goodwin's Regiment
           William Waller's Regiment
           Arthur Heselrige's Regiment

Following his quarry closely through Newbury and into Hampshire, the Parliamentary soldiers apparently '*plundered every Minister within 6 miles of the road without distinction, whether of their own party or of the others.*' Grandison, '*fearing to be caught napping by active Sir William Waller and his forces, and the better to protect himself and his Cavaliers from the pursuit of the Parliament's force, retreated to Winchester a place more likely to give him kind entertainment, being full of malignant spirits, who indeed were not a little glad at his coming, thinking themselves now secure from danger, being under the wings of a bird of their own feather*'. [12]

Sir William Ogle, the castle's governor, was dining in the Chequers inn when the news of the peer's approach was brought to his well-stocked table. But a letter from Grandison reached the governor soon afterwards; in it he offered to bypass the city

---

12 Vicars .p.227

completely and attempt to draw the enemy after him into Sussex, rather than subject Winchester to probable assault by Parliament's punitive army. Ogle, fed by reports that Waller had '*only loose parties of horse*', saw no reason for fear and resolved to meet Waller in the open field. '*Conceiving it altogether unsafe to keep themselves within the town, and so give the Parliamentary forces opportunity to besiege them, they resolved therefore to march out and to give them battle abroad, and so accordingly they issued out and prepared for a pitched field.*' [13] Two regiments of foot, one a regiment of the King's Lifeguard under Sir John Smith, the officer who had recovered the Standard at Edgehill, were ordered out from the city to serve as Grandison's shield and escort.

At Wherwell, ten miles west of Winchester, the Royalist foot found that the noble peer was in trouble and his brigade already breaking. Half an hour later, the Cavalier strength was scattered, pierced by a furious Roundhead charge, about which Waller was personally to crow in his account of the engagement:: '*...we cut off two regiments. One of horse and another of dragooners, 600 of whom were gallant horse......The Parliament men took close order, and commenced a very hot engagement by a charge of cavalry. In half-an-hour the cavaliers began to retreat towards the city, in pursuit whereof we took fifty commanders besides Viscount Grandison......*'.[14]

This report of Grandison's capture might have been mere wishful thinking or perhaps a misreading of the day's events. Other contemporary accounts carry Grandison unharmed into Winchester and place him at the side of Ogle, his retreat protected by the brave action of Sir John Smith and a rearguard of just 18 men, '*men of undaunted resolution....(who) stood whilst Lord Grandison with other forces made good their retreat, and being thrice charged by entire troops, still bravely repulsed the enemy and broke them, in Winchester.*' [15]

---

13 'A True and Exact relation of a Great overthrow given to the Cavaliers in Winchester' Hampshire Records Office

14 Vicars p.228

15 'A True and Exact relation of a Great overthrow given to the Cavaliers in Winchester' Hampshire Records Office

'SWEET CATHEDRALISTS'

A lone horseman had brought the first news of the rout, and the castle's commanders prepared for inevitable assault. That same day, the 12th,, as anticipated, Waller's men attacked, targeting the castle defences between the West and North gates. But solid walls on steep grass banks would be a difficult combination to rush. Vicars gives an account of what then happened: '*Notwithstanding the exceeding high and very steep passage up to the walls, even so steep that they had no other way to get up but of necessity to creep up upon their knees and hands.......the enemy playing all the while on them with their muskets, and yet slew but three men in this their getting up, so at last......our soldiers got up and plied their business so hotly and closely that they had quickly made a great breach'*.[16]

Colonel Browne's regiment forced the breach at noon and entered the city, driving '*the Cavaliers before them into the midst of the town; who, having no place else to shelter, fled apace into the castle.....so our men beset the castle round with musketeers and horse and lay perdues under the wall, so that not a man of them could stir*'.[17]

And there they were allowed to remain while Roundhead punishment of the town could take place. Several townsmen had chosen to assist the defenders and would now be forced to pay for their blunder. Hurriedly they collected the £1000 demanded for their deliverance and most of the city's secular fabric remained unhurt.

But clerical property would be far less fortunate, and three whole days of vandalism commenced. '*They...sweet cathedralists, in whose houses and studies they found great stores of popish books, pictures and crucifixes, which the soldiers carried up and down the streets and market place in triumph, to make themselves merry - and then afterwards cast them all into the fire and burnt them'. And thus the Lord most graciously began in some measure to revenge the wrongs of his poor people of Marlborough*', Vicars

---

16 Vicars p.228

17 'A True and Exact relation of a Great overthrow given to the Cavaliers in Winchester' Hampshire Records Office

18 Vicars p.229

commented in obvious satisfaction.[18]

The Royalists penned in the castle could do little to help. They could merely watch the flames of revenge and wonder what could have caused such rage. Four cannon abandoned by the Cavaliers in their hurry from the city streets were now being turned to fire on their former owners. At 10 or 11 p.m. that night, *'conceiving themselves to be all but dead men, they cried for quarter upon any terms'.*[19] Preservation of the castle was Lord Ogle's main concern.

Waller chose initially to refuse. At dawn, piles of faggots and barrels of tar were stacked against the castle's gates and soldiers stood ready with lighted torches to burn the entrance down. In the streets beyond, smoke from the previous night still drifted, and Parliamentary soldiers were dressed irreverently in the surplices of clergy and the robes of clerical office.

At 8 a.m. on the 13th, the surrender was negotiated - the third of Hampshire's towns had fallen. 42 officers and 600 soldiers, Grandison's entire regiment and Colonel Edward Carey's unit of dragoons, were taken captive in one quick sweep. Most were pillaged as savagely as the houses in the Cathedral Close. One eyewitness claimed that he saw *'four or five* (Parliamentarians) *pulling at one cloak, like hounds at the leg of a dead horse'.*[20] Grandison seems to have escaped on his way to custody in Portsmouth, *having, as was supposed, charmed their keepers with a good sum of money'.*[21] Colonel John Urrey, (or Hurry) commander of the escort, would be held in deep suspicion for apparently helping them on their way.

Desecration of Winchester Cathedral followed. On December 14th, Parliamentary horsemen rode through the nave ,*'as if they meant to invade God himself'.*[22] Guided by fine-sounding principles and the new iconoclastic norms of war, men had become dehumanised, programmed like harpies to vandalise the symbols of the living and the dead. A statue of King Charles 1 was desecrated

---

19 'A True and Exact Relation'

20 'Truth in Two Letters' Hampshire Records Officce   21 Rushworth Pt.111 Bk.1

22 Mercurius Aulicus

beyond recognition when soldiers apparently tried to remove the crown from the proud man's head. *'These monsters of men'*, wailed Mercurius Aulicus, the Royalist news sheet. *'To whom nothing is holy, violate these cabinets of the dead and to scatter their boxes all over the pavement. They threw down....the bones of the Bishops; the like they did to the bones of William Rufus, of Queen Emma, of Hardecanute, and of Edward the Confessor..... Those windows which they could not reach with their swords, muskets; or rests, they broke up by throwing at them the bones of Kings, Queens, Bishops, Confessors, or Saints'.* [23]

Yet some of those who witnessed this collapse of the old order saw a likely strengthening of Royalist nerve as a result: *'I must confess (it) was an unlucky blow'*, says one ardent Cavalier. *'But it discourageth not, rather adds vigilance to a just cause'.* [24]

The college was fortunately saved from a similar fate. Captain Nathaniel Fiennes, an officer of Horse and probably in the pay of the college's friends, apparently stood at the open door with sword in hand and some faithful soldiers at his side - and not a stone of the establishment's fabric was chipped. He and his men were said to have been paid more than £29 15s 6d by the college's friends for their efforts. The larders remained almost intact too; just 60 loaves were taken for the men's breakfasts and 12 bushels of the college's malt were fed to the Parliamentarians' horses.

Waller was thanked by Westminster for his services in the south. £2000 was voted for his soldiers' comfort. The system of paying rewards for service had begun. But Waller also paid a price, the cost of his unsullied reputation for honour and the later loss of his Winchester home. Writing years later in a mood of guilt for permitting his soldiers to desecrate at will, he claimed that God had been just *'for the punishment of my giving way to the plunder of the City of Winchester, to permit the demolition of my house at Winchester.'* [25]

Few other Hampshire towns were occupied in those early winter days. A semblance of normal pre-war life could often

---

23 Mercurius Aulicus 24 MSS Earl of Ancaster Hist. MSS. Comm 411 25 Waller W. 'Experiences' p.63

Sir William Waller

Portrait of William Waller

continue. Stockbridge residents in December were unaware of the war's start, and two villagers in Minstead thought that a Spanish army had invaded England.

The more involved bemoaned the passing away of more gentle times. Sir John Oglander, now politically muted at his home on the Isle of Wight, sadly commented: '*Thou wouldest think it strange if I should tell thee that there was a time in England when brothers killed brothers, cousins cousins, and friends their friends.....To murder a man held less offence than to kill a dog, and they would glory in their actions as if they had done a pious deed...*'[26]

And another of the King's dispirited men was just as observant in his comments on the bestiality of the war's early days. '*In our army we have the sins of men (drinking and wenching), but in yours you have those of devils, spiritual pride and rebellion*'.[27]

Several Hampshire towns were visited by soldiers on the move, convenient stopping places for tiring forces. Petersfield and Fareham were sacked by marauding troops in December, and damage was done to properties in Bishop's Waltham. The culprits are not identified, and both sides might equally be held to blame. The countryside suffered as much as the towns. Lord Stourton, one of Wiltshire's great landowners with estates bordering Hampshire, complained of the '*great unruliness of the soldiers of Hampshire*'. They had apparently broken his gateposts to pieces, charged him for the repairs, and then charged him a further sum to protect the posts from damage.

Clashes between the two sides were still relatively uncommon. Some slow moving Royalist fugitives from Winchester were punished in December near Andover, several of the victims cut to pieces in a ditch when their horses became trapped in the mud. And some gentlemen, hunting near Petersfield, found themselves galloping for their own lives when a troop of Roundhead horse recognised a Papist amongst their company.

---

26 'The Commonplace Book of Sir John Oglander' 27 Memoirs of Sir Philip Warwick p.253

'Sweet Cathedralists'

Royalist activity further east attracted Hampshire's Parliamentarians. In early January, Waller, with the county's assembled forces, moved into the neighbouring county of Sussex, and the pulse of Hampshire's war slowed down. But Royalist sentiment lived on in Hampshire, dwelling in the hearts of aristocrats, gentry and clerics; men like the Marquis of Winchester, whose home would soon be visited. Hampshire, beaten into apparent submission in the first autumn and winter of war, would soon provide the stage for one of the war's most dramatic and stretched out sieges.

7

'In a state of great combustion'

NO county's war could ever be self-contained, the errors and successes of local campaigning spilled almost inevitably over adjacent borders. The cathedral city of Chichester, in neighbouring Sussex, was as divided in its loyalties as Winchester, split ideologically into two embittered factions that scowled malevolently at each other over the Close's walls. The townspeople were largely Parliamentary in hue, guided by the same materialist interest as laymen elsewhere, and largely Puritan in sympathy. Opposing them were the city's clergy, the traditionalists of robe and mitre, and the men upon whom kings and archbishops could always rely.

On August 19th, Chichester's Recorder, the Royalist Christopher Lewknor, one of the city's 2 M.P.s, demanded the surrender of the city's magazine for the service of the King. Henry Chittey, commander of the trained bands, refused this request and placed a strong guard over the ammunition and weapons that both sides desperately wished to possess. Three days later, the royal standard was raised in Nottingham, and bitterness hardened into steel.

'IN A STATE OF GREAT COMBUSTION'

The clergy railed from the pulpit tops, employing the Word of God and His Prophets as allies for their cause. Branded as Papists, they were, however, rebuked in the streets and taverns of the city, and the war of words became almost as savage as the future clash of swords. Collecting food, horses and supplies, and with still strengthening passion, the Cavaliers drilled in arms within the Cathedral Close and prepared to fight.

Initially they identified closely with Goring's heroic defence of Portsmouth. Men, money and letters of support flowed towards the Hampshire port and, briefly, the two Royalist struggles almost became fused into one. £1000 was raised by Chichester clergymen for Goring's use and Chichester men served within Portsmouth's small garrison. Sussex Parliamentarians served in the investing lines, aware that success or failure beneath Portsmouth's walls would determine what happened in the county that lay to the east.

The Westminster nerve centre realised that too, ordering Colonel Chittey and the trained Band units to disarm all Papist suspects and the King's Commissioners of Array. Colonel Herbert Morley, one of the M.P.s for Lewes, was sent down from London '*to disarm all such as shall refuse to join in securing the county*'. That aggressive act merely started a competition for the hearts and minds of the still uncommitted. On 7th November, Charles issued a proclamation, offering pardon to all the county's inhabitants if they instantly submitted to his authority. Only two men, Chittey and Morley, were excluded, and the process of proscription started. Parliament responded by providing 7 guns and 10 barrels of powder to the townsmen of Chichester and ordering the arrest of Sir Edward Ford, '*not three days old in his place as High Sheriff of Sussex*' and a man who had recently promised to obtain the county for the King.

He looked likely to succeed. On 15th November, the county's Royalist gentry and their armed retainers appeared in arms at Chichester and forced the new mayor, Robert Eaton, to hand over the keys of the armoury. Chittey, outnumbered and outwitted, chose not to resist and he and his followers departed during the night. A report to Westminster in the following week announced gloomily that the *county of Sussex is in great combustion, and that there are some thousands of the Papists and malignants in the county gathered together in Chichester* '[1].

Swanley was the first to respond to this upsurge of Royalism in the east. Landing 200 men on Thorney Island, he sent a messenger to Ford in Chichester, demanding the surrender of the keys and magazine, the property, he claimed, of the Parliament which he served. Ford penned a brief and dismissive reply. Swanley, without the means to press his threat, wisely departed.

Ford went on to attempt more ambitious deeds, pressing men into joining his ranks with threats of severe punishment for those who refused. He was eventually defeated on December 8th at Haywards Heath with the loss of more than 100 men. Lewes, his intended target that day, could sigh with relief. But Chichester still lay firmly in his hands, and the Parliamentary hold on neighbouring Hampshire suddenly became as brittle as drying clay.

Hampshire's Roundheads were forced to intervene. On December 10th, the Earl of Pembroke, Lieutenant of Hampshire, turned to face the threat that was building in Devon and the west. Waller, searching for new adventure since his pounce on the city of Winchester, was ordered to deal with the crisis in Sussex. On Monday, 17th December, after nearly three days of plundering in the Hampshire city, he prepared to leave, his officers whipping up the regiments into a new zeal of frenzy with hints of renewed plunder in the Sussex cathedral city.

Resting briefly at Upham, where his men apparently used the church as a cavalry stable and urinal, Waller approached Havant and turned towards Chichester. With him were his 4 regiments of horse, the county's trained band and Sir James Ramsay's cavalry brigade, the latter a part of Parliament's field army now at winter quarters in Windsor. One of the war's early heroes and an able leader of men, he had ridden south to help those Parliamentarians still

---

[1] Godwin p.54

active in the field.

Circumstances, however, were not always to favour Sir William and his followers. At Havant, he was attacked by Cavalier forces, probably men from Chichester intent on mischief. His advance guard took the brunt of the malice, engaged in a frost-packed field for almost 7 hours by little bands of well-drilled Royalists. Sergeant-Major Philip Skippon, another unit of Lord Essex's slumbering army on the Thames, arrived with 11 fresh troops of horse - and the Royalists, at last, rode off. Two hundred of their number, it is claimed, lay dead or dying upon the ground.

The Earl of Essex chose to deal Waller an even more devastating blow. Always jealous of other people's success and without the width of vision needed to develop an overall strategy, he now recalled Hurry's, Browne's and Goodwin's regiments, claiming that they had only been lent! This left Sir William with 300 dragoons and 1000 horse, mainly Sir Arthur Heselrige's curiously armed 'Lobsters'. And some of these were now deserting, complaining that they had not received their promised pay.

The Roundhead general stood on the county's boundary and possibly also on the brink of disaster. He was acutely aware that the future of Parliamentary hopes in the south lay in his hands. He sent 100 men, all he could spare, to take Arundel castle, only poorly garrisoned for the King. The owner, Thomas, Earl of Arundel, had gone abroad before the war's start, leaving his son, Lord Mowbray, to decide the castle's wartime allegiance.

The tiny Parliamentary force split into two, part moving directly against the castle, while 60 men engaged the angered townsmen in the narrow streets. Placing a petard on the castle's main gates, the storming party forced an entry, '*surprising all there, amongst whom they took.....a great Papist, raising men and arms in Sussex to assist the malignants in Chichester'.*[2] 100 horses, valuable arms and stores, and 70 prisoners were taken, but not a single life was lost.

---

2 Godwin p.56

On the night of December 20th, Waller halted on the Broyle, the high ground north of Chichester; and his chaplains prayed to Heaven for victory. On the morning of the 21st, he was joined by 3 troops of horse and 2 companies of foot, men raised in Sussex by Herbert Morley and Sir Michael Livesey, nearly 4000 additional soldiers if Vicars is to be believed. God had answered the chaplains' prayers.

Chichester was to fall 8 days later, gunned into submission by Waller's artillery positioned near the North Gate. *'We got possession of the Almes Houses, within half musket shot of the North Port, and then planted our ordnance very advantageously, which played through the gate into the Market Place',*[3] wrote Vicars. Parliamentary musketeers occupying houses near the West Gate were less successful. Flushed out of their concealment by fire and smoke, they retreated and played little further part. Soldiers in the church of St. Pancras, near the East Gate, however, kept their positions and *'galled the enemy extremely in so much that they durst hardly any of them appear upon the wall'*[4] And ultimately Lt. Col. Nicholas Roberts, bringing two troops of horse and some foot from Arundel, arrived at the South Gate. The encirclement was complete.

On the night of Monday, the 25th, Waller moved his culverin to the vulnerable East gate and simultaneously planned to burn down the gate in the west. *'But while we in our quarter were debating about the order of our falling on, there came a trumpet to me at about ten of the clock, with a letter, desiring that to save further expense of blood I would admit of a treaty the next morning by nine of the clock'*[5]. Two commissioners dutifully arrived from the city the next morning and the negotiations began. Waller offered the customary quarter, an offer which was surprisingly refused, *'and so we parted, they with a protestation rather to sell their lives than to yield to so low a condition'*[6]. Waller resumed his planned assault, secure in the knowledge that the threatened gates could never keep

---

3 Vicars p.237   4 Vicars J. 'Jehovah-Jireh' p.235
5 Waller W. 'Experiences' p.65' 6 ibid

him out.

At 7 a.m. on the 27th, the city finally submitted, prepared apparently to accept the exact terms that were negotiated the day before. *'But that very afternoon'*, continued Waller in his personal account, *'when I was ready to enter the town, some of the Scottish officers of my Lord Crawford's troop grew into a rage at the strictness of the article concerning the yielding of the Horse and arms, and they vowed rather to die than to submit to it'*[7]. Cooler passions, however, seem to have prevailed within and the surrender was eventually made. Sixty officers, amongst them Sir Edward Ford and Mr. Christopher Lewknor, were sent as prisoners to London and paraded like a line of chained bears in the city's streets.

Waller personally appealed to the lesser men, those without declared allegiance to King or Westminster. He offered them liberty in exchange for their support, and many are believed to have accepted. Loyal townsmen were given positions of responsibility for their steadfastness. *'the first thing we did was to release and fully set at liberty all the honest men of the town.....who being thus enlarged, we employed in places of trust'* reported Waller in his 'Vindications'. But, during the evening after the surrender, a trail of powder and a lighted match was found in the cellar of the house where Waller was dining - and some of the honoured loyalists of the town lost the positions of responsibility that they had only gained that day.

No rain had fallen during those 8 days of siege, enabling the besiegers to drag their guns towards the city's northern walls and construct earthworks and trenches. Now, within an hour or two of the surrender, the heavens opened and the works were flooded - proof, some Puritans claimed. of the *'good hand of Providence'*.

But, if God had been on Parliament's side, His soldiers showed little respect for His holy church. The victors, according to a contemporary account, left *'not so much as a cushion for the pulpit, nor a chalice for the Blessed Sacrament.....As they broke*

---

7 Vicars p.238

down the organs and dashed the pipes with their pole-axes'. Waller and his commanders were held responsible for their leniency, condemned in the same account for *'having in person executed the covetous part of sacrilege, they leave the destructive and spoiling part to be finished by the common soldiers'.*[8]

Insult was added to injury, the service of thanksgiving in the Cathedral being marked by further acts of vandalism and indecency. Men, it is stated, *'ran up and down the church with their swords drawn, defacing the monuments of the dead, hacking and hewing the seats and stalls, scratching and scraping the painted walls.....Men of cauterized consciences, and given up to a reprobate sense, thus not only to take the name of God in vain, but damnably to blaspheme it, as if He were the patron of rapine, blood and sacrilege'*. Poor Sir Arthur Heselrige is accused of entering the Chapter House and stealing what was left of the Church plate.

Henry King, Bishop of Chichester, was permitted to retire to his brother-in-law's residence in Buckinghamshire. Many of the lesser clergy were less fortunate, some fined heavily for their crime. The city suffered for its complicity with a disfavoured cause: the needle-making industry, concentrated largely in the eastern suburbs, was almost wiped out when the houses around the Church of St. Pancras were demolished. Those dispossessed of their homes in the east and west were never re-housed. Colonel Anthony Stapeley was appointed to govern the shattered city and a garrison was installed. The citizens, to avoid the sad fate of their cathedral, paid the soldiers handsomely, offering food, clothing and plate to those who now made the city's laws. Waller, of course, was elevated to the ranks of the Parliamentary titans, his actions exalted by John Vicars: *'He took the City of Chichester ......, with Sir Edward Ford, High Sheriff of that county for the King, a most desperate malignant, Bishop King, as bad as the worst, Sir John Morley, together with many prime commanders, and at least 60 other eminent officers, very many brave horses, about 400 excellent dragoons, with 3 or*

---

8 'The Letters of Dean Bruno Ryves' Chichester Cathedral Collection

400 foot soldiers' [9]

The over-bearing arm of Westminster now reached towards the pulpits and altar rails of rural Hampshire, upsetting established religious practice wherever its ruling shadow fell. Clergymen's unguarded utterances were seized as evidence of delinquency, and the ejection from ministries commenced. For those dispossessed, a life of semi-exile or vagrancy might begin. Those tainted with the marks of possible Papism suffered most, detained in prison *'during the pleasure of the Commons'*. Thirty-two clergy in Andover alone were rejected during the course of the war. The Rev. Henry Edmundson, the rector of Holy Rood in Southampton, served a longer sentence for similar crimes against the re-ordered church. Some of those detained were held on board a ship in Portsmouth harbour, *'and there booed and even pelted as they were at prayers'*. The wives and children of those imprisoned became conditioned to a life of poverty or petitioned the Corporation for Ministers' Widows for financial relief. Parliamentary puppets, *'men of sane conscience and sound enunciation'* were put in the place of the clerics evicted, and the style and fabric of religious practice was radically transformed.

The social fabric was also starting to fall apart. 4000 Hampshire men had gone to war, leaving wives without husbands and children without their fathers. With no men folk to protect them, the vulnerable would be open to depredation and the savagery of plunder. The gentlemen of the manor houses went away, too, leaving lesser men in uncertain control of their estates. Rents were unpaid, fields were left untilled, workbenches unmanned and the horses taken from the stables to provide the mounts for war. Both sides were just as active, securing horses, harness and iron goods from farm and blacksmith, often underpaying or paying nothing at all. Thirty shillings a horse was the going rate for those who were paid. Four pounds an animal had been the pre-war market rate. Royalist parties from Andover raided as far as Stockbridge in the opening

---

9 Vicars 'England's Worthies' p.78

weeks of war, leading away 30 horses in a single night while their owners slept. Villagers in the Meon valley were paid fifteen shillings for each of their animals and then forced to provide the feed for the sustenance of their former property. 3000 sheep were taken by Royalist thieves from the fields around Odiham in the space of 12 days - and not a penny was offered in payment. And Portsea farmers were directed to grow hay instead of food for their family's consumption.

These first distasteful effects of bitter war were felt that autumn, even before the passing of full-scale armies brought added miseries to those that lived along the paths to war. Bishops Waltham residents in 1642 could speak of war in dismissive terms, regarding the demands of both sides as more a nuisance than a threat to survival. But just weeks later, they would see their homes destroyed, their barns set alight and their womenfolk raped in gratification of the basest of human desires.

The bells of London rang out on January 4th in celebration of the fall of Chichester. Waller and Morley received the special thanks of the Commons for *'great service in the taking of Chichester'* and money was voted for the maintenance and support of Hampshire's Parliamentary defence- £1500 for Sir William Lewis and his Portsmouth men and £1000 for the benefit of Waller's roving army.

Raising such money, however, had not been easy, and the Commons had recently legislated to extract cash from all those with money in their purses. In November 1642 the Commons appointed a Committee for the Advance of Money, its prime task being to negotiate a loan from the City merchants. The resulting loan was largely forced, the Londoners obliged to contribute twenty per cent of the value of their property. Southampton merchants were asked to contribute voluntarily. But those who refused were held in deep suspicion or listed amongst the damned. Taxation in principle, if not in name, this was initially the method by which Westminster would bleed money from the areas which it controlled.

Loans and gifts, however, would soon prove to be insufficient, and London searched for more effective methods. On February 24th 1643 Westminster passed an ordinance *'for the speedy raising and levying of money for the maintenance of the army'*. Each county would be required to pay a certain amount weekly to commissioners appointed for the purpose. All persons and corporations were to be assessed for their ability to pay; only church ornaments, servants' wages, people with annual income below £10 or with property worth less than £100 would be exempt. On these criteria, Hampshire was ordered to pay £750 weekly, the responsibility for collecting these taxes falling on the shoulders of a committee of county men. And so a second crushing burden was heaped on Hampshire folk, and for many this would become a weight far too heavy to bear.

Parliament's hastily passed measure was immediately condemned by the enemy as illegal. Yet an almost identical system was soon installed by the King's men, and, passed by the King's remaining loyal rump of M.P.s, was constitutionally no more legitimate than the London decree. But taking up arms against one's monarch was hardly lawful, and the moods and opinions of the time were unlikely to be influenced by such legal niceties. Fifty-five commissioners were eventually appointed in Hampshire, specifically to process and expedite the collection of the taxes due.

In May 1643 a further ordinance was passed to speed collection. The politically 'sound', often the constables of the Hundreds, were chosen by both sides as the agents of collection, and the chance existed for the dishonest and unscrupulous to line their pockets. Able to rely on locally billeted troops to enforce their demands, such men frequently became tyrants in their own communities. A hint of their power is portrayed in this rhyme from the Welsh borderlands:

> *'Here is the sealed demand of a saint, pray*
> *Pay without delay.*
> *Lest the saint (his lust he conceals not)*
> *Becomes an angry devil'.* [10]

'IN A STATE OF GREAT COMBUSTION'

The Cavalier tax system was apparently never as severe as that of its rivals. Known Parliamentary supporters were naturally taxed most heavily, many robbed of as much as 40% of the value of their estates. Yet wholesale confiscation of property was a thing of the future and most Roundhead estates remained untouched - apart from the fleeting visit of passing horsemen and the shallow probes of inquisitive officers.

The burden of contributions fell equally upon town and country. The Oxford Parliament set a 10% rate on income and property, and appointed regional administrators to collect what was due. But the Royalists were generally more sensitive to local government machinery and seemed anxious to remove any genuine cause for grievance. Grand juries or county meetings were often appointed at which the taxed could air their views.

But even these painful extractions from people hardly able to afford the necessities of life failed to fill the bottomless coffers of war. In desperation, the insatiable cormorants in Oxford and London looked for other sources of income. Trade and commerce, the basis of the nation's life, was still an untapped reservoir. On July 22nd 1643 the House of Lords approved a new ordinance which would give almost unlimited powers to Parliament's excise officers. A governing committee was set up in London with offices in all the major towns and ports within Parliament's empire. Local officials were responsible for registering tradesmen within their regimes and the commodities on which they depended. Almost at will, these men could decide the rate to be levied on goods for sale. 3d on a bale of raw wool, 6d on finished cloth and 4d on a barrel of salted freshwater fish were typical rates. The Royalists were far more selective in how they operated. For a long time the tin mines of Cornwall and the flow of money from foreign sympathisers kept the monetary pipeline full. The capture of Bristol in the summer of 1643 handed the resources and wealth of this major port to the King - and taxing of the nation's interior trade was then less

---
10 Carlton C. 'Going to the Wars'

necessary.

Both sides were now preparing for an escalating war. On 21st January 1643, Parliament resolved that the forces of Kent, Surrey, Hampshire and Sussex should operate as one body for the defence of Southern England. Hampshire and Surrey Roundheads were reluctant to combine and argued for county autonomy. Days of bitter arguing took place before an association eventually emerged.

Farnham Castle, slighted on December 29th by order of the Commons, served as Parliament's forward base. From here, Roundhead soldiers would patrol in groups as far as Aldershot and Odiham. The Portsmouth garrison policed S. Hampshire, visiting Petersfield and Fareham in search of Royalists and hidden supplies. Articulate Cavalier opposition seemed confined to Basing and Andover. Elsewhere, muted Royalist sympathisers wisely stayed at home, their hearts and thoughts with the King in Oxford, but with their swords still sheathed and their mouths firmly shut.

On 5th January, Mayor Seale and the Corporation of Southampton were forbidden by Westminster to publish the King's most recent proclamation, prohibiting the transfer of tonnage and poundage to the port's authorities, but again offering 'grace and favour' to all those who submitted to his will. On 11th February, in a mood of increasing ferocity, the Commons voted that money should be found for the equipping of 2 troops of horse and a regiment of dragoons, all under the command of loyal Sir Thomas Jervoise, and specifically engaged for the defence of the county. On the 23rd, Waller was made responsible for the administration of martial law, and the questioning of Royalist suspects began. On the following day, the newly associated four counties of the south agreed to raise 300 horse and 3000 foot for Parliament. Hampshire agreed to raise and equip 3 regiments of foot to serve the common cause. On February 11th, William Waller was made commander of Parliament's Western Association and given the task of relieving the hard-pressed Parliamentarians of Bristol and Gloucester.

An unseasonally mild February would encourage early

campaigning and the end of winter slumbers. The Royalists struck first, pouncing on Cirencester on the 2nd, a town close enough to Hampshire to send shock waves of horror through the county's Roundhead leaders. Further Cavalier aggression was to follow this unexpected Royalist success. Hearing that Sir William was about to advance towards the west, Prince Rupert himself rode out of Oxford on the 24th with 1500 horse and dragoons, determined to intercept a train of guns and ammunition that were reported to be travelling from Farnham.

Yet 1500 men in a winter landscape could hardly ride unnoticed, and news of the Prince's approach reached Waller near Guildford. He immediately ordered the wagons and soldiers to return to Surrey. Most of his scattered detachments pulled back in time, grouping for defence on Hampshire's eastern boundary before Rupert had the chance to swoop. 200 lone troopers, patrolling ahead of the main convoy, however, had already reached Alton, unaware of the danger that lurked ahead. Dismounted and in search of accommodation for the night, they were hit by the full impact of the Royalist cavalry force.

Accounts of the first Battle of Alton are sketchy and brief, but are full of suggestions of Parliamentary vigour. With horses unsaddled and carbines unready, the 200 Roundheads initially asked for quarter, claiming that they were merely scouts.

Their request was refused, and the threatened soldiers prepared to resist. Loading their sole field piece with grapeshot, they grouped at the end of the street and awaited their heavy punishment.

Eighty Cavaliers fell in the first frontal charge, shattered by the well-timed blast of the single Parliamentary gun. Another charge followed, 40 more Cavaliers were tumbled from their saddles and frightened horses locked on galloping hooves. 200 carbines were aimed at Royalist breasts and the casualties continued to mount. Hand-to-hand fighting then took place in the winter dusk, the number and pressure of Rupert's Cavaliers forcing the Parliamentarians back

Caricature of a plundering soldier

towards the town's edge. During the night, the little band escaped, hurrying back towards the parent body camped near Guildford. A few horses and muskets remained in Alton's streets as Royalist prizes. So, too, did the little gun that had fired with such punitive effect.

On February 28th, Waller returned to Farnham to prepare for his advance to the west. In a letter to the Earl of Essex, he complained bitterly of a shortage of men. Robbed of most of his infantry arm, he would be forced to rely on his dragoons and cavalry, 10 small troops of horse of his own regiment, *'which being put together will make three good ones'*, and Sir Arthur Heselrige's Cuirassiers, *'which were so completely armed that they were called by the other side the regiment of lobsters, because of their bright iron shells with which they were covered,......and were the first so armed on either side, and the first that made any impression on the King's Horse, who, being unarmed, were not able to bear a shock with them'.*[11]

From here he set out as ordered with his diminished army and four cartloads of muskets to be distributed to any recruits who might be persuaded to join his standard on the way. Reports of his likely absence from Hampshire sent tremors of excitement through the enemy camp, enough to tempt Bishop Ogle to consider plans for the re-capture of Winchester and Chichester if or when the opportunity arose. Hampshire and Sussex, where Parliament had seemed to rule supreme, seemed suddenly likely to be in contention again.

---

11 Waller W. 'Recollections'

8

'We are both upon the stage'

ROYALIST mischief was fortunately delayed. On March 3rd 1643, Waller and his army re-entered Winchester. In a public display of sympathy for the city's inhabitants and their property, he *'promised that no man should suffer any loss or damage by him, and he performed it for as much as it concerned himself, but when he went away (the next day), he left behind Sergeant-Major Carie with a troop of horse, to levy £1600 upon the same'* [1.]

Another bout of pillage consequently began. The college was fortunately spared the punishment that occurred in Waller's absence. An autumn ordinance had exempted places of secular learning, stating that *'none of the revenues assigned for the scholars and almsmen of those colleges may be stopped - notwithstanding the ordinance of sequestrating the rents and profits of Archbishops, Bishops etc.'* [2] And in a move to rid these places of near-Popish clericalism, a later decree ordered that students need no longer wear surplices, *'it being against law and liberty of the subject'*.

Winchester's townspeople, plundered of so much of their plate, money and linen during Waller's earlier visit, found the new

---

1 Commons Journals, Vol 11, p.172   2 ibid p.827

demands impossible to bear. People hid what they could, concealing valuables in holes in the ground or sending them hurriedly for safe-keeping to relatives in the country. A cleric's son hid his horses in a wood, leaving his servant on continuous vigil at the animals' side. Neighbours chose, however, to betray his crime, and the poor lad was brought before the stern-faced soldiers to answer for his sins. Questioned about the horses' whereabouts for more than three hours, he stubbornly remained silent, and the inquisitor's anger slowly grew. Placed for punishment in a halter in the stable of the 'Old George' inn, the young man was hoisted into the air and left to dangle for more than a day.

On 4th March, Waller's army entered Romsey, defacing the Abbey in another bout of Bible inspired fervour. Seats, organ and windows were hacked to pieces, God himself apparently guiding his self-appointed saints in their work of desecration. During their hours of activity, a zealous brother of the ministry '.....*got into the pulpit and for the space of two hours in a furious zeal applauded that religious act, encouraging them to go as they had done'.* [3] Gunners used the outer walls for target practice - the walls of the northern transept still bear the marks of the savagery. And soldiers were paid to search for the Abbey's silverware, much of which had been hurriedly hidden when Waller's men arrived.

From here, the Roundheads marched the fifteen miles to the city of Salisbury, recruiting on route and disarming the enemy. In the Wiltshire city, Sir William ordered a muster in the name of the King and Rupert - and nearly 3000 responded to his call, swearing loyalty to their monarch, 'Charles the wronged'. Waller disarmed them all and 'borrowed' their horses ' *'til the war doth end'*. Such euphemisms hardly righted the crime; the indignant owners protested to the King in Oxford, sadly still believing that the monarch's men were responsible. Some of those robbed in Salisbury even joined Waller's Parliamentarians in sweet revenge for the 'Royalist' misdeeds.

---

3 Quoted in Luce R. 'Pages from the History of Romsey and its Abbey' p.81

War was now to be like a sequence of intermittent tides breaking periodically on a sun-strewn beach. In between these sudden flows, life could almost resume its regular monotony, untouched by military or political affairs. Men and women, unconsciously programmed to be part of Hampshire's daily life, might listen with disinterest to the distant rumblings of war or look up briefly from their daily work when a sweat-covered horseman galloped hurriedly through their village. For most of the county's inhabitants, governed by the changing seasons and the cruel demands of nature, war was an alien quality, the hobby of the upper classes. The war so far had failed to be all-embracing, except for those who chose to let it be.

Spring took Waller and the centre of local war well beyond the borders of Hampshire, eventually pitting him against his pre-war friend, Sir Ralph Hopton, whose late winter invasion of Devon had almost secured the peninsula for the King. On 22nd March, the Roundhead general, whose energetic movements in the winter had elevated him to the status of a legend in the minds of friends and enemies alike, attacked Malmesbury, held by timorous Royalists since early February. Three weeks later, the Earl of Essex, waking from his winter slumbers in Windsor, pounced on Reading, garrisoned for the King by Sir Arthur Aston.

Sir Arthur's men had been materially assisting the Marquis of Winchester at Basing, providing weapons and men for the defence of the great house. In early March, a contingent of Aston's Cavaliers, sent to raid the homes and villages of N.Hampshire, had rested for the night at the Marquis's home. Riding into neighbouring Basingstoke the next morning, they relieved some travelling clothiers of the contents of their carts - £10,000 worth of material destined for the London markets. The merchants apparently travelled to Oxford to complain to the King. The clothing was eventually returned to its owners on payment of a small fee and the signing of an oath of allegiance. Some horses rounded up during a raid towards Aldershot were briefly held in Basing's stables pending their transfer to Oxford. And travellers passing below Basing's high walls were frequently shot at by the Marquis's soldiers.

Other Hampshire Royalists were slightly more circumspect and kept the peace. Those held in suspicion, men in probable secret correspondence with the King or with Papists in their households, were closely watched, their movements monitored by Portsmouth units. Detachments of Parliamentary horse halted outside the suspects' gates or quartered for a night or two in a nearby village. In the tavern that night, they would listen to the locals' talk, seeking for every word or utterance that might incriminate their squire. Suspects were sometimes arrested or questioned, and their homes disarranged by curious soldiers. But the Marquis of Winchester, with a miniature army of his own at his back and walls at his front, ruled with impunity and never concealed his Royalist credentials.

On May 4th, the quietened Royalists were weakened again. Two ships from Dunkirk and destined for Ireland, were forced into Portsmouth and robbed of their load. Within their holds were guns and ammunition, purchased by the Cavaliers from continental sources. A few days later, they were financially haemorrhaged again, this time by vigilant Roundheads policing a Hampshire lane. Two soldiers captured a rider carrying messages from the King to the Earl of Carnarvon. One of the seized papers contained details of a cache of silver recently collected to finance the royal cause. Lord Essex immediately sent 80 men from Kingsclere to search for the valuable booty. At Prosperous farm, six miles from Andover, they found the plate, later valued at £1200, hidden in a barn. The commander of the party was given a new saddle as a reward for his efforts; it, too, had been intended for the King. Charles, informed of what had happened, made fruitless efforts to find out the name of the erring captain, declaring that, if the Roundhead officer were ever taken prisoner, he (the King) would '*sit on his skirts*'.

On that same day, the Commons acted politically as well, decreeing that all fines and revenues from Royalist estates in Hampshire should be made available for the repair of the defences of the castles in Portsmouth, Hurst, Calshot and Southsea and for payment of the garrisons. Probably in response to Westminster's uncharacteristic generosity, the townspeople of Portsmouth declared their *'readiness to serve the Commons in the defence of that place with the last drop of their blood'*, and asked that Sir William Waller, still absent in the west, should serve as their military governor.

But Waller was fully employed elsewhere. Sir Ralph Hopton's victory over the Parliamentarians at Stratton in Cornwall raised hopes of a national Royalist victory and galvanised the King into fresh initiatives. On 25th May, Charles despatched the Marquis of Hertford with two entire regiments of horse and two regiments of foot, their mission being to combine with Sir Ralph on Somerset's damp levels and together conquer the west. At Chard, on 4th June, the two armies combined. Hopton, with 500 horse and 3000 foot, had taken considerable risk in leaving Cornwall and agreeing to march through largely untamed Devon to a union with Hertford and Maurice - for Waller hovered near Bath, ready to exploit any uncoordinated Royalist movements.

Sir William was too far north, however, to assist the Somerset Roundheads and he could do little to prevent the spectacular Royalist successes that took place during the next few days. Taunton was surrendered on 5th June, less than 12 hours after the Royalists marched from Chard. Bridgwater's surrender followed soon afterwards, just part of Parliament's collapsing house of cards. Colonel Edward Popham, one of the county's more energetic Roundheads, managed to weld the scattered forces of east Somerset into a significant force at Glastonbury, but could do little to stop the Royalist advance, which continued with little interruption towards Wells and the Wiltshire border.

On 5th July, Waller and Hopton closed in combat on Lansdown Hill, just beyond the modern reach of Bath's northern suburbs. Days before this early summer clash on slopes rich with campion and foxgloves, Hopton had written to Waller and proposed a private meeting. War, the framework for many acts of shameful violence, might still leave untouched those deep sentiments of honour and friendship that beat within the hearts of decent men. Waller's gentle reply exhibits literary skills and stoic reality:

'Certainly my affections to you are so unchangeable, that hostility itself cannot violate my friendship to your person.....that great God who is the searcher of my heart knows with what a perfect hatred I detest this war without an enemy. We are both upon the stage, and must act such parts as are assigned us in this tragedy. Let us do it in a way of honour and without personal animosities' [4]

Lansdown was to be a battle full of personal heroism and resolute strategy. The Parliamentarians lined the top of Lansdown Hill, successfully resisting the Royalist assaults. Sir Bevil Grenville, a Royalist Cornishman, saved the day for the King's men. Reaching the top of the hill, his pikemen stood *'as unmovable as a rock'* and refused to be tumbled down the slopes. Sir Bevil was killed in his hour of glory. Features of that summer battlefield still remain unchanged. The wooded drop, the lane up which the Cornishmen climbed and the summer colours have so far defied the northward expansion of Bath's crowded suburbs - and a monument still commemorates the spot where Sir Bevil fell.

Ten days later, the two pre-war friends and their armies were to clash again, this time near the town of Devizes. Waller pursued Hopton after Lansdown, following him through Chippenham and Pewsham Forest, and eventually boxing the Royalist fugitives within Devizes. During this eventful retreat, an ammunition cart blew up, maiming Sir Ralph. For some time he was to be rendered incapable of leadership and even physical movement. It was a cruel reminder that God was an undoubted Roundhead and an enemy of kings. Sir William certainly saw it as as Providential interference and as a much needed tonic for his men.

'When Sir William Waller had intelligence of this blowing up of the powder, of which he well knew there was a scarcity before, and of the hurt it had done', wrote Clarendon, *'he infused new spirit into his men and verily believed that they had no ammunition,*

---
4 Quoted in Adair J. 'Roundhead General' p.75

and that the loss of Sir Ralph Hopton (whom the people took to be the soul of the army....and at this time believed to be dead), would be found in the spirits of his soldiers'.[5]

Aware that there was insufficient food and accommodation in Devizes for the army and all its horses, and conscious of the dangers of close siege, the Royalist commanders in Devizes decided to appeal to Oxford for help. '*......it was unanimously advised and consented to, that the Lord Marquis and Prince Maurice should that night break through with all the horse to Oxford and that Sir Ralph Hopton....with the Earl of Marlborough, the Lord Mohun, and other good officers of foot, should stay, there with the foot and cannon.....till the generals might return with relief from Oxford'*.[6]

The arrival of these fresh units from Oxford, the cream of the King's cavalry, brought on the Battle of Roundway Down, one of the war's major actions and Waller's worst disaster. '*My dismal defeat, the most heavy stroke of any that did befall me*',[7] he later wrote in his memoirs. Six hundred Parliamentarians were killed, 800 captured, and the rest put to flight. Many of those killed cascaded to their deaths over a steep drop at Roundway's western end. His entire army virtually ceased to exist, something which no amount of brave polemics from London could ever hope to conceal. Clarendon crows comfortably, placing Roundway amongst the most celebrated Cavalier victories: '*This glorious day, for it was a day of triumph, redeemed the King's whole affairs, that all clouds that shadowed them seemed to be dispelled and a bright light of success to shine'*[8]

News of the defeat disheartened the Roundheads of Hampshire - and warnings of impending calamity were issued from the pulpit. A priest named Strickland, ministering at Hursley, was seen to wring his hands: '*O Lord, Antichrist has drawn his sword against Thy Christ, and if our enemies prevail, Thou wilt lose Thine honour'*. Others concluded that God had just changed sides.

---

5 Clarendon Vol. 111 Bk.7 p.110   6 ibid p.113

7 Waller J. 'Experiences' p.123   8 Clarendon Vol. 111 Bk.7 p.119

Hampshire lay precariously open to a Royalist surge. Waller, without an army at his back, wrote to the Parliamentary commanders in Dorset and Somerset, asking for troops to assist the efforts of Colonel Richard Norton, on whom the county's defence would probably depend. By June 1643, Norton, relying heavily on the energies of Francis St. Barbe of Broadlands, Romsey, and Richard Major, had put 400 men in the saddle, 6 troops of nearly 70 men in each, and furnished with carbine, pistols and buffcoat. Sir Thomas Jervoise's much smaller regiment was also active in the field, patrolling the Southampton area. But few records exist of the whereabouts of Robert Wallop's unit.

Troop commanders of Norton's regiment

Col. Richard Norton
Capt. Thomas Bettesworth
Capt. Francis St. Barbe
Capt. John Pitman
Maj. Robert Stewart

On July 15th, when the unwelcome news of Roundway Down eventually reached Westminster, appeals went out to the City of London and the 4 associated counties to provide money, men and horses for the creation of a new army in the south, 7000 men or more, fully equipped to meet the growing Royalist threat. Westminster authorised the raising of 500 fresh cavalry and 1000 foot within Hampshire, ordering *'the Deputy Lieutenants and Committees ...to take care for the listing of the said horses, and bringing them to their several rendezvous, and to enable them*(the Committee) *to seize and sequester the estates of such persons as shall be refractory to this service'.*[9] Norton's and Jervoise's regiments together absorbed the entire cavalry contingent. Sir William Waller was again given the command, Westminster's faith in his capabilities

---
9 Commons Journals Vol.3 p.172

hardly diminished by his summer disaster on the Downs.

Winchester Castle was, by now, again in Royalist hands. At some unspecified moment in the Spring, Sir William Ogle and Robert Tichborne conspired to re-occupy the empty fortress. With just 8 Cavalier gentlemen at their sides, they took possession - and the sense of relief in the damaged Close and Cloisters was almost tangible. But, on the 19th July, Norton and his regiment naughtily plundered Winchester, the city's third desecration since the war began, and seized the arms and horses that had been collected there. Then, under the mistaken impression that Waller was triumphing in Wiltshire, the Roundhead colonel took his men into Wiltshire with the intention of meeting his superior near Devizes.

Suggestions that Norton still remained ignorant of Waller's defeat are hard to accept. Westminster and the entire south of England had received full details within 5 days, and Norton must have journeyed fully aware of the facts. Perhaps he thought that he could single-handedly take revenge, somehow punishing the entire Cavalier army with just 400 men. He found Wiltshire hostile to his presence and Parliament's appeal in tatters everywhere. He briefly stayed in Wardour Castle, the Catholic Lord Thomas Arundell's peacetime home, and now about the only place in the county where the Parliamentary beacon still shone. Passing back through Wilton, he retired to Hampshire along a circuitous path that kept him well beyond the reach of Oxford and Basing Royalists.

Norton, however, hungered for personal glory. That summer, reports of the Basing Royalists' misbehaviour, particularly of the shooting of two travellers who had stopped to talk outside Basing's gate, unleashed a spate of requests to Westminster to draw the teeth of the Marquis and his Cavaliers. '*This House hath not only been in great annoyance to all the country round about, but hath been a means to stop the trading out of the west to London by robbing and pillaging the carriers and clothiers that come from them*',[10] an M.P. reported to the Commons. Fuelled by such complaints, and regarding

---
10 'The Weekly Account' Parliamentary newsletter

Basing House *'as being a place in which he hoped to find much spoil and little opposition'*, he personally threatened the Marquis with punishment.

The peer, taking the threats seriously, journeyed to Oxford and asked the King for 100 musketeers *'for the well-being of the house doth depend upon expedient action'*. Charles promptly dispatched Lt. Col. Robert Peake, an engraver by trade, with the required soldiers and prayed that Basing would continue to defend his crown.

Norton, however, got there first. On July 31st, a *'fair summer day, not given to the spending of energy'*, Parliamentary dragoons under a silk merchant named Harvey took up positions in the Park with units of infantry posted in the village of Greywell to protect the rear. But he had under-estimated the size of the task. According to a contemporary description, *'Basing Castle......stands on rising ground, having its form circular, encompassed with a brick rampart, lined with earth, and a very deep trench, but dry. The lofty Gatehouse with four turrets looking northward on the right whereof without the compass of the ditch, is a goodly building, containing two fair courts.....The south side of the Castle hath a park, and toward Basing town a little wood, the place sealed and built as if for Royalty'.* [11]

The Marquis intended to hold it for royalty. In a letter of pompous adoration to Charles during the previous winter, he had promised that *'if the King had no more ground in England than Basing House, he would hold it out to the last extremity'.*[12] And to inspire his family and those who were pledged to defend the house, he etched two words with a diamond on the glass of a window 'Love Loyalty' - the two words which had been the family motto and the everlasting name of this house.

Other members of the Paulet family were just as active in their efforts for the King. In August 1643, aware that Henry Paulet was having difficulty recruiting in N.Hampshire, Charles directed a

---
11 Money W. 'Description of the Siege of Basing Castle'
12 Walker, Sir Edward 'His Majesty's Happy Progress and Success'.

second appeal to the churchmen of Winchester: *'Whereas we are very well assured of the fidelity and good affections of our right trusty and well beloved Henry, Lord Paulett, to us and our service, and out of that assurance have granted him our Commission for the raising of one regiment of horse for our defence and for the settling and security of this kingdom and principally our county of Southampton against this unnatural rebellion, which regiment by reason of the present condition of his own fortunes he is not so well able to raise at his own charge, we do therefore hereby recommend him and this affair unto you, desiring you to assist him with the voluntary and free contribution toward the raising thereof'.*[13]

At Basing the odds at the time were fully in Norton's favour. For, when his men arrived and surveyed the impressive towers, there were, beside the household servants, just 6 gentlemen with muskets, all that remained of the once great armoury. Mercurius Aulicus speaks briefly of this summer assault, reporting that *'Colonel Norton, with Capt. St. Barbe of Broadlands, Romsey, with his troop of horse, and .... with a ragged rabble of dragoons, begirt the house and pressed the siege exceeding hotly'.* Twice his men were repulsed, forced back from the walls by the energetic firing of just 6 muskets!

Norton's challenge was to be short-lived, almost farcical, and showing little of the fierce determination for which this Roundhead officer was later to be applauded. He had timed things badly: that same afternoon Lt. Col. Peake's musketeers arrived and cleared a path to the door of the castle. Behind rode Sir Henry Bard with several troops of Royalist horse, his hard-riding and hard-fighting men lunging at the Parliamentary troopers as they swept towards the house.

A day later, Rawdon's soldiers visited Greywell, forcing the hurriedly made brushwood defences that Norton had placed across the Greywell road. The Roundheads withdrew first, heads and pride smashed in an hour-long fight on a rain drenched field. Col. Richard Norton retreated that night to Farnham and from thence fell back to

---

13 Document relating to the History of the Cathedral Church of Winchester' Hampshire Records Society p.54

The Layout of Basing House

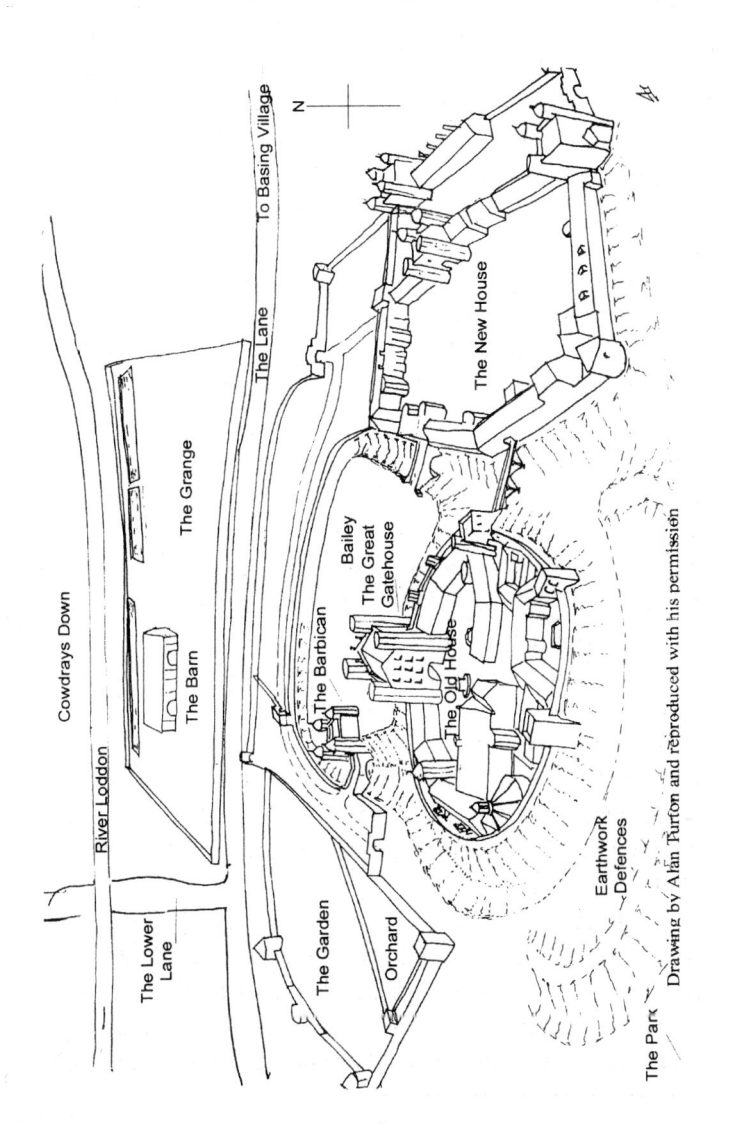

Portsmouth. He was acidly criticised by Mercurius Aulicus for *'plundering all the country as they passed along, for fear it should be thought that he had made so long a journey, and lain out so long, to undo nobody'*. Just as viciously, the news-sheet, commenting on his perceived lack of stomach at Basing, described him as a *'very valiant gentleman where he meets with no resistance'*.

The chance of taking Loyalty House without a major struggle had now gone, swept away with the falling leaves of early Autumn. Throughout the remaining weeks of summer, the defenders of Basing were busy, abandoning musket and carbine for pick axe and spade, and the newer fortifications *'is (sic) then begun, according to the quantity of men now added, to be fortified'*. Batteries and earthworks would spread throughout an area of nearly 15 acres - and the later siege of Basing House would consequently be one of the bloodiest of the war.

Much of the South and west now lay in Cavalier hands and a wind of pessimism blew through Hampshire. On 26th July, Bristol, the nation's second wealthiest city, fell to the King's forces. Nathaniel Fiennes, the town's Roundhead governor, was sentenced to death for surrendering, but was later reprieved. Following so soon after Roundway, Bristol's fall rocked the gossamer foundations of Parliament's southern platform, and triggered a bout of accusations about who was really responsible for these summer setbacks. Waller was quick to blame the Earl of Essex for failing to come to his assistance. Essex, still hovering inactively in the Thames Valley, was equally quick to exonerate himself, reminding the Houses of the smallness of his army and of the vital need to defend London.

Weeks later, it would be the turn of Exeter to taste the weight of the Royalist resurgence. On 4th September, after more than a month's siege, the Devon city fell to Maurice's troops - and another coastal city was in Cavalier hands. Further west, Plymouth still held out for Parliament, but, along the English shoreline from Exeter to Southampton, only Weymouth, Lyme and Poole defied the King.

Poole's allegiance to Westminster had never been in doubt

and had been one of the first towns in England to articulate its support for Parliament. Despite the protests of its Royalist mayor and several of his Corporation, a Parliamentary committee for the defence of the town was set up by leading townspeople and private money was spent on building defences. On June 23rd, Sir Walter Erle, a local M.P., had been given overall command, and, with the assistance of Hampshire men, he had set out to reduce the Royalist stronghold of Corfe. Forced to abandon the castle's siege on August 4th, he had retired to Poole to assist the defence. A few days later, Crawford haughtily demanded the town's surrender, reminding the townspeople that they were in unlawful rebellion against God's anointed King. Erle's response was just as haughty. Penned in the contemptuous style that was later to become the standard response to demands for surrender, he informed his Lordship that the town *'was already very well fortified and provided with ordnance, horse and foot to oppose any malignant whomsoever, that therefore they would not trouble his Lordship to send any forces to assist them, but if he did send any without their consent, they would deny them entrance'.*[14] Adding further insult, Erle reminded Crawford that the latter's commission was illegal…*'and therefore they sent his Lordship word, that since he pretended to assume that power, they hoped ere long to have him by force brought to the Parliament, to be made an example to posterity'.* Isolated from the rest of the Parliamentary south by Lord Crawford's cavalry that patrolled Hampshire's western borders near Ringwood and Fordingbridge, Sir Walter appealed to the Parliamentarians of Portsmouth and London for help, claiming in his letter that *'there is no place remaining that there is any hope of making it good but the town of Poole.'*[15]

But Portsmouth's commanders felt equally vulnerable and had already written to the Earl of Essex, requesting immediate help, *'lest we be felled like corn before the reaper'.* Westminster was a little more supportive, voting £300 on August 15th for Poole's

---
14 Vicars J. p.136   15 Tanner MSS. 62 f.218

defences, and directing Waller to arrange for the town's protection. The following day, two tons of lead from the roof of Lulworth castle were sent to the town with instructions about how to melt the metal down. Poole was to be reprieved for more than a month. During this interval, Crawford's Royalists raided Ringwood, Fordingbridge and Lymington, impressing horses and farm labourers into service for the King. Emboldened by their presence, a kinsman of the Marquis of Winchester led a party of horse, probably part of the garrison of Basing, into Winchester on August 12th, briefly occupying the castle and raising money from the city's clerics. Informed, however, that parliamentary dragoons from Southampton were riding north to deal with this mischief, he and his friends hurriedly vacated the city, leading 40 outspoken Parliamentarians in chains to Basing. Three miles from Winchester, the Cavaliers were attacked and the prisoners released. In this brief skirmish near Hursley, Paulet was killed and his entire force was captured.

But Southampton's Roundheads still felt vulnerable, and the military authorities reacted to dissension and treacherous comments within the town with threats of immediate imprisonment. Governor Peter Murford publicly chastised a townsman for openly sympathising with the Queen and then threatened to sequestrate the man's property *'for it will discourage the well-affected to hear that the Queen is beloved in any place.'*

Colonel Whitehead, itinerant policeman of Parliament's cause, was amongst those recruited by the governor to hold the peace. Arriving with a number of officials from Portsmouth, he ordered suspected Royalists to pay large fines. Those who refused were taken away to an uncertain fate in Portsmouth - and all their property was seized and sold.

The religiously disaffected were rooted out, too, and deported to New England. Elias Jones, a pamphlet writer and a man of impious influence, was bustled on board ship without trial and *'without allowing speech of his wife, or necessaries from his friends'*. Colonel

Whitehead, intemperate and extreme, argued that *'cruelty to Cavaliers was acceptable to God and His divine wish too'*. Armed with such reasoning, unreasonable men could now do anything, twisting the text of the Old and New Testaments to their advantage when the opportunity arose.

Murford's Puritan chaplain, Nathaniel Robinson, for example, was one of the more vociferous. Making no attempt to justify his narrow stance, he condemned the Cavalier out-of-hand as a man who *'delighteth in blood'*. In a prayer to the 'saved', he asked God to strike down these enemies of the Church. *'Let Thine hand, we pray Thee, O Lord, be on him and his father's house'*. Many of the more secular-minded were just as narrow. St. Barbe, who had left his house in Romsey to follow Parliament's standard, was unwilling to distinguish between the politics and religion of the day. Committing himself publicly to the service of Westminster, he was heard to utter that he would rather see the Kingdom in a flame than that the King should prevail against the Parliamentary cause. His troopers patrolled the villagers of Millbrook and Nursling, interrogating anyone who was held in suspicion. A labourer, armed only with a *'prong and a good heart'*, had a cart of hay with a crate on top. Supposing that the latter contained weapons for the King, two Parliamentary soldiers started to break the container open. But, felled from their horses by his strong rustic strength, they were beaten almost senseless by this man of the fields.

Reports of this miniature insurrection reached Murford in Southampton. Convinced that Royalist elements would soon mount an attack upon his town, he pressed the inhabitants of the town and its neighbouring villages into construction of new defences. The tythingmen and constables of the hundreds were ordered to supply men and money; those that refused were threatened with the gallows. Three men from Stoneham were staked to the ground for hours, a notice at their heads announcing their disloyalty to the common good - and all this for merely failing to arrive with their axes and shovels at the time required.

Portsmouth, too, shared this passion for building defences. Lady Norton, Richard's mother, seems to have played a leading part in directing the operations. Mercurius Aulicus, normally acidic in its comments, seems to have mildly admired her Boudicca-like activities. *'The Lady Norton, mother to that most noble colonel who hath done such wonders of late days, and governess for the present of the town of Portsmouth, for the committee dare do nothing without her advice, was very busily employed in making some new works about Portsea Bridge; and was not only every day in person amongst the workmen, but brought with her also every day 30 or 40 maids and women in a cart......to dig and labour in the trenches......It was further signified from thence that the Committee by her direction had caused a dungeon to be made there as dark as hell, that if the liberty of the subject should be laid up there nobody should have hope to find it intended for such malefactors, as it now appears, who either do refuse to take the new oath or to pay their taxes or otherwise shall show any good affections to his Sacred Majesty....'.*[16]

Defending the towns alone would not be enough to stave off the Cavalier advance. New armies would have to be formed, strategies sculpted and a sense of greater purpose and unity developed. Westminster edicts in July had promised Waller a new fighting force, but had not redressed the disunity and mistrust that caused disharmony in the high command. Waller, undoubtedly a better general than Essex could ever hope to be, resented his subordinate position and openly showed his disdain for the Earl. Lord Essex reluctantly agreed to confer greater autonomy on his subordinate, grudgingly stating in a letter to the Commons that *'he would begin upon a new score, and give Waller the best encouragement he can'*. Waller, in return, consented to take broad orders from the peer. The London press had been quick to point out the likely long-term consequences of this clash of personalities. *'Can the plough go where there are no men to hold?'* a pamphlet asked

---

16 Gates W. 'Illustrated History of Portsmouth'.

in July, capitalising on the lack of direction that had now become clear.

But rhetoric or wishful words were insufficient to physically mould the new army which Westminster desperately required. Short-term contracts, the sort of arrangement that had allowed soldiers to lay down their arms at the very moment when they were most needed, had long bedevilled the recruitment efforts of both sides. For Parliament, relying almost entirely on voluntary enlistment, it was a particular weakness. On September 13th, a Westminster ordnance permitted the recruiting generals to impress anyone between the ages of 18 and 50, with the exception of clergy, scholars, the sons of widows, members of the trained bands and the servants of peers still attending the Upper House. On that same day, Waller was appointed to the vacant governorship of Portsmouth, but simultaneously was ordered to be ready to '*march at once, wherever the needs must be*'. Far too vaguely worded and without any sense of specific direction or urgency, it hardly seemed to be a realistic basis upon which to build a fresh campaign.

9

'Disorder is the confusion of both'

THIS act of impressment, something that challenged all the notions of freedom and voluntary enlistment that had underpinned recruitment so far, enabled Waller to impress 5000 soldiers with which to commence his undefined campaign. £4000 was paid into the coffers for the support of his new army. The nucleus of this new force was formed from the 3 regiments of horse which had crashed to destruction on Roundway Down. Waller's own regiment, the oldest of the three, had been amongst those routed at Edgehill. Sir Arthur Heselrige's 'Lobsters', formed only weeks before the Lansdown campaign, re-emerged, phoenix-like, in all its quaint splendour, and the regiment of Col. Robert Burrell was now reformed under the command of an able Dutchman, Jonas Vandruske. A fourth regiment, the London Horse of Col. Richard Turner, would serve periodically with Waller in the campaign that followed.

The infantry regiments were all new creations. Six fit units, a total of 5000 men, evolved. They were paid, armed and organised by loans from the London merchants. Cavalry and foot, 7000 men, were ordered to parade at Windsor on September 22nd.

Almost simultaneously, the King began to remodel his western army. But, unlike the woolly semantics which atrophied Parliamentary decision making, Royalist strategy now developed more clearly than at any previous time. Sir Ralph Hopton, fully recovered from his injuries, was appointed to the command and given specific instructions to clear Wiltshire and Hampshire, and then strike towards London from the south.

And yet before either army could flap its fledgling wings, Lord Essex and the King had clashed at Newbury. The capture of Bristol seemed to have unleashed an unstoppable spate of Royalist energy that swept, like the Severn bore, up that river's valley. On 10th August, the investment of Gloucester, held for Parliament since the war's start by Colonel Edward Massey and 1400 men, began. Charles had good reason to be confident. When fully mustered, his force might have numbered as many as 30,000 men, and the city's defences were nowhere as formidable as those at Bristol. Moreover, his army had full command of the Severn and its local daughter streams, and the besiegers were able to divert the flow and deprive the town of its water supply.

Every conceivable military and psychological weapon was to be employed. Enormous mortars, wide-mouthed beasts capable of propelling missiles weighing more than forty kilograms, were dragged into action by the besiegers during the opening hours. Fearsome in appearance, however, they were frequently ineffective in operation: *'That night the enemy shot several granadoes out of their mortar pieces,'* states one account of the siege, *'they all broke, but did no harm; we have since received intelligence that their biggest mortar piece broke at the first discharg-ing of it; they say the biggest in England.*

This siege was to become one of the war's most eventful, exhibiting all the dramatic characteristics of siege warfare: sporadic sorties by the defenders in search of a specific objective, bombardment of the walls by besieging guns, frantic repairs to blistered defences by the city's women and girls, insidious attempts to undermine both the walls and morale of the besieged, and the unrecorded suffering of the innocent. Gloucester was ultimately saved by public opinion as much as by political action. The fall of Bristol had paralysed Parliamentary thinking and blown morale to bits - and few politicians in London saw any hope of victory. But, aiming at these weak hearts, a deluge of pamphlets appeared on the capital's bookstalls during that final week of August and the pen was to spit with poisoned rhetoric. One leaflet particularly put mettle into the watery veins;

> *'What is the matter, noble citizens, that your hearts are down, do you think the day is lost? Do you think England is lost because Bristol is lost?...Strive to set yourselves in order, for order is the strength of an army, and of a city, but disorder is the confusion of both...strive therefore to find them (malignants) out, give them the Covenant, if they refuse to enter into Covenant with you, let them not live in the city with you...sec-ure them and banish them...cast them out, spare none...'*

An ordinance in the same week authorised the London military commanders to mobilise six regiments of foot and 1500 horse, specifically to rescue Gloucester from catastrophe. But this alliance between the politicians and military was rooted in barren ground - for there was no money with which to pay the freshly raised troops. Additional appeals were therefore made to the City, the cause's wealthy paymasters. They responded immediately and the following day members of the London trained bands assembled in arms on Hampstead Heath.

On 4th September, buffeted by the heavy winds, the Roundhead force climbed Prestbury Hill and looked down on the blighted rooftops of Gloucester. Few of those present were ever likely to forget the scene below. Parliament's colours still fluttered above the city's battered walls and a maze of empty trenches broke the level ground to the east. For the besieging guns had gone, dragged away by the dejected lines of Royalist soldiers that could be seen merging with the distant mist. Charles, unable to dent the besieger's metal will, had ordered a withdrawal.

Three days later, Parliament's army at last entered Gloucester, greeted by a message pinned on the south gate which read: *'A city assailed by men but saved by God'*. Providence, not Essex, had been given the credit for the city's deliverance. Massey had just three barrels of powder left when the Royalist guns at last fell silent. Yet, Essex, advancing so far west, had uncovered London. Charles was to take full advantage of this fleeting opportunity. The campaign that followed was consequently never planned, having emerged as the result of sudden circumstance. Instead of returning to Oxford as his more cautious commanders advised, the King headed north towards Pershore, hoping to entice the enemy still further from London.

Essex was fortunately too wise to take the bait. Noticing that the King's northward movement had again unblocked the path to London, he decided instead to return to the capital by a more southerly route than the one he had followed on the outward journey. But to deceive the King, he first headed north to Tewksbury on the 10th, hoping to convince the Royalists that he was intending to fall on Worcester.

This began a territorial game of chess, each trying to outwit the other by carefully staged moves. Five days of Parliamentary subterfuge followed. On the night of the 15th, Essex at last dropped his mantle of deception. Taking advantage of the dark, he suddenly swung south on the first leg of his march to London. Charles, sitting indecisively beside the Severn, had been wrong-footed.

The chess game now became a race. The Royalists, fifty miles to the north, found themselves engaged in a race towards London. Soon the two armies were marching south-east on roughly parallel tracks, the King's men at least two days behind their quarry.

The cavalry of both sides were to clash at Aldbourne on the 18th. It is difficult to unravel the threads of Aldbourne. Rather than a setpiece action, it was a schoolboy brawl, a sort of spontaneous free-for-all, but probably inevitable. Notions of superiority filled the minds of the horse soldiers of both sides, convincing them that they were better than the infantry arm with which they were obliged to co-operate. Socially this is largely true: the cavalry consisted primarily of gentry and their retainers, the elite of pre-war England. Militarily this claim to superiority is far more doubtful. At Edgehill it had been the infantry that had shown constraint and greater staying power, and subsequent clashes had done little to dispel this unpalatable fact. But cavalry vanity flowed more deeply than this surface rivalry with the foot: the mounted bodies of both sides wished also to prove themselves as superior to the opposing horse. Few opportunities had presented themselves recently for testing this conviction: Aldbourne had become the jousting ground for which these men had so long sought.

The verdict of Aldbourne seems generally to favour Parliament, eroding the view that the Royalist horse were indomitable. Sir Philip Stapleton had shown his skills as a commander and his men had rivalled the dash and style shown by Rupert's men at Edgehill. From now on, until the professionalism and training of the New Model Army swung the advantage in favour of Parliament, the cavalry of both sides seemed generally well matched.

Heavy rains the following day were to be even more effective in slowing the Roundhead retreat, and it was to be the Cavaliers who reached Newbury first. The Parliamentary army, seeking only the Kennet valley's direct route to London, found their way blocked at Wash Common, just one mile south of the town. This was to bring on the war's second major battle, an action that would be coloured by the consequences of missed opportunities and too hasty planning.

Failure to occupy Round Hill in strength, a gentle prominence that commanded the field, was Rupert's first mistake. Essex, slower moving but quicker thinking, drove the small Royalist detachment from the hill and, by establishing a battery, stole the field of action. But beyond, deployed between Round Hill and the Kennet's banks, lay the Royalist cavalry, solid packs of mounted men that held the road to London. The King's infantry had not yet arrived, but Essex realised that an attack across this narrow neck of rain sodden ground would be bound to fail. Throughout the remaining hours of daylight the field commanders of both sides considered their restricted range of options.

Charles retired to rest in Newbury at midnight, confident that he could now deal Essex's army a lethal blow. His rest might have been untroubled. For Essex, however, searching for the key to victory in tiny Bigg's Cottage, his Enborne H.Q., the flickering lights burned endlessly. Riding at the zenith of his reputation, but dogged by suspicions about the true depth of his loyalties, Essex knew that defeat on the morrow would deliver him into the hands of his critics. To the Lord General of Parliament's armies and his subordinate commanders, huddled around the little table in the parlour, Round Hill was clearly the fulcrum upon which all conceivable strategies might hinge. At some point during those hours of darkness, Skippon's infantry regiment was sent forward to secure the hill's heights and two further regiments were later advanced in support. The entire army slept that night in the open, most bivouacing on the yellowing grass of Skinner's Green, less than one mile from the enemy's quietened ranks. Dawn's grey light exposed their huddled shapes, men in their thousands on the dew sparkled ground, and Parliament's colours flying solidly on the summit of Round Hill.

Lord Essex's strategy largely evolved from what he observed that morning, the 20th. The elite of the Royalist horse, perhaps 4,000 men under the personal command of Rupert, had now drawn up on Wash Common. Essex's immediate response was to reinforce Philip Stapleton, who had only 2,000 men with which to confront this Royalist strength. But the heightening daylight also revealed the sturdiness of the Royalist right, where four entire brigades of infantry manned the eastern edge of Skinner's Green from Round Hill to the

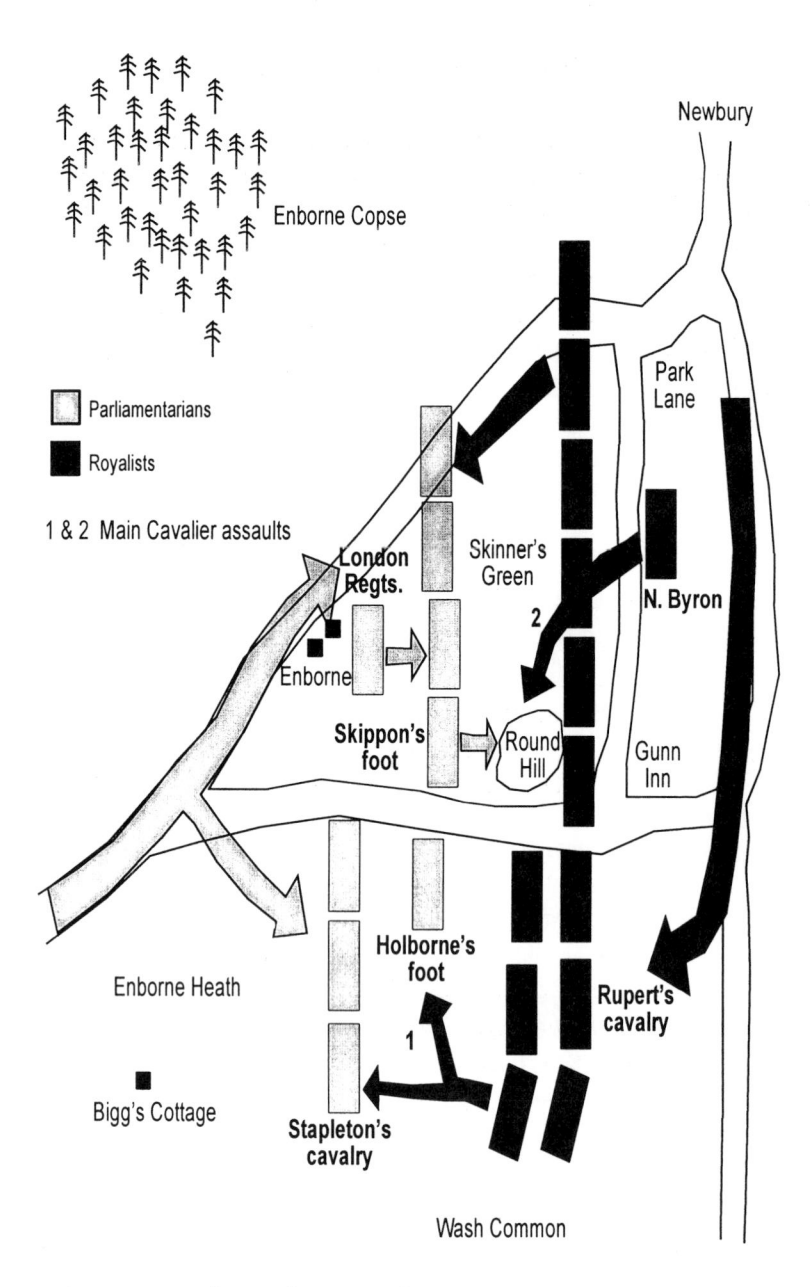

1st Battle of Newbury

winding Kennet. The remaining infantry were consequently sent northwards to secure the river's banks, leaving only Holborn's three regiments to anchor Stapleton's position on Wash Common. The six regiments of the London trained bands, unwilling to fight so far from home, formed the reserve, drawn up in mass behind the Parliamentary centre. Twenty-eight thousand men stood on the field, roughly equal numbers on either side, and an ominous silence reigned.

The King's army at Newbury

Horse:
Prince Rupert's brigade
Lord Carnarvon's brigade
Lord Wilmot's brigade
Sir John Byron's brigade
Col. Charles Gerrard's brigade

Total: about 6000

Foot:
Col. John Belasyse's brigade
Sir Nicholas Byron's brigade
Sir Gilbert Gerrard's brigade
Sir William Vavasour's brigade

Total: about 8000

Parliamentary army at Newbury

Horse: The Lord General's Troop and 14 small regiments.
Formed into two wings:
- left flank under Col. John Middleton
- right flank under Sir Philip Stapleton

Total: about 4000

Foot: 6 regiments of the trained bands of London (Red, Yellow and Blue regiments and 3 auxiliary regiments)

12 regular regiments formed into 4 brigades:

Left flank (Philip Skippon)
Lord Robarte's brigade (3 regiments)
Skippon's brigade (3 regiments)

Right flank (Lord Essex)
Barclay's brigade (3 regiments)

Holborne's brigade (3 regiments)

Total: about 10,000

Both commanders thought that they had been disadvantaged. Essex, visiting his troops on a morale-raising quest, was forthright, claiming that the Royalists were better positioned. They had, he admitted: '...the hill, the town, hedges, lane and river'. But at almost the same minute, Sir John Byron, a Royalist brigade commander, was criticising the Prince for not occupying the Round Hill in time, '...though we had day enough to have done it'.

Parliament's two guns on the Round Hill sounded the call to

arms, their sudden reports sending breakfasting rabbits scuttling for cover. Minutes later, the Royalist artillery on Wash Common responded. The resulting duel is said to have been one of the most prolonged and savage of the entire war. But separated by more than 300 metres from their targets, these guns were merely part of the war of angry words.

Rupert, like an impatient hunting dog on the leash, was ready to tear his Roundhead quarry to pieces. Resplendent as ever at the head of his well-formed lines, he saw battle as a frivolous sport, structured only by the laws of the chase with personal glory as its single goal. Separating him from Stapleton's smaller force was almost ideal cavalry country, sloping grassland split by the occasional edge or unkept enclosure. Soon after 7 a.m. a Royalist skirmish line of musketeers advanced across Wash Common and engaged the Roundhead cavalry. Minutes later, Rupert's troops charged through the musketeers' open line against the raised pikes of Holborn's brigade. These men, locking pikes in an instantly impenetrable wall, held the assault and deflected the Royalist aggression southward against Stapleton's waiting horse.

Aldbourne was avenged in the next few minutes. Stapleton's men were swept away, little stronger than corn before the reaper, and the brigade was to play no further part in the action. Richard Norton's regiment was part of this broken brigade, and Francis St. Barbe of Broadlands one of those killed during those fateful moments. In the centre of the field, Sir Nicholas Byron, one of a prolific family of Royalist supporters and uncle of Sir John, led his infantry towards the northern slopes of Round Hill. Parliament's two guns were promptly swung to face this new threat and the assailants were forced to take cover behind a bank at the south end of today's Dark Lane. Sir John, called to their assistance, scouted the hedges along the hill's northern slopes in search of enemy weakness and found a gap wide enough for one horse to pass through at a time. Lucius Carey, Viscount Falkland, the King's Secretary of State, was riding with Byron's men. In the act of passing through the narrow gap, both he and his horse were killed. His death, probably the most memorable feature of the battle, is commemorated by a memorial near the road to Andover.

Sir John Byron and his men, having broken down the flanking hedge, now stormed angrily up the hill, thrusting at Skippon's infantry with sword and carbine. The defenders, according to Byron's own report: *'entertained us with a great salvo of musket shot, and discharged their two drakes upon us laden with case shot'*. The punishment was devastating, and the proud Royalists were forced to withdraw, leaving many of their comrades dead on the hill's northern slope.

Revenge, however, followed swiftly. Sir Thomas Aston's fresh regiment of horse combined with Sir John's in a further charge and the double fury of their ascent shook the defenders from the summit and back towards a high hedge that lay on the western rise. Temporarily trapped by this product of peacetime farming, Skippon's men, according to Byron: *'...poured in another volley of shot upon us, when Sir Thomas Aston's horse was killed under him, and withal kept us off with their pikes'*. Skippon, watching his tormentors regroup, and surveying the now noticeable gaps in his own lines, fell back to a narrow lane and called on the Londoners of the reserve to assist.

The most savage killing of the day was now to occur. The Royalist horsemen were faced by an unbroken line of lowered pikes. When finally the Cavaliers withdrew, more than 100 horsemen lay dead at the foot of Parliament's unflinching ranks. This prolonged dialogue between horse and foot had again contradicted the established pattern of warfare and a long held axiom that cavalry normally excelled. Military conventions were overthrown on the little hill; ill-disciplined infantry had weathered the blasts of well mounted cavalry.

The sequel was even more impressive. Skippon, determined to hold the hill at any cost, posted two of the London regiments near the summit. The Blue regiment, placed on the right, was suddenly assailed by Rupert's horsemen. The trained bands stood,

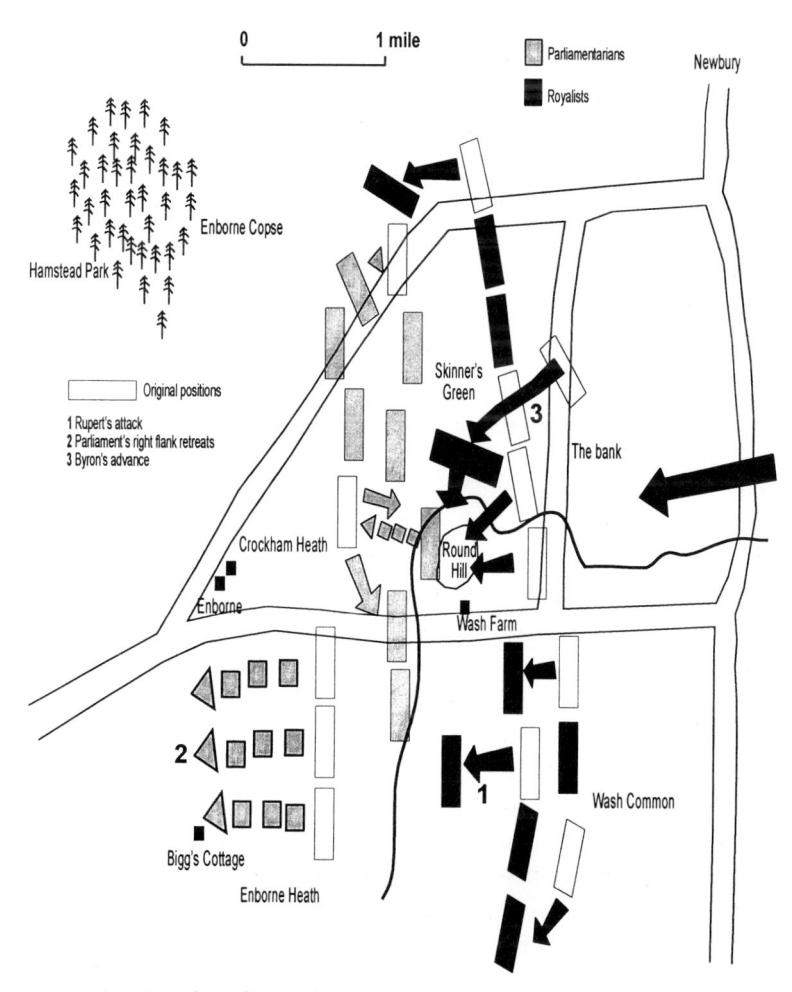

1st Battle of Newbury
The Moves

'DISORDER IS THE CONFUSION OF BOTH'

'...undaunted like a grove of pines in a day of winds and tempests...they kept their footing sure'. Faced by such stubborn resistance, Rupert's attack faltered and his personal pride ebbed. The day's conflict faded soon after 7 p.m. Nothing momentous or decisive had happened on the battle's northern front. Fighting throughout the field seemed to end by common consent, both sides disengaging before the first hints of darkness fell across the field. It had been a cocktail of missed opportunities and mixed success, one of the war's many indecisive and haphazard battles. Neither side had been forced from the field and the Royalist army still blocked the road to London.

But only for a little while longer. In the hours of darkness, Charles held council. Influenced by a *'foolish and knavish suggestion of want of powder'*, he decided to quit the field. Some of his advisers, amongst them Rupert, argued for remaining at arms on the field and resuming the battle the next day. They were overruled by the faint-hearted King. At midnight the Royalists quietly fell back through Newbury, unwitnessed by the enemy who lay all night on the field. Early the next morning a single shot was fired into the Royalist positions of the night before, but the last of the King's tired men had already gone. Charles's withdrawal had turned stalemate into Roundhead victory and the road to London lay open.

Recriminations were bound to follow in the Royalist ranks. The cavalry perhaps were beyond reproach, but the infantry, with the exception of Sir Nicholas Byron's brigade, had done too little and became the object of criticism in the days to come. *'Had not our foot'*, Sir John later wrote, *'played the poltroons extremely that day, we in all probability had set a period to the war, our horse having behaved themselves with as much gallantry as could be.'*

He might well have been correct. Nothing but Essex's army stood between the King and his capital and the probable end of war. But perhaps the single biggest flaw in the Royalist war machine was the King himself. With Charles at the helm, the ship of state would increasingly flounder. Faced by this certainty, many of her crew, in order to save their skins, would abandon ship and swim to foreign shores.

10

'Considering the forwardness of the gentlemen'

NO amount of military posturing or battle waging on a distant field, however, could alone be relied upon to save Hampshire for the cause. For a county's allegiance depended less on the success of national campaigning and more on the vigilance and determination of local partisans. In the autumn of 1643, the Parliamentary defence of Hampshire still lacked structure. It was blown to pieces when Winchester fell to Oxford's ever lengthening arm. Sir Richard Tichborne and Lord Ogle again visited the city in late September or early October, this time in the company of Lord Charles Gerrard and 120 horsemen. Raiding luckless Andover on the way, the Cavalier party rested until nightfall at Wherwell. At midnight they paraded noisily outside Winchester's North gate, a showy display designed to unnerve the gate's few sentinels. It was promptly opened, allowing the horsemen to ride in silent triumph into the castle.

Clerics, townsmen and traders seem to have welcomed the intruders and willingly made known the names of Parliament's adherents in the city. Some of those named were taken from their beds that night and others were visited at their breakfast tables on the morning following. Most of William Waller's furniture was taken from his house and ceremoniously destroyed in public. A few small pieces were spirited away by one of Sir William's friends and sent to Rotterdam for safety. Lord Ogle was able to strut triumphantly like a peacock, self-installed in the small gallery of Royalist heroes who would be applauded by the King.

Having gained his prize, he looked for the means to hold it securely and *'render it as inaccessible as art could invent, widely considering that as its situation rendered it the principal key of the whole western county it might be made a serviceable rendezvous for his Royal Master'*[1] By Christmas, it was heavily manned: 2 veteran regiments of foot and a troop of horse brought over from Ireland, and western England units raised by Ralph Hopton and Sir John Berkeley.

Oxford's arm also reached towards Poole. On September 18th, Lord Crawford, inactive since the start of the month, but now instructed to reduce the town, chose the most underhand methods to secure his goal. One of his officers intrigued with a woman of Wimborne to 'negotiate' with Captain Francis Sydenham, an officer of the Poole garrison, and persuade him to assist his King. Amongst the enticements offered by this wily woman was an offer of a commission in the King's army and £140 in return for opening the gate when the Royalist soldiers appeared. Sydenham, adopting a double role, accepted all of Crawford's and the lady's offers, but simultaneously kept Governor Bingham of Poole informed of these shadowy arrangements.

At 2 a.m. on the 24th, Crawford, his confidence sharpened by his backstairs intrigues, stopped in front of the town's principal gate with 2 regiments of infantry and 8 troops of horse, never even suspecting that Sydenham might be serving two masters.

The scene is almost imaginable. 300 expectant Cavalier

---
1 Godwin G.N. p.123

horse and foot, crowded into the curious 'half-moon' defence works that lay outside, like crowds in front of a football stadium waiting for the turnstiles to open. They probably never noticed the dust-covered chains that lay across the pathway or the determined looks of the defenders above the gateway. Sydenham failed to act, and the gate remained stubbornly closed.

The full force of the town's musketry and ordnance was unleashed instead. Horses reared, men fell, and panic swept like an epidemic through the compressed masses of men and horses. All semblance of order and dignity disappeared, and the lessons of military training were lost as men tussled with their companions in a frantic effort to escape. But the chains across the road had been pulled tight by hidden townsmen and the victims were effectively trapped. Terror fed on panic, 100 horsemen already lay dead or wounded, and the muskets still fired on. Well to the rear, like a theatrical backdrop, the peaceful waters of the harbour sparkled with emerald green. The slaughter would have been even greater if the guns, high on the town walls, had been able to lower their angle and sweep the ground beneath. Three-quarters of Crawford's force, 300 men, were either killed or captured. The peer was amongst the minority of survivors. Felled from his horse when the harness split, he had to crawl to safety. But Mercurius Aulicus chose to play down the disaster, claiming that only 10 men were dead and another 4 lay in chains.

Bells rang out in London. Distant Poole, the defence of which up to now had been regarded as unimportant, was transformed into a symbol of defiance, something for which Parliament had so long searched but, until now, had never found. On October 24th, the Commons voted £200 for the garrison's use and a special committee was appointed to consider measures for the town's long-term protection Four ships were fitted out to provide Poole with a naval arm, the captains and crews ordered to intercept any vessel that might attempt to enter the harbour. Cargo seized from gauntlet runners in the weeks following were sold in London, and the revenue

'Considering the forwardness of the gentlemen'

Poole in the 17th Century

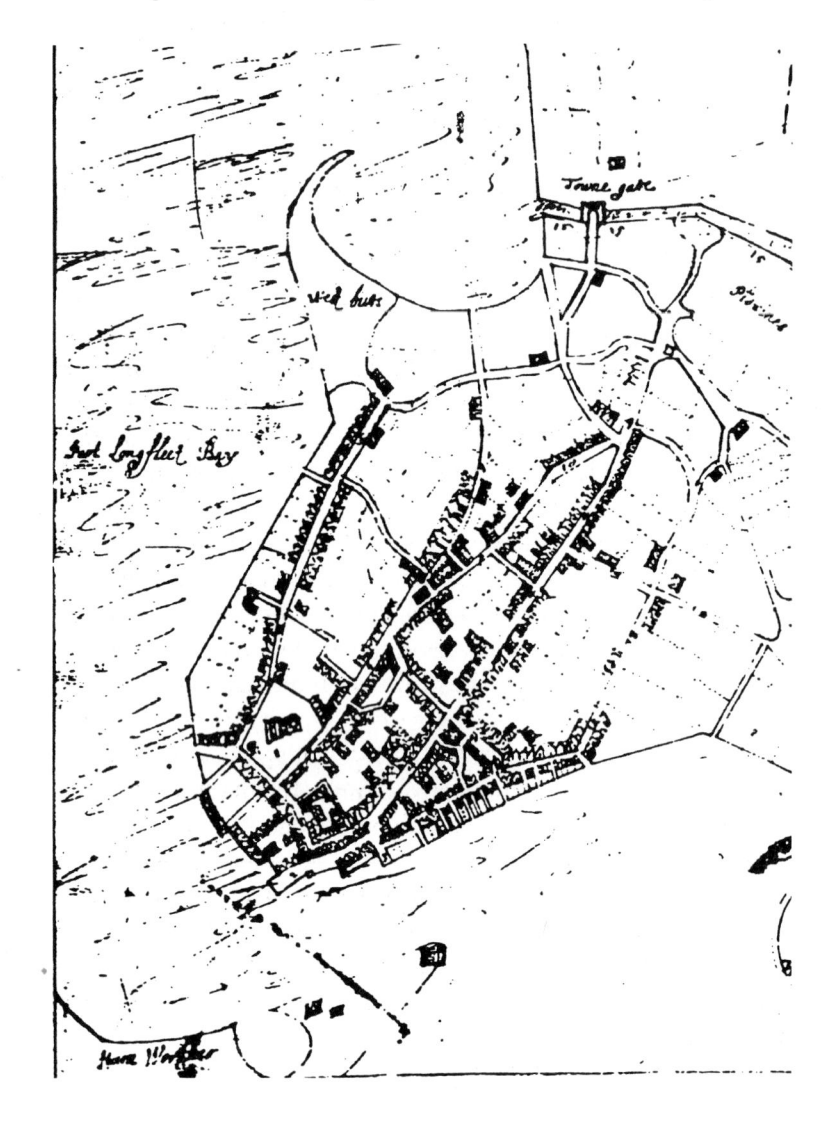

Reproduced with the kind permission of Poole Reference Library

made available for use in Poole.

The Earl of Warwick, in command of these ships and the rest of Parliament's scattered fleet, was obliged to be everywhere at once. With only 8 men-of-war in the south, and a coastline full of coves and bays in which privateers and Royalist vessels might lie undetected for days, the aristocrat saw his mission as near-impossible. *'They must send out more ships'*, he had written to the Admiralty in August. *'If they would employ so much, for in my life I was never so much put to it for want of ships, and there was but three on the west side of the channel'*

Fears of a Royalist resurgence on the Isle of Wight added to his burdens. The mainland castles nearest the island, Hurst and Calshot, were woefully undermanned and were failing to prevent Royalist schemers from crossing the narrow Solent. This, together with the utterances of some of Wight's unsilenced Cavaliers, contributed to a state of near-paranoia. As early as May, John Hall, an articulate resident of Swainston, voiced the general feeling of insecurity that existed.

'The Cavaliers coming so near these parts (Salisbury) *have put us in some fear here.....When the Cavaliers were come to Salisbury, Hurst castle, the very key of the island, was very much unprovided both of men and victuals, and most of the platform so much decayed for want of boards and other necessaries, as the ordnance can hardly be made use of there.....If that castle should be taken, the Island would quickly be in a dangerous condition'* [2]
Insecurity on the mainland deepened as well, becoming near hysteria in June when leading Southampton residents, fearing a Royalist assault on the city, hurriedly sent their valued possessions by boat to the island for safekeeping. The Newport town watch was strengthened and two newly raised militia units, nearly 300 strong, took possession of some barns near Cowes. And calls went out to Westminster in August for 100 barrels of powder to feed the defenders' guns.

---

2 'Letters to the Earl of Northumberland' Private MSS

Sir John Oglander was amongst those most closely watched. In May, he had been injudicious in his comments during questioning by Parliamentary officials, arguing that the fleet belonged to the King and that he *'would have given £500 of his own purse, so as the King's ships were in the right owners' possession'*. He was arrested by Carne on June 22nd and sent to London. *'I have sent up Sir J. Oglander and sufficient matter to keep him a while by the leg, if you will do him that justice; without it, peradventure the place will be the better for his absence'*.[3] The Lieutenant-Governor, Thomas Carne, had written in his indictment. Sir John claims that he was only summoned to attend at Westminster and could have chosen to refuse. *'I obeyed, and on that day undertook my journey. God send me health to perform it, and his blessing. Then I doubt not, if I may have justice, my own innocency will bring me back again. If not, I commend my soul to my redeemer'*[4]. He had remained in prison for two months. Eventually released, he now saw the advantages of a more guarded tongue and the benefits of compliance. Other Island Royalists chose to follow his example, and the Isle of Wight would become noticeably quieter.

But the true strength of Royalist sentiment on the Island was still ungauged. In an attempt to identify the malignants, Col. Carne, a zealous enthusiast for the cause, called a meeting on September 18th all the leading gentry, asking all present to sign a declaration of loyalty to Westminster. Sir John, wise enough to attend the summons, reluctantly signed, justifying his reasoning in his own record of events: *'I confess I wished myself away, but that could not be. Then, considering the forwardness of the gentlemen, and how I was counted a great malignant, and that all their aim was at me, and that by setting my hand I might gain a better opinion, and be thereby better enabled to do his Majesty service when occasion served; and that if I did refuse it I was certain to be banished the Island, I did unwillingly set my hand'*[5] Punishment, however, still followed. Sent again to London under escort, he was kept for three

---

3 'Letters to the Mainland' I.O.W. Collection in private ownership
4 The Commonplace Book of Sir John Oglander, Pt. IV p. 106   5 ibid. p.107

weeks in a house '*at the farthest end of Cabbage Lane in Westminster*'[6] and frequently interrogated.

In October, the Islanders petitioned Westminster for more support, colourfully suggesting that French ships were about to land soldiers near St. Catherine's Head. Jolted by the possibility, the Commons ordered Warwick to place some of his ships at the island's disposal and Col. Carne was summoned to London to discuss what needed to be done to maintain the island's Parliamentary purity. Amongst his recommendations were the strengthening of the garrison and the stockpiling of shot and weapons. Eleven culverins and twenty sakers were promptly ferried across the Solent and trees were felled in the New Forest for the construction of new gun platforms. John Lisle, Winchester's energetic M.P., introduced the necessary legislation into the Commons while Leigh and Worsley, two of Wight's M.P.s, petitioned the Earl of Essex to grant Sir Gregory Norton a commission to raise a force of 100 men for the island's defence.

The mainland remained just as vulnerable to Royalist insurgence. Every house, field, village or town was a potential haven for latent Royalism - and, like bacteria breeding in a cesspool of filth, such malignancy had to be rooted out. Norton, Murford and Jervoise were to double their efforts for the cause, searching the homes and galleries of even the quietest of the Hampshire gentry, looking for those little germs that might favour the discredited King. In October, a warrant issued by the Marquis of Winchester for the raising of money was intercepted. On the 18th, this was read out in the House of Commons, causing a storm of anger and immediate demands for the peer's arrest on the charge of high treason. Westminster then voted to provide additional money for the county's defence and, on the 22nd, announced the names of the Parliamentary committee who were to take responsibility for Hampshire's defence. 52 politicians, landowners and merchants, men whose Roundhead credentials were clearly beyond any doubt.

---

6 ibid. p.107

Acts of pure vindictiveness sometimes followed, the innocent punished as much as the guilty. In November, the Earl of Southampton's Titchfield house was seized and turned into a gaol. Basing was watched from a distance, Norton's soldiers sometimes patrolling on Cowdray Down or riding in clusters through the streets of Basingstoke. Some prattling priests, who talked too loudly of their enthusiasm for the King, were seized while fishing near Romsey Abbey. On November 6th, three Roundhead troopers, claiming that money for the King was concealed within a cask of wine in a barn near Stockbridge, broke the container open and drank it dry. In a more constructive frame of thought, the Earl of Warwick was ordered to prevent the landing of any strangers or aliens on English shores.

The Hampshire Committee

George Baynard	Thomas Bettesworth	John Button
John Bulkley	Arthur Broomfield	Henry Broomfield
Henry Campion	William Carrick	Thomas Chandeler
Thomas Clerke	William Collins	Thomas Cresswell
John Doddington	Edward Doddington	Thomas Dowse
Thomas Evans	Arthur Evelin	John Elliotte
Edward Exton	John Fielder	George Gollop
Thomas Gate	Edward Goddard	William Gore
Thomas Hanbury	Robert Harward	John Hooke
Edward Hooper	William Jephson	Richard Jervoise
Thomas Jervoise	John Kemp	John Kitwell
William Lewis	John Lisle	Nicholas Love
Richard Love	Richard Major	Thomas Mason
Richard More	Richard Norton	John Pitman
Ralph Riggs	Francis Rivert	John St. Barbe
James Tull	Robert Wallop	Richard Whitehead
Alex Wilson	William Wither	William Woulger
Henry Worsley		

'Idle Dick' Norton was the real star of the hour. After serving with distinction under Sir Philip Stapleton at Newbury, he and his regiment retired to Southampton, pausing briefly at Romsey to lay Captain St. Barbe to rest in the Abbey. Southampton was constantly threatened by roving Cavalier forces which somehow refused to be contained. In these autumn weeks of danger, immediately after the fall of Winchester, the Southampton Parliamentarians clamoured for a stronger, more charismatic governor than Murford, and Norton was suddenly hoisted into office while Murford found himself demoted to the post of the garrison's Sergeant-Major.

The former governor's excesses had been praised or criticised, depending on the view of the commentator. Some saw him as a deliverer from evil, others, more commonly, viewed him as little better than the devil himself. Mercurius Aulicus, of course, was the most condemnatory, seizing any opportunity for vilifying the man, a tailor by trade: *'Murford, the pretended Governor of Southampton (nine of whose profession make one man), hath power to fine that town as seemeth best to his greatness'*, states the Royalist news letter in its September 1643 edition. Referring to the costs of financing a banquet arranged by Murford, the newsletter pointed out that *'the poor townsmen paid for all, it so pleasing this mighty Governor that he assessed the town to £650, which they were forced to pay suddenly to avoid plundering, which he threatened, especially the old mayor, who was constrained to ransom his goods for £40'*. The carping writer then hastened to pull into the open another of Murford's political and religious misdeeds, something which even the townsmen would find hard to forgive: *'.....this infamous Governor pulled down the picture of Queen Elizabeth from over the north gate of that town (called the Bar Gate), saying that the Queen was the occasion of all these troubles, for if she had made a thorough reformation all this fighting would have been spared. But if nothing but religion had stirred this good man's spirits, he might still have governed the shears and thimble and let corporations alone'*.

Norton and he were probably jointly responsible for the decision to convert the Earl of Southampton's house at Titchfield in November into a gaol for the disaffected, and for the seizure of Lord Hertford's Netley home. But Murford alone was denounced

Portrait of Lord Ralph Hopton

by Mercurius Aulicus, '.....*though I know not the man, is resolved still to trouble me with his weekly actions. For, having decreed to make the Earl of Southampton's house a prison, this week he sent in fifty prisoners to take possession, and to show his mightiness, he assembled his committee.....where, after a serious debate, it was concluded that all the coal in Netley House, a house belonging to the Lord Marquis of Hertford........should be removed to Southampton'*.

Norton, however, was no less a zealot than his predecessor, and some of his methods of forcing the co-operation of the townspeople seem to have been equally questionable. In his own account of his government of the town, he boasted that he soon persuaded most of the more prominent townsmen to sign an oath of loyalty to Parliament, adding that, although *'some devilish spirits there are that have refused it, but I shall pare their nails'*.

But he needed to be constantly vigilant. In November, Col. Sir Humphrey Bennet, Royalist sheriff of Hampshire and only recently commissioned by Charles to raise a regiment of horse, took quiet possession of Romsey *'to the end they might be always in action against the garrison of Southampton'*.[7] By Christmas, nearly 500 men had become established in the town; Col.Bennet's regiment of nearly 200 and a sizeable regiment of foot under the command of a Colonel Courtney. Norton and Murford, fully distracted by mutterings of discontent in Southampton, would find little immediate opportunity for dealing with this dangerous presence and more than a month would elapse before Norton felt able to challenge the supremacy of the two Royalist colonels.

First he would have to assist in the reduction of Basing and the expulsion of the Cavaliers from N.W.Hampshire. The taking of Winchester had merely been the Royalists' opening move. In the weeks since the capture of Bristol and the destruction of Waller's army on Roundway Down, the Cavalier tide had become almost unstoppable. Dorset, Wiltshire and the entire west of England had

---

7 Hopton, Sir R. 'De Bellum Civile' p.69

fallen in the summer storm. But, until now, the threat had stopped just short of Hampshire, and the rebuilding of Parliament's forces had been unhindered. Waller's new army was able to grow at Farnham, and the periodic cases of Royalist insurgency in S. Hampshire were minor and detached; Crawford's apparently purposeless gestures in the New Forest were fully disregarded.

The first warnings of a full-scale Royalist advance came in late October 1643, when Crawford, repulsed so indecorously at Poole, re-entered Hampshire: '*There are about 2000 foot and 2000 horse of the King's forces...... there are 1000 horse also quartered at Andover and Whitchurch and 7 colours of horse at Alton*'. Sir Samuel Luke records in his journal on the 26th, adding: '*...and 'tis thought that they intend either for Chichester or Southampton*'.[8] Advanced units had apparently reached Odiham. At Winchester, Ogle had by now strengthened the defences of the city by employing 1000 men to dig entrenchments, and the services of an unnamed Dutch engineer. And *"by virtue of a letter sent from His Majesty; Mayor, alderman and merchants were deprived of their plate for the maintenance of the army."* For Ralph Hopton had already summoned all Hampshire males between the ages of 16 and 60 '*to appear in arms for the King at Winchester*'. Charles, having secured the allegiance of the counties of the west, had now decided that Hampshire and Sussex would be the new routeway to London and the reclamation of his capital.

---

[8] Journal of Sir Samuel Luke pp.175-176

11

'One company of Blue Coats with snap-han muskets'

OCT 30 We marched to a green about a mile from Windsor, where we... rallied our men, each regiment drawing into a regimental form where likewise our train of Artillery and waggons of war came to us, and so we marched towards Farnham through Windsor Forest, where in the afternoon we met some of Sir William Waller's Troops of Horse, his own regiment, and one company of Blue coats with snap-han muskets'.[1]

With Elias Archer that day were craftsmen, apprentices and the *'tosspots'* of the London taverns, men of every trade and none, with no particular religious or political persuasion and largely unskilled in the arts of war. A sense of duty imposed from parish pulpits, a promise of adventure and the pressures of a rigid system had pulled these men from cellars and workshops, and from all the humdrum certainties of daily life. With boyish enthusiasm, they gathered under the standards of their regiments, few, if any, having any notion of the sort of dangers that lay ahead. The pain of wounds,

---

1 Archer E. 'A True Relation of the marchinh of the Red Trained Bands of Westminster, the Green Auxiliaries of London and the Yellow Auxiliaries of the Tower Hamlets'

the death of friends, and dismal nights in damp fields would dispel the sense of mission. Thoughts of home and happy memories of London's alleys would appear instead in vivid and unerasable colours. For those trapped in long-term service, desertion from the ranks would be the only way home, and Parliament's manpower problem surfaced again.

The three London trained band regiments marched to Farnham the next day. The carnival atmosphere was enhanced by the colours of the standards: red with silver stars for the Westminster regiment, yellow with blue rays for the Tower Hamlets Auxiliaries and green with wavy golden rays for the Cripplegate Auxiliaries. In later weeks of the campaign, they would be joined by other provincial regiments, each dressed in the colours chosen by the commanding colonel: Ralph Weldon's red coats from Kent, Herbert Morley's blue coats from Sussex, William Springate's white coats and Samuel Jones's green coats from Surrey, the latter regiment forming the garrison of Farnham Castle. Dull winter campaigning would at least be lightened by a kaleidoscope of colours.

On Wednesday, November 1st, Waller, his slouch hat pulled over his face and a sense of purpose on his brow, reviewed his assembled army: 16 troops of horse, 8 companies of dragoons, 16 pieces of artillery and 36 companies of foot - a total of more than 5000 men. At his side was Sir Arthur Heselrige, whose reborn Cuirassiers provided the bulk of the cavalry arm. For many of those in the lines that day, Waller had already become a legend, a man of deep principle and unswerving determination.

The army remained at Farnham until the 3rd, drilling and practising all the skills of soldiering. Breathless scouts periodically rode in, and a thousand inquisitive faces looked up from their drill and speculated on what the messages might convey. During this time of partial inactivity, a soldier was hanged from a tree in full view of the assembled army for, apparently, inciting mutiny in the ranks. And carts rumbled in throughout the day, carrying provisions and clothing for the troops from grateful Londoners.

Crondall, five miles west of Farnham Park, was now to play a major part in the Hampshire war. Garrisoned intermittently from that time onwards until the tide of Royalism had been finally stilled, the church was to be sadly abused by irreverent men. Entries in the Parish register hint at this savage maltreatment; one records a payment of five shillings to a John Chandler for *making clean of the Church when the soldiers were here'*. A trooper apparently still rides at night along the avenue to the church's main door.

'Friday, November 3rd, ' continues Archer. *'We marched out of Farnham towards Alton, where by the way at Bentley green...... where, having refreshed ourselves about an hour, we marched away to Alton, but our regiment was quartered two miles thence at two little villages called East Worldom and West Worldom'.*[2] Situated just two miles from Alton, the Londoners forced one hundred of Crawford's troopers to withdraw from Alton and fall back towards Andover and Salisbury, where the Royalist strength was beginning to assemble.

Lord Hopton seems to have been like a man caught out in an unexpected gale. Unable to mould events in the way that Waller could, he had, at least, the skill to react spontaneously and pluck advantage from imminent disaster. But now he seemed non-plussed, remaining without purpose at Winchester until scouts confirmed the scale and direction of the Roundhead advance. On 3rd November, he, too, fell back to Andover. Hopton, in his own account, tries to justify his decision, but unwittingly alludes to his own uncharacteristic hesitation.

'He resolved to march with what he had to Andover, where Colonel Gerrard with his brigade was then quartered. Depending upon his intelligence for the state of the enemy in that country, he came as he had designed, into Andover three or four hours within the night, and there kept his men in guard, till he had consulted with Lord Gerrard, who came immediately to join him at his lodging, and the Earl of Crawford with him'.[3]

---

2 Archer   3 De Bellum Civile p.64

'One company of Blue Coats with snap-han muskets'

The church at Crondall

The Marquis of Winchester would be consequently obliged to depend upon his own resources and the manpower already at his disposal. Hearing that the King had written to Lord Percy, the general of the Royal Ordnance, to send *'ten barrels of powder* (to Basing) *with match and bullets proportionable'*, he followed up with his own request on November 3rd, personally urging Lord Percy to respond: *'I therefore desire your Lordship to command carts for the conveying of the said powder from Oxford to this garrison, standing not only in great want of the same, but also daily expecting the enemy's approach... And if any arms have been brought into the magazine, I desire your favour in the furtherance of 100 muskets to be sent with this conveyance'.*[4]

Saturday, November 4th, was an impossible day for campaigning: cold, wet and windy with squalls of snow. An ordinance passed in distant Westminster that day placed Sir William in command of the associated forces of Hampshire, Kent, Surrey and Sussex, and ordered the commanders of the four counties to march to Waller's support. Theoretically, it would have doubled his army's size. In practice, however, reluctance, lethargy and county politics combined to slow any rapid union of such far-flung forces. Units of Waller's troops uncomfortably trudged some distance along the road to Winchester, huddled figures protecting themselves against the elements and without any of the dignity of an advancing army. They retired to Four Marks Hill in the evening, thawing themselves deep into the night over campfires that could be seen as far away as Winchester.

Waller's second army

Horse: Sir Arthur Heselrige's Regt.
Sir William Waller's Regt.
Col, Jonas Vandruske's Regt.

Total: 1800

4MMS Rawlinson, D.395, fol.147 Bodleian

A fourth regiment, Col. Richard Turner's regiment, paraded with Waller at Windsor in October, but was then diverted north for service in the south midlands.

> Foot: The three London Trained band Regts.
>
> Sir William Waller's Regt. (commanded by Sir James Ramsay)
> Andrew Potley's Regt.
> Sir Arthur Heselrige's Regt. (commanded by Col. John Birch)
>
> Total: 3100

Sunday was brighter and calmer, and the Roundhead army could advance again, reaching Alresford, just 7 miles from Winchester, in the afternoon. But, instead of continuing towards the cathedral city or bivouacking for the night in Alresford's cold fields, Waller ordered his men to swing to the right and take up quarters at Chilton Candover, midway between Alresford and Basingstoke.

Waller was possibly employing a cloak of deceit, intentionally masking his long-held intentions to strike at Loyalty House. The showy push towards Winchester might have been a feint, a plan contrived in the campaign tents to confound the enemy's reasoned thinking. There might, however, have been a genuine change of plan that night, induced by erroneous reports that a large Royalist army was advancing south against the Parliamentarians' left flank and rear.

Fog shrouded Basing House on the 6th, preventing the Londoners from viewing the fortress that was challenging Parliament's claimed hold on Southern England. From the rooftops and look out points of the great house, the Parliamentary army was invisible, too, the regimental units completely undetectable as they tramped in semi-silence towards their quarry. The marquis and his retainers listened all night, the peer himself climbing to the roof of the gate house in a futile attempt to catch for himself any tell-tale sounds that would pinpoint the exact location of his adversary. The rumble of cannon and baggage trains on the gravel of the adjacent roads soon after 7 a.m. on the 7th sent the garrison rushing to arms and earthworks. Here, at last, was the Parliamentary fist, the long-expected assault to punish the marquis and rob him of his home. *'The Lord Marquis and the rest could not yet get sight of him through the greatness of the mist, till about one of the clock, when the sun, breaking and dispersing the mist, discovered Waller's whole body to the garrison'* reported Mercurius Aulicus. Amongst the colours flying provocatively in the thinning mist was Waller's personal standard, showing a tree in full leaf and the motto 'fructus virtutis' (fruit of valour). Within the house's defensive perimeter were just 500 men, the peer's family retainers, the soldiers of Marmaduke Rawdon's regiment and several civilian gentlemen, *'resolute and desperate'*, according to the True Informer, *'by reason that many of them, being Papists of great estates in those parts, have secured the greater part of their treasures and riches in that house'*.

The men of the Tower Hamlets regiment seem to have made the first move, occupying a small lane that crossed the River Loddon. This, however, was purely deceptive, a mischievous tactic to distract the defenders while the artillery was unhitched on Cowdrays Down. The Londoners maintained a brisk musket fire from behind the roadside hedges, to which Royalists on the northern defences replied until dusk took their targets away. At 4 p.m., Waller's 6 guns on the Down belched out. Suddenly everyone in the house was involved: kitchen maids, stable hands and the marquis himself - trapped, like figures in a Doom painting, in the jaws of approaching Hell. Rank and social station meant nothing now as peer and retainers, equalled by danger, sought protection within the masonry's extensive bulk.

But minutes later, the bombardment halted. Waller, sensing a whiff of possible victory in the smell of gunpowder that hung in the air, chose now to send a well-phrased ultimatum. *'Sir William Waller, being present in person, hath sent to demand the castle for the*

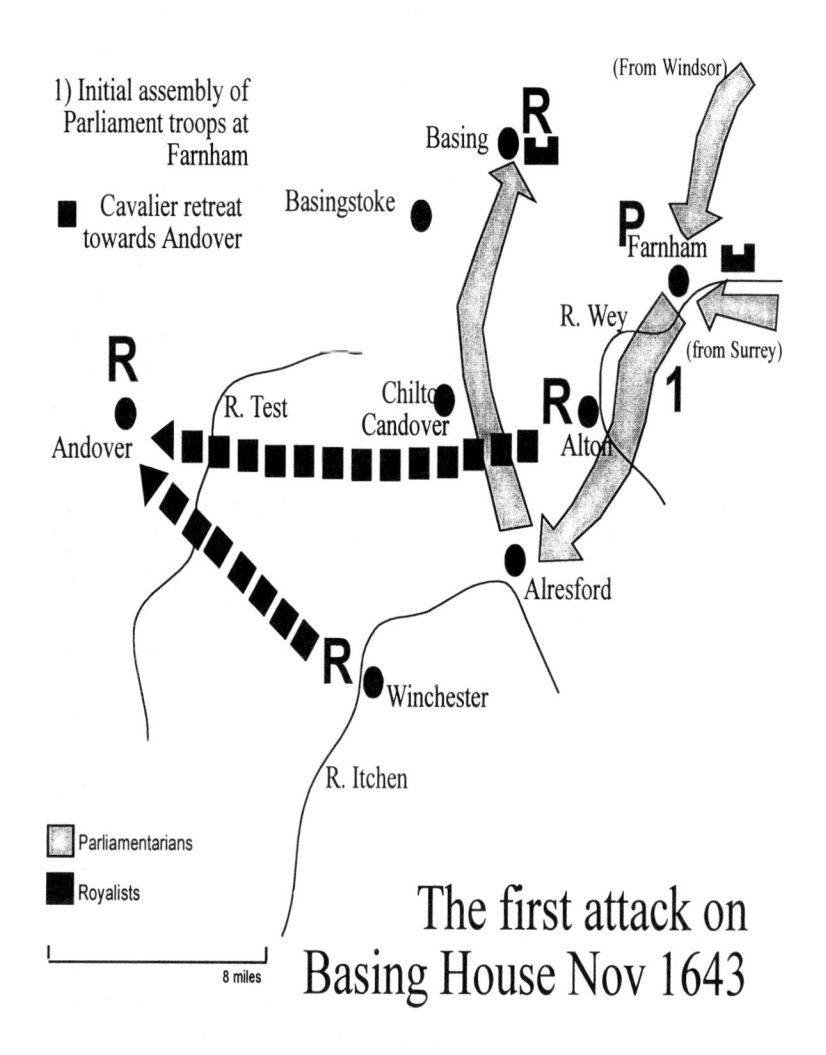

The first attack on Basing House Nov 1643

1) Initial assembly of Parliament troops at Farnham

■ Cavalier retreat towards Andover

- Basing **R**
- Basingstoke
- (From Windsor)
- **P** Farnham
- R. Wey
- (from Surrey)
- **1**
- **R** Andover
- R. Test
- Chilton Candover
- **R** Alton
- Alresford
- **R** Winchester
- R. Itchen

☐ Parliamentarians
■ Royalists

8 miles

King and Parliament'.[5] A single gun on Cowdrays Down suddenly discharged during the silence of the moment, apparently reinforcing the Roundhead demand. It had, apparently, been fired accidentally. Lord Paulet, remembering his earlier firm promises to his King and now rightly angered by cannon fire during a time of truce, was more provocative in his reply. Trusting to his men's fortitude and the strength of Basing's old walls, he refused to surrender his home, reminding his foe that *'the law told him he might keep it against any man'*. Re-asserting his legal right, he added: *'That it was now particularly commanded by his Majesty, who had put a garrison into it, beyond which command he knew no obligation'*.[6]

The musketeers in the lane, having expended all their ammunition in a largely pointless show of provocation, retired. Their place was taken by a troop of dragoons, and the shadow shooting continued. Two hours later, Waller tried diplomacy again. First apologising to the peer for *'the rudeness of his disorderly guns during the parley'*, he offered free passage to Marchioness Honoria and the women and children of the household. She proudly refused the Parliamentarian's chivalrous offer, pointing out that her place was at her husband's side and she was *'resolved to run the same fortune as her Lord, knowing that there was a just and all-seeing Judge above, from whom Sir William Waller could pretend no commission'*[7.] Armed with this courteous but haughty reply, the Parliamentary messenger was escorted from the house through a rear exit. Trying to find his way back to the besiegers' lines, he fell into a marsh and lost a boot.

Each of the 6 cannon was fired six times that night, deliberately robbing the defenders of sleep - just part of the psychological warfare that both sides had learnt to employ. And throughout the night, illuminated by fragile torches, the Londoners worked, throwing up breastworks along the northern side of the house, watched, no doubt, by the nearest Royalist soldiers.

---

5 Waller 'Recollections'

6 Godwin p.112   7 ibid p.112

'One company of Blue Coats with snap-han muskets'

View to the north from Basing House

'ONE COMPANY OF BLUE COATS WITH SNAP-HAN MUSKETS'

At dawn on the 7th, the Roundhead guns on Cowdrays Down opened again, continuing to fire for most of the morning. The house and its windows, protected by earthworks and high walls, were almost unassailable, and a lot of Parliamentary ammunition was used fruitlessly. Royalist soldiers were not inactive; small numbers reinforced the defenders of the barn and torched all the more distant cottages that might have been used for cover by the besiegers.

Waller performed most effectively when he was in control of his own timetable, unworried by fears of enemy counter moves or the imminent arrival of relieving forces. But substantiated reports had already reached him of Lord Crawford's busy activities in Andover and the apparent departure of large forces from that town in the direction of Basing. His strategy that day seems consequently to have been flustered by these reports and careful planning seems absent. While most of his cavalry was sent to detain Crawford, 500 men were launched against the north front at 9 a.m. with instructions to occupy the outhouses of the Grange and flush the defenders from the ancient barn. A single Royalist cannon on the roof of the house attempted to halt their advance. '*We fought from ten till six, but two of our company wounded*', one of the combatants later wrote. '*Never in the world was there such desperate service on the very mouths of cannon with so little loss*'[8]

Musketeers surged down the narrow lane, edging across the River Loddon to avoid exposure to Cavalier bullets. The defenders in the barn had made holes in the building's walls, and finding a Parliamentary breast for a target was hardly difficult.

Other Parliamentary detachments attacked the Grange and the casualty rate began to mount. Waller, seeing the shadows of failure looming and anxious to dilute the Royalist effort, ordered three guns to aim at the New House, the enormous shape of which must have appeared as attractive to the gunners as a lamp to a mischievous child with a catapult.

Sir William's captain-lieutenant, a Captain Clinson, at the

---

8 Godwin p.113

'ONE COMPANY OF BLUE COATS WITH SNAP-HAN MUSKETS'

The 1st Attack on Basing House

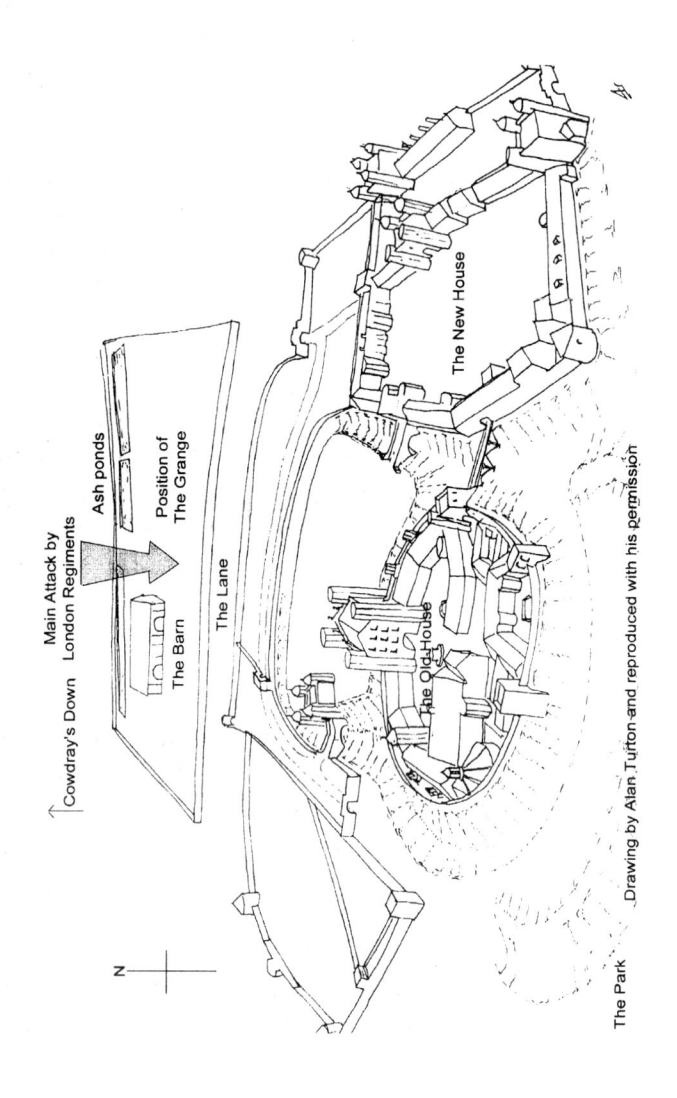

Cowdray's Down
Main Attack by London Regiments
Ash ponds
Position of The Grange
The Barn
The Lane
The New House
The Old House
The Park
Drawing by Alan Turton and reproduced with his permission

head of 500 men, eventually took the grange, the outhouses of which were full of food *'and divers sort of household goods'*. Still determined to secure a victory that day, the Roundhead general extended his fighting front as far as the village church, and at least 1000 men were now fully employed. *'Our army had no shelter not so much as a hovel, nay not so very many trees, save only by the Park side, some few young groves which could not shelter them to any advantage....yet did nothing to discourage their resolution'*, a slightly biased report suggests.[9] The Grange's outhouses provided that well needed shelter and the weary and wounded lay down to rest. The red brick walls of the New House beyond were hazed in the man-made mist of gunfire. The soldiers of both sides, forced to throw away their fears and personal passions, had become almost mechanical, methodically loading and firing, each choosing the target which he thought was the most vulnerable.

Sir Marmaduke Rawdon helped to steel the nerves of the besieged. Somehow present wherever the attack was greatest, this pre-war importer of wine from the Canaries, coaxed and encouraged.

He was later to be knighted by a grateful king in acknowledgement of his efforts. Sir Robert Peake, whose father had been court artist to James 1, was almost as effective. Derided by his enemies as a *'seller of picture babies'*, he was never regarded by them as a competent tactician of war despite his personal heroism and charismatic style.

The Parliamentary soldiers were tiring now and the assault became as spasmodic as waves breaking on a shore. Resting men dined on what they had found in the storehouses of the grange: beer, salted bacon, cream and peas; unit commanders joined their hungry men at this banquet under fire. But the attack never fully faded; those that had eaten resumed the fight and others took their place at the feast without a table.

Parliament's soldiers were soon at the Marquis's gates. But the unwanted guests had come unprepared and had no grenades or

---

[9] 'The Soldier's Report'

'One company of Blue Coats with snap-han muskets'

The 'Bloody Barn' at Basing

petards with which to break the gates. Yet the sight of so many Roundhead troopers eating their way, like voracious slugs, through the garrison's well-stocked larder, was too much to bear. Clearly unable to claw back the provisions themselves, Rawdon and Peake determined to destroy the stock and deny to the enemy what had been intended for Royalist stomachs. With these two senior officers were Lieutenant-Colonel Johnson and 25 chosen men - and a volley of supporting musket fire to support the soldiers on their way. Successfully they fired the barns and the summer's wheat crop was soon consumed in flames. Dashing into the yard of the Grange to punish the raiders, Johnson engaged Clinson in hand-to-hand combat and a theatrical display of swordsmanship.

Clinson was killed a few minutes later, not by the hand of Johnson alone, but by the accummulated weight of those who rode at Johnson's side. Not prepared to observe all the niceties of fair play and balanced advantage, his Royalist friends came to his help, and Parliament's champion was savagely felled. *'The loss of the garrison was only two slain'*, boasts Mercurius Aulicus. The Parliamentarians lost far more, several possibly roasted to death in the flames that devoured the crop.

Heavy rain and winds served on no one's side, dampening powder and resolutions alike. At some point during the afternoon, it is reported that the Marquis again asked for terms, but was instantly refused. Waller called a retreat in mid-afternoon, withdrawing his troops half a mile from the house to refresh his men and give the Royalist peer time for thought. They slept in the open fields that night, Waller himself resting with his troops on bales of straw. Archer voices the discomfort of them all: *'Our lodging and our service did not agree, the one being so hot and the other so cold'.*[10]

Two days of torrential rain and sad autumnal weather followed, effectively preventing any renewal of the assault. Sir William, placing a strong detachment on the nearby Downs, charitably withdrew his entire army to Basingstoke to rebuild their

---

10 Archer

strength and feed their nerves. Some of the more fortunate were accommodated in the Vyne, the home of the Royalist colonel Sandys, and amused themselves by shooting his deer. In the same spirit of compassion, the marquis sent a cart load of the Parliamentary wounded to the town.

The three days following were full of rumour and as yet unconfirmed reports that Sir Ralph Hopton, having reviewed his forces at Amesbury, was advancing into Hampshire again with the solid intention of forcing battle and liberating the house. Reports of a similar nature reached London, but with the unwelcome details of Waller's withdrawal from Basing and the strengthening numbers of the Cavalier hordes. Many in the capital viewed these stories gloomily, construing withdrawal as weakness or pure cowardice. During this indefinite reprieve, the marquis wrote to Sir Edward Nicholas, the King's Secretary, detailing the events of the past week: Nicholas relayed the news to Rupert in a practical and almost journalistic style: ' *Monday last Waller sat down before basing House, and Wednesday last he drew off his ordnance and forces to Basingstoke,...where he now lies with all his forces, and threatens to return thither to assault the place again and hath sent for scaling ladders to Windsor for that purpose. The Marquis of Winchester writes cheerfully...and that he hath lost only one man and one hurt. Sir F. Berkeley was, on Wednesday last, at Huntingdon, twenty miles on this side of Exeter, with four regiments of foot, and will, we hope, be at Winchester on Monday next'.*[11]

He spoke accurately: Waller had indeed sent to London for ladders and the equipment needed for a sustained siege. On Sunday 12th, Waller, supplied with petards, grenades and ladders and a fresh regiments of dragoons, returned to Basing House, determined to achieve what the weather, Royalist determination and stout defences had combined to prevent the week before.

The cavalry drew up before the house at noon, taunting the garrison with a barrage of unkind words. For an hour, this verbal

---
11 Godwin p.116-117

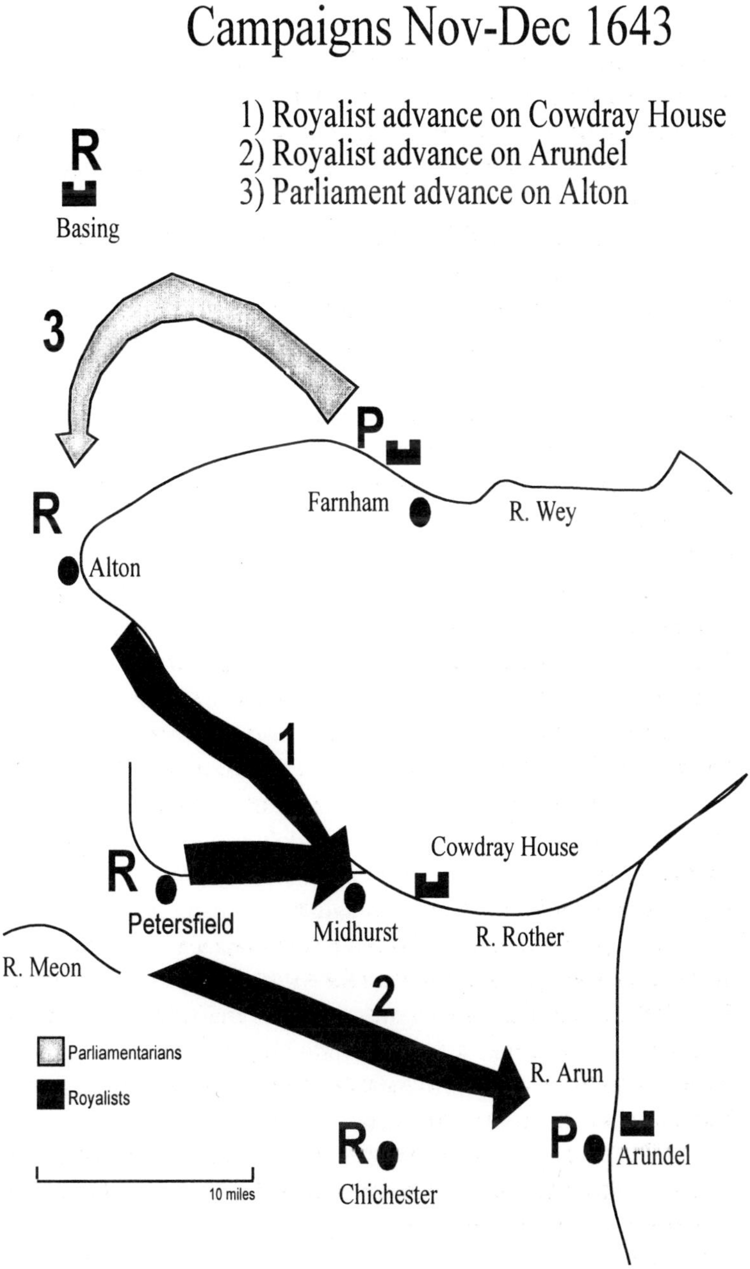
Campaigns Nov-Dec 1643
1) Royalist advance on Cowdray House
2) Royalist advance on Arundel
3) Parliament advance on Alton
R
Basing
3
P
Farnham
R. Wey
R
Alton
1
Cowdray House
R
Petersfield
Midhurst
R. Rother
R. Meon
2
Parliamentarians
Royalists
R. Arun
R
Chichester
P
Arundel
10 miles

war continued, petty comments about the commanders of each side with the occasional scream of 'Papist' from the throats of Parliamentary zealots. Waller's guns were simultaneously unhitched on Cowdray's Down and the infantry shuffled into positions on three sides of the great house.

A single gun fired out and resting crows took flight. Another of Waller's 10 weapons on Cowdray's Down followed, then all the rest, obsequiously following the leader's signal shot. For almost two hours, the punishing weapons discharged, aiming their missiles largely at the windows and walls of the New House, where the marquis and his wife were believed to be. A gun on the roof answered back, the gunners crouching low to avoid detection. At about 2 p.m., the infantry went in, perhaps 3000 men in three divisions, launched almost simultaneously - '*a hot and desperate charge*' - according to Archer. On the north and north-east, 2000 alone, many weighed down with ladders, surged towards the New House, the Westminster and Tower Hamlets Auxiliaries, taking advantage of the cover of a copse that the marquis had failed to remove. A detachment reached the outer walls and gained possession of the garrison's 'half-moon'. A unit of dragoons followed at their heels and placed a petard on the 'garrison gate'. The crushing of Loyalty House seemed imminent. The other assaults achieved far less and no heroes were made. Advancing clumsily with their ladders across the Park from the south, 500 Londoners reached the earthworks of the Old House and placed their standard in the ditch. But a well-placed gun on the ramparts shattered them with case shot, and the spirit of dash was instantly exorcised. A dozen men were killed in the trenches in those opening minutes and others were injured by bricks and tiles hurled by the marchioness and the household's angered ladies. Military drill and firing techniques were forgotten in the panic of the moment; the rear lines of musketeers fired wildly before the front lines had retired, causing 70 casualties to their own men. A sudden sortie of Lieutenant-Colonel Johnson and a handful of Cavaliers added to the Londoners' discomfort. Parliamentary apologists were quick to excuse their limited effort: *'We must forgive them being young and raw soldiers, and not yet frosted abroad'*, the Complete Intelligencer explains.

One hour later, the elements attacked instead. Driving rain and forceful winds compelled the besiegers to retreat and the besieged to huddle at their stations. Out in the open, where the fighting had been fiercest, were two small guns, the regimental standard and countless scaling ladders, all abandoned in the drama of retreat.

Waller scowled that evening, anticipating the lash of censorious London tongues that would capitalise on his defeat. While reviewing his troops in the evening rain, he was greeted *'with a mutinous cry among the city regiments'* and so *'was forced to threaten to pistol any of them that should use that base language, and an enemy in the field so near'.*[12] At 10 p.m., he sent some of the Auxiliary regiment to rescue the guns, pointing into the darkness to the direction in which they should go. Screened by night and blanketing rain, they edged their way, like grounded insects, to where the cannon were believed to be. Ahead, some of the wounded called out; for some, the very last utterances they would ever make. The guns were retrieved and, with them, the bodies of some of the young men of London. Waller, waiting for the party to return, was the last to rest that night, joining his dispirited men in the open field less than half a mile from Basing's battered walls.

Monday, the 13th, was wetter than the day before. Muskets failed to fire and cannons refused to be coaxed into life. Some of Waller's dampened soldiers deserted during the night, leaving their pikes and muskets where they had briefly rested. He had lost more than 300 killed or wounded during the previous week and perhaps twice as many during the nocturnal desertion.

Far too few remained in the morning to attempt a new attack and painful reports reached the general of the imminent arrival of Ralph Hopton, his sparring companion at the head of nearly 5000

---

12 Waller 'Recollections'

men. A letter from the Lord marquis had been carried to Sir Ralph by a woman with a basket of apples. In the hurried note, Basing House's owner had spoken of near-exhaustion and *'gave him notice of the last day that he was able to hold out, which (as the Lord Hopton remembereth) was the 12th day after Sir Wm. Waller's coming before it'* [13]. The Cavalier commander *'sent back the woman with assurance of relief by that time, and writ (sic) to Oxford to devise what assistance might be spar'd out of Reading for that service'*. Charles had responded promptly, ordering Sir Jacob Astley, governor of Reading, to join Hopton at Kingsclere with 900 of the town's garrison. Lord Henry Percy's Horse regiment was also instructed to ride to Hopton's support. Parliament's scouts witnessed the junction of these forces and rushed the unwelcome news to Waller in his field near Basing. Reluctantly, Parliament's miracle worker retired again to Basingstoke in a mood of near-devastation. Two days later, Hopton reached Basing House; music and laughter took the place of gunfire that night. The marquis wrote triumphantly to Oxford, playing down, almost politically, the hurt to his home and family, while Waller had *'dishonoured and bruised his army,whereof abundance were lost and without the death of more than two in his garrison, and some little injury to the house'*. The delighted Queen, who knew the house so well, gave the messenger four pounds and ten shillings, *'all that she had in her purse'*.

On November 15th, the Parliamentary army reached Farnham and began to count the costs of injury and desertion. The names of all those absent were recorded and sent to a Commons committee sitting at Worcester House in London. Many of the listed were eventually sent back to Farnham in chains, flushed from cellars and homes while their loved ones cried out for mercy. Councils of war sentenced several of the deserters to death as an example to those who might still be tempted to leave the ranks.

Hopton did not remain as the marquis's guest for long, duty and a recognition of his immediate advantage eventually taking him

---

13 *De Bellum Civile p67*

eastwards as far as the defences of Farnham. But first he claimed ownership of most of Hampshire, placing infantry and cavalry in Winchester, Andover, Basingstoke, Petersfield, Romsey, Long Sutton and Alresford to back up his claim. Then, in a deliberate effort to protect his advance, he ordered Lord Crawford to occupy Alton, with Colonel John Bolles and his regiment of infantry in support. Hopton took up residence in Odiham, a position from where he could plan his next aggressive moves.

William Waller had been wrong-footed by his former friend and his supply of resourcefulness had almost run dry. While Cavalier patrols moved without hindrance through Hampshire's leafless lanes, the Parliamentary army became largely confined to Farnham and the Surrey border. Hopton's troopers knocked at the doors of cottages and wayside inns, calling on the able-bodied to serve the King or feed his passing troops. Semi-legal devices were used to persuade the more reluctant farmers to part with their crops, seemingly direct orders from the King himself which few men dared to disobey. '*This is to require you in his Majesty's name*', one of the December summons began, '*to furnish and supply his Majesty with such quantities of hay and oats as you have for the horses to our quarters this night at Warnford for which hay or oats you shall receive payment out of the weekly contribution of this county*'. [14]

Parliament's bullies employed similar arts of persuasion on the people of S.England with thinly veiled hints of punishment against those who might refuse. A warrant issued by Colonel Samuel Jones, the Governor of Farnham Castle, was delivered to Lord Paulet's tenants. '*... except you send into Farnham Castle, by Monday next, without further delay, the several proportions of wheat, malt, barley, and other things assessed and charged upon you, ... you are to expect the same penalty with which the Marquess of Winchester threatens you, there being more reason that you should serve a Protestant before a Papist*'. [15] Some of the more unfortunate were visited by the soldiers of both the warring sides and, for most,

---
14 and 15 Documents Hants. Records Office 22M75/1

the double demand was a cross far too heavy for rustic backs to bear. Daily musters and energetic training in Farnham Park failed to halt the flow of deserters from the regimental ranks. Travellers on the roads near the capital were frequently stopped by Roundhead troopers and accused of desertion in a time of war. Those with money in their belts or a plausible tale at hand might continue on their way, but the poor and less convincing might find themselves in Farnham with a rope around their necks. Thirty men swung one day from a tree near the castle's gates, but probably none had tramped to Basing in the week before or had ever heard the sound of angry cannon.

The stomachs of those who remained in service were generally full and few would ever complain of hunger at night. '*There came to us much provision of victuals and strong waters to our regiment, which was very thankfully received, although...... we had no great scarcity before*', wrote Archer on the Sunday after arriving in Farnham.

Stomachs might have been filled, but not the soldiers' purses. Many in the ranks had not been paid for weeks and hints of mutiny amongst the more loyal were almost as tangible as the morning frosts. Sir William had written frequently to London, spelling out the consequences of a failure to pay. In his *Vindications*, he justifies his stance morally and practically -as any sensible general would. '*And for the payment of arrears I may say I was for it to the utermost farthing....And, truly, herein I did but discharge my conscience, for I was ever of opinion that a soldier's pay is the justest debt in the world. For if it be a crying sin to keep back the wages of an hireling, that doth but sweat for us, it must needs be a roaring sin to detain pay of the soldier that bleeds for us*'.

More in gratitude for his efforts than out of sympathy for the sufferings of the soldiers, Westminster voted £5000 for the immediate use of Sir William and his paymasters. Seduced by the pen and logic of the London pamphleteers, the Capital's merchants had opened their coffers again.

This encouraged Waller to grow far bolder and more eloquent. In language just as colourful as his earlier appeal, he wrote to the Speaker on the 27th to acquaint the honourable members with the state of his army: '*Want of money and want of clothes have produced want of obedience and want of health... working like a malignant fever upon the spirits of our men, and dulling the edge of our swords, though I am confident the metal is unaltered. I cannot but take notice with humble thankfulness of 5000l voted for our supply, but I beseech you give me leave without offence to tell you it is impossible for this sum or less than double the proportion of this sum to stop the clamorous wants of our soldiers.... God knows, I write this with a sad sense, but I have reason to doubt what command I shall be able to retain upon those, whom I can neither reward nor punish'.*[16]

Lured by confirmation that immediate pay was promised, 400 horsemen from Kent appeared in the park at Farnham on the 19th, followed hours later by Colonel Herbert Morley's regiment of Sussex Foot, Norton's Hampshire regiment and Sir Michael Livesay's Kentish men. 7000 men stood at the gateway to Surrey, positioned to repel any sudden enemy thrust towards London's soft underbelly.

Royalist optimism at that moment would have been justifiable. A succession of victories in the north and west had flowed, like an unstoppable tide, and few outside London now doubted that God was a true Cavalier. Hopton's army, when it mustered at Amesbury in the week before entering Hampshire, was numerically not far inferior to Waller's, but the sense of well-being that prevailed was far greater. And now reports were broadcast throughout the south that the King himself was marching to Basing at the head of 2000 men with some of the western regiments following.

But hints of disharmony and personal acrimony appear within Basing's walls. Sir Marmaduke Rawdon, united militarily with his Lieutenant-Colonel in recent days, accuses Peake in a letter of

---

16 Waller's 'Vindications'

Royalist army at Amesbury

Foot:		Horse:	
	Sir Ralph Hopton's Regt.		Sir Horatio Carey's Regt.
	Prince Maurice's Regt.		Sir John Covert's Regt.
	Lord Hertford's Regt.		Earl of Crawford's Regt.
	Col. Arthur Griffin's Regt.		Sir Nicholas Crisp's Regt.
	Col. Allen Aspley's Regt.		Sir Edward Dering's Regt.
			Sir James Hamilton's Regt.
			Sir Edward Ford's Regt.
			Col. Richard Spencer's Regt.
			Lord Hertford's Regt.
			Sir Ralph Hopton's Regt.
			Sir Edward Stawell's Regt.
			Sir George Vaughan's Regt.
	Total: 2000 men		Total: 1600 men

Note: Maurice's regiment does not appear to have participated in the Hampshire campaign despite being present at the Amesbury muster. Lord Henry Percy's Horse regiment, Lord Gerrard's regiment, Sir Thomas Byron's Horse and the infantry regiments commanded by John Bolle, Sir Jacob Astley and John Berkeley joined the Royalist army in Hampshire. They were joined by a contingent of Irishmen under the command of the marquis's kinsman, Sir John Paulet.

misconduct and seeming dishonesty. *'I was commanded by his Majesty to send 100 musketeers into Basing, which accordingly I did; appointing Robert Peake my Lieut-Col., to command them. My said Lieut-Col refused to give me any account of such moneys as he received for the maintenance of these men.'*

In a further wave of bitterness, Sir Marmaduke denounces the noble Marquis for treachery or even something worse. The peer had recently been commissioned to raise a regiment of his own *'for the arranging whereof he drew from my said Lieut-Col.without my knowledge, and so armed men without my consent'.*[17]

Despite these strained relations, the strengthening of Basing House continued unchecked, trees being felled in the park to firm the earthen banks. Waller, however, had now adopted a purely

---

17 ' The Humble Petition of Marmaduke Rawdon ' Hants● Records Office

defensive role and Lord Paulet's house was no longer Parliament's prime target. On November 16th, more out of mischief than with any serious intent, Parliamentary units attacked Hopton's new headquarters in Odiham. The Royalist commander had taken pains to prepare for such a possibility, lining the hedges with musketeers, who provided a shield of defence while Hopton and his staff withdrew to Alton.

Encouraged, perhaps, by signs of a weakening of the Cavalier heart, Waller sent infantry to Midhurst on the 17th, a place where Royalist sympathies were known to be strong. *'It was thought that if we came not (to Midhurst) with a very strong party, the town being very malignant, and store of Papists in it; would have risen against us'.*[18] Less than 50 men took part in the daytime task, searching houses, church and stables for any person who might be enflaming passions for the Royalist cause. Some lamed horses and three drunken soldiers were found, the latter *'so much taken with drink that they could neither stand nor sit'*. More valuable than these prizes were some yards of cloth, *'taken from Papists and malignants there to clothe the foot'*. Men had learnt to justify their thefts from the defenceless; simply labelling those who owned what one wanted as rebel, malignant or papist would be sufficient grounds for depriving the legal owners of all that they possessed.

Two days later, the soldiers clashed again, this time upon Beacon Hill, a mile from Farnham. Hopton's cautious approach had taken his troops to Pirbright and Petworth - and Chichester's Parliamentarians had become alarmed. Scouts had fed Waller with a surfeit of reports throughout the 18th, most erroneous and even far-fetched, but all received with anxiety by the general in Farnham Park. On the morning of the 19th, perhaps 1500 of Hopton's men appeared in arms outside the park's gates, causing breakfasting Roundheads to rush for their weapons. For much of the morning, the two armies watched each other, like curious children on their first day at school.

---

18 Waller 'Recollections'

Hopton broke the trance just before midday, ordering his cavalry to canter forward. Parliament's guns opened in response and felled several troopers with the first discharge. Caught like animals, the horsemen neither retreated nor advanced, and again saddles were emptied in the subsequent cannonade. Waller's horsemen, having formed behind the artillery, were ordered to test the Royalist nerve. Evening twilight brought on the main action, a brief and disorganised affair in which the Parliamentary cavalry charged, followed by most of the infantry. The Royalist cavalry, numbed by the earlier bombardment, *'wheeled about and fled down the hill, and their foot, being always behind the horse on the side of the hill,......retreated while their horse stood for the reserve'* [19] Pulling back through Crondall, Hopton left a rearguard of musketeers to hold the enemy. Waller, disinclined to fight at night, also withdrew, ordering his men back to the safety of Farnham Park and to well-earned suppers.

Hopton, however, was as active as the hunting owl that night, ordering a party of horse to ride through the Roundhead camp. Parliamentary scouts, misleading their general during the day, proved more reliable at night and brought Sir William a timely warning of the impending Cavalier arrival. The Parliamentarian cavalry had already mounted, carbines ready; 60 Cavalier prisoners were taken and almost as many killed or wounded. Boosted by their nocturnal success, the Roundheads gave chase, riding recklessly through a shadowy world in pursuit of an invisible quarry. They were eventually brought to a halt by Royalist musketeers behind the road's high hedges and *'the purchase proved not much worth, costing some men's lives, a few of whom being worth many horse'*.

On the 20th, Sir Arthur Heselrige's regiment of foot arrived to swell the Parliamentary army, the last in the line of immediate reinforcements that had recently marched to the assistance of Waller. With their arrival and the simultaneous appearance of some men from Kent, the Parliamentary army at camp in Farnham again

---

19 Waller 'Recollections'

outnumbered its enemy.

Yet Waller had been forced into a purely defensive role and could only guess at his opponent's intentions. Strategically, then, the advantage lay with Hopton, who could strike at will and in which ever direction he chose. Ahead lay Parliamentary Kent and another route to London. Bypassing Farnham and passing through Sevenoaks and Tonbridge must have appeared as an attractive option. Sir William, expecting this to be his adversary's likely move, summoned the men of Surrey to muster at Guildford while the stout hearts of Kent also took precautions.

But Hopton was to throw away his God-sent opportunities, concerned, it seems, about possible Parliamentary activity in his rear. His energies were spent instead on further strikes at Farnham, intending, in his own words, *'to see the countenance of the enemy'* and to keep the Roundhead hordes detained while the repairs to Basing's defences were completed.

The most pronounced skirmishes of the autumn's campaign took place on two consecutive days. On the morning of the 27th, Parliamentary gunners in Farnham Castle opened fire on a party of Royalist horse and killed 15 of the intruders. Determined to draw the fox from his lair, Hopton prepared a far larger bait on the morning of the 28th and *'presented himself in battle upon the nearest part of the heath towards Farnham, and drew out 1000 musketeers and some parties of horse to advance towards their quarters to draw them out. But Sir Wm. Waller, resolving not to hazard a battle, drew out his foot into the little park, close under the castle, and kept his horse close, playing only with his cannon out of the castle, and resolving, as he did afterwards, very soldier-like, to take his advantage upon our retreat'.* [20] Hopton was again cheated of a clear victory in the field of battle for which he had so long planned.

Waller did take advantage of the enemy's retreat, pursuing them through Odiham to Hook. But he claimed no victory from the day's events and throughout the day had sensed a possibility of

---

20 De Bellum Civile p.67

disaster. A thick mist had enveloped the park in the afternoon, blunting the fierceness of the cavalier aggression. Sir William, convinced that Hopton's entire army lay beyond the park's walls, believed that this providential mist had rescued him from almost certain defeat. The less realistic of the Parliamentary elite construed the action as an undoubted Roundhead victory. The messenger carrying reports of the action reached the Westminster legislators while they were attending prayers in St. Margaret's Church, and God was thanked for his involvement.

Waller's strategy, in avoiding battle, was sound, and seems based on the hope that Sir Ralph would tire both himself and his army in almost purposeless assaults against a well-entrenched foe.

One of Waller's officers was a little more assertive than his superior. Colonel Van Druske (or Van Rosse), a flamboyant Dutchman bent on making his mark, took *'note that Sir Edward Stowell with his regiment, and a troop, or two more, quartered at Sutton (a quarter very untenable) and therefore the Lord Hopton had given Sir Edward Stowell an officer of his own with 30 dragoons, to help to strengthen it. The said Van Druske, with a strong party of horse and dragoons, attempted that quarter about two hours before day (*probably the 25th*), but he was at the entrance so well entertained by the dragoons, and so handsomely charged by Sir Edw. Stowell himself in the middle of that quarter, as he was broken, routed, and chased some miles homeward, having left behind him 7 or 8 of his own men dead in the quarter…..Van Druske carried nothing away with him, but 2 pistol bullets shot in his shoulder...* '[21] The wounded Dutchman claims to have fought alone, deserted by most of his men at the moment of fiercest combat. Others wishing to be labelled as heroes would make similar claims in the weeks to come, asserting that a lion's heart within their breasts would force them to engage in single-handed combat whatever the odds. Odiham was re-occupied the following day by Sir John

---

21 op.cit p.67

Berkeley and his entire regiment of horse. Two days later, his regiment of infantry, 1000 strong, joined him in this tiny Hampshire town.

On November 29th, Parliament's horsemen raided again, a token demonstration towards both Odiham and Basingstoke. Numerically insufficient to drive the King's men from the towns, the aggression merely demonstrated a fact of which both sides were now fully aware: Parliament's domain extended no further west than Hampshire's eastern border.

12

'A runlet of sack and a fattened ox'

'*IT appearing that..... there was little good to be done upon the enemy, being so sheltered under the castle of Farnham, he removed his own tertio to Alresford, Sir John Berkeley with his horse and foot to Petersfield, and left Sir Jacob Astley's Foot, and the Lord Crawfords's Horse and dragoons at Alton, intending speedily to remove them from thence to Midhurst, and Cowdrey House.....*'.[1] In this dismissive paragraph, Sir Ralph attempts to justify his sudden change of tactics while simultaneously identifying alternative targets for attack. Politically, this was astute, designed as much to maintain the polish on his reputation and ward off the critics who would be bound to exploit even one military failure or unexplained withdrawal.

An invasion of Sussex was entirely logical. Sir Edward Ford and the shire's other Royalist activists had kept the county's political waters disturbed since Waller's earlier capture of Chichester. Through that more sympathetic county might lie a softer path to London and Charles's recapture of his lawful capital. Lured by promises, then, of a rising in support of the King and the sweet taste

---

1 Hopton R. *'De Bellum Civile' p.68*

of likely success, Hopton instructed Royalist forces to attempt the speedy capture of Arundel and Chichester. He consolidated first, placing much of his army in Winchester while his colonels put down temporary roots in Hampshire's smaller towns. Supporting the brigades now in occupation of Alresford, Petersfield and Alton were Sir Humphrey Bennet's 700 men in Romsey and mobile units which patrolled daily through the Test and Itchen Valleys.

Cowdray House, near Midhurst, was seen as the key to the Downs, and its early occupation was considered to be essential. Each of the 3 brigade commanders, Berkeley, Astley and Crawford, were ordered to contribute dragoons for that purpose and take possession of the building before Parliament became aware of their intentions. *'But by great misfortune the design was discovered, and the enemy put men into Cowdrey House that night'*, lamented Hopton in his account. *'Which failure proved to be the beginning of the Lord Hopton's misfortune, for till that time, it had pleased God to bless him from the beginning of the war with reasonable good success, without any considerable disaster'.* [2] Colonel Edward Apsley, placed in command of the parliamentary garrison installed in the house, would take no chances; few opportunities occurred again for the cavaliers to contest Cowdray's wartime ownership.

Chichester and Arundel proved to be easier bolts to snap. Sir Edward Ford had taken occupation of the cathedral city on November 22nd while youthful Colonel Jospeh Bamfield (or Bampheild) was sent to challenge Parliament's hold on Arundel. On December 6th, *'being favoured by a g.reat mist, without any discovery, about four of the clock,......we surprised, and forced the town.'* [3] But, without experience of the arts of siege or assault, he saw little hope of taking the castle. He wrote, therefore, to Lord Hopton for assistance and the advice of more senior years. Sir Ralph, *'being loath to quit the hope of that place, took a sudden resolution to draw a stronger party of horse and foot out of Petersfield, and*

---

2 op.cit p.68   3 Col. Joseph Bamfield's 'Apologie'

marched with them himself (through Harting and Marding) *to Arundel, where coming in the morning with show of as much terror to the castle and new endeavours upon it as he could make, the captain delivered it up to him that day, and marched out with about 80 men, with reasonable conditions'* [4.] Hopton retured to Petersfield, leaving a garrison under Sir Edward Ford in occupation of town and castle.

Yet he faced exasperations, too. Injudicious voices in Oxford had called for Lord Gerrard's recall to assist elsewhere, and Sir Ralph had written to Rupert in protest: *'May it please your Highness. Your Highness's comments concerning Col. Gerrard's regiment, as all other your commands, I shall ever be most ready to obey. I shall only offer to your Highness my present difficulty, which is, that we being here, near the enemy, and our horse decreasing much, I am doubtful lest, in sparing a good old regiment, I may give the enemy too great an advantage upon me..'* [,5] His entreaties fell on deaf ears and the 'good old regiment' was withdrawn.

Like a rusted machine coaxed into sudden life, the Royalist momentum, unleashed by easy and probably unexpected victory in Sussex, had to be refuelled and the momentum somehow sustained. Hopton consequently had need to find new purpose and fresh targets - houses and towns to charm into surrender and local people to be persuaded of the merits of the royal argument. Colonel Bamfield was to be the King's crusader in Sussex, patrolling towards Lewes at the head of 3 regiments of horse and 700 foot. Edward Apsley, the local Roundhead responsible for resisting this offensive, attempted to snatch Arundel back on December 8th, a futile act by desperate men to whom Waller could offer no help. Assembling on Harrow Hill, east of Arundel, Sussex's parliamentary squires and their retainers tried to blockade the town as a preliminary, perhaps, to an intended siege.

Bamfield's men, however, quickly broke the barriers and the enemy's shallow morale. Apsley was captured during an evening

---

4 Hopton p.69   5 De bellum Civile p.70

brawl, and Roundhead resistance turned quickly to water. Only the men of Surrey and Kent, and Waller's more solid force at Farnham stood between Hopton and the capital. Waller was forced to wake from his brief winter slumbers. Stung by criticisms of his inactivity and conscious also of his unquestionable need for more artillery, Waller visited London in early December, spending much of his time in discussions with the Earl of Essex, whose loyalty to the cause was sometimes held to be suspect. On the 5th, he returned to Farnham, accompanied by some ordnance with barrels made of leather and held together by iron hoops, '*which will carry a bullet of a pound and a half weight, and do execution very far*' [6.] Likely to split after only a few discharges, the weapon would have a limited life. Following the general on the road back to Farnham were 500 men from the Windsor garrison. On the 13th, the White and Yellow Auxiliary Regiments were ordered by the City paymasters to join Waller; any soldier who refused to march was fined or even imprisoned. Negotiations with the Earl had clearly earned dividends as well; Sir William Balfour's experienced cavalry brigade, 1000 strong, was detached from Lord Essex's army to take up service in the south.

Two simultaneous setbacks for the Royalists now took place at almost opposite ends of Hampshire. Retention of Alton was vital for Hopton's long-term strategy, protecting Winchester from frontal assault and securing Hopton's route of advance into Sussex. In his account of events, he openly concedes his doubts about his ability to hold the town against a determined Roundhead assault and confirms the instructions given on December 11th to his two colonels to abandon the town if the enemy pressure became too great. '*The Lord Hopton, viewing the large extent and unsecurity (sic) of that quarter, left express order with the Earl of Crawford, and Col. Bolle, to keep as good guards and intelligence upon the enemy as possibly they could, and that, if ever he found that the enemy moved out of Farnham with a body; they should presently quit that quarter, and*

---

6 The True Informer 7 De Bellum Civile p.69

retreat to him'.[7] On the evening of the 12th, battered by a deluge of reports of unexplained activity in the park at Farnham, the Royalist general repeated his instructions, leaving nothing to the discretion of the officers in Alton town.

Lord Crawford also sent messages that day. Guided by the established principles of social conduct that distinguished a gentleman from his inferiors, he sent a messenger to Farnham, asking Sir William for a runlet of sack in exchange for which he would provide a well-fattened ox. Waller promptly complied, sending a hogshead of drink and his compliments to Crawford while reminding his Lordship of his obligations in return. Crawford, in spontaneous jest, replied by messenger that he would personally deliver the carcass to Sir William.

At 7 p.m. on the 12th, 5000 Parliamentarians set out, resting briefly on the heath between Brundon and Farnham before turning in the direction of Basing. Then, *'on a sudden they were appointed to face towards the south, and towards Alton, till they obtained within half a mile of the said town, altogether undiscovered by the enemy; our scouts being so diligent, that not a person stirring in those passages was left at liberty, to have any opportunity to inform the enemy of our proceedings'.*[8] At 9 a.m. on the 13th, the Parliamentary army approached the town from the west where they had *'both the wind and the hill to friend'.*

Hopton paid tribute to his rival's stealth and style, conceding that Crawford and the men of Alton remained unaware of the Roundheads' approach until the hour of attack. *'But Sir Wm. Waller had very politically, and soldier-like taken advantage of the woodiness of that country, and drawn his men, and his light-leather guns into the woods, and with the pioneers, made his way through them, without coming into any of the highways; and so, notwithstanding the advertisement and orders the Lord Hopton had given, and all the diligences of the officers upon those orders, Sir Wm. Waller was drawn out the next morning with his ordinance,*

---

8 'A narration of the great victory, through God's Providence, obtained by the Parliamentary forces' Hants. Records *Office*

and all his forces into the next field to Alton, before they had the least notice of his moving'.[9]

Lord Crawford had placed his scouts to the north of Alton, the direction from which he naturally expected his enemy to come. He was consequently non-plussed by the sudden appearance of Waller's men where they were least expected. Lacking both the stomach and the strength to take on the massed might of the Parliamentary army, Crawford and his 300 horse, mindful of the clear instructions given by Sir Ralph, galloped out of the town towards the east, leaving John Bolle and his less mobile infantry to hold Alton for the King.

Waller, however, had cast his net widely, sending parties of horse to seal the routes of escape, *'so that the enemy could not have the benefit of their accustomed running away... Our foot in the meantime behaving themselves like men, with great expedition; beat the enemies out of their works of the north-west and east parts of the town... here grew then a very hot fight, by reason of a malignant, who willingly fired his own barn and other houses, thereby to offend our men with the smoke'.*[10] The peer's men, confronted by Heselrige's stern faced 'Lobsters' drawn up across the road, turned hurriedly to the right and galloped southward through the still closing net in the direction of Winchester. Heselrige gave pursuit, his men reminded by their colonel of less glorious times on Roundway Down when Royalist cavalry swords had broken the Lobsters' skulls. Thirty riders were dismounted in the chase and their horses captured.

With Crawford's departure, Bolle was forced to become the King's champion instead. Most of his 700 men had taken up untenable positions in the market place, still unaware of the direction from which the attack would come. Some now sensibly occupied the adjacent houses or crowded into the churchyard, like sheep penned against their will and unable to escape. Three Parliamentary regiments were approaching from the north and north-west, but were, according to Archer, reluctant to attack until the slower- moving

---

9 Hopton   10 'A narration of the great victory'

London regiments and Col. Jones's four companies of Greencoats arrived.

Parliamentary forces at Alton

Andrew Potley's Regt.	Sir Arthur Heselrige's Regt.
James Carr's Regt.	Samuel Jones's Regt.
London Green Auxiliaries	London Yellow Auxiliaries
London Red Auxiliaries	

The Cavaliers, therefore, fired first and *'bent all their force against those three regiments, and lined divers houses with musketeers, especially one great brick house* (probably a barn) *near the church was full, out of which windows they fired very fast, and might have done great prejudice to those men, but that when our train of artillery came towards the foot of the hill they made certain shot, which took place upon that house, and so forced them to forsake it'* [11]

The London and Farnham regiments eventually arrived, enabling the attacking forces to lengthen their line of pressure. There was to be no bid for personal valour or sudden rush towards the enemy fire, and no posthumous heroes were made. Most sheltered for protection behind low hedges and walls, conscious of their vulnerability to a bullet in the chest.

An isolated breastwork and half moon had been constructed the week before, the only substantial defence structure on the town's perimeter. From within, 30 or 40 Royalists held back an entire regiment, the London Reds, in a display of ordered teamwork. The defenders were only displaced by the Green Auxiliaries' flanking advance, who, *'being in the wind of the enemy, fired a little thatched cottage, and so blinded them that this regiment marched forwards, and coming in part behind the works, fired upon them, so that they were forced to forsake the said half-moon and breastwork, which they had no sooner left but presently the Green coats and part of*

---

11 Elias Archer

The Attack on Alton

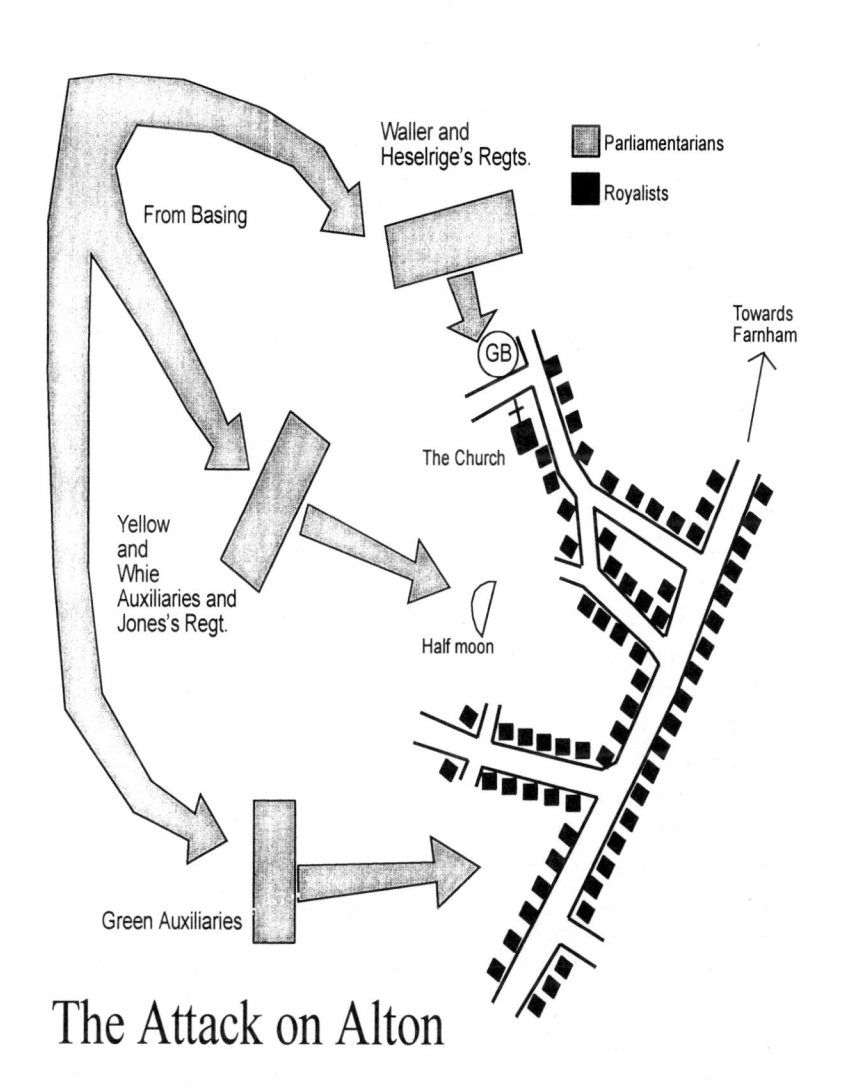

the musketeers of the Red, and our Yellow regiment entered while the rest of our regiment marched into the town with colours flying.[12]

And so, Archer pithily describes the morning's struggle, glorifying the deeds of amateurs and playing down the efforts of the defenders. The White and yellow Auxiliaries, attacking from the west, broke through makeshift breastworks and pushed forcefully along the main street towards the church while Col. Birch led Heselrige's five companies into the town from the north. The Green Auxiliaries, suddenly free of enemy musket fire, torched a cottage on the edge of the town to form a smoke screen behind which they could advance in order against the Royalists huddled in the market square. Green coated musketeers and the supporting lines of the Yellow Auxiliaries followed close behind, and the last of the Royalist resistance was driven from the square.

Smoke became part of the urban battle scene. The barn's owner, a zealous Royalist, fired his own building when it, too, became untenable. Royalist soldiers took immediate advantage of its cover, dashing into the churchyard before the temporary pall lifted. Those of Bolle's men who were left to fight lined the yard's low wall and a breastwork to the north of the church or manned the scaffolding in the church itself, 400 men or less with an unwanted obligation to defend an unseen King's wish to rule.

For two hours, according to some accounts, the defenders held the enemy at bay, crouching behind the churchyard wall while their commanders yelled hoarsely in their ears. The Red Regiment of London concentrated in force at the south-east corner of the yard, every musket coming to bear on this single section of the wall. Battered at close quarters and outnumbered by four to one, the Royalists fell back, *'leaving their muskets standing upright, the muzzles whereof appeared above the wall as if some of the men had still lain there in ambush, and our men seeing nobody appear to use those muskets, concluded that the men were gone, and consulted*

---

12 Archer

'A RUNLET OF SACK AND A FATTENED OX'

Interior of Alton Church

among themselves to enter two of three files of musketeers, promising Richard Guy, (an officer), who was the first that entered the churchyard, to follow him if he would leave them'. [13] The southern and western sections of the wall were still in the hands of Royalist musketeers.

Only one man initially followed Guy's advance. Just two Parliamentarians stood within the defended precincts, swords raised, the first and only real heroes of the day's battle. And somehow they survived; their unreal courage had melted the Royalist resistance and not a musket was aimed at their unprotected chests. A minute later, two hundred or more Parliamentary soldiers had flooded in and the Royalist defenders of the wall had gone, hurrying back into the church for personal survival. A dozen Royalists were felled at the doorway by Parliamentary pikes, halberds and musket stocks, probably the highest rate of casualties of the day so far. The defenders of the earthworks on the church yard's north side were less infected by the panic of defeat. Leaving their works, they advanced aggressively, pike men in the rear and muskets at the front, and began to argue with the front Parliamentary ranks.

The best and worst of human nature now emerged; men fought with fists, weapons and even stones, targeting any enemy soldier who stood within reach. Musket stocks rendered men senseless, pikes snapped on impact, and grenades were thrown at windows. Men cried for quarter; it was freely given, and the wounded were sometimes helped. A dying Cavalier aided by a youthful Roundhead, raised a carbine and shot his helper through the throat. Another, giving quarter to his fallen victim, was slashed across his back and arm.

For the Royalists, the fighting was just a splendid gesture of defiance, meaningful, spirited and dignified, but hopeless. Two hundred men, with their backs to the wall and seeing the church behind as their only chance of survival, pulled back towards the open doorway, still fighting, and hearing throughout the cries of the

---

13 Archer

Facsimile of cover of contemporary report of the action

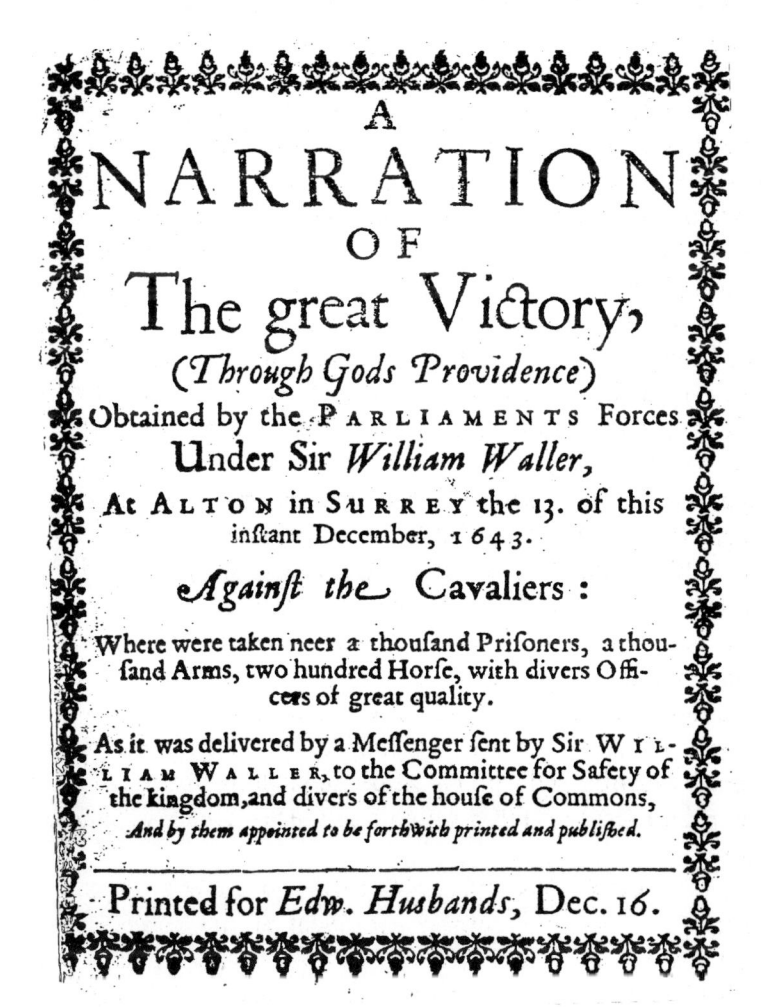

A NARRATION OF The great Victory,
(*Through Gods Providence*)

Obtained by the PARLIAMENTS Forces Under Sir *William Waller*, At ALTON in SURREY the 13. of this instant December, 1643.

Against the Cavaliers :

Where were taken neer a thousand Prisoners, a thousand Arms, two hundred Horse, with divers Officers of great quality.

As it was delivered by a Messenger sent by Sir WILLIAM WALLER, to the Committee for Safety of the kingdom, and divers of the house of Commons, *And by them appointed to be forthwith printed and published.*

Printed for *Edw. Husbands*, Dec. 16.

dying. Pikes were snapped in the low doorway, and those within the church were already attempting to close the doors. But the pressure of the distressed outside forced the doors open again, and the last of the sanctuary seekers went inside.

So, too, did some of their assailants, following at sword's length. The Royalists, however, had already reformed inside, whipped into calmer discipline by Bolle, who *'threatened to run his sword through the heart of him which first called for quarter'*. Parliamentary soldiers died in the doorway, victims of a sudden salvo and a vicious thrust of pikes. ...... *'dreadful to see the enemy opening the door, ready to receive you with their pikes and muskets, the horses slain in the aisles of which the enemy made breastworks, the churchyard, as well as the church, being covered with dead and wounded.... You escaped with a few dry blows from the stocks of the muskets of those who afterwards.....were carried prisoners to Farnham,'* Colonel Birch, one of the Parliamentary officer wrote in his diary. [14] Colonel Bolle, *'valiantly defended himself, till, with the death of two or three of the assailants, he was killed in the place,* (possibly in the pulpit) *his enemies giving him a testimony of great courage and resolution'*. His epitaph still hangs within the church, worn by age but with its memories still clear:

'His virtuous life fear'd not mortality,
His body must, his virtues cannot die,
Because his blood was there so nobly spent,
This is his tomb; that church his monument'.

And a memorial brass in Winchester Cathedral still rekindles the grief felt by the King when he heard of the colonel's death; *'Bring me my mourning scarf, I have lost one of the best commanders in the Kingdom'*.

Resistance ended soon afterwards, and the counting of the dead and wounded could begin. Waller claims to have lost less than a dozen men and to have taken nearly 900 prisoners. Estimates of Royalist casualties vary between 20 and 60. Whatever the actual

---

14 'The Memoirs of Lt. Col. John Burch'

numbers slain and captured, the fight in Alton churchyard sapped the Royalist nerve - particularly that of unhappy Hopton. On December 16th, writing personally to Waller, he admits: '*This is the first evident ill success I have had: I must acknowledge that I have lost many brave and gallant men: I desire you, if Colonel Bolle be alive, to propound a fit exchange; if dead, that you will send me his corpse. I pray you send me a list of such prisoners as you have that such choice men as they are may not continue long unredeemed: God give a sudden stop to this issue of English blood*'[15].

The captives, amongst whom there were, apparently '*divers Papists and Irish men*' were housed in the smouldering ruins of the barn that night and then, tied with match, they were taken in pairs to Farnham in the morning where '*they may hear better doctrine than they have heard at Oxford or among the Irish rebels*'.[16]

Crawford, too, wrote to Waller, but in less courteous tone than Hopton. '*I hope your gaining of Alton cost you dear. It was your lot to drink of your own sack, which I never intended to have left for you*'.[17] He left his hat, cloak and his personal physician in Alton as well. Waller, remembering that he should have received a fattened ox in exchange for the sack, promptly boasted that he, '*instead of a beast, brought away 565 (or more) prisoners.*'

Sir William's reputation soared. A grateful House of Commons wrote to their general, thanking him for the '*great service he has done*'. It was followed by a steady stream of supplies: horseshoes, swords, ammunition and weapons, the equipment for which he had been asking for weeks, but only victory, it seems, would release. His army swelled slightly as well, augmented by two or three hundred erstwhile Royalists, men captured at Alton, who promised to take up arms for Parliament in exchange for their freedom. Those who refused, mainly Irishmen, were taken from Farnham to secure accommodation within the capital.

Those scarred by the fight often sought compensation for

---

15 'The Memoirs of Lt. Col. John Burch 16 'A Narration of the Great Victory (through God's Providence) at A Alton in Surrey' Hants. Records Office   17 King's Pamphlet E.78 No.24

injuries received. Hampshire's court records are full of their claims: the Parliamentary soldier who lost his arm and, as a result, his peace time employment as well. Another, whose left hand was never found, lost his right arm as well. Rendered clumsy and useless by his injury, he later dropped boiling water on his new born baby. The courts awarded both men nothing. But a lieutenant in Sir Arthur Heselrige's regiment with a minor wound caused by a pike appealed directly to the Commons. He was awarded £20 and a coat of grey cloth. But an Alton civilian, whose chairs had been destroyed in the fight, was merely informed that he had *'served the Parliament well'*.

Fanciful reports reached Westminster of the enemy reactions to defeat. The King himself was rumoured to be marching from Oxford to Reading at the head of an impressive force, presumably to link with Hopton before testing their combined strength against Parliament's Farnham army. Frustrated by the Earl of Essex's continuing lethargy at St. Albans and his lack of leadership, Westminster's politicians were forced to adopt a more active role. In almost daily letters to the peer, they urged him to send infantry to Waller's assistance, *'otherwise he will not be able to prosecute this advantage which he has now gotten, for the King's forces increase in Hampshire and Sussex, and divers new regiments are raising there'*. [18] Grudgingly, the Earl responded, sending his rival 600 cavalry and a brief letter of support. Winter was just commencing and Lord Essex preferred to hibernate instead.

The King was unsupportive, too, doing little to assist his energetic champion in the south and the *'desired supply came not'*. Petersfield and Alresford were both abandoned in those dizzy hours of panic and the entire Royalist house of cards began to collapse.

Southampton's Parliamentarians were as active as Waller so that even Winchester seemed to be in danger. Romsey, lying half way between the two towns , became Norton's immediate target. On December 12th, at the very moment when Waller was prowling in the neighbourhood of Alton, Norton and Murford, hearing of

---

18 Commons Journals Vol.3 p.345

Courtney's and Bennet's absence from the town and the disordered state of the Royalist garrison in Romsey, took two companies of the Southampton garrison and set out to extinguish the Royalist presence in the Test side town.

Just one hour after a lingering dawn, a forlorn hope of 50 men confronted Cavalier pickets on the bridge, possibly Broad bridge, and *'fell upon their strong traverse, which was presently quitted by their sentinels'.*[19] Murford and Norton followed close behind and together, with 150 men, they forced their way towards the market place where the Royalists had hurriedly gathered.

Thirty men were killed in the close hauled brawl, the men of both sides clashing brutishly and without any sense of discipline. No ordered ranks or calm commands prevailed; each man was forced to act alone in a frantic bid for personal survival. More than 25 Royalists were taken captive, amongst them Colonel Norton's brother, who had chosen to serve on the King's side. The survivors streamed towards Winchester with the Roundheads at their heels. Norton called the hunters back and the town was savaged instead. The plundering soldiers broke enemy muskets to pieces and threw several barrels of powder into the river. Well supplied by the fleet, the garrisons of Portsmouth and Southampton seemed to feel little need for additional stocks of such heavy essentials of war.

Norton's forces ranged yet further afield in the week following, capturing a force of 200 Royalist cavalry that had taken up quarters in Twyford. And vague reports exist of two December skirmishes at Harting, the Parliamentarians and Royalists winning one apiece.

Hopton, in occupation of Winchester with most of his force, had been strategically blanched by these concurrent defeats at Alton and Romsey. Like a sailor caught in a foreign port by a storm at sea, he could only sit tight and speculate on tomorrow's weather. Guessing that Arundel must be in the hurricane's path, he ordered Colonel Bamfield, still governing at Arundel, to return the three

---

19 'Letter from Norton to Speaker Lenthall' Private collection

regiments of horse that served him there, *it being needful only to make good the castle*', a defensive task for which cavalry would be wholly inappropriate. Bamfield, still to win his place in the King's esteem, wrote boastfully to Hopton that he could hold both town and castle and resist the enemy's demands. But, inwardly not so confident of his ability to resist, he sent back only Sir William Boteler's and Sir William Clark's fine regiments, keeping Lord Belasyse's horsemen and 800 foot at his side.

Hopton had correctly divined his peacetime friend's intentions. Waller left Farnham on the 17th, advancing through Haslemere and Midhurst in search of fresh glory. Cowdray House was a tempting target on the way. Informed that Royalist Horse and Foot were camped within the grounds, he proposed to attack at night and rob the campers of their sleep. Warned of his approach, however, the soldiers and their mounts escaped and only some bedding was found. On the night of December 19th, Waller's army pitched camp on the downland north of Arundel. The London regiments had returned to their city homes, but a fresh Kentish unit, 1000 foot and horse under Sir Henry Heyman, had taken their place. And it is vaguely claimed that 500 Royalists captured at Alton had joined the Parliamentary ranks.

Bamfield had good reason for his boastful confidence. The castle which he had sworn to defend lies on a major spur of the Downs, at the eastern end of which the River Arun meanders lazily. West of the fortress, the low roofs of the town's houses offered an impediment to an attack from that direction, while a ditch and earthwork skirted the castle's northern approaches from where Waller's army were now gazing down.

Sir William rose before dawn the next day, almost the shortest day of the year, and studied the towers and parapets of the massive building. Recollections of Basing probably flitted through his active mind, vivid pictures of failing troops, barbarous gunfire and eventual defeat; the haughty jeers of Lord Paulet's men were heard again. Two hours later, the attack went in, a 3 pronged assault against the well-manned earthworks to the north. By early afternoon, earthworks, park and town were in Parliament's hands, and every man active for the King's cause had taken refuge within the castle's heart. ' ... *we fell on upon the north side of the works, which we did so scour a weedy hill in the park on the west side of the pond with our pieces, that we made them too hot for them* ', Waller explains in a letter to the Lords. ' ... *at the same time we fell on upon a narrow passage by the mill, where they had likewise a double work, and very strong. In a short time, by the good hand of God, we forced both, and entered the town with our horse, notwithstanding a brave sally made* '.[20]

Lacking the will and ability to flush them from their lair, the Roundhead chose to keep them in instead. In that same letter to London which recounted the victory, he pours out his woes and worries: low morale, general weariness and a shortage of soldiers. *'I am very weak in Foot, and my Horse so hacknied out that they are ready to lie down under us....being so weary and in so weak a condition I am forced to keep home for a while and to watch the nine* (troops of Royalist horse)*that are in the castle* '.[21]

Cold winter weather, frozen wells and the tediousness of enemy watching did nothing to improve his soldiers' morale; desertion began again. Those same factors, however, must also sap the Cavaliers' will to resist. Moreover, within the fortress were soldiers, townsmen and horses, and far too little food for all to feed. The siege would consequently be short - or so Waller and his officers optimistically assumed.

So began one of those frequent dramas of individual and collective suffering. In support of periodic musket discharge and long-range artillery bombardment, hideous psychological weapons were brought into play: the banging of drums at night to keep the defenders awake, the vocal taunting from below the castle's walls, the roasting of succulent pigs in full view of the hungry garrison and the draining of the pond which served as the defenders' main

---

20 Lords Journals Vol. V1 p.350   21 ibid p.351

supply of water. They were to be deprived almost completely of water to drink when an ox fell into one of the castle's wells and contaminated the water that lay within. On the 21st, the Parliamentarians were joined by three fresh regiments: Colonel Herbert Morley's Kentish Foot, Sir William Springate's infantry from the same county and Sir Michael Livesey's regiment of Horse. All were paraded in front of the castle in a further bout of teasing.

On Christmas Eve, the first of the garrison fled, flitting like bats in the half-light of dusk. Parliamentary pickets saw them go and fired their muskets in mock salute. Some horses, too, were released, the half-crazed animals forced through the gate by pikemen in their rear. On Christmas Day, 30 mounted riders tried to sortie, or perhaps to escape. Roundhead musketeers, in mischievous mood, forced the back.

The King's general had the determination, but not the means, to relieve the unhappy garrison. Friction between Irish Catholics and stout English loyalists led to evening brawls, the cracking of several skulls and a dangerous loss of purpose. Yet he was duty bound to answer the garrison's call and stirred his fractious men accordingly. He appealed again to Oxford for reinforcements, this time specifically for infantry, far more useful than mounted men in counter-siege operations. Almost perversely, he received the services of Lord Wilmot and a 1000 cavalry troopers, experienced fighters trained in the mould of Prince Rupert and accustomed to dash, but of little value for service in waterlogged trenches.

Hopton first sent men to break down the bridge over the Test at Redbridge in a deliberate attempt to prevent Norton from following too closely on the Royalists' heels and also, it can be presumed, to prevent supplies from entering Southampton. Sure that his impish men had achieved their task, he set out from Winchester on December 26th at the head of 1200 Foot and 2000 Horse with the breaking of Waller's hold on Arundel as his only aim. Passing through Petersfield, until so recently the lair of one of his cavalry detachments, he was engaged in a brief skirmish with one of Waller's far-flung patrols. On the 29th, his army bivouacked near West Dean, 5 miles from Arundel, hovering close to the enemy lines in the obvious hope that his presence would undermine Waller's tenacity and send him beetling to Farnham or beyond.

In his rear, however, Norton had become mischievous, advancing towards Winchester with the entire Southampton garrison. Winchester, of course, was far too robust for Richard's puny force, but some cattle in a field near Hursley were easy targets. Intended for Royalist cooking pots, they were only lightly guarded. More than 50 were driven off and the animals ended up hanging in Southampton's larders instead.

Countless Royalists had now abandoned Arundel castle, some crossing the river at night in an ox-hide boat. On the 28th, the first white flag appeared above the parapets, fluttering briefly before an incensed officer tore it down. Written messages then showered from the walls, requests for tobacco, cards, wine and mercy. Parliamentary soldiers risked life and limb to collect the papers, the more straight laced calling first for surrender as the price for providing the precious commodities which were so earnestly required.

Hopton had now moved on again. Three miles from Arundel, he was met on the road by a Captain Cox, one of the garrison and sent by Bamfield *'to let the Lord Hopton know that they were all very well resolved, and that they had made a computation of their provisions, and found they should have no want for 14 days'*. When asked if he had seen the provisions, the captain replied that *'he had the day before seen a heap of wheat in a room, which as he described was computed not to be less than 40 quarters'*.[22]

What Bamfield hoped to achieve by this untruth is not entirely clear. Possibly he wished to defeat Waller on his own and so deflect Hopton from his goal. If so, he brilliantly succeeded: Hopton promptly fell back to Westbourne to await the arrival of two regiments of Irish soldiers under Colonel Charles Mynn, now

---

22 De Bellum Civile p.73-74

on route from Gloucestershire where they had achieved little glory. Sir Ralph, robbed of any sense of urgency, looked for something else to do. Richard Norton, still mobile in Hopton's rear, placed about 60 men in Warblington House during his present bout of wild audacity. Lying midway between Portsmouth and Chichester, Warblington, the peacetime home of the Royalist Cottons, was in a position to dominate Chichester's vital harbour. Lured by its charms and angered that his enemy had got there first, Hopton now regarded its capture as a dress rehearsal for Arundel's relief and as a chance to polish up his recently tarnished glory.

He seems, however, to have first argued with Norton in the open field on December 30th. Leaving a token force in residence in Warblington House, the Southampton colonel followed in Hopton's rear. Heavy mists, however, blunted his enthusiasm and concealed the enemy's movements. That night he camped with his regiment close to Westbourne, totally unaware that most of Hopton's cavalry were in bivouac less than a mile away.

Hopton reacted as any quick-thinking general should. Sending his dragoons to block the retreat route to Warblington and a detachment of cavalry under Sir Edward Stawell of Hinton Ampner to guard the road to Chichester, he ordered 120 horse to nail down Norton in his camp, instructing the rest of his force to follow when they were ready.

The Parliamentarians were clearly disadvantaged, but not dismayed, by the enemy's sudden appearance in the mist. Conscious that every moment of delay would add to the Royalist numbers, Norton wisely withdrew in the direction of Chichester. Stawell, keen to make his mark, led his regiment in a charge as soon as Norton's fugitives appeared. The Roundhead colonel, finding the routes to Warblington and Chichester both blocked, decided to make a stand and rely on the goodness of God.

There is little evidence of what actually happened on the open heath. Chased, no doubt, by superior numbers, Richard and his men seem to have headed towards Warblington, his nearest haven in this time of trouble. Colonel Horatio Carey and 80 horsemen were sent in pursuit and the besiegers of Warblington were placed on full alert.

Caught between the closing jaws of two Royalist forces, Norton's small force should have suffered for their sins. But Carey failed to catch his quarry, and the besiegers of the house would be forced into unsupported action on the track to the park. The unnamed commander of this besieging force failed too, *'upon what unfortunate apprehension I know not, for he was an old soldier, and in many other occasions before and since maintained a very clear and good reputation, but then upon the first discovery of Col. Norton with his frighted party, he unfortunately quit the pass, and retreated, and thereby gave Norton the opportunity to charge and rout him'.*[23] Other Royalist troopers, however, had been sent in Carey's place. These, arriving at the close of the miniature skirmish, captured 24 of Norton's force, the commander himself only narrowly escaping.

Richard Norton and the residue of his force galloped insanely towards Havant and apparent safety. Two powerful regiments of Cavalier horse were near at hand. *'I had not long been in my quarters, but my scouts brought me in word of a party drawing towards me'.*[24] Norton explains in a letter to Westminster. Realising that it would not be sensible to engage a mobile force of unknown numbers, he ordered 80 of his men to ride to Chichester while he remained with just 50 troopers to guard the line of retreat towards Southampton.

Ludovic Lindsay, Lord Crawford, the Royalist general who had lost his promised sack at Alton and fortuitously the commander of this Cavalier brigade, saw the means for instant revenge. Spotting the tiny Parliamentary force through the shifting mists, he sent his men thundering across the frosted fields to stop the Roundhead retreat. Norton, as quick thinking as his adversary, pulled back his rearguard, but *'at the entering of a town called Havant'*, he was

---

[23] 'De Bellum Civile' p.75 [24] 'Good news from Portsmouth declaring how Col. Richard Norton met my Lord Crawford's regt.' Hants Records Office

confronted by the entire Royalist force.

'There was then a necessity of going forward, whatever the danger was', he explains in his letter. *'I apprehended it to be far greater than it pleased God to suffer it to be; they stood and faced us with some of them while the rest marched by; for they were coming out of a cross lane, they stood till we came within half-pistol shot of them, and when they saw that we were resolved to fall on them, they fairly (trusting it seems more to their horses than their arms) ran away. We fell upon them, I think, with the more anger, having been crossed before, and truly we spoiled too many of them...they were most in red coats, but they were quickly all of a die,......I think there escaped few without broken pates'* [25.]

Royalist accounts make no mention of this engagement. Certainly it coincided with Hopton's brief investment of Warblington. Norton's isolated garrison surrendered soon afterwards and marched away with honourable terms. Sir Ralph Hopton had gone some way to salvage his earlier reputation, and now, at last, could turn his mind fully to the relief of Arundel Castle.

But on Saturday, 6th January, the fortress fell, held by the Royalists for only 25 days and defended for only 15. On the day before, according to a contemporary account, *'the enemy........being extremely punched with famine,......sent a message to our Major General of the west, the generous spirited Sir Will. Waller, with more humble expressions than formerly: desiring a treaty, by means of 3 persons from either party; and that the Lady Bishop, with her daughters, and waiting gentlewomen might have liberty to come forth and refresh themselves'.* [26] Sir William, always chivalrous, invited Col. Bamfield and the ladies to dinner while 3 of his officers visited the castle to negotiate terms.

No agreement was reached in the first bout of discussions. The ladies, however, continued as guests of the Parliamentarian and, for a day at least, politics took second place to social niceties and sweet-humoured conversation. Late in the evening, the earnest talks

---

25 'Good News etc.' 26 'A full relation of the late victory at the taking of theCastle of Arundel' TT81(10)

began again and terms were reached when most of the non-involved had gone to bed. Castle, garrison and weapons passed into Westminster's hands at 9 a.m. Amongst those taken were recalcitrant Sir Edward Ford and Sir Edward Bishop, the two most wanted of the Sussex Royalists. *'Thus God brought about this great work, without bloodshed, and Sir William Waller is possessed of the said town and castle of Arundel with about 100 officers and commanders...besides, about 2000 arms, with ammunition and good store of riches to encourage our valiant soldiers in their further service'.*[27] concluded the letter that carried the news hurriedly to London and caused the capital's bells to peal again. Bamfield followed soon afterwards, led in chains to brief imprisonment in the Tower. He was to be released during the summer, receiving his freedom in exchange for Sir Ellis Layton, a Colonel of Horse in the Parliamentary army.

The King's fortunes might have been laid low in Sussex, but rural Hampshire still held stoutly for the King. Basing and Winchester were seemingly impregnable and, from both places, Royalist soldiers rode out almost daily to exact the tributes of war. The widow of a Royalist officer killed at Reading and now a resident of Odiham, was one of those who complained of the heavy exactions of Lord Paulet's Basing soldiers. She, at least, received a hearing; her complaints reached the King in Oxford. Lowlier beings received a beating instead and lost possessions or liberty for their temerity. An Aldershot carpenter was forced to make 60 chairs for the Cavaliers' use and then convey them to Basing at his own expense. And a Royalist captain who had equipped soldiers for the King had all his horses 'borrowed' for the duration of the war by Major General Jacob Astley. Informed that the officer had written to Rupert to complain, Astley attempted to justify his theft and vilify the captain. In a letter to the prince, he states that the officer had *'oppressed the people,... ...and he went under my name, which he used falsely, as giving it out he did it by my warrant.....As upon*

---

27 'A full relation of the late victory at the taking of the castle of Arundel' TT (81(10)

complaints of the county and the Committee here, I could do no less than commit him'.[28]

Hopton now felt forced to adopt a dual strategy: limited aggressive moves wherever the chance arose and a simultaneous posture of defence which would keep open the lines of communication between Winchester, Oxford and the west. In the grounds of the priory at Wherwell, near Andover, he constructed a fortified post, an outpost of solid construction with artillery bastions and a semi-resident garrison of varying numbers. A redoubt was started about a mile west of Winchester on a site marked today by the spot known as Oliver's Battery. Waller, meanwhile, had left Arundel, entrusting it to the care of Sir William Springate and Col. Herbert Morley. Sir William and many of his garrison were eventually carried away with typhus, an affliction which caused far more suffering than the siege and bombardment had ever done. Travellers avoided the town, stopping well beyond its reaches to stare in awe and pity its wretched citizens.

In mid-January, the milder weather of earlier winter broke. Heavy snows took its place and stilled the clash of weapons. Both sides sought instead the comfort of roaring fires in wayside homes. Waller, with little else to do, wrote frequently to Westminster, reminding the politicians of his successes in the field and the dwindling resources with which he had been forced to do so much. In one, he asks specifically for the proceeds of the sale of booty taken from a Dunkirk privateer to be made available for the use of his army and the payment of his troops. '*I humbly desire there may be a speedy supply of money sent, without which I have no hope to march. I shall presume with all humbleness to be a maker of requests unto you in the behalf of this poor army, that out of the sale of these wares, we may have our arrears discharged, the surplusage if there be any, to be accounted to the state'.*[29]

When war emerged from its hibernation and spring flowers bloomed again, the clash of weapons was to grow even louder. In a

---

28 Warburton p.212   29 'Letter from Waller to Speaker Lenthall' Tanner MS.62

'A RUNLET OF SACK AND A FATTENED OX'

Hampshire field, where sheep graze unknowingly today, 10,000 men locked in battle, and one of the war's five major actions was fought. Late winter, with its skirmishes and defiant posturing, was to be a dress rehearsal for the battle at Cheriton.

13

'All the country store eaten up'

CHARLES had never chosen to submerge his reign within a forest of political and military uncertainty. But, for more than a year now, he had been forced to battle his way through choking woodland. For a brief while, in the autumn of 1643, he seemed to have emerged at the other side, and ahead, on a sunlit and treeless plain, lay his crown, his throne and his dignity.

Yet it had been only a clearing and the woodland grew again. Both sides had fought themselves to a virtual standstill, victory in one area offset by defeat elsewhere, and a military solution seemed increasingly unlikely. A diplomatic settlement perhaps remained possible, and the two arguing sides explored every constitutional and semi-legalistic device at their disposal to win the war of words.

For Parliament, it was largely a matter of securing credibility, of convincing the nation and the outside world that it spoke with constitutional authority in place of a discredited monarch. But the Great Seal, the symbol of legitimacy, was in the possession of the King in Oxford, and the resulting decrees of the two Houses were usually dismissed as invalid.

Charles, too, worked under a constitutional handicap; the

absence at his side of the nation's elected representatives. In an effort to maintain the legality of his rule and actions, he issued a summons on December 23rd 1643 to all members of either House to assemble in Oxford on January 22nd. This 'Parliament in exile' would, because it met at the King's wish, be more legal than its rebellious counterpart still sitting at Westminster. A promise of 'grace and pardon' was offered as an incentive to all those who responded to the summons. And so, by different means, both sides attempted to stamp the mark of legal sanctity that would make their actions constitutional.

The weapon of loud abuse was also well employed. Over 40 peers and 200 commoners obeyed the King's call and dutifully assembled in Oxford on the date required. Their treachery called forth a tirade of vituperation and they were described in London in inhuman terms as *'unnatural monsters, who, like vipers, to make way for their own safety, would destroy the womb that bore them; and because themselves are justly cut off as rotten and destructive branches of the representative body of the kingdom, would therefore pluck up the tree by the root, and destroy both Parliament and kingdom'.*[1]

Almost at a stroke, things changed militarily in Parliament's favour - mainly as a result of Parliament's bold political moves. In August 1643, Westminster's leaders asked Scotland to provide an army, offering in return a religious settlement in both countries *'according to the Word of God and the example of the best reformed Churches'*. Drafted to protect the various sects into which the church had divided, these words hinted at the establishment of Presbyterianism in England, the very thing for which the men of Scotland had so long worked. In September, both sides accepted the Solemn League and Covenant, a virtual commitment to fight together for unspecified and still unclear aims. On February 16th, 1644, a Committee of Both Kingdoms was instituted to assume direction of the war. It was denied the right, however, to negotiate directly with the King without the prior consent of Parliament.

---

1 O.P.H. XIII p.82

Charles reacted explosively to the signing of the Covenant, countering with two measures that were ultimately to lose him the support of many of his more loyal English subjects. First, in clear bad taste, he concluded a truce for one year with the Irish Catholic Confederation, the so-called 'Cessation', an act which released Royalist troops for service in England. Then, accepting the plan long advocated by James Graham, Earl of Montrose, he agreed to rouse Scotland from the north and emotionally set the Highlands alight. With their homes and hearths threatened from behind, the Scottish Covenanters would be unwise to march south from their homeland and leave their families at the mercy of Royalist reprisals.

Strategically, both of these moves might have been sound. But, politically, they would provide welcome fuel for the Parliamentary propaganda machine and help to topple him from his throne. His next move was even more injudicious and ill-advised. Having already recruited hundreds of Irish men to his standards, he now chose to employ mercenaries from the continent, men of few principles and almost no scruples. The Thirty Years War had generated the need for such men and had provided a diet of blood and a licence to murder. Large numbers of these men were still available in the inns, taverns and alleys of the continent, ready to serve any general, king or prince with money to spend. *'The King need not scruple to call in the Irish or the Turks, if they would serve him'*, Lord Byron had written to Ormonde, the King's general in Ireland, in stoic acceptance of this foolish policy. *'The English, excepting such as are gentlemen, not being to be trusted in this war'*.[2]

His gamble was soon seen to be unravelling. On 18th January 1644, the Scottish Covenanting army, over 21,000 strong under the command of Alexander Leslie, Earl of Leven, assembled at Berwick and began the crossing of the Tweed. The Marquis of Newcastle, Royalist commander in the north, received the news in gloom. Believed to be capable of military miracles, he urgently wrote to

---

[2] Carte's Original Letters 1.36

Prince Rupert to remind him of his frailty. *'I know they tell you, sir, that I have great force; truly I cannot march 5000 foot, and the horse not well armed....Since I must have no help, I shall do the best I can'* [3].

On the 28th February, after involvement in a number of running engagements, the Scots eventually crossed the Tyne, and the drive towards York began. Northern England, solid, safe and previously reliable, was suddenly seen to be vulnerable. Victory in the war now seemed likely to go to whoever won in the north, a point which the Marquis of Newcastle made in a letter to the King: *'If your Majesty beats the Scots, your game is absolutely won'.*[4]

He clearly underestimated the need to hold Lancashire and Cheshire, one of the most valuable recruiting grounds for the Royalists in the early weeks of war. Threatened by purely local forces under Sir William Brereton, the longer term Cavalier domination of this vital area seemed beyond any doubt. But on January 25th, Lord John Byron's Royalists were thrashed at Nantwich, and the King's ownership of the English north-west was far less secure.

What happened in Southern England's chalky downland and clay vales seemed far less important, almost irrelevant beside the great surge of events in the north. Winter's grip that year had been more vicious in the south. While Leven stormed the Tyne and Brereton's Roundheads spilt enemy blood in Cheshire, Royalist and Parliamentarian almost comatosed in the south and only very minor skirmishes are reported. During the early weeks of February, Hopton received orders from his King to retire to Marlborough. Sir Ralph remonstrated, pointing out that all his hard-won Hampshire gains, including Winchester, would be lost. Charles relented, Hopton stayed and the King's colours continued to fly over Winchester.

And they were soon to fly over Romsey. Milder weather in the first week of February and accusations in Oxford of Royalist inertia roused Hopton to sudden activity. Preferring *'not to be*

---

3 Warburton E. 'Memoirs of Prince Rupert' Vol.111 p.225   4 op.cit p.227

altogether idle',[5] he forcibly impressed men in Wiltshire and West Hampshire, adding more than 2000 men to his ranks in February alone. On the 5th, he took possession of the Abbey town, killing several of the Parliamentary garrison and capturing 80 others. Frenzied by such easy victory, he cast covetous glances towards Southampton, the capture of which would have earned him a hallowed place in the gallery of the King's champions.

Military assault would be an act of self-destruction, and more subtle means would need to be employed. Deceit, bribery and gentle persuasion, widely practised elsewhere, might be more productive and far less wasteful of human life. He recruited the services, therefore, of a distinguished Winchester lawyer, Jasper Cornelius, and embarked on a course of corruption.

Cornelius selected a Robert Mason, a Southampton merchant, as the target for his bribe, and asked him to offer Murford £1000 and the King's high favour in return for betraying the town. Murford, less corruptible than his earlier behaviour might have suggested, informed Norton of the Cavalier offer. The governor, following established precedent, joined the web of intrigue and asked Murford to negotiate further.

Murford played his double role admirably, dragging out the negotiations to buy Norton time to acquaint Waller and Essex with these murky affairs. The promised pardon arrived from Oxford, but not the money; the King's councillors had decreed that the reward would be paid when the city had been delivered. Seven more letters changed hands and further candlelit plotting took place.

At last the trap was sprung. Mason was arrested and charged with treachery. Escaping before justice could be done, he fled to Winchester and took service with the King. Hopton took prompt revenge, blockading Southampton from the north. The Earl of Warwick, hearing of the town's sudden plight, sent the *'Henrietta Maria'* into Southampton Water and kept the channel open for supplies. Cattle, sheep and winter fodder were stolen from barns

---

5 Hopton p.77

and the roads to the town securely held. Norton's men sometimes struck back, riding out in force to relieve the pressure and the monotony of a semi-siege. A well-respected Parliamentary officer was taken captive during one such outing. His furious soldiers rode after the captors and chased them as far as Twyford. Here the Royalists eventually stood at bay, placing their captive in the front line with carbines pointed at his head.

For a moment, the tension of indecision prevailed, a semi-silence of hard stares at a distance of yards. The Parliamentary carbines were slowly raised, a volley rang out, and 8 Royalists were toppled from their mounts. The others reined off immediately, taking their captive with them. A further short ride, another warning volley, and the captive broke free when the horse of one of his guards stumbled and threw the rider.

Waller emerged at last from his short winter hibernation. Disturbed by reports of Hopton's sudden aggression, he ordered Major-General Richard Browne and his City Brigade to garrison Petworth's ancient manor house. Units of Parliamentary cavalry also occupied Petersfield and the Tichborne family home at West Tisted. And where Parliamentary rule prevailed, the spiritual zealots in the Roundhead ranks governed too. Self-appointed guardians of other men's souls, they searched for evidence of religious malpractice. The church at Odiham was visited during morning service and the minister was ordered from the pulpit for blasphemous preaching. A minister of a neighbouring community was chained to the door of his church for '*utterances contrary to God's True Word*', and his congregation encouraged at sword point to denounce his wickedness.

Sir William tried periodically to curb their overflows of enthusiasm, aware that their loud utterances and violent intrusions would violently stir the normally tranquil waters of village life into open hostility against the Covenanting cause. Throughout the struggle, he chose to steer a middle course, convinced that individuals should work with a clear conscience and with a sense of the attainable. '*My principles (I may speak it freely and truly) were grounded upon the public interest, and had no other ends than what are laid down in the declaration of Parliament, and the National league and Covenant, that religions might be reformed and maintained, the person, dignity and honour of the King preserved, and the peace and safety of the kingdom settled*', he explains.[6]

While Episcopalians in Winchester fought back with condemnation of Presbyterian mispractice and '*their incitement to Babel*', the military arms of both sides strengthened their grip on the fields of war. On February 5th, the day on which the '*Henrietta Maria*' sailed into Southampton's harbour, Waller moved infantry to Bishop's Waltham, only 6 miles from Hopton's Winchester. Sir Ralph employed the services of a Dutch engineer to rebuild the castle's ailing defences and concentrated all his forces within the city and its suburbs.

This moment was like the prelude to an expected storm, when angry clouds above a tropical island cause the frightened inhabitants to hurriedly barricade their houses and gather their crops. The stretched intensity of February days was periodically dissipated in sudden squalls of minor fighting. On the 15th, Hopton again made a dangerous move towards Southampton, sending 2 troops of horse through Nursling on a mission with no particular aim. Norton sortied instantly, taking the Royalist horsemen in the flank and, according to the only accounts available, robbed them of 120 horses, most of their weapons and much of their dignity as well.

Colonel Norton, however, chose not to be baited further. Despite the Royalist presence in Romsey and along the road to Winchester, he remained with most of his men within Southampton's medieval walls, awaiting the call from Waller that must surely come.

Sir Ralph again took revenge, this time punishing Hampshire folk for the crimes committed by his enemy. Desperately short of mounts for his men, he ordered farmers in possession of horses to

---

6 Waller W. 'Vindications' p.7

deliver them to the stables of the Royalist cavalry, offering to pay £10, well above the pre-war market price, for every horse provided. Sheep commanded a lower price, 20 shillings at most, and poultry were bought at 10 pennies 'a neck'.

But, despite these attractive prices, the farmers were not always paid. Oversight, poor record keeping, and intentional dishonesty all contributed. Money might have jingled at the belts of the luckier of the county's inhabitants and, for them at least, immediate hunger might have been postponed. A lack of horses, however, meant that fields would soon no longer be tilled and next season's flour and vegetables could not be grown. The economy of rural England, subsumed by the needs of war and the demands of unwanted armies, was in danger of grinding to a tragic halt.

And the money in the generals' coffers was usually taken from those who could least afford to give. Those with land of their own were taxed by the Royalists at 25 shillings each week, more than the weekly income of nearly all. The Parliamentarians insisted on a similar amount, and double taxation was frequent. Trodden into the Hampshire mud by the military boot of those who believed that they were performing God's will, the inhabitants of town and village were deprived of their self-respect and often the means to survive.

By contrast, Cavalier bellies seem to have been well-filled. Troopers patrolling near Odiham are stated to have consumed 3000 sheep in 12 days without paying a shilling for the privilege. Mutton and pork hung in the larders of Winchester castle, and Hopton's army consequently ate well - more than a pound of meat, 8 ounces of bread and an average of 2 pints of beer per soldier per day. The bill of fare of Parliament's soldiers was probably just as impressive.

The sense of impending climax clearly affected both sides, causing hearts to flutter in Oxford and London, and mobilisation of fresh units to begin. In early March, long promised reinforcements left Oxford, the Queen's own regiment of 800 horse and 1200 foot. Accompanying them were two noblemen, the 21 year old Lord John

Stuart, brother of the Duke of Richmond, and the 70 year old Patrick Ruthven, the Earl of Forth, an experienced veteran of the Thirty Years War. His arrival at Winchester unleashed a flurry of speculation that Hopton was about to be replaced.

Waller had reinforcements too. Col. Ralph Weldon's Red regiment of Kent joined him on March 4th, 800 untested but well-needed infantry ordered west by Parliament's express command. Very little moral support from the Commander of Parliament's armies, however, flowed in Waller's direction. Letters had passed from Westminster to the Earl of Essex, asking him to co-operate with the campaign in the south. The Earl had replied diplomatically, but jealousy of Waller's successes underlay every utterance and not an extra soldier or gun was provided. Waller, less discreet perhaps than a serving politician should be, comments acidly in his 'Experiences' of the peer's seeming malevolence: *'It had bitter endings, for the Parliament wrote to Essex to join me, intending that we together should do a mighty work, but the General would not, to their no small displeasure; for which no good reason could be given, but that he would have his great name stand alone'.*

Alarmed by the build-up of Royalist strength, he personally wrote to Essex on 21st March, suggesting some bolder Parliamentary initiative in the midlands towards Oxford that might serve to draw away the Cavalier strength from Hampshire. The Lord General's response was frustratingly non-committal and vague: *'I....have been considering of that proposition you make, but when I look upon the posture of my own army and the distance the Earl of Manchester's forces are at being so divided,....I think the motion may admit of so much delay as to let me know the ground you go upon, what certain intelligence you have, for the report is uncertain whether Ruthven be there or towards Gloucester, and how you conceive this can be effected up by me in this season by these forces you propose...I shall desire you therefore speedily to let me know your thoughts upon this fully, and I shall so frame my resolution after as may be most the good of the kingdom. This is not any way to retard you from your advance towards the enemy as you find advantage'.*[7]

Another dramatic skirmish had meanwhile taken place near Romsey on March 9th, the result, it seems, of Hopton's unceasing desire to punish the citizens of Southampton. For the third time since the year's start, Sir Ralph sent cavalry towards the town, and, for the third time, Richard Norton came out to meet the threat. Confronting the Royalists on a low hill, possibly Pauncefoot, Sir Richard sent a detachment of his men on a long detour to the west with orders to fall on the Royalists' rear. Perhaps 100 Cavaliers were killed or captured and their horses taken to stables in Southampton.

On the 12th, Romsey was snatched from the Royalists during a day of wild confusion. Some of the garrison, while patrolling in the New Forest, were attacked by fellow Royalists, and carbines discharged at close quarters. Informed of these wanderings in the Forest and aware, no doubt, that the abbey town was consequently only poorly guarded, Norton sent troopers under Cap. Thomas Evans to take possession. Hardly a soldier or his musket barred the Roundheads' advance or remained in the Market Place when Evans and his men arrived.

On Wednesday March 13th, however, the returning Cavaliers quickly ended the Captain's moment of triumph. Awakened in the early hours, the Parliamentarians were forced to fight where they had slept and *'with their breeches undone'*. Amongst the men taken captive were 6 deserters from Lord Hopton's army, one of whom still owed his former colonel a small sum of money. Condemned in a hurried session in the market place, they were hanged from the still-existing wrought iron signpost of the old Swan Inn.

This frivolous sparring on the banks of the Test was hardly the way to win the county. Both sides, plagued by myopic thinking at their respective headquarters, seemed incapable of long-term vision. Instead of an aggressive forward drive, Royalist movements in early March seem uncoordinated and without clear purpose. Units

---

7 Lords Journals Vol.V p.363

of cavalry moved east, west and south simultaneously, while Ogle and Hopton were known to be discussing imminent withdrawal from the city of Winchester. Waller seemed just as indecisive, wondering whether to stand his guard in vulnerable Farnham or carry Parliament's colours into England's west.

And so, more by chance than careful design, they eventually clashed in a major battle. Hopton, despite his doubts of the wisdom of remaining, stayed in Winchester with most of his army. Satellite units lay all around; in Southwick, Fareham, Andover, Alresford and in Bishop's Waltham. Waller, still agitated, visited the Commons and asked personally for horses, weapons, powder and the remaining military resources of the four associated counties. He returned with promises of a battery of guns and the news that Sir William Balfour and 4000 horse had been sent from Windsor to help him in his still unspecified aim.

The Scotsman Balfour was far from mercurial. Yet he possessed an eagle's eye for strategic advantage and seldom missed an opportunity in the field. Together, the two Parliamentarians, Balfour and Waller, might move mountains, both equally cautious but unhesitating, both passionate believers in the cause, but both equally philosophical about how the Covenanters' aims should be achieved.

Balfour's men occupied Newbury on the way, a detachment from here riding out to expel the remaining Royalists from Andover while a small force of 200 men was sent to observe the Royalists in Basing. The general's movements then become conjectural - reports of a skirmish near Odiham taking place almost simultaneously with an action near Basing House, during which 6 cart loads of malt, bacon and beef for the Marquis's garrison were supposedly taken. Later his men were seen near Winchester, their sudden appearance causing Royalist cavalry to sortie in response and attack a Parliamentary camp at Bramdean. The carts and their contents were apparently recaptured, some Roundhead prisoners being forced to repair the shattered sides and broken wheels.

'ALL THE COUNTRY STORE EATEN UP'

On the 16th, the Royalist muster began near Tichborne, most of Lord Ruthven's regiments being evident in the ranks that day. On the very same day, Parliament's London brigade moved from Petworth to Midhurst, probably to shield the transfer of 100 barrels of powder on route from Surrey to storage in Arundel Castle.

The first real murmurs of discontent were recorded at this time. Dispossessed farmers and pillaged villagers, wronged by both sides for someone else's gain, would eventually unite in tangible resistance, and the murmurs would become an earthquake of revolt. But, for now, the sufferers relied upon petitions, humble and deferential, asking only for the redress of their grievances. On March 19th, Hopton received a letter from the poor of the Hospital of St. Mary Magdalen, near Winchester. They informed the peer that one-third of their flock of sheep, on which they depended so heavily for an income, had already been killed by Royalist soldiers. Now the plunderers had swooped on their barns and *'have not only devoured nine quarters of their seed barley for this season,.......and have broken down and burnt up the great gates, all doors, table boards, cupboards, gyses, timber partitions, barns and stables there, but have also used violence to the House of God.......and have converted the said House of God into a stable for horses and other profane uses, to the great dishonour of God and grief of soul of your poor petitioners'*. Hopton was said to have promised immediate protection and punishment of the offenders.

Psychologically, as well as militarily, a battle seemed inevitable. Hopton, searching for revenge after his humiliations at Alton and Arundel, would probably have ignored the cautious whispers of any in the King's court who might have advised against a major challenge to the enemy. Lord Ruthven, however, concurred entirely with Hopton's new belligerence and, together, the two men forged their plans for the intended fight.

Sir William Waller, equally assertive, laboured under a far greater indignity - the defeat at Hopton's hands on Roundway Down in the previous July. He had never fully recovered his self-esteem

'ALL THE COUNTRY STORE EATEN UP'

and nursed a strong conviction that only a major victory over his former friend would cure the injury that hurt his inner self. The rapid build-up to battle in the coming week was as much his work as that of his Royalist adversary.

Both armies were soon at each other's throats. On the 19th, after a full day's fast and a lengthy service of thanksgiving, Waller advanced his forces towards Catherington, intending eventually to unite with Balfour's cavalry at Petersfield. Short of horses with which to pull his expanded array of artillery, he force purchased the animals of local farmers and so damned himself in the eyes of Hampshire folk. Surrey's Parliamentary forces simultaneously grouped at Godalming and began their journey to an uncertain future in Hampshire. On the 21st, Browne's Petworth forces received their new orders: *'to advance towards Winchester to a town called Treyford, which accordingly he did with incredible spped, almost at an hour's warning, and that night arrived there, which we found to be a small village, not above seven or eight houses to quarter all our men'.* [8] Similar orders went out to the cavalry, Balfour's brigade between Romsey and Winchester, and the various regiments of Hampshire, Kent and Sussex that lay in camps between Arundel and Chichester, all to unite in the fields near East Meon.

That evening Balfour gave instructions to his men. *'You are hereby required herein provided which is that no officer or soldier shall ransom or conceal any prisoner of prisoners, but within twelve hours shall make them known unto the General ...Be it also, that if any officer or soldier shall wilfully fail to appear at the rendezvous at the hour or time appointed, he the said officer shall be forthwith cashiered, and taken from his charge......And it is further declared that no soldier upon any pretence whatsoever shall dare to stay behind or straggle from his colours'.* [9] Hearing of these dramatic moves, Hopton and Ruthven hurriedly called a council of war in Winchester. Only Sir William Ogle dissented from the decision made in Eastgate House - an immediate advance towards the east to

---
8 'News Indeed ,Together with a Fuller relation of the Great Victory obtained at Alresford' Hants. Record Office

9 Quoted in Adair J. 'Cheriton' pp.214-215

confront Waller's growing army. Arguing for caution and pointing out the facts, he was reported as saying that ' *if Waller should come within a mile or two of Winchester, you might if you thought fit, draw out and fight having this garrison to back and supply you...but if you march six or seven miles to fight, you must carry your provisions and in this extreme hot weather you will weary the soldiers'*. Mandated by the rest of those present, the Earl of Brentford, ' *having at that present a fit of the gout, commanded the Lord Hopton to draw out the whole army and trains.....and to take his quarters that night in the field three miles towards the enemy upon the way of the plain'* [10]

The Londoners moved from Treyford to West Meon on the 25th, probably the first of the infantry to reach the place selected by Waller for the union of his forces. A minor skirmish followed in the evening. A dozen or so of Sir Ralph's men had visited West Meon that day and were apparently still present when Waller's quartermasters rode in. Some of the Royalists stayed briefly to argue, firing their carbines as they hurriedly mounted their horses, and their commanding officer was taken when his bridle broke. The unlucky man was found to be in possession of a bag of money and a written order for some supplies of rope. Six men are said to have been buried standing upright beneath the floor of East Meon church, some of the broken victims of this dusk time fight. West Meon's village cross was hacked to pieces later that night.

Colonel Walter Slingsby and Elias Archer, Royalist and Parliamentarian respectively, both have accounts of another near encounter on the 27th. Royalist forces had entrenched in strength on the chalklands of Tichborne Down by the 23rd. Hearing that Parliamentary cavalry had taken up quarters in nearby Warnford, Royalist units attempted to surprise them there, but *'having discovered one of our parties the night before were drawn out, and embattled upon a hill about 2 miles behind their quarters in woodland country,'* [11] they wisely decided against an evening assault.

---

10 Hopton p.78   11 op.cit p.78

'ALL THE COUNTRY STORE EATEN UP'

East Meon

This 'drawn out' unit was, apparently, the White Regiment, following in the footsteps of the London Brigade. The Cavaliers stayed in the vicinity all night, intending to engage as soon as the dawn's light broke. *'Next morning (we) early advanced in hopes to have surprised them in this quarter, but when we came thither, not a man was to be found. Yet we spied a full regiment with white colours stand in order facing us upon our left....*(and) *could by no means discover where the enemy's body lay'*, Slingsby reports. [12]

Archer refers to the good grace of Providence in his account of what is presumably the same episode. Believing that the Parliamentarians had assembled for morning thanksgiving, the Cavaliers planned to attack when the act of worship began. *'But, it pleased God, who foresaw the plot, to prevent the danger, directing us to keep the Fast of the Wednesday before, when we lay still at Midhurst, so that we were provided to entertain them, and drew our men into a body near the town, which done, orders came to march away, which accordingly we did,... expecting the enemy every hour to fall upon us, so that we were forced to make a stand a mile or so from the town in extreme danger....'..* [13]

The 27th was also involved in a race for possession of Alresford, *'a reasonable strong quarter'*, and a town that lay astride the road from Winchester to London. Waller, with his army now drawn up on the wooded downland of Westbury Forest, was just as aware of the town's strategic value. Balfour was consequently ordered to take possession and so deny the enemy a chance to protect its vulnerable left flank.

The Royalists, however, got there first, largely as a result of the mercury mind of Sir Ralph himself, and something for which he claimed full credit.*'Hereupon, by the advice of the Lord Hopton, a resolution was presently taken to march with the whole army, with as good speed, as could stand with good order, towards Alresford, and the Lord Hopton and Sir Edward Stowell's brigade of horse, and his own regiment, one of horse, and another of*

---

12 *Colonel Walter Slingsby's Account (printed at end of Hopton's Bellum Civile)* 13 Archer E. 'News Indeed'
Hants Record Office   14 Hopton p.79

dragoons, advanced with as much speed as they could to possess Alresford before Sir William Balfour'. [14] Observing Balfour just one mile to the south of the town, Hopton, at the head of 800 men, quickened his pace and rode into the town only minutes before the Roundheads arrived. For the last half hour, the two sides had ridden in full view of one another, almost at shouting distance and separated only by thick patches of yellow gorse.

Parliamentary regiments at the East Meon muster

Horse:	Foot:
Sir William Balfour's brigade (22 troops)	Browne's London brigade
Balfour's regiment (c. 400 men)	The White regiment(c.1200 men)
John Dalbier's regiment (c.250 men)	The Yellow regiment(c.1000 men)
Sir John Meldrum's regiment (? men)	
John Middleton's regiment (? men)	Sir William Waller's regiment(420 men)
	Sir Arthur Heselrige's regiment(? men)
Sir Arthur Heselrige's regiment (7 troops)	Col. Andrew Potley's regiment (? men)
Jonas Vandruske's regiment (6 troops)	Col. Ralph Weldon's regiment (760 men)
Edward Cooke's regiment (4 troops)	Col. Sam Jones's regiment(? men)
Sir Michael Livesey's regiment (4 troops)	
George Thompson's regiment (4 troops)	
Richard Norton's regiment (4 troops)	
Sir William Waller's regiment (11 troops)	

Source: Harley's letter, Portland MSS.
Reprinted in J.Adair's 'Cheriton'.

Those vital minutes of speed had gained Hopton the choice of ground, and would now force the Parliamentarians to advance from their sheltered positions at the Meons to fight the Royalists in the open. Barricades were hurriedly thrown up across the approaches

'ALL THE COUNTRY STORE EATEN UP'

to Alresford. And here Lord Hopton seemed content to stay, placing his army '*on a rising ground joining to the town fronting towards the enemy*'. Only Lord Ruthven, still suffering from his gout, took up lodgings within the town itself.

Waller seems to have been briefly confused by the enemy's whirlwind movements. Discomforted by the terrain which he had been forced to occupy, he pulled his army back and bivouacked for the night in Lamborough Field where today's road from Petersfield passes through the village of Hinton Ampner. Several London soldiers were frightened by a herd of cows which gazed in curiosity at the passing troops. Sir William took up more comfortable quarters in the manor house, the home of the Stukeley family. Few on either side now doubted that this was the evening before a great battle, a Spring evening of lingering dusk and fluttering hearts. Just two miles north of the house, on the high ground of Sutton Common outside Alresford, the Royalist soldiers, too, were settling for the night, their conversation and thoughts similar to those in the opposing army.

Skirmishing began early next morning, Thursday the 28th. Sir Ralph, curious to pinpoint the exact positions of his adversary, sent out a scouting party. The two sides clashed near the headwaters of the Itchen in a meadow of yellow celandine.

Other skirmishes followed later, some centered on two barns which lay between the two armies. Full of corn, they naturally attracted visits from both sides. By nightfall, the Royalists had undisputed possession of both buildings and their valuable contents, much to the annoyance of one of Waller's officers, who saw Parliament's failure to take the buildings as a '*great oversight......we might with a few foot have maintained it until we had fetched away the corn, which was much wanted in our army.*'[15]

Strategically, the Royalists were now to gain even more, suddenly robbing the Roundheads of the chance to take possession of the long ridge of East Down, only high ground nearby. Early in

---
15 Harley R.'A Letter...to his brother Col.Edward Harley' Portland MSS Vol.3

1 Parliamentary rendezvous at E. Meon
2 King's army and western army rendezvous at Tichborne Down

The advances towards Cheriton

the evening, just when Waller's officers were preparing for supper and another night in bivouac, Hopton and Ruthven, *'viewing the advantage of the ground they had gotten, and that there was a little wood on the top of that hill with a fence about it, placed Sir George Lisle there with 1000 musketeers, and a guard of 500 horse upon the way by him, and laid out the quarters for the whole army upon the same hill where they had stood in arms the night before, with command to every horseman to rest by his horse, and every footman by his arms...'*.[16] Royalist soldiers could now look down on the flickering light of the Parliamentary campfires, knowing that they had the advantage of position.

Waller and his senior officers held a Council of war in the manor house that night. Messengers had ridden in from London with tales of disaster in the midlands and fears that the Royalists might advance on London. Weaker hearts around the table advocated retreat to avoid the possibility of defeat.

Waller, however, had earlier viewed the ground on which the battle must be fought and his well-honed strategic skills spotted the advantage offered by Cheriton Wood, the still unoccupied forest land that lay to the left of the cavalier positions. Supported by a small majority of the council, he issued orders for the wood's occupation.

But deception followed first, a night-time ruse to convince the enemy that the Roundheads were abandoning the probable field of battle. Sir William ordered his wagons and baggage to depart, and the sound of wooden wheels and muffled hooves in the early hours of morning served his purpose well.

'....that night Sir George Lisle being very watchful upon the enemy's motions, and giving of them several alarums, and being so near as he heard them span and drive their waggons, conceived they had been drawing off, and so advertised the Lord Hopton, who presently sent the intelligence to the Earl of Brentford, and he forthwith directed his orders to command Jo. Smith to draw out a

---

16 Hopton pp.80-81   17 op.cit p.80-81

party of 1000 horse to be ready to wait upon the rear of the enemy....' [17.]

In reality, however, Waller had sent Colonel Andrew Potley's infantry regiment and part of the London Whites to occupy the woods. Under the command of Lieutenant-Colonel Walter Leighton and supported by 300 horsemen, this force of 1000 musketeers, standing earnestly to arms in Cheriton Wood, must have gravely unnerved the Royalist generals when reality arrived with the dawn. And well to the right, near where the tiny houses of Hinton Ampner still lay hidden in partial night, Colonel James Carr and a unit of dragoons had silently taken up positions in the hedgerows.

The soldiers of both sides were waking now from their troubled rest, bodies and souls weighed down with a sense of dread and possible death. Few probably talked during their hurried breakfasts, each preferring to dwell for a moment in a personal world of past memories rather than face the realities of the morning. Sweethearts, childhood, a muddle of sweet thoughts - all desperately trying to crowd out the horrors of the hours ahead. *'To some it was a trusty awaking from a cold sleep, to others it stroke more terror than the earth had done cold before',* Harley wrote in an unusually sensitive survey of men's minds. *'In the morning when I went to view the army, I saw such a cheerfulness in every one's countenance, that it promised either victory or a willingness rather to die than lose the field'*.

Friday, March 29th, had dawned misty. Late winter dampness hung over the ridges and the 'arena' on which the battle would be largely fought. The terrain between Alresford and Hinton Ampner is shaped like a horseshoe; two ridges join at the eastern end to enclose a hollow nearly one mile wide. The northern ridge behind which the Royalist army was positioned is slightly higher than its southern neighbour, handing to the Cavaliers the theoretical advantage of the day.

It had become a contest of wits and cool determination between two able generals, both equally matched in the skills of

'ALL THE COUNTRY STORE EATEN UP'

The Royalist army at the Battle of Cheriton

Lord Forth's contingent

Horse: (800 men)
Lord Forth's regiment
The Queen's regiment
Prince Maurice's regiment

Foot: (1200 men)
Col. George Lisle's Reading regiment
Col. Sir Henry Bard's Oxford regiment

Col. Thomas Howard's regiment

Col. Richard Neville's regiment

Lord Hopton's contingent

Horse: (2200 men)
Sir John Smyth's brigade

Foot: (3000 men)
Sir Allen Apsley's Division

Sir John Smyth's troop
Sir Humphrey Bennet's regiment
Col. Andrew Lindsey's regiment
Col. Sir Edward Waldegrave's regiment
Col. Sir George Vaughan's regiment

Sir Allen Apsley's Redcoats
Lord Hopton's Bluecoats

Sir Edward Stawell's brigade

Sir Bernard Astley's Division

Lord Hopton's regiment
Lord Hertford's regiment
Col. Edmond Peirce's regiment
Col Edward Stawell's regiment

Sir Bernard Astley's regiment
Col. Francis Cooke's regiment
Sir Gilbert Talbot's Yellowcoats

Lord John Stuart's brigade

Walter Slingsby's Division

Lord John Stuart's regiment
Col. Sir William Boteler's regiment
Col. Sir William Clerke's regiment
Col. Sir Nicholas Crisp's regiment
Col. Dutton Fleetwood's regiment
Col. Sir Edward Ford's regiment

Walter Slingsby's regiment
Henry Shelley's regiment

Sir Matthew Appleyard's Division
Sir William Courtney's regiment
Sir John Paulet's Yellowcoats
Sir Charles Vavasour's Yellowcoats

campaigning. But timing, not greater competence, seemed to have provided Hopton apparent dominance of the field. Yet time was a fickle ally and no man's friend for long. The new day, chosen by circumstance for the date of a great battle, would see whether Sir Ralph could take full advantage of that dominance.

Notes: Prince Maurice's cavalry regiment was commanded at Cheriton by Major Robert Legge.

Astley's Foot regiment had previously been the Marquis of Hertford's

Vavasour's regiment was now commanded by Appleyard.

Source: ' Cheriton' by J.Adair

14

'With a fair pair of heels'

PARLIAMENT'S soldiers were probably the first to prepare. Waller, forced to be content with the southern slope and his recent occupation of the dark expanse of Cheriton Wood, had made his detailed plans before dawn. His guns had been placed on the higher ground behind his main position, most of the weapons pointing menacingly at the prized ground of east Down, from where Lisle had just been forced to withdraw. Leaving their bivouac points along the road, Waller's infantry deployed along the southern slopes of the ridge, their movements partly masked from the enemy by the rise in ground, but fully divined by Hopton and his officers. Heselrige's cavalry lay behind the left end of the infantry and Balfour's brigade lay on the right, as if to protect the foot from the threats and pressure of an encircling movement.

During the course of the morning, both units were moved forward to lie in front of the infantry. In ordering this move, Waller departed from normal textbook procedures, which tended always to place the horse on the flanks of infantry and not in front or behind. Contentious to those brought up in the conventional strains of military discipline, this forward positioning of the horse would enable Parliamentary cavalry to dominate the 'arena' and control the movement of enemy units that attempted to cross the area.

Forth and Hopton, possibly more from an after thought than any innate perception of the wood's true value, placed some artillery beyond the wood's north-east corner, and set about driving Leighton out. And so this was where the battle started, soon after 8 a.m., when the morning mists had cleared. Colonel Sir Matthew Appleyard and 1000 musketeers were given the job of attacking the wood and protecting the Royalist left flank.

Dividing his task force into four parties, Appleyard zealously obeyed his orders. *'But the bodies of our men no sooner appeared on the top of the hill, but the enemy showed how well they were prepared for us, and gave fire very thick and sharp, which our men very gallantly received and returned'.*[1] Hopton, versatile as ever in the face of trouble and *foreseeing that our party could not long out upon so great disadvantage, and observing an opportunity to cast men into the wood upon the flank of the enemy, he drew off Lieutenant Col. Edward Hopton with one division of the commanded musketeers, and commanded them to run with all possible speed into the wood upon the enemy's flank'.*[2]

The young lieutenant colonel took his party eastward around the northern edge of the wood and fell on Leighton's exposed right flank. One volley, it seems, was sufficient to put the Londoners to flight, and grant the Royalists possession of the valued woodland. Both sides had adopted the same war cry 'God with us', causing the confusion of the opening minutes. The Roundhead commander changed the cry in the minutes following and his troops went into battle with shouts of 'Jesus with us' on their lips instead.

1300 Parliamentarians were soon in full flow, hurrying from the forest land like bats driven from a cave. Harley watched them leave, and his comments about their conduct are far from sympathetic: *'no sooner they did see that the bullets would come otherwise than they would have them but they made a foul retreat......I am confident I smelt them... with a fair pair of heels, which did so discourage the rest, that they all left their charge with*

---

1 Hopton p.81   2 Hopton p.81

The battlefield of Cheriton today

a shameful retreat.... and the soldiers put the fault on their officers, and the officers on the soldiers'.[3]

Hopton and Forth seemed now to disagree about the tactics to be employed. Sir Ralph wished to seize the favours of the moment and punish Waller's disordered right flank. Forth, the senior of the two, preferred first to consolidate and then advance on mass. The entire Cavalier army was ordered to move forward and take up position on the reverse slope of a small ridge that lay within the 'arena'. Cheriton Wood, now bristling with Royalist muskets, covered the left flank, and most of the horse was massed nearby. Hopton's forces occupied the eastern extension of the Royalist line, separated from Forth's units by the little lane that ran south across the field of battle to join the Bramdean road.

But both generals had lost control of events - and possibly the field as well. Having made his dispositions, Hopton rode over to confer with Forth on the timing of a Royalist attack. By the time he arrived, however, Forth's flank was fully engaged, *'and so hard pressed, as when he came to the Lord Brentford, he found him much troubled with it, for, it seems the engagement was by the forwardness of some particular officer, without order'.*[4]

Colonel Sir Henry Bard, an impetuous and undisciplined young officer, *'with more youthful courage than soldier-like discretion'*, seems to have been the culprit. His infantry were probably part of the force of 1500 men placed on the Royalist right flank, their apparent mission being to tease the Roundhead defenders from Hinton Ampner if the opportunity arose.

Bard must have sensed his chance. Ordering his men forward, he and his men were soon setting fire to hedges and outhouses, determined to flush the enemy from their cover. Leading his men too far and too energetically, Bard and the regiment became isolated within the smoke and were to tragically pay for their error. Heselrige was the first to see his chance. Within minutes, he had sent his horse against Bard's flank and rear, *'and there in the view of our whole*

---

3 Harley MSS   4 Hopton p.82

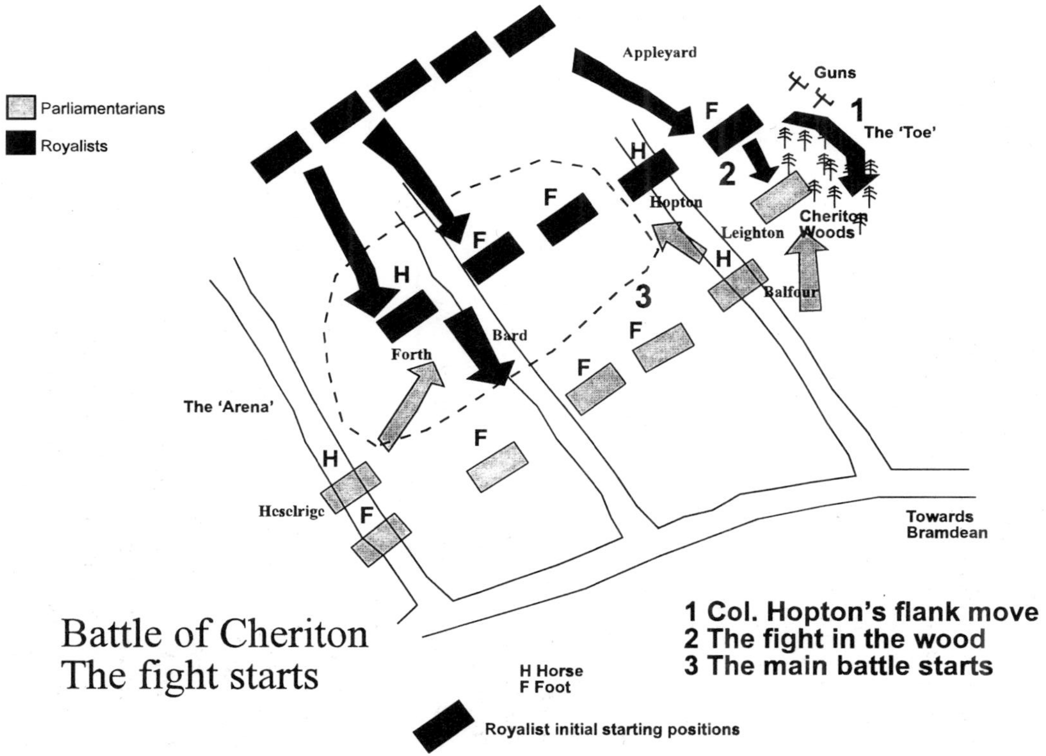

Battle of Cheriton
The fight starts

1 Col. Hopton's flank move
2 The fight in the wood
3 The main battle starts

H Horse
F Foot

■ Royalist initial starting positions

□ Parliamentarians
■ Royalists

army....kills and takes every man'.[5] Bard, his arm severed by a Roundhead sword, was taken captive, while his closest companion's skull was almost split in two. The other Royalist units, just as confused and dislocated by the changing wind and capricious smoke, were pounced on by Colonel Norton's men in a moment of glory that Harley chose to record: *'Our men, seeing the advantage set them to a disordered retreat, our horse seeing it, sent a party of a hundred horse under the command of Captain Butler to charge them, and another under the command of Colonel Norton to second them. Captain Fleming commanded another party. They all of them performed their charges so well that through God's blessing, they routed them all, slew about a hundred and fifty and took a hundred and twenty prisoners with divers commanders of quality'.*[6]

The battlefield's other flank had, by now, also locked in action. Walter Slingsby's two Cavalier regiments stood on East Down, pikes and muskets ready to defend the lane to Bramdean and the western edge of Cheriton wood. No command to engage seems to have been given here. Spontaneously, just before midday, like two youthful lions contesting leadership of the pride, Royalists and Parliamentarians clashed, and every ounce of sinew was fully employed.

Slingsby claims that Parliament's cavalry and infantry attacked first. Sir Michael Livesey's men of Kent and Balfour's horse, supported by Heselrige's infantry and a London regiment, charged three times along narrow Bramdean lane. They were repulsed each time by the solid determination of Slingsby's Cavalier foot, who *'not firing till within two pikes length, and then three ranks at a time, after turning up the butt end of their muskets, charging their pikes, and standing close, preserved themselves, and slew many of the enemy'.*[7]

Stalemate then ensued, the annoying state of affairs that all generals try hard to avoid. With both flanks brought to a standstill and with no sign of God's expected intervention, Forth resorted to

---

5 Harley MSS   6 op.cit   7 Slingsby

more drastic strategies. His cavalry so far had been totally inactive, passive bystanders with no obvious role to play. At about 2 p.m., Sir Edward Stawell's 4 regiments, nearly 1000 men in total, were brought forward and positioned for action at the head of Bramdean Lane, one troop at a time, an obvious mistake in the opinion of Slingsby: *'Then we drew down most of the horse.....but having one lane's end only to pass into it, they came upon great disadvantages, for by that time one body was in the ground and drawn up,....it was over charged with number*'[8]. Despite this clumsy strategy, the Royalist horse achieved some success, a few penetrating as far as the distant Roundhead guns. But success bred over-confidence, and soon the body of Royalist cavalry had been completely fragmented, broken into little pieces by the narrowness of the front over which they moved and the fierceness of the Parliamentary opposition. Sir Edward, wounded five times, was amongst those taken captive.

Forth was yet to make his greatest blunder. Seeing the desecration of Stawell's brigade, he ordered further regiments to follow the same path to destruction. Only Sir Humphrey Bennet's regiment remained in reserve, watching unhappily as a further 1000 men performed a series of unplanned charges and wild extravagances that later caused Clarendon to lament: *'The King's Horse never behaved so ill on that day.....and left their principal officers to shift for themselves'.*[9]

Secure behind the enclosures on the hillside, Heselrige's foot soldiers could pick their individual targets and sally at convenience. Reining only yards from the Parliamentary muskets, the Royalist horsemen had little chance to fire their carbines or use their swords. Further back, Waller's artillery belched hostility, the gunners keeping both their aim and their nerve throughout. They were later to gain commendation for their activity.

Individual acts of heroism took place, personal and often unnoticed within an impersonal and shapeless mass of struggling men. Sir John Smith, sergeant-major-general of Hopton's army, led

---

8 op.cit   9 Clarendon Vol.111 Bk.Viii p.14

his brigade forward almost as far as the Roundhead guns, but was sadly killed by a cuirassier when his horse reared sideways. *'With this wound brigade he falls,'* an eye witness lamented, *and with him the fortune of the day and the courage of our horse. Sir John Smith's troop resolving, to die rather than lose such a brave leader, advanced and brought him off, his horse and arms, while one of his lieutenants rode up to the armed monster (the cuirassier) and shoots him in the eye, sending him to answer for his detested feat, in so base a manner, wounding to death a gentleman every way accomplished and worthy'.*[10]

But Forth still glimpsed the possibility of success on his right, the still smoky fields near Hinton Ampner. Heselrige's cavalry had been diverted to the centre of the field and, without adequate support, Colonel Carr's London regiment holding the western section would be imperilled by an energetic Royalist push. Supported by small units of cavalry, Forth's infantry began to push the Londoners back *'to a disorderly retreat, at which time the day was doubtful if not desperate'* [11]. At 3 p.m., with Parliamentary success on the right flank matched by possible disaster on the left, the days's laurels could have gone to either side or to none. Men prayed as they rode or fought, and the Parliamentary password 'Jesus help us' assisted them on their way.

Perhaps he did. For, even on the western edge of the field, Parliamentary muscle and nerve began to excel. Major-General Richard Browne who *'who was ever known to be a valiant man, and must be looked upon as a special instrument in the work, drew off 100 men from the hedges, and in his own person led them on to charge the horse, which they did most gladly and courageously, and forced the enemy's horse to wheel about'* [12]. Colonel James Carr led his infantry around the edge of the enemy right and pushed forward to the northern ridge, the previous night's resting place for Hopton's army. Heselrige and his cavalry, having little to do in the Parliamentary centre, now returned to the army's left. Sweeping

---

10 \Britticae Virtutis Imago TT. E.53.10   11 Military memories of Col. John Birch   12 Op. Cit.

around the Royalist units on that sector, they took the enemy infantry in the flank. It was now about 3 p.m and Parliamentary victory was emerging from the smoke and the blood.

By 3.30 p.m., a pincer was developing with Roundhead success on both flanks. On the Cavalier left, Hopton's cavalry had broken and only the musketeers in the hedges of East Down held Parliament's horse and foot. Heselrige's infantry under the command of Lieutenant-Colonel John Birch re-entered Cheriton wood, and some of the most vicious fighting of the day took place. And sometime during the afternoon, the time and place not fully reported, Lord John Stuart, Lieutenant- General of the Royalist Horse, led the Queen's Regiment in a counter attack, but was killed in his moment of intended glory.

On the Cavalier right, events were no more favourable for the King. *'Colonel James Carr and Major Strauan* (Strachan) *had so plied their business on the left of our army that they forced the enemy to draw off their ordinance, and quickly engaged all the enemy's foot on them, but they seeing their horse to retreat would no longer abide the charge of our foot and dragoons, but made a speedy retreat to a hill a little beyond the place where we did fight'*, Harley states in his account, recognising Carr as one of the architects of eventual victory.

By 4 p.m., with the Roundhead foot breaking through at both ends, the pincer had almost closed. *'These two great parties went on with such success, that in one hour the enemies' army was between them, all our horse and foot coming on in the front of them'*. The Royalist soldiers reacted in different ways. Some pulling off their identifying colours, *'thrust them in their breeches, threw down their arms, and fled confused'.*[13] More mettled men, Hopton amongst them, fought on, conscious that the consequences of defeat would be more dishonourable than heroic death on the field.

And then, inexplicably, the Parliamentarians on East Down halted, ordered, it seems, to pursue the enemy no further. Who gave

---
13 'News Indeed' Hants Records office 14 Birch

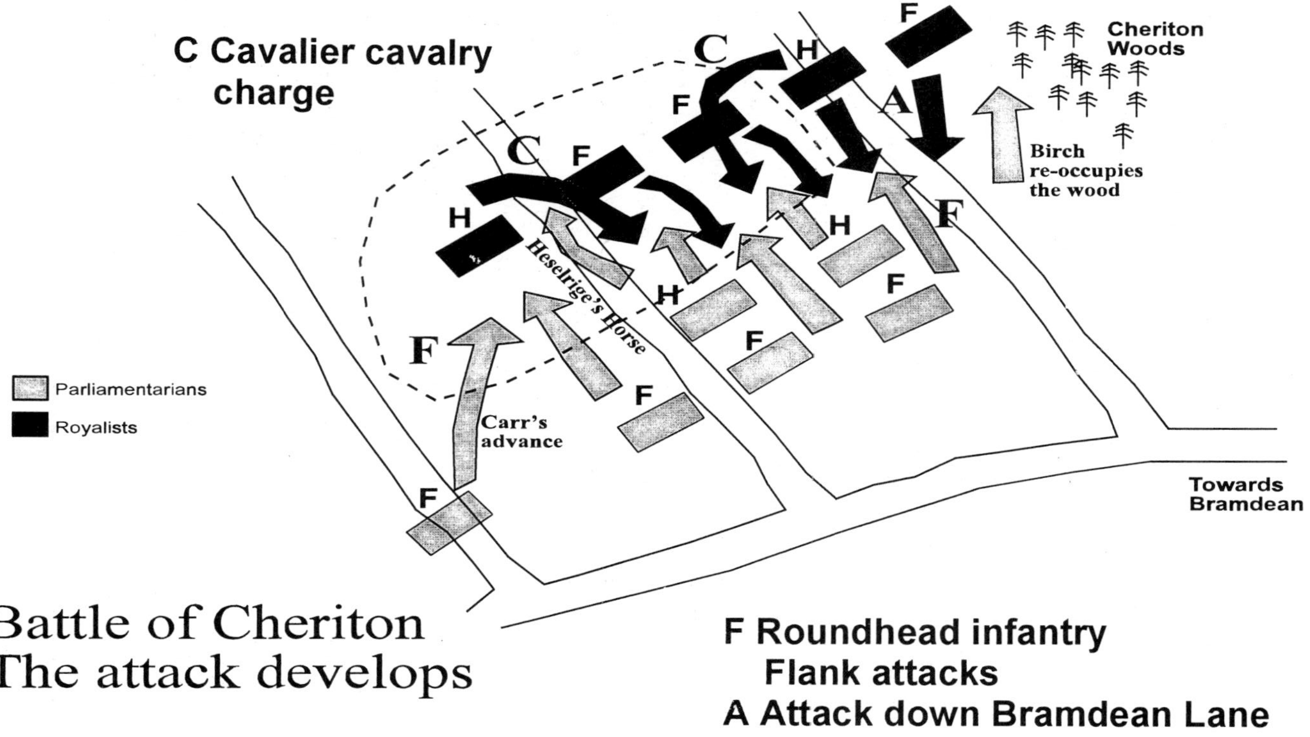

Battle of Cheriton
The attack develops

C Cavalier cavalry charge
F Roundhead infantry
Flank attacks
A Attack down Bramdean Lane

Cheriton Woods
Birch re-occupies the wood
Heselrige's Horse
Carr's advance
Towards Bramdean

Parliamentarians
Royalists

the command might never be known, but the reasons for his order and the possible consequences became the subject of debate for weeks to come. '*The reason is too deep for me to give*', says Birch's secretary in his memoirs. '*Only this I am sure of; had the enemies' commander in chief been there, he could not have commanded anything more advantageous to them. Thus was that day's victory gained, into which I make bold to add, that it was indeed a victory, but the worst prosecuted of any I ever saw*'.

The forty minutes delay allowed the Royalists to partially regroup and withdraw their cannon. Counter instructions fortunately arrived in time to order the Roundheads forward again, and Parliamentary victory was soon beyond any doubt. At some point during this hectic fighting, Waller was nearly captured. Personally leading his troops, he became detached: '*The enemy having by a charge given upon some troops of mine shut me off from my own men*', Waller explains. '*I having then but three in company with me, but it pleased God they were repulsed again, and thereby a way opened for my retreat.....I reckon it a mercy that....., charging without my headpiece, ...I came off safe and unhurt*'[14] Harley gives credit to General James Wemyss, commander of Waller's artillery, for the order to continue the pursuit: '*To him next under God doth belong much of our victory. Through his persuasions it was ordered we should again fall on them and give them a general charge*'.

A series of staggered actions took place as the Royalists withdrew to the crest of Tichborne Down, just south of where Alresford's railway station stands today. The Queen's Regiment and Col. Richard Neville's men, the former officered by several Frenchmen, took the brunt of fighting during the twilight hours of the battle. Capt. Raoul Fleury, one of these ostentatious fighters from the continent, lost a foot and later died. He had fought without any mishap throughout the day's action, suffering only a broken harness. Archer chooses to give an account of one of these brief

---

14 Waller W. 'Experiences' p.19-20

tussles: '....*it pleased God to raise up the spirits of some few, not above 300, and to put such courage into them, as to adventure out of the closings , to charge the main body upon the plain, which they did so resolutely that they put them all to flight, our horse pursued them two miles at the least, till the enemies' horse overtook their own foot, who cried out....Face them, face them, once more face them; which they did, but to small purpose; our horse came up, and at the first charge they were all routed and fled....some fled to Basing, some to Alton, and some to Winchester, and by the way they cried out, theKingdom's lost, the Kingdom's lost'.*

Waller's humiliation on Roundway Down had been fully avenged. Hopton, whose own horse had been shot in the shoulder during the sad minutes of withdrawal, describes the defeat in an almost journalistic style: '*and the enemy pressed in that part so hard (especially with their musket shot) that it was with great difficulty that we got off all our cannon; and making our rear as good as we could with some of the best of our horse and dragoons, we recovered our first ground upon the ridge of the hill by Alresford town, with all our army, cannon and carriages; from whence we showed so good a countenance towards the enemy, that they gave us some respite, unwilling (as it seemed) to hazard their whole army upon us*'

The two Royalist generals executed their withdrawal with far more skill than they had ever shown on the battlefield that day. Believing that Winchester was an '*indefensible ill provided place, and utterly unsafe for an army in that condition*', Hopton advised retirement to Basing and then ultimately to the greater security of Reading.

But Alresford, lying on the chosen route of escape to Basing, had to be secured first. Sir Ralph took personal command of the 1000 musketeers that stole into the town at sunset. Colonel Richard Feilding, commander of the artillery set off next, heading with the remaining 9 guns and the baggage initially towards Winchester, and then turning north to Basing. The bulk of the infantry left soon afterwards, protected by a tiny rearguard of 100 horse. Passing through Alresford, the regiments took the more direct and largely wooded route through Preston Candover.

Hopton and his musketeers followed at their heels, units of dejected men whose sense of purpose had been savagely dashed. Part of the town was torched as they departed in a desperate attempt to slow the enemy's pursuit. But none of the soldiers could be sadder than aged Lord Forth, remaining alone on the evening field with only his page for company until the last of the cavalry had set off across the Downs to Basing. Surveying the darkening field over which he had held command, he must have wondered how his King would receive the news. Then, only minutes before Parliamentary cavalry rode up the slope on which he stood, he turned his horse and rode away towards the north.

Reports of Cheriton probably reached London and Oxford simultaneously, garbled and unsubstantiated accounts in the first few hours supported later by the letters of those who had been present on the field. Sir William Balfour's letter to the Earl of Essex was one of the most authoritative; it was read aloud in both the Lords and Commons.

'... *It hath pleased Almighty God to grant us a great victory over our enemies, beyond all expectation, we having taken a resolution to be wary, and cautious to engage ourselves in a fight with the enemy but upon advantage... ......The enemy coming on towards us, were received with such dexterity and valour, that it pleased Almighty God to give us an unexpected and great victory, by beating both their horse and foot out of the heath before our quarters, and following the victory, not only to their quarters, but put them by Alresford, and followed them within 4 miles of Winchester; their whole body of foot which they have been so long a composing totally routed, and so broken, that Hopton cannot make up his foot army I am confident most part of this summer; their foot were so dispersed up and down through all the fields,*

---

15 Hampshire Magazine Vol.1X 1884

that they swear they will never serve again...'.[15]

The Committee of Both Kingdoms responded publicly in almost regal terms. '*We acknowledge the great goodness of God for so seasonable a mercy after the unhappy business at Newark. We are very sensible of the great advantage that will come to the kingdom by a careful and diligent improvement of this success against the enemy for the recovery of the west*'[16]. Several days of celebration followed and church bells rang throughout the capital.

Mercurius Aulicus, reliable supporter of the regal cause and eloquently caustic in its defence of the King's affairs, poured open scorn on Parliament's versions of events and offered their own instead: '*And the truth is, they are so full of Sir William Waller, that they have no leisure to hearken to ambassadors; whose late deliverance (for so Sir Arthur Heselrige called it to their faces) is blown up into an unparallel'd victory. Scaffolds were set up, and two men placed on them, who gaped half an hour, that the Lord Hopton was totally routed and overthrown, ten thousand of his men killed and taken, ALL his ordnance taken, ALL his arms, ALL his ammunition, ALL his baggage, ALL his commanders killed and taken, the execution followed nine miles, General Forth shot all to pieces, and the Lord Hopton escaped with only ten men to Reading. To all which we can say but this, that ALL these are most abominably false; and we dare the devil and all the Covenanters to show so much as one piece of ordnance, one colour, or one carriage of ammunition, arms or baggage that you gained in this service...... And whereas they triumph, that His Majesty had three Lords, and four Knights kill'd and taken, we can answer them, that we killed all their Lords and Knights but Sir Arthur, and the two Sir Williams; and left not one alive of all the Gentlemen of quality, but Sergeant Major General Browne the Faggot-man*'.

But whatever the version the propagandists wished to pursue, Cheriton had been a disaster for the Oxford cause, even Clarendon admitting that it '*broke all the measures, and altered the whole*

---

16 Hopton

scheme of the King's Counsels and....he now discerned he was wholly to be upon the defensive, and that was like to be a very hard part too'.[17]

Waller appeared at Winchester's gates on Saturday, 30th March, confident that Ogle and the mayor would grant him quiet possession of both castle and city, the former of which Waller still claimed by right of his wife's inheritance. Lord Hopton had left Winchester to its fate, retiring for one night to Basing before withdrawing to Reading. And few of the King's men within the city's walls considered that they could hold the place in the absence of Hopton's Royalist muscle.

Ogle had more private reasons for agreeing on an immediate surrender. He felt that Waller would be satisfied with the city as a prize and would leave Ogle at peace within the castle. The mayor and corporation consequently met Waller outside the gates, handing him the keys and freedom of the city in exchange for his protective hand and a promise of kindness towards their ancient castle. Ogle and about 100 men sat stubbornly within the castle while Sir William and his army camped in the cathedral precincts.

Parliament's general, however, felt that both castle and city should be his to command. Sending ambassadors to Ogle, he threatened to burn the Royalist lord's house at Stoke Charity and the city as well if he chose to keep the castle gates closed. The Cavalier merely retorted that the site of the fired city would make a spacious garden for the castle, *'upon which answer he (Waller) plundered five or six of the houses of the best affected citizens for the King, and marched out of the city at Kingsgate, and drew up his army in the meadow about a half mile from the city'*[18]. Waller was now convinced that clearing Hampshire of scattered Royalists was more important than occupation of its principal city.

Romsey had been abandoned by the Royalists in the days before Cheriton, its tiny garrison called into the field to augment Hopton's army of foot. But Andover, the town represented by Waller in the Commons, had been occupied by Colonel Neville's regiment

---

17 C.S.P.D. 1644 p83   18 'A True Relation of my Lord Ogle's Engagements' Add. MSS 27402 f.82

of horse, 300 men, and seemed in need of immediate salvation. Consequently Sir William Waller led his army towards the upper waters of the Test, determined to rescue his beloved town. He rested that night in Stockbridge, and from here he sent Sir William Balfour and a party of horse to drive the intruders out.

But the town was to be spared the anguish of a Springtime skirmish. Balfour's cavalry appeared near Wherwell, persuading most of the Royalists to hurry away in the direction of Newbury.

Waller ordered Balfour in pursuit. *'Monday, the 1st of April, our regiment, Sir Arthur's regiment of horse, and Sir William Waller's regiment of dragoons were commanded to fall on the enemy's quarters at Newbury'*, Harley writes in his account of the post-Cheriton days: '*A little before sun setting we began our march; half an hour before daylight we came before the town; Captain Fincher, having the disposal of the business, desired me to second him with my troop in charging first with the forlorn hope into town…Another way there was a small party which went before Captain Fincher's party……Not long it was before the other party of ours had entered the town and were come to this barricade, and then our fear was ended, we took some horses and about an hundred prisoners'.*

Almost as exhilarating, perhaps, as this action in Newbury was the capture of Lady Hopton outside the town. Residing in Winchester throughout her husband's recent campaign, she had chosen to leave when Waller arrived, accompanied by two coaches, one of which was full of her jewellery. Scouts carried word of her movement to Balfour at Andover and she and her escort was taken on the road, attempting, it seems, to join her husband who had now gone to Marlborough. Chivalry fortunately still ran through the veins of Englishmen despite the culture of the time. She was permitted to continue to Oxford with all her valuables and her retinue of maidservants.

Waller now set out to extend the frontiers of Hampshire's war, heading west through Salisbury to assist the Parliamentary effort in neighbouring Dorset. Balfour, marching from Andover on the 2nd, joined his commander at Wilton, leaving just 2 regiments of horse to contain the remaining Royalists still lingering near the Test. Splitting his forces as he crossed into Dorset, Waller sent a detachment of 1000 horse and dragoons over Cranborne Chase to challenge a Royalist contingent ensconced in Blandford while he personally dealt with the larger enemy units that operated from Christchurch and Weymouth.

The Cranborne force experienced almost no opposition, the Blandford Royalists melting away like snow in a warming wind. Near Ringwood, however, Waller was confronted by a force of Cavaliers that had hastily assembled to block the Parliamentary advance. Deftly, he swept them away and the path to Christchurch lay open.

Sir John Mills, the King's governor in Christchurch, had been injudicious in his support for Charles, drawing attention to his loyalties by loud utterances of praise when discretion might have been a better poise. Waller arrived outside Christchurch at the very moment when several of Dorset's most eminent Royalists were present in the town and so trawled a bigger net of Cavalier prisoners than he might have expected. Three hundred men surrendered and were taken into custody, amongst them 22 men of quality. *'Our governor advanced towards Poole to relieve it, and in the way have taken Christchurch, I hope not in name but in truth... '*, states the terse report penned in Ringwood on April 7th. The writer gives brief praise to an unnamed lady of the town, *'a valiant Lady Captain, which would have been sharp work, had all the rest had that magnanimous spirit she had, but God be thanked, this was without the loss of blood.'*.

Waller is even less informative, boasting only that he took the town *'without firing a shot'*, a claim contradicted by the surviving comments of those who might have fought on the other side that day. These speak of spirited resistance, first near the Portfield and the town's leper hospital, and then on the bridge at Iford, where local Cavaliers under Stephen Hooper of Hurn Court held the enemy for an hour or more, eventually surrendering in order to prevent likely damage to the Priory Church.

But this was to be the limit of Waller's advance. His supply lines from Farnham were in danger of being snapped by the Royalists in Basing, and an isolated Parliamentary army in Dorset would be a liability to Westminster. Waller, never a man to chase after objects that lay beyond his reach, pulled his army back to Farnham. On the 5th his troops reached Romsey, spoiling the abbey again during three evenings of mischievous fun.

Winchester lay temptingly near. Ogle's Royalists had recently disarmed the small Roundhead force left within the city despite Waller's looming shadow just nine miles away in Romsey and Stockbridge. Waller set out on Monday, April 8th, to resecure Winchester for the Parliament.

Roundhead spies within the city had also been at work. One, a Mr. Callaway, resident of the city, had been in regular communication with the Roundhead general himself, and a plan had been forged *'that whereas my Lord Ogle did quarter all his soldiers...in the city and there being a good space of ground betwixt the city and castle in which my Lord kept only three score soldiers, and the South gate opening betwixt the city and the castle, that if he could by pretence open the gate, then all my Lord's soldiers in the city would be cut off and he having so few of them in the castle, it must of necessity be taken'*.

Ogle discovered their intentions, possibly from the careless prattle of Mrs. Callaway. Dressing the defenders in new coats sent from Oxford and bribing them with promises of strong drink, he prepared to defend his charge. Waller, criticised by many for his earlier leniency to the castle's defenders, placed petards on Winchester's southern gate and blew it open.

Defending musketeers stood their ground, playing on the Parliamentary soldiers and prompting them into reprisals when the opportunity arose. Eventually taking full possession of the town, the Parliamentarians set fire to buildings and plundered without mercy, seizing women's clothing as well as the furniture of the rich. *'We lost one common soldier in taking the town'*, Harley pithily states, summing up in just two sentences a night of drama and distress. *'We took above a hundred horse and a hundred prisoners; we plundered the town and so returned to Romsey'*. Waller, despite his intentions to hold the town until the end of hostilities, had decided to withdraw again. And the castle still remained in Ogle's hands.

Parliament achieved more lasting success on the following day. In what was to be their last service in this campaign, Browne's Londoners, having remained near Southampton for a week after Cheriton in apparent refusal to travel with Waller to the west, marched through Botley towards Wickham to assist Southampton forces in besieging Waltham House, the Bishop of Winchester's Palace.

The siege lasted three stretched days, 200 Cavaliers inder one of Sir Humphrey Bennet's kinsmen initially holding the building against a Parliamentary force of similar numbers. General Browne's guns, however, tipped the balance, a day of bombardment shattering masonry and Royalist morale. On the 9th Bennet surrendered. His small force were permitted to *'pass away with their horses, and their swords by their sides, and the common soldiers only with a rod or staff in their hands'*. The palace suffered viciously in the aftermath, plundered as far as the rafters but with little of value found. The garrison, according to Mercurius Aulicus, were robbed of their clothes and their dignity, stripped almost naked and left only with their shirts. Bishop Curle, apparently resident in the palace throughout the siege, hid under some manure and escaped in a farmer's cart.

Odiham, too, was the scene of skirmishes. Occupied almost continuously by units of Parliamentary horse since the winter of the previous year, it was inevitably a target for the men of Basing, who searched for easy pickings and the chance for glory. On April 20th ten Parliamentary troopers, sent from Odiham to gather timber, were

Bishop's Waltham Palace

watched for an hour by Paulets's Cavaliers. In the shadows of a little copse, a fight took place and the collected timber was spilled along the road. Four days later, Odiham men took revenge, seizing sheep and cattle destined for Royalist larders. The forty accompanying soldiers were forced to serve as drovers. And, on May 7th, Waller was to be personally involved, leading men almost to the walls of Basing House itself, and taking a casket of money and bag of plate that lay poorly guarded in a carriage near the gate. Amongst those taken was the marquis's apothecary, a man well known in London in more peaceful times. Charged with Papism and probably much more, he was taken to Farnham Castle and *'there lodged in so noisome a hole... 'tis not conceivable how a man should breathe in it above two hours'* Petty scores and personal quarrels were being settled in a miniature war in Hampshire's secluded lanes and vaults.

Westminster reacted to news of Cheriton during that week. Orders went out to the four associated counties to raise additional soldiers for Waller's army: 500 dragoons, 1200 horse and 3000 foot, the troops to be paid and armed from fines on Papists and delinquents, and from a newly imposed tax on the common people of all four counties. Hampshire's contribution was set at over £680 weekly, a burdensome obligation on an innocent people. Sir William Waller was newly styled as Sergeant-Major-General of the Parliamentary army, and lesser honours were placed on his colonels' shoulders. The newly recruited were to be bound to the cause by the Solemn League and Covenant, a political and religious cement to which all fighting men were forced to subscribe. Parliament, dependent until now on an army of the politically indifferent, was trying to instil a contractual commitment to the cause.

The commitment of some of the existing forces, however, was now in doubt. The Londoners, despite service at Bishop's Waltham, had begun to disband, and a sum of £1000, hastily raised in London to purchase their continued service, failed to materialise in time. Heselrige himself visited London on April 1st to disentangle

'With a fair pair of heels'

Odiham

the web of confusion that held the money back, but it was to be another fortnight before the vital funds left the capital. Three fresh regiments of Londoners and a regiment of horse from Kent were mobilised during this period, while a strong message was sent to Browne and his disgruntled Londoners near Southampton that desertion at this time would *'not only prove very prejudicial to the public, by discouraging our own party, and encouraging the enemy, but dangerous to yourselves, to be cut off in their march, being without horse'*. To compound difficulties, Colonel Harvey, the designated commander of this new London brigade, refused to march south, professing a deep and personal animosity towards Waller and claiming that he *'would rather carry a musket under His Excellency* (the Earl of Essex) *than any charge under Waller'*. Sir James Harrington was appointed in his place, and the brigade set out.

Remonstrations were also made to Waller himself. Several eminent members of the House collectively attempted to dissuade Sir William from returning to Farnham as he now intended. *'It is evident your coming back gives the enemy encouragement and opportunity to recruit, and we hear Romsey is a place of security and great advantage, which the enemy is likely to be possessed of, if not prevented. It would lose the country lately gained, which will presently declare again for the other side, the enemy will recruit there, the counties on this side will receive great discouragement'.*

Waller ignored their warnings and retired to Farnham. Here he remained until early May, spending his time corresponding with the Houses on the subject of men and pay. A further ordinance on April 16th associated Hampshire with Berkshire and Wiltshire and so gave Waller further grounds for complaint. For now his troops were to police the Thames as well as the Test, and the flow of letters between Farnham and London increased.

Detailed reports of these enemy activities and the build up of forces at Farnham were interpreted by the King's circle as evidence of an intended Parliamentary push towards the west. A Royalist army assembled at Marlborough within days to block this anticipated

Report of the action at Cheriton

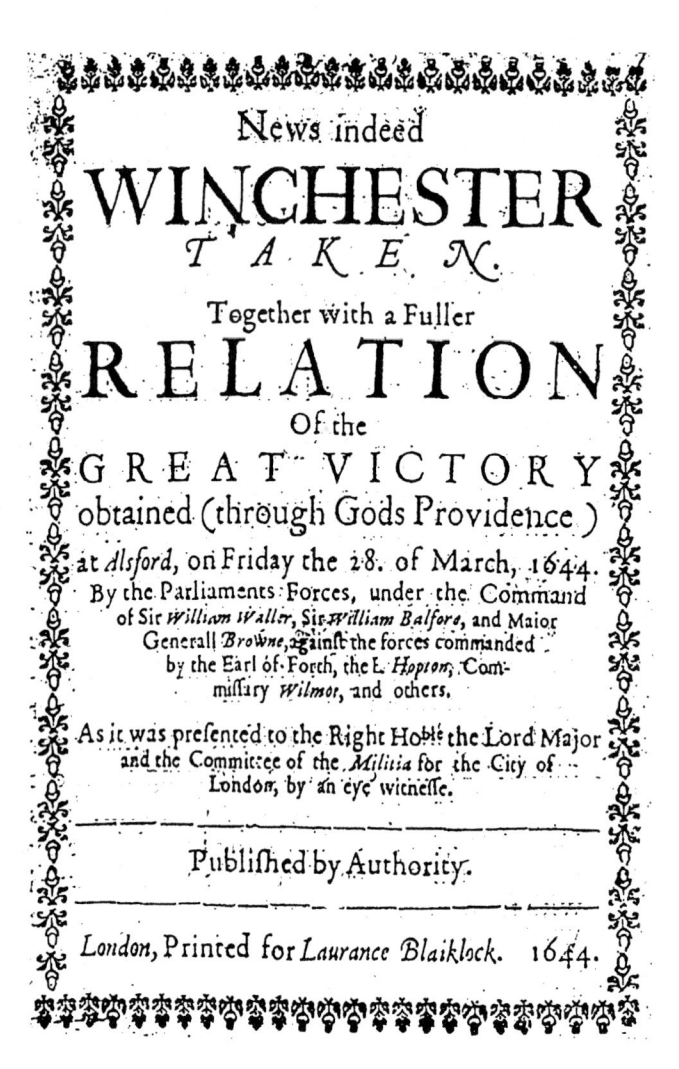

News indeed
WINCHESTER
TAKEN.
Together with a Fuller
RELATION
Of the
GREAT VICTORY
obtained (through Gods Providence)
at *Alsford*, on Friday the 28. of March, 1644.
By the Parliaments Forces, under the Command of Sir *William Waller*, Sir *William Balfore*, and Maior Generall *Browne*, against the forces commanded by the Earl of *Forth*, the L. *Hopton*, Commissary *Wilmot*, and others.

As it was presented to the Right Ho^{ble} the Lord Major and the Committee of the *Militia* for the City of London, by an eye witnesse.

Published by Authority.

London, Printed for *Laurance Blaiklock*. 1644.

move, days of activity in Wiltshire being justified by Parliamentary movements further east. Cheriton had neither terminated war in the south of England nor dashed the King's hopes for glory, despite what Clarendon chose to say.

Charles, less candid than Clarendon, frivolously dismissed the setback at Cheriton in a letter to Prince Rupert of the Rhine. Writing to his nephew immediately after the scale of defeat had been measured in Oxford, he says: '... *though the loss was very inconsiderable, except the loss of some few brave officers, 400 being the most in all, both of horse and foot, the rebels loss being certainly more......I hope in a few days to be able to venture on another blow, for my foot came off in good enough order, and now I hear that the appearance of horse is better than we expected*' [18].

With the sources of recruitment still open to both sides and neither prepared to consider the possibilities of defeat, partial destruction of armies on a field of battle might do little to halt this lengthening war. It would take defeats on a larger scale than Cheriton and the haemorrhaging of support to eventually bring Charles to his knees. Waller, Essex and Westminster had not yet found the means.

---

18 Warbuton E. 'Prince Rupert's Diary' Vol. II p285

15

'The blast blowing off his hat'

WALLER spent most of the next three weeks in Westminster, personally coaxing men and supplies from a reservoir that was in danger of running dry. For Parliament's two earls, Essex and Manchester, had been tapping it too, demanding powder, guns and men in an endless flow of letters. Politician and paymaster, working in tandem for the common good, sent money and powder to the Earl of Essex and letters of encouragement to Sir William Waller.

The South's Parliamentarians therefore took measures of their own. Colonel Norton raised additional horse and paid for the harness and weapons himself. Sir Arthur Heselrige was now governor of Southampton and it was probably he who instigated a sudden raid across the border into Royalist held Wiltshire. On May 10th, hearing that two troops of Prince Maurice's cavalry were carousing in Salisbury, he sent 120 of Southampton's horse to test the Cavaliers' will to fight.

At 3 a.m. on the 11th, guided by locals who knew where the visitors slept, the Parliamentary party attacked and scattered the handful of men who had been assigned to nocturnal duty. Forty or so other men, billeted in the homes of Royalist sympathisers, were either turned from their beds or sought safety in the night time streets. One, taking refuge in a loft, tried to fight off his assailants with a wooden crucifix and large pewter bowl. Heselrige's men returned to Southampton that night, taking the unfortunate man, bowl and crucifix with them as tangible trophies of the knockabout fight.

Royalism, in the late Spring of 1644, was like a serpent cowed by the snake charmer's music. Except in England's west, where Maurice was besieging Lyme and where the King's writ was still heard clearly in every town, Charles's cause had become vulnerable. In the north, the Scots pushed relentlessly on and the siege of York was about to begin. And the King's Oxford heartland, pulsating without hindrance through the war so far, was about to shrink, more in reaction to the possibility of sudden disaster than to any forceful Parliamentary aggression.

And it seemed that Royalist defeat was indeed possible. Two large Parliamentary armies were poised outside London; the entire Oxford heartland lay within easy reach. On May 15th Essex moved out from his Beaconsfield base, paralleled south of the Thames by Waller, who had been ordered by Westminster to assist in operations against the King's capital. Halting for the night at Bagshot to await the last of the promised reinforcements, Sir William rode over to Henley on the 17th to confer with the Earl of Essex. It seemed that at last the two Parliamentarians would operate with an uncharacteristic unity of purpose and the chance of a pincer movement against the King's capital emerged. Reading was evacuated the following day, abandoned by the Royalists in the fever of the moment, and the regal frontier began to recede. On the 25th, they abandoned Abingdon as well, causing even die hard Cavaliers to comment on what might soon occur: *'And now the rebels thought their game sure having without a blow got the possession of Reading, Abingdon, and so all of Berkshire'.*[1]

It seemed possible that Basing might also be included on the

---

[1] 'His Majesty's Happy Progress' by Sir Edward Walker

list of fallen garrisons. The core of Waller's army was still waiting at Bagshot on May 20th for the arrival of Colonel Ralph Weldon's Kentish regiment and the even slower moving units from London. With smaller detachments stationed at Odiham, Greywell, Alton and Basingstoke, the Parliamentary hold on central Hampshire seemed beyond any doubt ; only the continued presence of the Royalists in Basing threatened this one sided dominance. And with little else to do until the expected forces arrived, a lightening strike at the Paulet home was a sensible proposition.

Waller had never had a better chance. A plot had been hatched within Basing's walls to deliver the house. Lord Edward Paulet, brother of the marquis, *'as unsuspected as a brother ought to be'* had been in secret correspondence with Waller for some time, sending letters at night and asking only for *'favoured treatment and the forgiveness of the Houses assembled'*. Sir William Waller, mindful of his orders to campaign on the Thames, sent Sir Richard Granville, his new commander of horse and just one regiment, to negotiate the terms of surrender.

Sir Richard was to be one of the war's black traitors. Setting out from London with his new commission, he left the Basing road near Staines and headed instead to Oxford to seek audience with his true master and tell the tale of Edward Paulet's treachery. On hearing the dreadful reports, the Marquis forced his brother to serve as executioner of all those involved in the plot, and the name of Edward has been one of shame to the family ever since.

Perhaps this near gain of Basing and evidence of discord within the garrison caused Waller to personally visit Basing on his way to the Thames. On the 21st the London regiments, untested in military action, were sent from Bramley to invest the house and so gain direct experience of war. *'They welcomes us with 2 or 3 pieces of ordnance and hung out three or four colours;'* one of the soldiers recounts. *'The ordnance did no hurt, only scared our under marshal; the blast blowing off his hat, our horse went round, faced the house; the defenders charged upon them, slew two horse and one man of* ours; we saw two men of theirs fall on the breastwork, but no more to our view. There we lay until evening and it not being thought convenient to lay siege to the house, we marched round the park to Basingstoke'.[2] Three days later, the entire Parliamentary army, with the London bands still unbloodied, marched out of Hampshire into Oxfordshire in accordance with the instructions received from Westminster. With their disappearance, Hampshire's war was to become a purely local struggle, county men pitted against their neighbours and with Basing largely at the focus.

The Marquis of Winchester struck first, buoyed by news of his adversary's departure. Aware that Parliament's hand on Odiham was weak, the peer and Rawdon, the *'decayed merchant of London'*, hatched a plan to take the town. All the able bodied of the garrison, 80 horsemen and 200 foot, were to participate, each to be paid five shillings in advance for his efforts and with personal instructions to *'fire the town of Odiham and put all to the sword'*.

At 11 p.m. on the 31st May, the party set out, guided by two local men who knew the way, one *'with a dark lantern and the other with torches to fire the town'*. But their intentions were already known in Farnham, the details carried to Colonel Samuel Jones by a Basing traitor who had listened in the shadows outside an upstairs room. The Parliamentary commander instantly sent 200 men galloping through the night towards the town and placed sentries on the road to Basing.

In a little lane above the mill at Warnborough the two sides clashed, in the total blackness of early morning. Alerted by the sound of hooves in the shallow waters of the Whitewater ford, a Roundhead sentry fired his musket and called out a warning to the cavalry that waited at his rear.

It is difficult to unravel the threads of the nocturnal melee, and reports are as confused as the fighting itself. Perhaps 100 Parliamentarian horse barred the Royalists' way, peering into the darkness in an attempt to identify their foe. Carbines were fired

---

2 ' a True Relation of the Progress of the London Auxiliaries since their joining with Sir William Waller'

hopefully as though night itself were the enemy. Then a further volley, a pause, and the night fired back, tongues of sudden light just twenty paces away. The warmth of horses' breath, the smell of leather, and Royalist swords were swinging savagely in search of Roundhead skulls.

But unfriendly night was a protector too; the small band of Roundhead horse, the Watch of Horse, pulled back unseen and only one man was felled. The Royalist horse rode on, scattering the line of foot that had been posted just outside the town. Ahead lay frightened Odiham and hours of probable pillaging.

Yet Parliament's resources had not been fully tested. Colonel Norton and some of his horse were in the little town - and so, it seems, was Jones and the Odiham infantry. *'Colonel Norton, in all this losing no time, had by this got most part of his horse and drew them into the field, leaving the rest for the town and, marching close to the enemy, very furiously fell upon them with great valour, which caused the enemy presently to retreat'.*[3] Nothing but raw courage could have fuelled this charge into uncertainty, where an enemy several times their number might have been waiting with unsheathed swords and carbines ready. But Colonel Jones was near at hand. Hurrying to Norton's assistance, he *'fell on this front with his foot, the horse came on in the rear, at which the enemy's horse fled, and all the foot with their arms were taken, and the horse pursued almost to Basing House'.* Amongst the six officers taken was a London mercer, but dressed *'more like a tinker than a gentleman',* he was allowed to leave. Perhaps ninety common soldiers were also taken, *'whereof some of them are such as have formerly run from the Parliamentary service, and are likely to receive their just reward'.*[4]

Twelve hours later, Colonel Norton led his men against Basing, summoning the Marquis by trumpet. The peer, with a garrison of less than 200 men after his setback of the previous night, chose to ignore the call and not a man appeared on the parapet

---

[3] 'A Great victory obtained by Col. Norton against Col. Rowden... near Walnborough Mill' Hants. Record Office

[4] 'A Great victory obtained... near Walnborough Mill

'THE BLAST BLOWING OFF HIS HAT'

Report concerning fighting at Warnborough

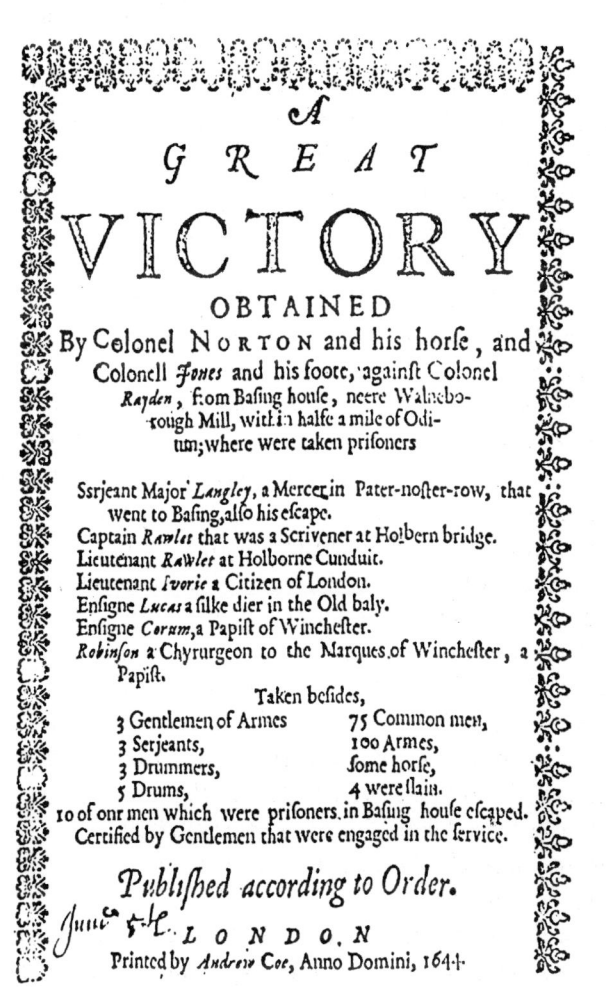

A
GREAT
VICTORY
OBTAINED

By Colonel NORTON and his horse, and Colonell *Jones* and his foote, against Colonel *Rayden*, from Basing house, neere Walnebo-rough Mill, within halfe a mile of Odi-tum; where were taken prisoners

Ssrjeant Major *Langley*, a Mercer in Pater-noster-row, that went to Basing, also his escape.
Captain *Rawlet* that was a Scrivener at Holbern bridge.
Lieutenant *Rawlet* at Holborne Cunduit.
Lieutenant *Ivorie* a Citizen of London.
Ensigne *Lucas* a silke dier in the Old baly.
Ensigne *Corum*, a Papist of Winchester.
Robinson a Chyrurgeon to the Marques of Winchester, a Papist.

Taken besides,
3 Gentlemen of Armes   75 Common men,
3 Serjeants,   100 Armes,
3 Drummers,   some horse,
5 Drums,   4 were slain.
10 of our men which were prisoners in Basing house escaped.
Certified by Gentlemen that were engaged in the service.

Published according to Order.

June 5th. LONDON
Printed by *Andrew Coe*, Anno Domini, 1644.

walls.

Parliament, however, would soon arrive in force; Norton's men of Hampshire were merely the skeletal outline on which Roundhead flesh would form. Richard Onslow, colonel of the Surrey regiment, was already on his way with five companies of foot. Samuel Jones, responsible for holding Farnham and Odiham in Waller's absence, supplied two companies of his greencoats for service at Basing and positioned three in Odiham as a garrison. Herbert Morley, a Sussex M.P., was soon to be present with six companies of his Sussex bluecoats. All were present outside Basing by June 11th, 2000 men according to the diary of the coming siege.

Norton now took overall command in Hampshire's little war, calling the tune to which the Cavaliers in Basing would be forced to dance. His cavalry took possession of the park to the south of the house, stopping supplies from reaching the ancient building and attempting to fence the garrison in. The Royalists were to be deprived of their sleep throughout this week, the opening days of a possibly long siege. For Norton, convinced that an assault would achieve nothing but bloodshed, had already decided to try to starve the defenders into surrender.

Alarmed by the enemy presence within his park and angered by their taunts, the Marquis re-organised the watch and allocated the duties of defence. The remaining garrison was split into three, fifty men or so per group with a captain or above in charge of each. Two groups were to be always on watch, 48 hours or more at a time, the south face towards the park being the area of greatest concern. Major Langley, the tinker mercer taken at Odiham, took charge of the house's north front where much of the earlier fighting had taken place. Only Colonel Rawdon was *'excused duty by reason of his years'*.

Parliament's nearby force spread out that evening, some taking up their quarters in the ruins of the ancient priory at Andwell, some in Sherfield and the bulk in Basingstoke. For two whole days, the 12th and 13th, they were hardly seen at Basing, but the watchers on

'The blast blowing off his hat'

Report on Norton's Siege

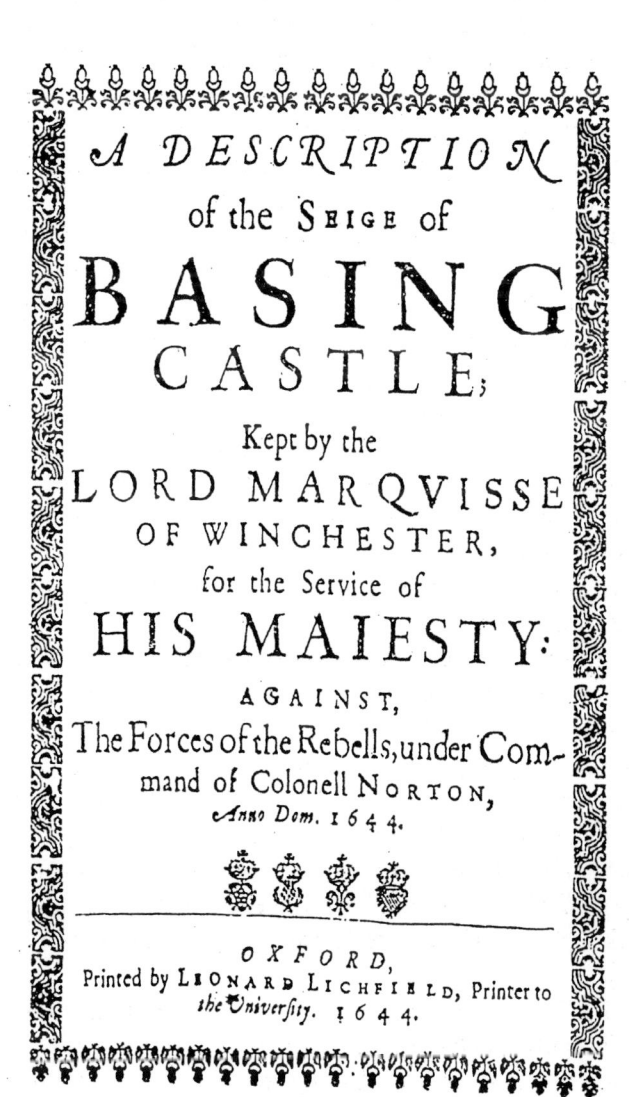

A DESCRIPTION
of the SEIGE of
BASING
CASTLE;
Kept by the
LORD MARQVISSE
OF WINCHESTER,
for the Service of
HIS MAIESTY:
AGAINST,
The Forces of the Rebells, under Command of Colonell NORTON,
Anno Dom. 1644.

OXFORD,
Printed by LEONARD LICHFIELD, Printer to
the *University.* 1644.

the house's walls were never allowed to relax their vigil. Yet survival depended on sustenance and fresh numbers as well as careful vigilance -sorties of the garrison consequently became necessary. Small bands of men hurried out at night, avoiding the park where Parliament's sentinels were probably keeping watch. Periodically a press gang went out, descending on nearby villages to force the sons of farmers into the service of the king. On the 15th, a larger party rode towards Reading to round up unwilling recruits and force contributions from the yeomen of northern Hampshire. Norton and Morley, still stationed at Basingstoke as though unwilling to develop the siege, heard of these Royalist activities and promptly set out with a mixed force of horse and musketeers to cut the enemy's line of retreat.

They arrived too late; the Cavaliers had ridden past and were a mile ahead, possibly with some new recruits in their ranks. The Parliamentarians gave chase and caught them at the broken bridge over the Loddon, almost at the gates of Basing itself. The prey chose not to fight, preferring instead to negotiate the muddy banks of the river and the water itself rather than cross swords with the enemy.

Days of rain had softened the mud and the earthen banks, trapping several horses before they reached the water. Fifty or so muddy Cavaliers eventually reached the safety of the house, but the abandoned beasts were left neighing pitifully on the far bank.

Norton departed that evening to deal with a shadowy Royalist presence in Andover, leaving Onslow and his regiment of horse to help the Parliamentary foot to contain the Marquis's over-active garrison. In Richard's absence, the skirmishing continued, mainly in the fields and lanes around the great house whenever a Royalist detachment tried to sally out to obtain supplies.

'*They have agreed amongst themselves to maintain forces to keep in those thieves and robbers*', the Kingdom's Weekly Intelligencer claimed, hinting at the mischief caused in past weeks by the predators of Basing House. '*This service will be of great advantage, for there is nothing to hinder the trade of the clothiers*

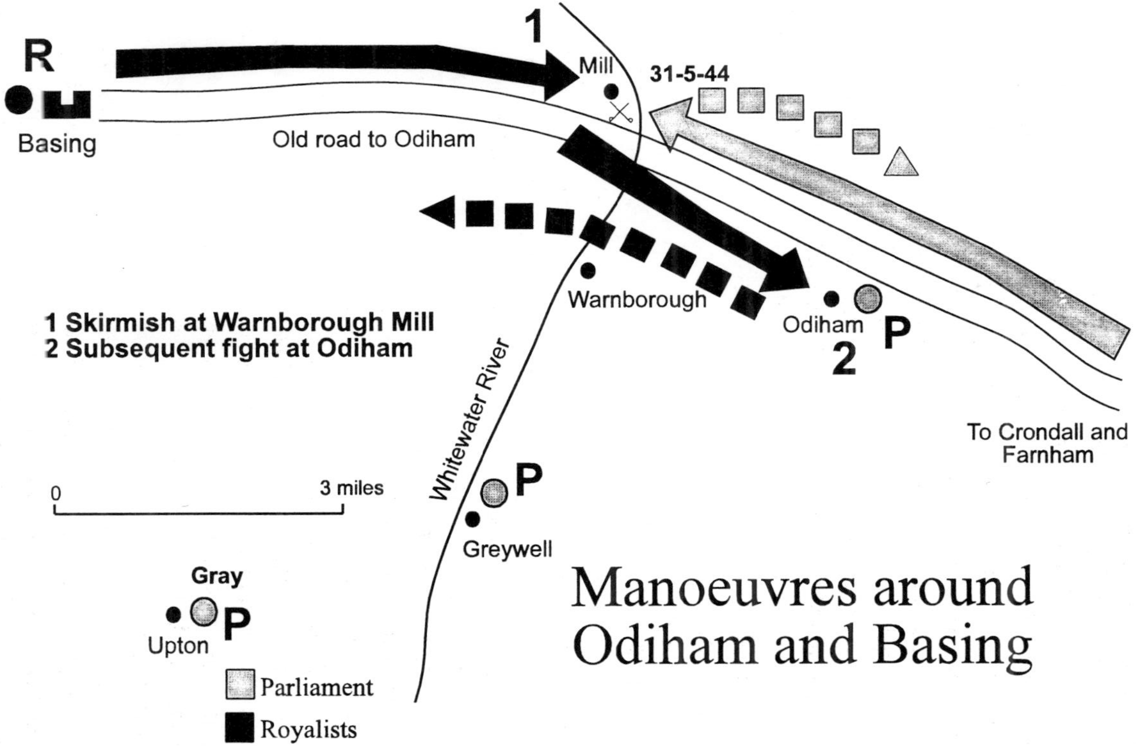

Manoeuvres around Odiham and Basing

1 Skirmish at Warnborough Mill
2 Subsequent fight at Odiham

Basing
Old road to Odiham
Mill
31-5-44
Warnborough
Odiham
To Crondall and Farnham
Whitewater River
Greywell
Upton
Gray

0 — 3 miles

Parliament
Royalists

of Wiltshire to London except that garrison'.

Robbing the innocent in homes or on highways was now an accepted rule of war. Travellers and villagers were like defenceless worms in a freshly ploughed field where hungry birds were gathering for a meal. Armies on the march and the garrisons of both sides - all would prey on those who had so little to give. Even richer pickings were to be gained from the nation's merchants, the men who trundled the highroads, their carts and packhorses piled high with their wares. From Trowbridge and Bath, from Andover and Salisbury they journeyed, attracted to the markets in London, a metropolis of insatiable needs and changing tastes. And the road to the capital lay close to Basing and Farnham's walls. As war became more intense and sentiments became more bitter, the road east grew as hazardous as the spice route to China.

Yet still they journeyed, bribing garrison commanders along the way to grant them free passage. Tales of mistreatment abound. Sir John Boys, Royalist governor of Donnington Castle near Newbury, was amongst the most notorious of these unprincipled highwaymen and his catalogue of crimes is more shocking than any committed by the men of Basing. In one well-quoted incident, Andover merchants asked the Marquis of Winchester to be allowed to sell tableware in London, promising to pay him fifty pounds on their return. The party, however, was intercepted near Newbury by Donnington's Royalists and ordered to pay a substantial fine. Faced by ruin, the victims borrowed money from friends in Marlow in order to pay the fine and then continued their journey to London. Hours later they were stopped again, this time by men from Reading. Unable to meet this new demand, the merchants and their baggage were held in custody, and the tradesmen only gained their freedom by parting with their wares at a tenth of the likely London price.

But the Cavaliers were not alone in engaging in these acts of terrestrial piracy. Parliament, too, needed provisions for sustenance; reports of Roundhead robbery on the roadside are plentiful. The contents of local barns were seized and little compensation was

2nd Attack on Basing House

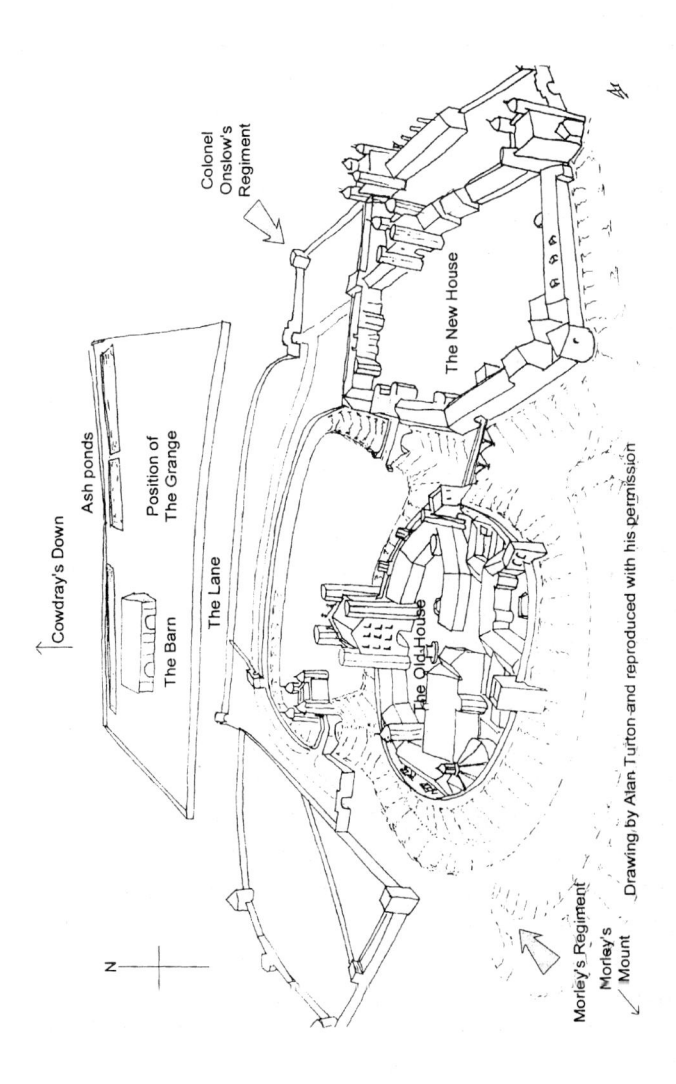

ever offered to the owners. Enough hay for 200 horses was taken from a farmer near Odiham in May 1644; the poor man received only twenty shillings for his crop with a vague promise of more to come. Near-theft of this kind was justified by the perverse reasoning of a society contaminated by war. Theft without compensation would be made equally excusable: the removal of produce by one side would prevent it from falling into the hands of the enemy, the less righteous, and the owner would still be dispossessed. *'Colonel Norton......seized on many cattle and much corn, which the Marquis of Winchester, a grand Papist, but nevertheless one whom His Majesty employs for the good of the Protestant religion, had provided to be sent to him at the garrison of Basing House, but it will now be better employed'.*[6] A letter states in an obvious attempt to legitimise such deeds.

On the 17th, Norton returned to take command of the investors of Basing House. Under his orders breastworks were constructed on Cowdray's Down and in the park; the line of trees upon which the peer and his wife had gazed in times of peace were felled to supply the wood. Parliamentary infantry took possession of the neighbouring houses, '*all of which lay within musket shot of Basing House'*. Coffins in the Paulet family vaults within the church were stripped of their lead or forced open for entertainment. For the second time in a year, the inhabitants of this unremarkable village were to find unwelcome strangers billeted in their lofts and soldiers drilling in their street.

The garrison now had an additional reason to sortie from the houses. Anxious to prevent the enemy from lodging too close, the Marquis's men slipped out at night on the 19th to burn the infested buildings and force the squatters out. '*..we fired all between us and the church, themselves at same time firing some beyond, by which their works grown hot some fly into the hedges, others further off'*, the Diary of the siege recounts. The Parliamentarians, forced to

---

6 Moderate Intelligencer

abandon the church when the flames and smoke engulfed them, first rang the bells as a call for assistance. Musketeers and horsemen descended from Cowdray's Down and eventually sent the Royalists home.

Norton's resourcefulness had at last run dry. In letters to London he appealed for money and weapons, supposing that an abundance of arms would magically force open the gates of Basing House and bring Lord Winchester to his knees. Letters of encouragement and gratitude came back in response, penned mainly by John Lisle, Winchester's politically active M.P., and a supply of saddles, swords and muskets arrived too.

The diary boasts of Royalist achievements and heroic actions, of tiny groups of well placed Cavaliers concealed in hedges, of sudden ambuscades on Basing's roads and of ever closer investment by Parliament's forces. Two companies of Portsmouth men joined the besiegers on the 24th and, *'resolving now more straitly to begirt us, ...the Regiment of Blue (*Morley's Sussex men*) is drawn into the park, and Colonel Onslow's to the lane (on Morley's right) and close towards Basingstoke, where having fixed their quarters they presently break ground, shutting us up on three sides with their foot, and on the other side their guards of horse keeping on Cowdray's Down'.* Waller's eroded earthworks were repaired and a line of trenches began to snake across the park in evident determination to uphold the siege. At night campfires flickered in the park and stretched northwards on to the heights of Cowdray's Down.

But Norton had left again, called to the midlands by Sir William Waller. *'Norton himself is gone to Sir William'*, Mercurius Aulicus reports derisively, *'and left the work to others, thinking it ill manners to attempt that for which his general was so handsomely basted, who found it as difficult to enter Basing as to get into his Worship's own castle at Winchester'.* This culinary term seemed appropriate to describe Parliament's earlier discomfort; the House was frequently referred to as 'Basting House' in future. In Norton's absence, Colonel Morley took charge with Onslow's horsemen serving as his more mobile arm.

As the Parliamentary pressure increased, the persistence of the besiegers grew, a fact recognised by the diarist in his entry of the 29th. *'Their work in the park is brought to some perfection, and by noon their cannon baskets placed made known they had a culverin there, giving us six shot thence. Next day being Sunday (their cause allows not now for Sabbath) doubling their diligence throughout the leaguer, forwarding the sconce at Morley's quarters in the park, and on the town-side towards a mill, drawing a line from the church. At Onslow's quarter raising a platform in the lane with so much speed that the next morning a demi-culverin plays from it'.*

Waller was to lose his guns, standards and reputation that very day in an action in Oxfordshire that should never have been fought. Royalism's capital had been threatened by Essex's and Waller's harmonised move along the Thames that had begun in earnest during the last week in May. The Earl's army had camped on Bullingdon Green on the night of the 29th just beyond the city's precincts; King Charles himself viewed the enemy's arrival from the tower of Magdalene College. But the Lord General of Parliament's forces made no direct assault on the city, preferring to cross the Cherwell at Islip and savage Oxford from further north. Waller, advancing from newly acquired Abingdon, had crossed the Thames on June 1st, only ten miles from where the Roundhead peer had pitched his camp. Pressured from both north and south, Royalism in Oxford seemed in danger of extinction.

But sustained co-operation between Essex and Waller was a concept which could exist only in frenzied Royalist minds. The personal quarrels had begun again, revealed in a two way flow of letters and in bouts of petty bickering that soon began to wreck their shallow rooted unity of purpose.

Westminster was to be responsible for the final break,

curiously ordering Waller to march to relieve Lyme in Dorset at the very moment when the pincer around Oxford seemed about to close. Yet it was to be Lord Essex who was the first to react, jealously insisting that Waller remain in the Midlands to tease the King while he, as the more senior of the two, took command of operations on the Dorset coast. *'Pardon me, if I make bold to order and direct my own Major-General for in truth, I do not see how Sir William Waller can take care of all the counties along the seaside from Dover to St. Michael's Mount. If you think fit... make him general and me the major-general of some brigade'* [7], he complained in a caustic letter to the Committee of Both Kingdoms to justify on strategic grounds his decision to override their orders. On 14th June 1644 he reached Blandford Forum in Dorset, ignoring all requests from Westminster to comply with their executive order.

And so Waller, left alone with an army outclassed by the King, suffered discomfort on the 29th June at Cropredy Bridge, an indecisive action perhaps, but one which again tipped the south midlands balance in the King's favour. Among the two hundred captives taken by the Royalists that day was Colonel James Wemys, Lieutenant-General of Waller's ordnance, a man who had been at Sir William's side throughout the recent campaigns in the south. *'Guid faith'*, declared the Scotsman on his knees before the King, *'My heart was always with your Majesty'*.

Waller's Army Summer 1644

Horse: Sir William Waller's Regt. (9 troops)
            Sir Arthur Heselrige's Regt. (8 troops)
            Jonas Vandruske's Regt. (6 troops)
            Richard Norton's Regt. (5 troops)
            Edward Cooke's Regt. (5 troops)
            Sir Michael Livesey's Regt. (5 troops)
            George Thompson's Regt. (4 troops)

Foot: Sir William Waller's Regt.

---

7 Lords Journals

Sir Arthur Heselrige's Regt.
Andrew Potley's Regt.
Ralph Weldon's Regt.
Tower Hamlets Regt.
Southwark Auxiliaries
Westminster Auxiliaries

News of the setback reached Basing on July 1st, carried by messenger from Oxford under cover of darkness. *'We echo it to our neighbours with volleys both of small and great'*, the diary euphorically records. *'They answering with their guns, battering our kitchen and gatehouse till a shot from our platform spoiling their carriage, silenced their demi-culverin'*.

Reports of Cropredy Bridge were not as well received by Parliament's agents in the south, and the tremors of concern passed over to the Isle of Wight. Partly prompted by the news, the island's Parliamentarians formed a Committee of Safety in July, granting this body powers to defend the island and to receive *'complaints or information against any minister whatsoever -officiating within the said island who is infamous or scandalous in life or doctrine'*.[8]

The Committee of Safety for the Isle of Wight July 1644

Captain Baxter	Sir John Leigh
Thomas Bowerman	John Lisle
William Bowerman	Sir William Lisle
Joseph Bulkeley	William Maynard
John Button	Matthews
Col. Thomas Carne	Bartholomew Meux
Edward Cheke	Sir Gregory Norton
Joseph Hobson	Thomas Wavell
	Sir Henry Worsley

Oglander was unimpressed, regarding the body as yet another sign of growing Parliamentary authoritarianism: *'We had a thing here called a committee which overruled Deputy Lieutenants*

---

8 'The Commonplace Book of Sir John Oglander Part 11 p.110

and also Justices of the Peace ... These ruled the Island and did whatsoever they thought good in their own eyes'. [9]

Less than 72 hours later after reports of Cropredy Bridge had reached the nation's furthest corners, Parliament's disgrace was lifted by news of victory on July 2nd 1644 at Marston Moor, the battle in which the King's northern army was wiped out. Cavalier reputations were destroyed that day. With Charles and Rupert were more than 21,000 men and the cream of the Royalist high command. Stretched out along a two mile front to the south of York, the King's army had seemed invincible, almost God-sent in the golden light of the summer evening. Yet five hours later, it lay dashed to pieces and several generals were amongst the fugitives. *'The runaways... were so many, so breathless, so speechless, and so full of fears that I should not have taken them for men',* states one of the Royalist officers. The 'immortals' of the Cavalier army, the Marquis of Newcastle's legendary Whitecoats, were the last to crumble, fighting on with pike and musket until just thirty men remained. The peer, who had expended so much energy in the service of his monarch, lost heart completely. Not prepared to endure the *'laughter of the court',* he abandoned the cause and took ship for the Continent.

In the battle's wake, the King's northern garrisons began to capitulate and soon active Royalism in the north of England was all but extinguished. Parliament and its Scottish allies, unlike Essex and Waller, had worked in tandem to secure that victory, and the combined weight of the victors could now move south to exploit their northern success.

The taking of Basing was a necessary ingredient of that searched-for victory. On July 10th, the Commons ordered the prompt delivery of 500 more muskets to Basing's besiegers; the Hampshire siege was suddenly elevated to a status of national importance.

Morley never faltered in his efforts to take the house or to snatch full advantage of what man and nature had provided. The Farnham and Southampton contingents held the church and nearby

---

9 Op, Cit. p.111

cottages, playing dice in the pews and defecating and cooking in the grounds. Yellow stains, still discernible today, on the building's inner and outer walls might be permanent marks of this period of disrespect. Morley's own regiment manned the park, careless in their daytime movements and frequently leaving the cover of their works to shoot rabbits for their evening cook pots. Onslow occupied the rest of the besieging line, responsible for guarding the road to Basingstoke. Frequently exposed to attack from the house and denied the protection of Parliamentary cavalry on Cowdray's Down by the river which lay in between, Onslow's men were cruelly treated.

Reports of Cropredy and Marston Moor had little effects on moods or resolutions, besieged and besieger acting out their tiny war with little regard for the wider struggle. Sometimes Parliament bombarded heavily, punishing the defenders for some earlier bout of aggression or purely as a form of entertainment for the men. *'They spoil us two or three a day, burning within our works'*, the diary reports on July 3rd. *'They now renew their battery on the house unto the detriment and topping of our towers and chimneys'*. And the poor marquis received a cannon ball in his room that morning, forcing him to leap from his bed and run *'into another room without his breeches, crying out that he wondered how the Roundheads could find him out, for he thought he had been safe in bed'*.

The culverin in the park was probably responsible for the man's embarrassment. Standing on Morley's Mount, a platform specially built in the park, the gun with its 5½ inch bore and 18 pound shots played almost continuously now. Another gun, a demi-culverin, was mounted in the lane, and the earthworks continued to grow. *'We are intrenched within pistol shot of the house, so that none can enter in or out'*, a letter to Westminster states. *'Since our throwing up a trench against them the enemy are very still, which before were lavish in their powder, though to little purpose'*.[10]

Aware that Norton was about to return, Morley sought to gain the glory that his superior might otherwise win. Reinforced on

---

10 Weekly Account news sheet

11th July by the arrival of another 140 Southampton men, he sent a demand for surrender. ' *To avoid the effusion of Christian blood, I have thought fit to send your Lordship this summons to demand Basing House to be delivered to me for the use of King and Parliament; if this be refused, the ensuing inconvenience will rest upon yourself'* [11].

But the peer's dignity only had been dented by the projectile in his bedchamber and his determination to resist remained unimpaired. His answer was characteristically terse, tossed back at the Parliamentarian after only a moment's deliberation. *'It is a crooked demand and shall receive its answer suitable. I keep the house in the right of my sovereign, and will do it in spite of your forces; your letter I will present as a testimony of your rebellion'*. [12]

Nothing therefore changed; the siege continued as before - day after day of bombardment, yelled insults and frantic sorties. Sentries and soldiers were shot dead during brief fights in Basing's leaf framed lanes, and the walls of village houses were pocked with musket balls. Men must have questioned the reasons, musing upon the circumstances that had placed them there. Within the house, a shortage of salt, flour and beer tapped the defenders' morale more effectively than any noisy aggression by the enemy outside. Lord Winchester's yellowing fields of corn around the house were being harvested by their new occupants and the crops used to make bread to fill the stomachs of Morley and his men. Reports to London speculated almost wistfully on the amount of likely suffering within the house: '...*the besieged say that they have plenty of meat, but so tainted by reason of the weather and for want of salt and seasoning, that it is very infectious, and many of them have died lately through the extremity of the disease it has bred'*. [13] Rotting meat was thrown from the windows. Evil smelling and ridden with flies, its sudden arrival near the Roundhead lines probably helped to drive the besiegers back.

Winchester Castle, the only other notable nest of Royalism

---

11 Siege Diary   12 op.cit   13 Parliamentary Scout

within Hampshire, was spared any form of siege at this time. Parliament's soldiers periodically appeared near the city's walls or stopped the flow of commerce towards the gates. *'The enemy often faces Winchester Castle, and are still repulsed'*, Mercurius Britannicus smugly reported in a summer issue. Lack of manpower, rather than the castle's impregnability was responsible for this lack of Roundhead success. Three thousand men now stood in arms around Basing's walls and only small mobile units of horse could be released to taunt Ogle's tiny force. The Committee for Hampshire received orders from London to raise yet more foot and horse, a tall demand for a small group of amateur politicians in a county grown weary of war and with so little money hanging at their belts with which to pay any additional troops.

Consequently Sir William Ogle and his supporters could become far more adventurous, issuing from the castle to show the King's colours in a countryside that wished to be left in peace. Stories of rape and murder are carried by Parliament's press, all reported to have occurred within just a few miles of Winchester's walls. Carrying a sword erect on which a woman's petticoat hung, Royalist forces were said to have ridden through Hursley and King's Somborne, emptying barns and poultry houses, and slashing the neck of a miller who tried to intervene.

On July 18th, on the very day that the Hampshire committee arrived at Basingstoke to view for themselves the siege arrangements around Loyalty House, Ogle's horsemen, 50 strong, rode into Andover in an attempt to re-arouse Royalist passions in the breasts of the town's inhabitants. A convoy of cloth and cheese destined for London homes unfortunately lay close at hand, far too tempting and vulnerable a target for men with an insatiable taste for plunder. Goods, oxen and carts were soon within Winchester castle's walls; their eventual sale would raise much needed funds for Charles and his slowly fading cause at Oxford.

The Committee of Both Kingdoms, alarmed at Ogle's continuing raids, wrote to Sir William Waller to request the return

Map of Alton

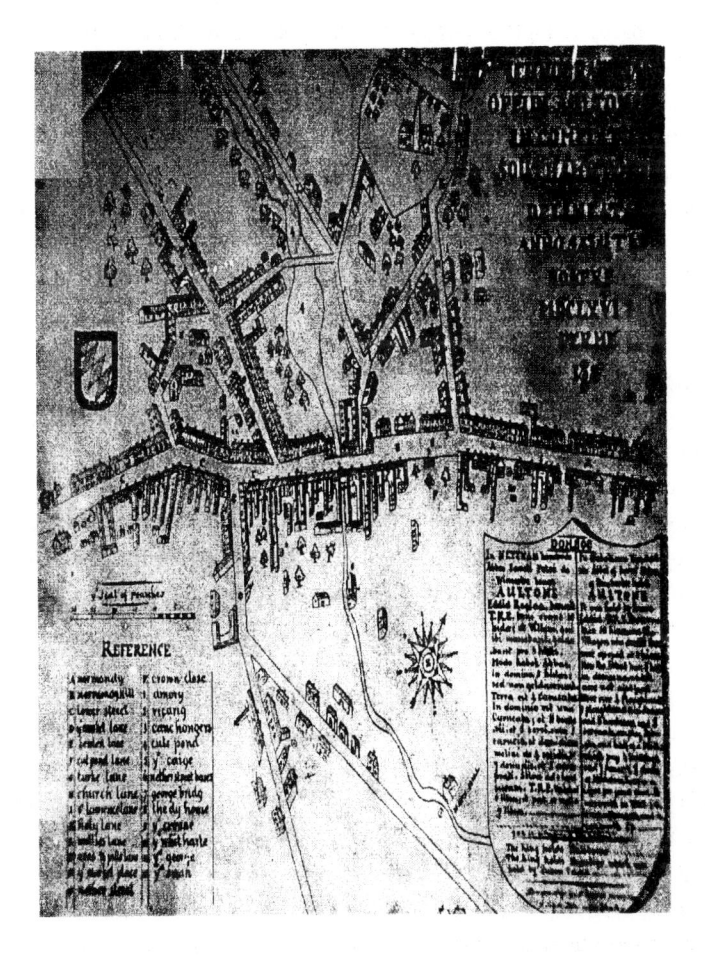

Reproduced with the kind permission of the Hampshire museum service

of Colonel Norton, the "great incendiary", from service in the Midlands to counter the Royalist's threat in Hampshire. *"Since the coming away of Colonel's Norton's regiment from Basing.....there has been a great loss of cloth in that county.....the county press for the return of this (Colonel Norton's) horse and urge the promise of this committee that they should return when the Associated counties were come in".*[14]

Colonel Norton consequently returned with all but two of his troops of horse. Informed about Ogle's harassment of the Hampshire countryside, Westminster reinforced the garrison of Portsmouth and sent 'Idle Dick' with his cavalry to the Winchester Downs. Southampton and Portsmouth men were to be added to this fluid force. Rarely meeting and seldom fighting, the two sides pursued each other's shadows throughout the rest of the summer, while Hampshire folk attempted to live their daily lives as though war were a phenomenon to be found only in more distant parts of England.

Ogle and the Marquis were in regular communication despite Norton's policing efforts. Royalist messengers wearing orange scarves passed as Parliament's men and travelled the roads almost unchallenged. One rider reached Basing with thimbles and thread for the ladies and candles for the night-time tables. Messengers from the besieged house rode just as easily to Oxford, carrying tales to the King of near-despair and the onset of disease. Edward Jeffreys, a servant of the Marquis, made the journey eight times at night with a crucifix in his hand, his horse's hooves covered in rags to muffle the sound.

Parliamentary prisoners, gathered during the garrison's sorties, also chose the cover of night to make their escapes. Eight broke out one night from the house, passing over two walls and through a garden gate to rejoin the besieging force. Later escapees found the passage even easier, and it is probable that Lord Paulet, concerned about the number of mouths to feed, deliberately relaxed his guard.

---

14 C.S.P.D. 1644 p.300

Morley and his officers had planned an assault that week, the penultimate week of July, jettisoning their strategy of gradual suffocation in favour of a weighted rush against the now fractured walls. 3000 men, armed with ladders and with the prayers of army chaplains to help them on their way, must inevitably break the stone defences and the will of the defenders to hold the fortress for the King. Two men with some knowledge of the plans, however, were taken captive and chose to tell their Royalist captors the details of what they knew. Cavalier vigilance was increased and Roundhead plans to storm the house were laid to rest under the soil and timber of the expanding earthworks.

Two mortars had now been brought into the park. Weapons of psychological warfare as much as agents of mass destruction, these could fire huge grenades that exploded on impact, damaging or destroying everything in the vicinity, more terrifying and deadly than a cannon ball which needed to find a definite target. A letter from Lichfield in Staffordshire describes the terror caused by these monsters' first appearance.: *'This day came their mortar piece which struck the poor citizens into an ague of trembling, and gazing on the strangeness thereof, not having seen the like before'.* [15] The Basing Diary, however, plays down the effect on morale, recording in the entry on Juy 27th, when the twins made their debut at the siege: *'they shot us six great stones sized with the grenade of 36 pounds, with each day continuing like allowance, these and the grenades for a while seemed troublesome, but afterwards became by custom so familiar to the soldiers, but they were called, as they counted them, baubles, their mischiefs only lighting on the house, and that the less, our courts being large and many.'*

The engineering skills of both sides played a far greater part as the siege went on. Parliamentary earthworks were countered by Royalist 'blinds', timber and earth structures with covered apertures for musketeers. Stretching outwards towards the besieging lines in an attempt to enfilade the enemy positions, they housed snipers

---

15 Hartleian MSS.2043

who preyed on Roundhead targets day and night; several Parliamentary officers and soldiers quietly passing their day in the Roundhead works fell unexpectedly with musket balls in their chests. But structures such as these merely spawned new counter works, men labouring like moles by candle flame at night to neutralise the structures of the enemy. Savaged by the Cavalier earthwork that reached towards the Basingstoke lane, Onslow's soldiers built a retaliatory wall that emerged in hours to command the entrance to the Royalist construction and soon made the latter untenable.

The engineers' great skills were sometimes undone by bouts of inclement weather which drove the besiegers from their lines. On the 24th July, the rain fell incessantly so that *the trenches on the town side in the meade float with the quantity of rain that fell, thereby forcing them* (the defenders) *to lie more open to our towers, from whence our marksmen spoiled divers'*.

The action-packed days of late summer were largely the result of spontaneous acts of bravado, attempts to alleviate the monotony of endless siege or the exploitation of sudden opportunities. The Royalists seemed generally to be the more resourceful, tackling the enemy in the open when they judged him to be most vulnerable. On the 28th, a miniature battle occurred in Parliament's inner trenches, brought on by forty well-mounted Cavaliers who thirsted to draw some Parliamentary blood. Twenty or more of Onslow's soldiers were hacked to pieces by the horsemen's swords and a Roundhead colour was snatched from its guard.

July 30th was marked as a special day in the diary of the siege - a cause for possible muted celebrations within Basing House. Just one year previously the Cavalier garrison had arrived and taken occupation of Basing for the King. A culverin near Basing church spoilt the day, joining the chorus of other guns during the morning and shattering the tower which stood within its range. The 31st was even more uncomfortable for the Marquis's men; a new platform connected by a trench to the church had appeared during the night

'THE BLAST BLOWING OFF HIS HAT'

Part of the defences of Basing House

and an out house containing much of the remaining corn was set on fire and partially destroyed.

Basing was now one of the war's more notable sieges and one of its most sustained. All the weapons and resources available at the time were employed: heavy guns, constant sniping, elaborate engineering schemes and the denial to the besieged of food and water. So, too, were the tactics feeding on fear: savage attempts to keep men awake at night and deprive them of well needed sleep, the oral or penned warnings of eternal punishment and the taunts that wafted over walls when the guns had ceased. Men lived in the shadows of life, a dark and futureless world of despair. Occasionally a ray of hope would flash, fuelled by rumours of impending relief or news of victory on a distant field. Then it would disperse and the shadows would again descend.

News of the Earl of Essex's early successes in the west did little to help. The Parliamentary general had entered Dorset on June 11th, endeavouring, according to Walker, *'by a counterfeit civility to draw the people to his party'*.[16]

Westminster, however, saw the dangers that loomed in this adventure in the west, and ordered him to return immediately to the Thames. Lord Essex's letter in response contained a threat to resign his command: *'If, after all my sad consultations and faithful endeavours…you shall call me back as one that is not fit to be trusted any further in a business of such high concernment I will come and sit in Parliament'*. And his advance was initially vindicated, prompting Prince Maurice to abandon the siege of Lyme while Weymouth capitulated on 16th June without a fight. Somerset's chief town followed soon afterwards. On July 8th, Colonel Robert Blake, the defender of Lyme, accepted Taunton's surrender, and the early memories of Parliamentary setbacks in the county were expunged.

But King Charles himself was soon in pursuit, reports of his advance filtering through to Basing's defenders. Cheered by his

---

16 Walker E 'Historical Discources upon several occasions'

near-victory over waller at Cropredy Bridge, the vengeful King was anxious to net an even bigger fish. On the 15th, his army entered Bath, throwing the county of Somerset into contention again. Westminster was consequently forced to a change of heart. Faced by prospects of the Earl's defeat or perhaps even seeing dividends from a push into Cornwall, the Committee of Both Kingdoms chose to forgive the Earl of Essex for his sins and voted £20,000 for the army's pay and provisions. The eyes of Parliament turned from Basing towards the Tamar valley where the Earl would soon be campaigning.

Norton and Morley still persisted in trying to win their little backwater war. The first three days of August 1644 were uneventful days, hours of drudgery and forced vigilance made worse by a period of hot, dry weather. The Royalist system of watch was changed. Fatigued by 48 hours of continuous duty, those fit enough for service were regrouped into two parts, each serving for 24 hours, *'our gentlemen and troopers doing the same'*.

Nocturnal sorties to snatch fodder for the horses served also to reduce the tedium of the times. Creeping out with the discretion of thieves, the garrison soldiers reaped and gathered in total darkness *'under the command of the rebels' works with hazard of their lives'*, and the valued horses were kept fed for at least another day.

Parliament's two colonels sent despatches to London with reports of the siege's progress and fanciful comments on the welfare of those besieged. Smallpox was known to be stalking within the house, bedding the defenders and sapping away their remaining strength. More mortars arrived that week, and the Marquis's officers periodically counselled an honourable surrender. The peer, however, considered the prospect of internment within the Tower of London to be far more distasteful than the daily barrage of poorly aimed guns. He replied, *'that under His Majesty's favours the place was his, and that he was resolved to keep it...'* [17] According to some Parliamentarians who escaped from the house when the smallpox

---

17 C.S.P.D

first struck, only 250 Royalists remained within the house, *'All sick and very weary'*.

A daylight sortie on August 4th swept away this perception of ailing cavaliers on the point of mass surrender. Buoyed by further news of the King's progress in the west and believing *'the intentions of the rebels rather to starve than storm us, and the doubt of a more potent army now removed, which hitherto had made us frugal of our men.....as well to animate our men dismayed through divers wants and reigning of the pox... we resolve upon advantage to make some sallies'*, the Diary reports.

Casual infantry on Cowdray's Down were the chosen target. A Lieutenant Cuffaud was to the agent of the day's snatched glory. Supported by a cornet with twenty men to shield the aggressive move, the lieutenant rode out with twenty more on a direct assault on the sunlit slope of the nearby Down.

Eleven Parliamentary infantrymen paid the price for their lack of vigilance, killed in the early moments of the Cavalier rush. Four others were taken captive, herded like cattle towards the house's still awesome walls. Neighbouring units of Roundhead soldiers, unaccustomed now to daytime savagery and conditioned consequently to near-inactivity in the summer sun, were swamped in sudden panic and did not stay to count the enemy strength. Twenty frenzied Royalists had swollen into an army, possibly the King's army itself. Drained of any rational judgement, men streamed from their places in the besieging lines as if dragons themselves were invading. Behind they left weapons, tools and self-esteem in a frantic search for personal salvation and the comparative protection of Basingstoke town.

But Royalism won little more than this assortment of discarded objects. Gradually becoming aware of the real size of the force that snapped indecorously at their heels, the Parliamentarians rallied, and *'again returning, they spend their heat at a distance with their guns and mortar-piece'* The moments of Cavalier glory were over.

Parliament enjoyed its own brief moment of glory that night in Winchester's near empty streets. Captain Thomas Bettesworth, a Winchester man whose peacetime home had been in the Close, was in command of a small force that had been detailed to police the city's approaches. Soon after midnight he and his men saw a pile of rubbish outside the city's walls and instantly seized the opportunity that this carelessness had provided. Climbing quickly over the unguarded wall, the Roundhead party hurried silently through the sleeping city in search of the mayor and several prominent men of the Cloth. More vigilant sentinels in the city centre, however, spotted their furtive movements and called the guard to arms. Bettesworth and his men retreated, climbing back down the ladder of rubbish with four insignificant prisoners as the only evidence of their efforts.

These two unconnected actions took place during a period of Parliamentary disaster in the nation's west. Convinced against all reason that his appearance in Devon and Cornwall would trigger a major uprising against the King and an enthusiastic dash to join the Parliamentary colours, the Earl of Essex took his army across the Tamar on 26th July and scattered the Royalist troops besieging Plymouth. Reinforced by Bristol and Somerset men, the King pursued, crossing into Devon on the 25th, only two days behind Westminster's invasion force. In the days that followed, the Royalist cordon was formed, enmeshing the Parliamentary army and solidly blocking the route of escape. Parliament's army was soon as helpless as a rabbit in a poacher's net. *'We now hear that 3 armies are marching against us from the east... we must expect another army upon our backs from the west... we shall sell our lives as dear a rate as maybe'* Essex wrote factually in a letter to London on the 27th, [16] the sanguine mood of recent weeks suddenly punctured by the errors of the last few days. In Exeter, King and Council met to discuss the art of 'Essex catching' and the final snares were carefully made. On the 31st, the Royalist army, 5000 horse and 10,000 foot, crossed the Tamar at Welltown and snapped Parliament's communications with London. The Earl of Essex, proud, unbending and entirely the cause of the disaster that was about to occur, was about to be humiliated for his determination to wage war entirely on his own.

16

'Only puddly and bad water to drink'

IN comparison with these fast-moving events, Basing's continuing siege drowned in tedium and insufferable indecision. Representatives of the London Parliament came sometimes to advise, closeted for a day with Norton and Morley in a siege field tent. But they seldom came to listen, choosing instead to lecture the experienced officers on the spot with abstract generalities and worthless platitudes of war. *'Basing is in a great want of match'*, they constructively remarked, *'If you keep them in continual alarm, they will not be able to holdout'* [1] *But* the wherewithal for this more intensive aggression was not provided during the later days of summer; only Colonel Whitehead's Southampton regiment of foot joined the besieging lines, his five companies reaching Cowdray's Down on August 10th and occupying the chalkpit known later as Oliver's Delve.

The Diary now becomes as monotonous as the siege; almost daily references are made to the battering of towers, swelling earthworks and the search for hay and provisions. It speaks of minor sorties, brief actions in the village lanes and Parliament's counter

---

[1] The Soldiers' Report

moves. A row of erect pikes had now been placed across the base of Cowdray's Down as a protective barrier against the Marquis's sortying cavalry.

On the 14th, Cuffaud and his cornet struck out again, targetting the men on the Down once more. With twenty horse and forty musketeers each at their backs, the duo slashed and hacked, dislodging the guardians of the Downs in an almost exact replay of their earlier success and capturing a lieutenant of horse and eight of his men.

The cornet, however, was to be denied a hero's return. Spurring his horse when the enemy rallied, he was overpowered and taken captive, compensation perhaps for the loss of Parliamentary soldiers and pride that day. *'The two next days were spent in parley for release of prisoners'*, the Diary states, *'They sending us one wounded, we return them three, offering Lieutenant Cooper and the Corporal (both stout men, wounded and taken fighting) for our Cornet, but would not be accepted, so much they valued him'*.

Those not called by God to be glorious heroes found other ways to serve their sides. Bravery in action, vigilance and steadfastness were the routes to recognition and rapid promotion. Morley, with a musket ball still in his shoulder and with commissioners from London skulking at his back, found the time to commend his men and reward those who had fought well.

Those failing in their daily duties might be savagely punished. Two deserters, caught hiding beneath the Lodden bridge, were flogged where they crouched and another was hanged by his feet. Captain Oram, commander of the guards on Cowdray's Down during this latter raid, was humiliated instead. Held responsible for the Royalist success and charged with neglect and cowardice, he was court martialled, disciplined and was then nearly deprived of his life.

Colonel Whitehead was militarily embarrassed a few days later. Warned by a deserter from the house that the chalkpit had been chosen for punishment, Morley placed another culverin there behind a line of protective works with Whitehead's three hundred as its protecting force. But, on the 7th, Basing's horsemen attacked on mass, scattering the Parliamentary newcomers like rats before a harvester. Encouraged by easy success, the Royalist troopers rode on, slashing at Whitehead's cowering soldiers in their desire for revenge.

But they rode too far and their numbers were too few to survive the weight and might of the Parliamentary infantry positioned further back. Saddles were emptied by musketeers placed behind the hedges near Holloways Mill, every volley seeming to find its intended target. The marquis's trapped men withdrew. Parliament's army, too timid and effete to dare to storm the house, had, at least, held solid in defence; the cordon around Basing House was hardly dented.

The culverin in the delve made its noisy debut that night, joining its scattered sisters in a new bombardment of the house. Few defenders dared to man the crumbling walls, and muskets were discarded in favour of spades and tools with which to repair the defences. The more sanguine observers in Parliament's camp smelt the scent of probable victory in the gun powder's smoke. And soon the soldiers were under orders to prepare gabions* and ladders in preparation for an early assault.

The signs of devastation within the house became more evident and the periodic shouts of defiance from walls and windows were soon to be features of the past. Prisoners escaping from the house at night talked of huddled, immobile men with eyes downcast and faced drained of hope. Deserters came with them, men jaded by lack of sleep and food. Three of Rawdon's men, detailed to labour at the outer walls during the hours of darkness, appeared in the Parliamentary lines with their tools still in their hands.

The sorties became fewer now and their outcome was less effective. Designed to feed the hopes and stomachs of men and to

---

* cylindrical baskets filled with earth or stones

'Only puddly and bad water to drink'

The church at Basing

test the foundations of the enemy strength, they had become nothing more than fiery shows of defiance, hollow gestures constrained by Parliament's strong line of works. And, with men incapacitated by disease and others deserting at night, the marquis could scarcely find the manpower needed for such outings.

A hint of warranted bitterness calls out from the Diary on the night of the 22nd. That night, starting as one of the quietest of the siege so far with no evening bombardment as the sun went down, was ruined by a bout of literary savagery. Soldiers in the Parliamentary trenches, *'whose baseness prompted them with hope to gain by craft what by their force they could not'*, shot notes fixed to arrows *'with proffers of preferment to the soldier persuading mutinies, and labouring divisions 'twixt the regiments, leaving no stone unturned, but all in vain'*[2].

Desertions increased in frequency despite the peer's denial, two or three a night, sometimes more, haemorrhaging through the cracks and gaps in Basing's collapsing walls. A show piece execution in the yard on the morning of the 25th of a would-be deserter temporarily slowed the stream. Two days later, after another hanging, the flow congealed and *'for a long time not one man that stirred, though our necessities grew fast on us, now drinking water, and for some weeks past making our bread, with peas and oats, our stock of wheat being spent'*.[3]

Norton and Morley had done all that humans could possibly do to seize the Marquis and his home. The containing earthworks now extended around the house, a mile of mounds, platforms and redoubts hosting culverins and demi-culverins and with ditches for the musketeers. In terms of labour expended and resourcefulness, the efforts to reduce Basing were as great as in any of the war's other great sieges. Diversion of the River Loddon followed at the end of August, an ingenious attempt to lower the level of the water near the Grange to facilitate the building's capture. Royalist ingenuity, however, matched their enemy's; a dam was constructed

---

2 and 3 Diary of the Siege

to maintain the river's level.

Norton's summons followed soon afterwards. Penned on September 2nd, it was the culmination of Parliament's summer efforts, delivered to Basing when the last of the stores of wheat was believed to have run out. '. *These are in the name and by the authority of the Parliament of England, the highest court of justice in this kingdom, to demand the house and garrison of Basing, to be delivered to me, to be disposed of according to order of Parliament'.*[4] The Marquis of Winchester was given just one hour in which to reply.

His answer was well rehearsed, delivered several times already to the faint hearts within the house who had counselled surrender during the weeks of August. *'Whereas you demand the house and garrison of Basing by a pretended authority of Parliament, I make this answer, that without the King there can be no Parliament, by His Majesty's commisssion I keep the place, and without his absolute command shall not deliver it'.*[5] Norton responded with his guns, ordering his batteries into instant retaliation. Towers and walls were shattered almost beyond repair that day, but still the defiance continued.

Yet, in private, the proud peer's spirit was almost as broken as his walls. Edward Jeffreys travelled again that night, sneaking through the Parliamentary cordon with another message for the King. It spoke of hunger, disease and a lack of will, suggesting that *'he* (the Marquis) *could not defend it above ten days, and must then submit to the worst conditions the rebels were likely to grant to his person and to his religion.'*[6]

September 2nd 1644 was a moment of bright glory for the King in the west, even if no sunlight of hope danced in the courtyard of Basing House. Parliament's army, led dangerously by the Earl of Essex, was ensnared beside the River Fowey in Cornwall and subjected to punishing attack. Concerned for his own safety, the Earl, sole architect of this defeat, took ship for Plymouth and left Philip Skippon to negotiate the terms of surrender. Essex was quick

4 and 5 Diary of the Siege   6 Op. Cit. p.49

to justify his escape. His value as a commander might well be debatable, but his political worth as a hostage would be considerable. *'I thought fit to look to myself'*, he wrote, attempting to unburden himself of blame, *'it being a greater terror to me to be a slave to their contempt than a thousand deaths'.*

Few of the 6000 Parliamentarians who surrendered at Lostwithiel ever lived to see their homes again. Robbed of clothing and dignity as they journeyed east and with injuries untreated, they died by the roadsides, their carcasses lining the route of retreat for months to come. Richard Symonds, who witnessed their departure from Cornwall, describes their distress: *'...prest all of a heap like sheep, none of them except some few of the officers that did look any of us in the face'.*[7]

The destruction of Essex's army sent Parliament's high command reeling, and nothing could have prevented Charles from striking at London if he had chosen to do so that autumn. The saddened earl, with just 3000 men, was sulking in Portsmouth. The Earl of Manchester's army of the Eastern Association had progressed no further south than Watford, and Waller had dissipated his forces in garrisoning the south coast. Irresolute since his mauling at Cropredy Bridge and lacking any sense of purpose, he had marched belatedly to the assistance of the Earl of Essex, advancing no further than Wiltshire when news of the disaster arrived at his camp. Unable to hold the King's expected return from the west on his own, Waller wisely withdrew to Andover, and the chance of another major clash in Hampshire suddenly grew large. *'You must not expect,'* Waller wrote to the Commons, *'to hear we have done any service, the best we can hope for is to trouble and retard the enemy's march and make them keep close together. Should we engage the horse before your foot come up, and they miscarry, your foot would be all lost, and the King could go which way he pleased'.*

News of the King's new latitude offered no real comfort to Sir Arthur Aston, Governor of Oxford, the man responsible for

---

7 R. Symonds Diary

holding the city in the King's absence. Throughout the summer he had remained stubbornly deaf to the stream of requests for help carried at night from Basing. Rumours that the Earl of Manchester was approaching Oxford deafened him still further and he openly argued in Council that to send precious soldiers from his tiny garrison to Basing, with Parliamentary garrisons at Abingdon, Newbury and Reading, would be *'full of more dangers and liable to more dangers than any soldier who understood command would expose himself'* and the King's service to and protested that he would not suffer any of the small garrison that was under his charge to he hazarded in the attempt'. [8]

The marquis's letter on September 2nd spoke in tones of desperation and imminent defeat, far less sanguine than the summer's early letters. Colonel Henry Gage, of whom *'the Lords of the Council had a singular esteem'* and a man still searching for a purpose, instantly gained the Council's support when he declared *'that though he thought the service full of hazard, especially for the return, yet if (the Lords would, by enlisting their own servants, persuade the gentlemen in the town to do the like and engage their own persons whereby a good troop or two might be raised he would willingly, there were no one else though fitter, undertake the conduct of them himself'.* [9]

The force that he assembled was impressive, evidence of the latent manpower that still lay at the King's disposal. Greenland House near Henley had recently fallen to Parliament's men, and the terms of surrender had permitted the defender, Colonel Hawkins, and his 300 men to return to Oxford with their colours, drums and weapons. This proud regiment, to which an additional 100 musketeers were quickly grafted, elevated in status by its heroic stand at Greenland, would provide the infantry for the expedition to Basing. Colonel William Webb, a soldier of experience, was placed in command of the 'gentlemen volunteers' and their retainers, 250 horsemen hurriedly enlisted for the purpose of rescuing Basing.

---

8 Clarendon Vol.111   9 op.cit

Sir William Campion, Governor of Boarstall House in Buckinghamshire, brought in 200 more, troopers with experience of fast moving combat and punishment under fire. Edward Jeffreys rode out that night, the 3rd, carrying in his boots the news that would cheer the garrison. Gage and his men, it was assumed at the time, would be only six hours behind, and every man in Basing House wanted to be the first to glimpse the horde of Heaven-sent soldiers that would end the weeks of torment and suffering.

But Gage could not master time; collecting supplies, provisions and 1200 pounds of match was to take another three days and consequently delay the date of departure. While Basing's defenders waited in hope, Cavalier officers in Oxford were still assembling their men and checking harnesses and bridles.

Soon after dawn on the 4th, Basing's garrison were drawn up in preparation for a day of expected excitement. Like countrymen searching the skies for signs of an approaching storm, they surveyed the Parliamentary lines for the slightest indication of sudden discomfort. But the Roundhead lines seemed undisturbed, with guns and infantry still in place and no hint of concern amongst a flock of sheep that still grazed on the edge of Cowdray's Down. It was disappointingly to be a day like all the others - and the siege would still go on.

The Marquis consequently decided to disrupt the Parliamentary lines from within. Noticing that the enemy's works in Onslow's quarters seemed almost deserted, he ordered out three columns, 90 men in all, on perhaps the largest sortie of the siege so far. Moving as a team, they captured a redoubt and the demi-culverin that had plagued the house for weeks.

Parliament, however, snapped back; guns beyond the Royalists' reach were activated just in time and the Royalists were forced to retire, dragging the cannon with them as they withdrew. Parliamentary musketeers were hurried forward to obstruct their endeavours - and the gun was overturned.

Waller himself seems to have witnessed this event. Riding

from Andover to Basingstoke earlier in the day, he had been reviewing cavalry on Cowdray's Down. A stray shot killed an officer at his side while another was wounded by stones thrown upwards when a cannon ball landed. And one account talks of a further daring Royalist outing in the afternoon towards the coveted Delve where Whitehead's men were still positioned. They went out from the house again that night, this time to possess themselves of the valuable stolen gun. Far too heavy for the men to turn, it was to remain where it lay in the ownership of neither side. Both sides appointed guards to watch over it and both sides were to periodically fight for its possession.

Parliamentary strategic thinking in the days after the surrender at Lostwithiel seem atrophied, unable to react to the Royalist aggression in the west. On September 7th, panicked by reports of further Cavalier successes in those distant counties, Sir William and the Earl of Manchester both received instructions to advance towards Dorchester in an effort to block the enemy advance. Waller had by now seen for himself the situation at Basing and would have preferred to take personal control of operations there instead. But his superiors ordered him on, reminding him of the dangers of leaving a Cavalier army unchecked. On the 10th, he reached Salisbury, leaving his tired Kentish infantry at Wallop while Edmund Ludlow's Wiltshire men patrolled the county boundary.

Lord Essex, despite his humiliation at Lostwithiel, had not yet lost the confidence of the Committee of Both Kingdoms. In September Westminster began to forge a new army for him to command, instructing its suppliers to send 500 pairs of pistols, shirts, shoes and hats to Portsmouth to equip the fresh recruits. England's south-eastern counties were asked to pay the bill: Hampshire and the Isle of Wight's contribution being assessed at £125 weekly for an unspecified period to come. And Colonel Alexander Popham received a commission to raise a regiment of horse with loose instructions to serve wherever the need arose.

In contrast with this period of near-stagnation in the

Parliamentary high command, the King and his nephews seem to have basked in a glow of self-satisfaction. Banbury and Basing might be in danger and Royalism in the north almost entirely eliminated, but the field army on which he relied had not been defeated and the flow of recruits had not yet dried up. And, despite the absence of any visible indication of imminent relief the men of Basing held firm, even when a chimney stack collapsed on the 5th and the New House was dangerously breached.

At 10 pm. on Monday, 9th September, Colonel Gage at last set out with 1000 men at his heel. Few townsmen saw them leave and not a soldier was permitted to speak. Wearing orange scarves and ribbands, Parliament's chosen colours, they were joined at Cholsey Wood by nearly 100 horsemen and infantry from the garrison of nearby Wallingford. From here they struck out in the direction of Aldermaston and an uncertain future at Basing House.

Major-General Richard Browne, commanding Parliament's garrison at Abingdon, was clearly wrong-footed or misinformed. Aware from his scouts that Royalism was on the move somewhere within the autumn night, he sent cavalry out to block their path. But the hunters were blinder than the hunted and never made contact with Gage's silent force.

A few unfortunate Parliamentary troopers unwittingly stood in the Royalists' path. Sent out from Reading, according to Mercurius Aulicus, to destroy a pile of surplices and prayer books, they rose from their overnight beds in Aldermaston when the Royalist quartermasters and their escort rode into town in search of food and water.

The Cavaliers might have avoided the ensuing fight. Greeted by the Reading men, Captain Walters and the Royalist escort rashly tore off their orange scarves and shot at the welcoming arms. Parliament's soldiers, some with *'their breeches still unloosed and their boots afar'*, returned the fire and a noisy brawl took place in Aldermaston's normally silent streets. A leather jug probably saved the life of one of the Roundhead soldiers. Picking up the utensil

Gage's relief of Basing

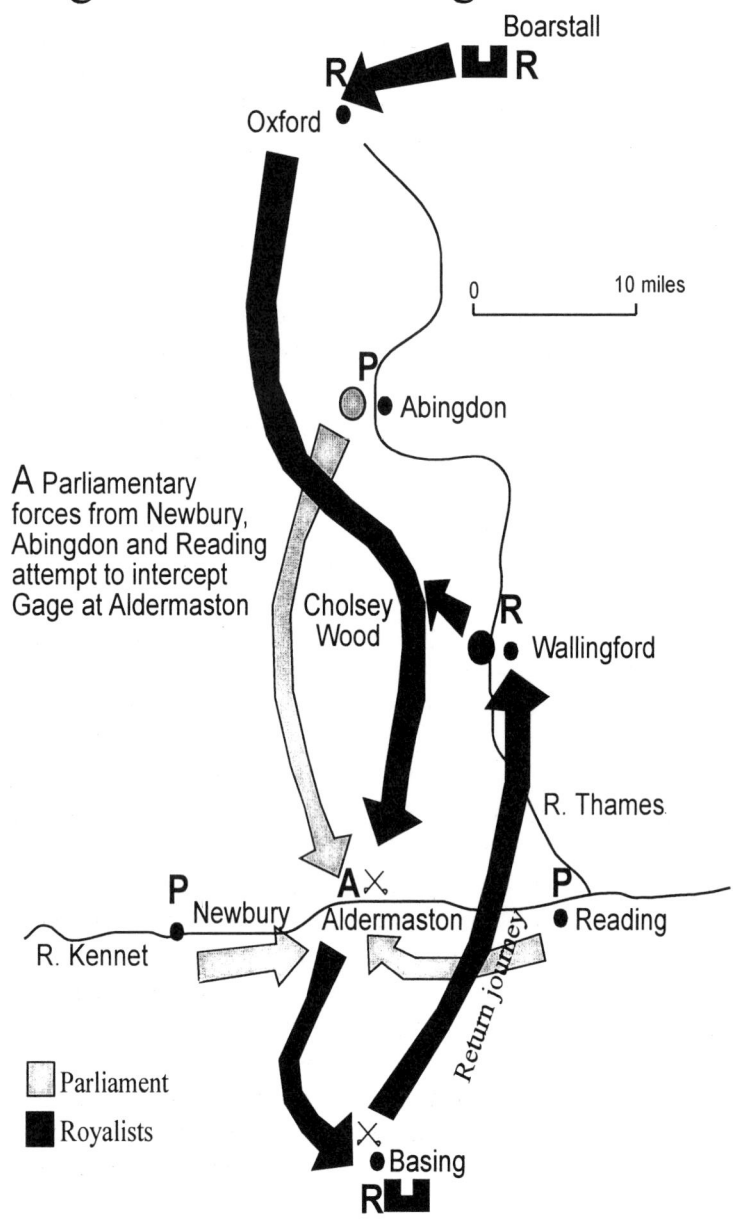

when a Royalist carbine was levelled at his head, he threw it at his assailant and deflected the ball. Two or three were killed on either side, and the Parliamentary horses, tethered in a yard, were taken.

Colonel Gage, informed of Walters's folly, chose to hurry his pace. He ordered his horsemen to dismount, and most of the weary foot soldiers were soon mounted on the cavalry's saddles.

At 8 p.m. Colonel Gage and his force of relief reached Aldermaston, *'a village out of any great road, seven miles distant from Reading, where I intended to rest and repose,'* [13] Three hours later, with an enormous moon lighting their way, the Cavaliers set out again, as silent as before but with their stomachs now full. Somewhere on that nigh time route, Gage stopped to despatch a message to Sir William Ogle, who had recently promised to assist Gage, *'desiring him with his men to fall into Basing Park, in the rear of the rebels' quarters there, betwixt 4 and 5 of the clock in the morning, being Wednesday, the 11th of September, while I, with the troops of Oxford, fell upon the other side'.* [10]

Reports of their slow approach reached the besiegers. Norton hastily disposed his men to meet the threat, thrusting forward a line of musketeers to give early warning of the enemy's arrival. And somewhere through that agitated line rose Edward Jeffreys, carrying news of the skirmish at Aldermaston and the imminent appearance of Gage and his men on Chineham Down, two miles from the Marquis's crumbling house.

More in euphoria than from any real need, the marquis and his men prepared bonfires of welcome and warning to guide Gage on his way, like lighthouses on a rocky shore. For a while, the house's battered silhouette stood out, framed against the flames, and Royalism seemed again to be shouting out.

But Gage, and even the Parliamentary cavalry waiting in readiness all night on Cowdray's Down, would never have seen the well-stoked fires. A thick mist fell before dawn and a light drizzle nearly doused the flames. And Royalist planning was to fall apart

---

10 'The Life of the Most Honourable Knight - Sir Henry Gage'

evenmore in the hours before dawn. Arriving as scheduled at Chineham soon after 4 a.m., the Royalist colonel was met by an officer from Winchester, bearing a message from Sir William Ogle that must have caused the Cavalier's lion heart to sink. The governor of Winchester, Gage reported, *'durst not send his troops to assist men, in regard some of the enemy's horse (Ludlow's regiment) lay betwixt Winchester and Basing, so that I was forced to enter into new Councils... we resolved not to dismember our forces and fall on in several places, as we would have done if either the Winchester forces had arrived, or we would have surprised and taken the enemy at unawares, but to fall on jointly at one place'.* [11] Instructing his men to tie a white handkerchief above their right elbow so as to be instantly recognisable as friends to the defenders of Basing, he promised them rewards and bounty for their efforts in the service of the King.

Everything would now depend upon Norton's reactions. The Parliamentary colonel had taken full advantage of time, night and the still heavy mist to dispose his men on Chineham Down. Morley's Sussex regiment of foot and five troops of horse had drawn up to meet the Royalist force, every soldier ordered into silence and every face searching keenly into the fog in the direction of the road that led from Andover.

Placing Colonel Webb in command of his right and Lieutenant-Colonel Buncle in charge of the horsemen on the left, he personally led the infantry that followed just behind. Parliamentary musketeers behind the hedges on Chineham Down fired first, shooting wildly into the mists at what could have been little more than outlines of swirling grey. Colonel Webb ordered an immediate response, sending his men crashing towards the hedges. Buncle followed on the left, probably targeting the lines of static Parliamentary horse so that *'after a shorter resistance than was expected from the known courage of Norton... the enemy horse gave ground and at last plainly ran to a safe place beyond which they*

---

[11] 'The Life of the Most Honourable Knight - Sir Henry Gage'

'Only puddly and bad water to drink'

Colonel Henry Gage

could not be pursued'. *[12]* Morley's soldiers, their pikes barely visible in the mists, stood firm, holding the line for two hours or more and only slowly giving way to the weight of the Royalist muscle, the closely packed lines of musketeers that surged like the risen dead from the greyness of Chineham Down.

The Marquis and his men listened from a distance and interpreted correctly the tell-tale signs that indicated Royalist victory: frenzied Roundhead horsemen, their animals bathed in sweat, the uncertain movement of the soldiers on duty near the house and the sudden appearance of men with white handkerchiefs at the gate of Basing House. The peer had men ready to assist, a body of musketeers that now broke out to maul the enemy rear. Sallying from the Grange, they mauled the breastworks on Cowdray's Down and then, for devilment, laid into the defenders of the Delve and cleared them from the works.

Colonel Gage entered the house in muted but ecstatic triumph while Norton's beaten men watched sullenly at a distance or collected the wounded that lay strewn like trampled flowers across Gage's path. Estimates of the numbers of the fallen vary enormously - Mercurius Aulicus, prone to exaggeration, claimed 120 killed, 100 more taken captive and probably as many wounded by the muskets and swords of the Royalist horde. Parliament's apologists, just as capable of exaggeration in the opposite direction, talk of the loss of just one man while Norton sustained a *'slight hurt in the hand'.*

Yet Gage's work was still not done. Stopping in the house only long enough to offer the Catholic peer the respects *'due to a person of his merit and quality'* and no doubt enjoy a celebratory drink, he took most of his force on an expedition to Basingstoke to gain food and provisions for the hungry men of Basing who had so steadfastly served their king. He left 100 of his musketeers to strengthen the garrison and supplies of match to bolster their defiance.

The scene at Basingstoke when the Cavaliers arrived is almost

---

12 Clarendon

imaginable. The weekly fair was in progress, as impregnable to the ravages of war as the weather itself. For ages past, men had travelled the roads to England's market towns, their livelihoods depending on what they might buy or sell. Quarrels between lords and princes made little difference, money still changed hands and the inns were invariably full. Men would look disinterestedly when a trooper or two rode into town on an errand of apparent importance. And during the long weeks of siege that had almost become part of the town's throbbing daily life, Parliament's men had become institutionalised, their appearance as routine as the fair itself.

Today, however, the slow pulse of market day life was to be briefly arrested by the sudden appearance of Gage's massed force at the market's edge. Farmers, countrymen and gossiping cousins were temporarily caught in a spell, immobilised in the midst of transactions and with money still clenched in their outstretched hands. From the windows of an upstairs room in a market place inn, Royalism's enemies had seen Gage's soldiers too. Gathering up papers and belongings, the Parliamentary officers hurried from the building, the sounds of departing hooves uncomfortably audible in the semi-silence. Here, just two days previously, commissioners and officials had been at work, hunched over lantern light at night to forge new plans for victory at Basing. They had left the night before, warned perhaps of Gage's intentions, leaving only Norton's more junior officers at residence in the inn.

But the Royalists were no policing force of occupation, intent on punishing those who stood out against the King. They had come to buy provisions, not forcibly extract from those who had come to sell. *'all that day I continued sending to Basing House as much wheat, malt, salt, oats, bacon, cheese and butter as I could get horses and carts to transport'*[13], Gage reported. He purchased livestock too, *'of which divers were excellent fat oxen, as many or more sheep. and 40 and odd hogs'*.[14]

---

13 'The Life of the Most Honourable Knight'   14 Mercurius Aulicus

Two simultaneous raids went out from Basing House that afternoon, both designed to take advantage of the disorientation in the Parliamentary ranks and prevent them from closing behind the visitors to the fair. The Marquis sent out two hundred musketeers on a raid towards Basing Village. Amongst those who went out were the Oxford Whitecoats, the men left by Gage and veterans of the midlands fighting. Royalist musketeers rushed the church, flushing out the handful of defenders who nested there and capturing the soldier son of Sir Thomas Jervoise, M.P. for Whitchurch, and thirty four lesser beings. From here they went on to more vengeful acts, torching the siege works around the house from which most of the defenders had already fled. And the overturned gun was pulled back to the house, about to serve its new owners as effectively as it had served its previous.

Lt. Col. Peake led out a party soon afterwards, targeting Sir Richard Onslowe's batteries in the park. Almost all of the siege works, with the exception of Morley's fort, were in Royalist hands, taken, not so much as a result of Royalist muscle, but as a result of the sudden paralysis and decay that had swept through the Parliamentary ranks. For almost the entire day, Cavalier infantry, wagons and horsemen had passed through the village, almost without hindrance, and the Parliamentary defence lost its structure and composure. Colonel Gage remained in town, buying provisions until the sun went down. The countrymen returned to their homes, purses full and their produce sold. War, so often the destroyer of livelihoods and patterns of living, would occasionally strew bounties in its path.

But Parliament had begun to strew obstacles in his path, barbing the way back to Basing in a sudden late evening expenditure of effort. Norton's horse, joined by a detachment of Browne's Abingdon men, had reformed and now, according to Gage, *'made a show of a desire to fight with us again, advancing for that purpose over a large champion almost within musket shot of our horse, which stood ranged in a field without Basingstoke, betwixt large hedges lined by me with musketeers'.* [15]

---
15 'The Life of the Most Honourable Knight'

Gage chose not to fight, sensing the tiredness of his men and the dangers of dusk-time fighting. *'I gave orders to the horse to retire by degrees and pass through the town (Basing village) towards Basing House whilst I with the foot, made good the avenues or passages on this side the town, where the enemy appeared. And when I understood the horse were all passed through the town, and put again into their squadrons on the other side towards Basing House, I myself with most of the foot, retired likewise through the town to our horse, leaving Captain Poore with 60 or 70 musketeers to make good that avenue.'*[16]

The colonel and his loyal force slept that night in the marquis's house, a fortress no longer under siege and with its larders replenished. But too many mouths to feed would quickly empty the larders again while Parliament's besieging net, if successfully flung, would catch too many men. Gage paced his chamber that night, composing his plans for withdrawal now that the garrison's war machine had been refuelled.

He sent his horse and foot into Basingstoke again in the morning, presumably to collect supplies which had been left in the town at the onset of night. He himself remained in the house to confer with the peer and drink King Charles's health. A detachment of those left behind tried their hand against Morley's fort, the only works untouched during the mauling of the day before. But Norton's men were back in force and Royalist hopes were disappointed. The raiders were recalled, leaving six dead on the ground, the only mortalities since Gage's arrival.

Spies came in during the day, carrying reports of Parliamentary movements in the vicinity of Basing House and their attempts to stop his escape. Major-General Browne was waiting at Aldermaston with 500 dragoons and cavalry. Three hundred of the Newbury garrison were watching for Gage at Thatcham while Reading men based at Padworth guarded the crossings of the Kennet. Likely to be noticed by every villager, milking maid or passing traveller on the road, his movements would be broadcast to the

---
16 'The Life of the Most Honourable Knight'

enemy - and he honestly cared for his men's survival. '*I resolved, therefore, in my own breast, without acquainting any man, to make my retreat that very night, having during the short time I had been at Basing House put at least a month 's provisions into the House'* [17]

First he threw deception into Parliament's path. Hoping that his written messages would fall into Norton's hands, he sent out warrants to the inhabitants of settlements further west, instructing them to supply quantities of corn, '*upon pain of sending them 1000 horse and dragoons to set their towns on fire before noon the next day... if they refused.'.* [18]

At 11 p.m. that night, the 12th, under cover of another welcoming fog, the Royalist force set out, led by two of the Marquis's guides and disguised, as before, in Parliament's now traditional colours. At Burghfield they crossed the Kennet, every cavalryman carrying a foot soldier behind him on his horse during the unpleasant crossing of the autumnal river. A few hours later, hidden in the dawn mists that lay across the valley, the Royalists crossed the Thames at Pangbourn and so reached Wallingford at 8 a.m.. Skulking somewhere in the vicinity was Parliament's Richard Browne with a force that matched Gage's in size.

But hunter and hunted were fortunately never to make contact - and Oxford lay just two hours march away. The city's courtiers were already aware of his approach and most were awaiting him at the gates. On the 14th, after a day of uneventful rest under the protective guns of Wallingford Castle, his men entered the city, feted by the ladies and applauded by the crowd. But Henry Gage was not amongst those who enjoyed the welcome. Having done his duty, he rode unnoticed to his lodgings, from where he penned the concluding words of his account: '*And thus, my lord, to comply with the order I received, I have troubled your lordship with a tedious relation, for which I humbly beg your pardon'.* [19] He was later to receive a knighthood for his endeavours.

17, 18 and 19 'The Life of the Most Honourable Knight'

17

'Being minded of his grave'

IN the wake of his departure, Parliament's colonels debated whether to continue the siege. Throughout Friday, the Royalist soldiers of the garrison travelled freely from house to village - or even beyond - transporting the provisions that had been purchased for Royalism's sustenance. Norton did nothing to stop their progress, keeping his men at their stations on the Down or in their fort within the park. One hundred Royalist musketeers roamed freely on Parliament's overrun works, like cockroaches on a piece of meat, taunting the besiegers to come out and fight.

Only once during the following week did Norton find the nerve to challenge them in the open. Celebration and drink had impaired the Royalists' fighting sense and so made them highly vulnerable to attack. The parliamentary colonel in person led the sudden assault against the carelessly held positions in the churchyard and village street.

Less inebriated soldiers from Basing House came to their drunken colleagues' assistance. The fighting that ensued was brisk and heads were savagely broken. Mercurius Aulicus poured scorn on Norton's less than noble efforts in the churchyard brawl, suggesting that *'being minded of his grave, he was the first man that ran away'*.

For a week or more, the Royalist cockroaches were permitted to swarm, untouched by Colonel Norton or his men. But the Roundhead colonel stubbornly held on, his soldiers drilling in the park and hunting the autumn hare. No one now spoke of a state of siege and hardly a gun was fired. Royalist and Parliamentarian mingled at the Wednesday fair in Basingstoke, eyeing each other from across the market stalls. Two men tussled over a lively pig that had broken from its pen and sought its freedom in the open streets. Falling on the animal to prevent its escape and claim it for themselves, the duo suddenly realised that they championed opposing hues and so fought with their pistols instead. The pig continued on its way.

Norton's orders became increasingly vague and even contradictory, evidence that Parliament's high command had devised no new strategy for bringing the peer to his noble knees. On the 9th, he received instructions to prepare for an *'advance into some other places of the Kingdom for the service of the State'* while a day later he was informed that barrels of powder were being sent to assist his execution of the siege. Four days later, he chose to punish the Cavaliers in an afternoon attack on their outposts in the village. By evening, Parliamentary troops were again in possession of the church and the Royalist garrison was confined to Basing House. Norton, having received no clear orders to the contrary, had decided to renew the siege.

The next few days are almost a replay of the past, minor Royalist sorties stopped by Parliamentary effort and the renewal of artillery bombardment. Succulent pigs grazing on Cowdray's Down tempted the Marquis's men out on the 24th. But the animals were being fattened for Parliamentary cooking pots and the Roundhead guardians fought more passionately as a result. Five troops of cavalry charged the Royalist raiders, forcing them back towards the cover of some hedges near the Grange where Royalist musketeers joined in.

And so the siege droned on, each day's events as unproductive as the previous - and with surrender no nearer. The battery at the Delve was visited again and its supporting timbers pulled down. The slow haemorrhage continued, two or three men daily wounded or killed, sacrificing their futures in an act of utter futility. On the very last day of September occurred the most profitless event of all - another Royalist attack on the church in which a dozen or more men were slain. The church remained in Roundhead hands.

Larger, more forceful actors were about to enter the local stage. On October 2nd, King Charles and the Royalist army reached Sherborne on their way back from Cornwall, the sudden appearance so close to Hampshire causing consternation in Parliamentary circles. But three Parliamentary armies lay close to Charles's likely route to Oxford, each in size almost as large as the entire Cavalier army that marched from the west. The Earl of Manchester, campaigning in the midlands throughout the summer, had arrived at Reading on September 29th, his movement south from Lincolnshire slowed by a fresh bout of characteristic lordly stubbornness. His lack of co-operation was to continue, dangerously frustrating any chances for concerted action against the King. *'My army was raised by the Association'*.(Eastern Association) snapped the Earl when ordered by the London Committee to prepare for action further west. *'It cannot be commanded by a Parliament without their consent'*.[1] On October 4th, he commenced a half-hearted siege of Donnington castle, the King's outpost near Newbury, citing this involvement as a further reason for refusing to obey the politicians' commands.

The army of the other Earl had not yet reformed. Quartered at Southampton, Portsmouth and on the Isle of Wight, it was still re-equipping after its mauling at Lostwithiel. Only William Waller, with units at Salisbury, Dorchester and Shaftesbury, seemed sufficiently mobile and willing to meet the Royalist threat.

Yet first he would need to know the direction of the Royalist movement and the motives which guided the King. Banbury, as well as Donnington, lay under siege, and Oxford seemed in almost

---

1 C.S.P. Dom. D.111 56, XI V

continuous danger. Salisbury, Newbury and Abingdon were positioned along the King's most obvious path -and Basing's besiegers were consequently a likely target for the King's aggression. Rumours of his approach naturally heartened the garrison, spurring them to periodically sortie towards Cowdray's Down and pick little quarrels with their enemy. In an attempt to break their hopes, Norton tried to be more forceful, bombarding the house with greater frequency and closing the road to the house.

He also sent requests for help, reminding all who might choose to listen of the frailty of his besieging line and the nearness of the King. Westminster heard his pleas and ordered the Earl of Manchester to send four troops of horse to bolster the cavalry on Cowdray's Down. Major-General Lawrence Crawford, an officer in high command in Manchester's army, made a personal appraisal of the besieging works and even offered to take command of Parliament's Basing forces.

But Manchester refused to lend his officer's services and remained as uncooperative as ever. Ordered on October 8th to rendezvous with Waller, he sarcastically complained that the instructions were far too vague and even failed to identify in which direction he should go: *'They would have me march westward and Westward Ho, but they specify no place. It may be to the West Indies or to St. Michael's Mount....'.*[2]

On that very day, the King left Shaftesbury at the head of 10,000 men. In a letter penned to Rupert in Bristol, his intentions to relieve Basing become abundantly clear. *'I am advertised by a despatch from Secretary Nicholas that the Governors of Banbury, Basing and Donnington Castle must accommodate, in case they be not relieved within a few days. The importance of which places hath made me resolve to begin my march on Tuesday' towards Salisbury, where Prince Rupert may rely upon the King of En gland shall be, God willing, on Wednesday next, where I shall desire Prince Rupert to come with what strength of horse and foot you can......*[3]

2 Lords Journals Vol.VI p.28   3 Warburton E. p..248

'BEING MINDED OF HIS GRAVE'

Charles's arrival at Salisbury on the 15th caused those in Wiltshire who rode under Parliament's colours to withdraw into neighbouring Hampshire. '*His Majesty leaving Somersetshire in so good condition*', explains October's edition of Mercurius Aulicus, '*advanced into Wiltshire... and came into Salisbury on Tuesday last, whence the rebels made such haste that they left good store of their friends behind them in the town which his Majesty's forces seized on*'.[4]

His appearance so close to Hampshire's borders caused shudders of fear in the county's two major towns. Southampton's Governor asked Westminster for supplies of powder and match while Portsmouth asked the Earl of Essex for protection from the regal storm.

The inhabitants of Hampshire's offshore neighbour felt vulnerable too. Concerned that Col. Carne, their able defender, was in London, members of the Newport council wrote urgently to the Earl of Pembroke, requesting the officer's prompt return. '*Yesterday late in the evening we had intelligence that the King's forces were advanced near the island to such places from whence by reason of many boats and barques they may without any difficulty annoy if not wholly endanger this island. And surely they never had a better opportunity than now, both in respect of our being utterly destitute of any shipping and also that the people here...are somewhat discouraged and discontented. And now, my Lord, suppose this island should be invaded....in what a sad condition were we, not having a man of known experience in military affairs to command us, and your Lordship may be confident that here would be as little resistance and as much confusion and destruction as can be imagined...we beseech your Lordship that Col. Carne's business may be suddenly heard and that he may be speedily sent down to us, which will again recover the spirits of your drooping islanders*'[4]

But it was Waller who lay in the storm's full path. Pulling back his scattered forces, he withdrew to Andover, single-handedly

---

4 Newport Convocation Book

attempting to block the royal path and praying, no doubt, that the Lords Essex and Manchester would support him in the hours to come.

Essex, however, was initially just as bull-headed as Manchester and refused to stir his limbs. Still semi-comatosed at Portsmouth, he wished to build his self-esteem and would do nothing until he felt completely ready. Yet both men were eventually obliged to respond to worsening conditions and, on the 16th October, they agreed to unite with Waller in the vicinity of Basingstoke.

A major battle seemed increasingly likely - only the actual location had yet to be chosen. Charles waited for three days in Clarendon Park, just outside Salisbury, awaiting the arrival of Rupert from Bristol. The Prince, however, felt unable to comply, fearing for the stability and welfare of Bristol in his absence. Buoyed by his enemy's failure to pull together and naively believing that he could yet avoid a major battle, Charles decided to relieve Basing and Donnington with the forces at his disposal, throwing his earlier cautions to the wind.

His decision to attack Waller's flimsy force was the immediate product of this spirit of newly-found optimism. Rather than hurrying to Basing and Donnington before Parliament's three forces could unit, he was persuaded by Lord Goring to snap at the suspended bait. Waller, with just 3000 dragoons and horse, had placed his men in battle order, just to the south of Andover's outer limits, purely to purchase time for the two earls' armies to begin their march to battle. Throughout the hours of the fog-soaked morning of the 18th, the Parliamentary ranks waited, listening for the sounds of horses and marching feet on the road from the west.

But no major battle was to take place outside this Hampshire town. Waller, aware that Essex and Manchester were still far too distant to present a united front, withdrew his men into the town, leaving only a rearguard to block the King's advance. Mercurius Aulicus provides details: *'Somewhat short of Andover a forlorn hope being sent out, met with another of the rebels very near their* *main body; both charged and kept their ground till two bodies of his Majesty's horse (*probably Goring's brigade) *came up and marched into the field where the rebels stood; at sight whereof the rebels' forces began to fly out at the other end of Andover town'.*

Colonel James Carr, the unsung hero of Cheriton, was one of eighty prisoners taken in the chase with another Scotsman, a man so badly wounded that, ' *a little before his death rose from under the table, saying he would not die like a dog under a table, but sat down on a chair and immediately died of his wounds'.*[5]

Portrayed as a virtual rout of Waller's army in Clarendon's brief summary of the afternoon's skirmish, the action was really little more than an embarrassment and a knock to Roundhead pride. Probably no more than two dozen were killed in total, and the fighting, watched by the bemused townsfolk, lasted for less than two hours. It was, however, like a tonic of spring water for the Royalist forces, infusing the King's colonels with notions of invincibility and '*so raised the spirits of the King's army, than they desired nothing more than to have a battle with the whole of the enemy, which the King meant not to seek out nor to decline fighting with them if they put themselves in his way'.*[6]

And so a major battle suddenly became inevitable. Until this moment, it had not been the King's intention to seek a battle with his enemy's field army or contest possession of the road to London. Sudden over-confidence encouraged him to reach for the heavens and attempt the near-impossible. Exposing his chest to three Roundhead daggers simultaneously, Charles had chosen to rely for deliverance on God and His angels. He slept that night in the town's 'White Hart' inn, intending to march towards Basing the next day.

Waller, by contrast, would have no sleep that night, using the cover of darkness to withdraw his army to Basingstoke. '*It was a great mercy of God'*, he later lamented, '*that when the King came suddenly upon me with his whole army at Andover and I had then nothing but a mere body of horse and dragoons with me, I made a*

---

5 Symond's Diary   6 Clarendon Vol. 111 Bk.8

fair retreat to Basingstoke'. [7] The Earl of Essex had marched from Portsmouth that day, briefly assembling his forces on Portsdown Hill before moving up to Petersfield. Manchester, too, had at last stirred. Leaving just one regiment to hold Reading in his absence, he marched with his infantry, intending to place his forces *'betwixt Newbury and Basingstoke, and there to meet with our Lord General'.* Oliver Cromwell and the cavalry of the Eastern Association had moved out the day before. Resting near Basing on the 17th, he was within a few hours riding distance of Andover when the skirmish took place in that town.

Had Cromwell and his cavalry been present at the fighting, the outcome might well have been different. The Earl of Manchester's critics were later to censor him for his lethargy - and Andover, not Newbury, might have been the site of one of the war's main battles. The Earl, of course, tried to belittle the whole affair, arguing that he had been quick to travel to Waller's assistance. *'yesternight late. I received a very hot alarm from Sir William Waller's quarters, that the King with all his army was come to Andover, and that he was upon his retreat towards me, whereupon I drew out my foot and those horse that were with me in order to help Sir William Waller, who reached Basingstoke with little or no loss'.* [8]

On the 19th Charles and his army moved to Whitchurch, still unaware that the Parliamentary hounds were closing for the kill. Essex's scouts watched him there, communicating all his movements to Skippon at Petersfield. *'The last night, about eight of the clock, went out about 4000 horse out of Whitchurch to give an alarm, and returned this morning about break of day....and that this day* (the 21st) *the rendezvous was to be kep upon Sevenborough* (Seven Barrows)', [9] one of these detailed reports announced.

The King's army moved on to Kingsclere during the morning of the 21st. In still unbridled optimism, Charles despatched James Compton, the Earl of Northampton, with 500 foot and 800 horse to

---

7 Waller W. 'Experiences'   8 Godwin C.N. p.271   9 op.cit p.273

combine with Oxford forces under the competent Henry Gage in an expedition to rescue Banbury from the enemy.

Parliament's three armies combined at Basingstoke on the 20th; 19,000 Roundheads, one of the largest forces assembled in the war, moving in to draw rich Royalist blood. Charles, in less sanguine mood now that his enemies were snapping so closely, abandoned any hope of relieving Basing and decided to concentrate at Newbury instead.

Personal animosities and long-standing jealousies might have stood in the way of this union of the Parliamentary armies. The two earls, unwilling to co-operate in the past, would now be required to work in total harmony, collaborating on the field of battle in a way they had never done before. Recognising the dangers of continuing discord, the Committee of Both Kingdoms placed the combined army's command in the hands of a committee of 8 men, the earls being just 2 of the number. Most prominent amongst the others were Cromwell, Waller and Heselrige, practical men with experience of field commands.

Detachments of both armies seem to have met in the vicinity of the Marquis of Winchester's crumbling home. Royalist cavalry were viewed on the 22nd from the roof of the house while the siege diarist states that some of Essex's infantry temporarily joined the besiegers' lines, his *army towards evening drawn in battalia that night keep the field, the van near Rooke's Down, the battle at Basingstoke, and rear by Hackwood*'[10]

But this was intended merely as an overnight stay, not as a reinvigoration of a rapidly collapsing siege. Reporting on an afternoon skirmish between part of the Queen's regiment and a detachment of Essex's cavalry, a fight which apparently favoured the King, Mercurius Aulicus caustically commented that '*they* (Parliament) *durst not adventure the bruising of their army upon Basing garrison, but left it on Tuesday last.*' By the 22nd, the van of the Parliamentary army reached Swallowfield, intending to secure

---

10 'A description of the Siege of Basing Castle kept by the Lord Marquis of Winchester' Hants. Records Office 15M84 2/3/26

the Thames valley and the direct route to London.

Charles meanwhile was being forced to respond to events which had not been entirely of his creation. On the 25th he drew up his army along the northern side of the River Kennet, his right flank protected by the river and his left by the course of the smaller Lambourn. The centre of the King's position, and effectively the front line, rested upon Shaw House, while the army's rear was covered by the defences of Donnington Castle, of which only the keep now remains. Lord Astley, one of the wisest heads at the King's table, was given command of the centre's 3 brigades; Maurice commanded the rearguard drawn up in Speen, and Goring's 4 brigades of cavalry lay close to the Lambourn's southern banks.

Parliament's army responded swiftly, swinging west from Swallowfield on the 24th when news of the King's deployments at Newbury became known. By the evening of the 25th, having brushed briefly with a Royalist screening force near Thatcham, Westminster's armies established their own positions of strength close to the confluence of the Lambourn with its parent.

This skilful deployment had taken place despite the new command structure, and not because of it. The committee system, scattering the responsibility for decision making over several shoulders, was bound to be cumbersome. Every decision and planned movement had first to be endorsed by London. Worse still, Lord Essex was struck by illness and was confined to bed in Reading, leaving the less able Manchester as the senior commander in the field. Beneath him, jealousies between the section commanders had almost become institutionalised, part of the rituals of the High Command, and the army was in clear danger of crumbling to dust. Cromwell, commander of the Eastern Association's cavalry, was convinced of his own merits and seemed determined to act independently if the chance arose. Balfour and Skippon, lesser stars in the Parliamentary constellation and generals of horse and foot in Essex's army, resented Manchester's usurpation, while Harrington and the City brigade were only prepared to accept orders from the

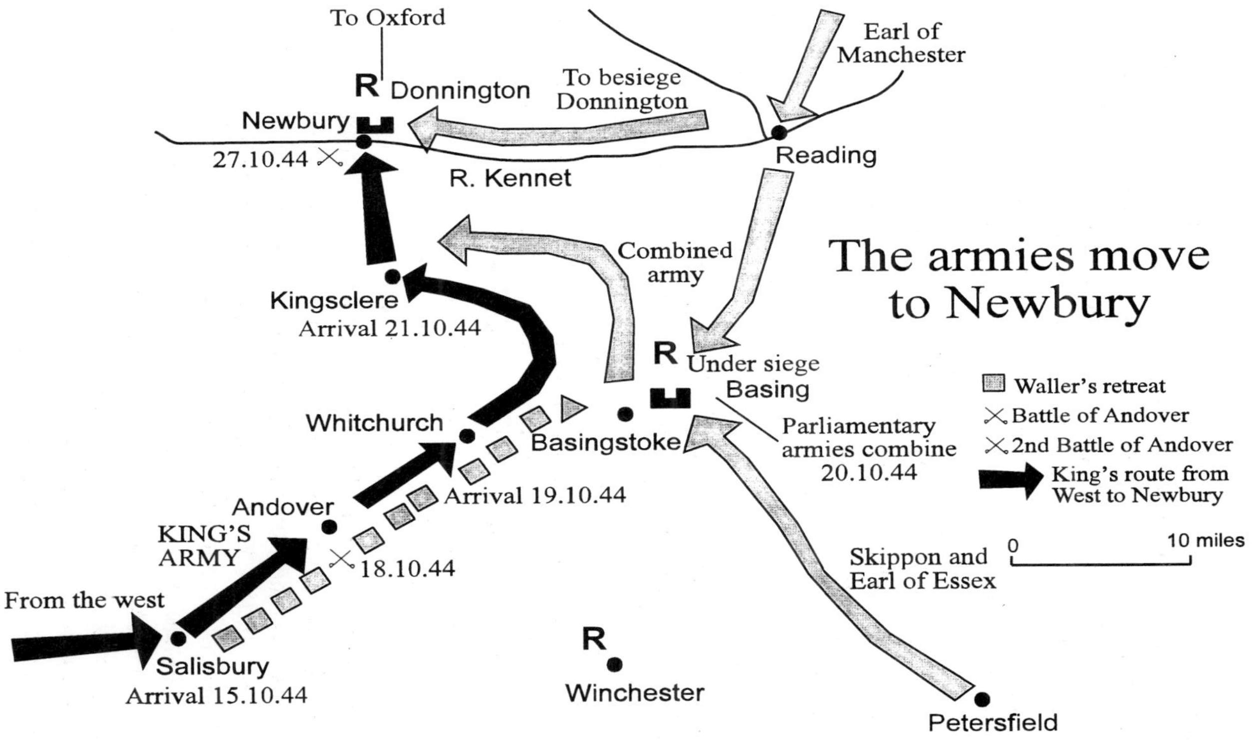

The armies move to Newbury

Legend:
- Waller's retreat
- ✕ Battle of Andover
- ✕ 2nd Battle of Andover
- ➡ King's route from West to Newbury

0 — 10 miles

- Petersfield
- Skippon and Earl of Essex
- Winchester **R**
- Parliamentary armies combine 20.10.44
- Under siege Basing **R**
- Basingstoke
- Earl of Manchester
- Reading
- Combined army
- R. Kennet
- To besiege Donnington
- To Oxford
- **R** Donnington
- Newbury **R** — 27.10.44 ✕
- Kingsclere — Arrival 21.10.44
- Whitchurch — Arrival 19.10.44
- Andover — ✕ 18.10.44
- KING'S ARMY
- Salisbury — Arrival 15.10.44
- From the west

councillors in London.

It is therefore remarkable that this poorly co-ordinated war machine assumed the offensive at all. That afternoon, the 25th, the Parliamentary soldiers took possession of the grassy top of Clay Hill and gazed down at the King's straggling positions below. Three brigades of Cavalier infantry, 5-6000 men, manned the ground of Shaw House, drawn up behind a line of ancient earthworks which served as ready made defences. Goring's horse, proud, well-disciplined, and with a sense of their own grandeur, strutted like peacocks on the meadows of the Lambourn, seemingly oblivious of the coming storm. More conscious, perhaps, of their vital role, the regiment of Prince Maurice lay in wait to the west of Speen.

King Charles spent the night in Shaw House, dangerously close to the enemy positions. But the significance of the coming day had already dawned: the drawn-out war might be about to end. *'This day will bring us judgement on our crown'*, Charles was heard to mutter that evening, *'and upon your shoulders lies the burden. See to your King and secure your peace with God'*. Alternatively his crown and his dignity might lie trampled underfoot in the blood stained mud of the Kennet valley. But, for the inhabitants of Newbury, there was less finality. War had knocked at their doors a year before and nothing had been settled then.

Some, no doubt, witnessed the first tentative movements of the Parliamentary army on the morning of the 26th. Manchester's foot probed the Royalist positions on the dew laden lawns of the great house. Colourless, fluid, and as silent as the grave in the half-light, they might have been the armies of the dead. Then the dialogue of distant guns began; Parliament's guns on Clay Hill roared in anger, answered in turn by the batteries of Donnington Castle. Here lay the real terrors of war for soldiers and civilians alike: the deafening discharge of foul-mouthed guns, the whine of shot, and the uncertainty that followed before the missile landed. For men accustomed only to the bellow of cattle, the sound of the lathe or the familiar roar of rushing water, the noise of battle was both devilish and terrifying. Hearts beat louder, blood pulsed faster, pikes were gripped in whitening hands, and the drifting shades became men again.

Yet the King's lines at Shaw House were far too dense to be taken by frontal assault. Parliament's scouts were already at work, searching for hidden chinks in Charles's impenetrable armour. It clearly lay somewhere behind - beyond the scattered regiments of horse and foot that constituted the Royalist second line.

The strategy that emerged from the battlefield conference that now took place was instant, forged from the materials of unfolding events. Waller was probably the author; it bears all the imprints of his quick-thinking mind rather than the slow methodology of the ponderous Manchester. A decision was made to send just part of the army on a wide detour to the north, penetrating behind the Cavalier positions in an attempt to find a crossing of the Lambourn and so fall on the Royalist rear. In its conception and execution, it demonstrates that Parliament had at last accepted that calculated risks would have to be taken if stalemate were to be avoided.

The King had assembled only 9000 men on the field that day, only half the size of the force which confronted him through the mists. Waller set out after dark at the head of 12,000, pushing his way through Hermitage, Chieveley and North Heath before bivouacking for the remainder of the night. Left behind on the slopes of Clay Hill was the remainder of Parliament's army, on its own equal in strength to the entire Cavalier horde. The first pale streaks of dawn coaxed Waller's force into motion again and the Lambourn banks were reached just as the first of the King's men began to stir.

Waller's movements were not detected until more than four hours later. Sometime during late morning, lookouts on the parapets of Donnington Castle spotted his columns in the meadows to the west - and the fortress's guns were fired in hurried warning. Maurice's men had worked like moles during the night, throwing up mounds and ditches on the Kennet's nothern banks. When the Parliamentary

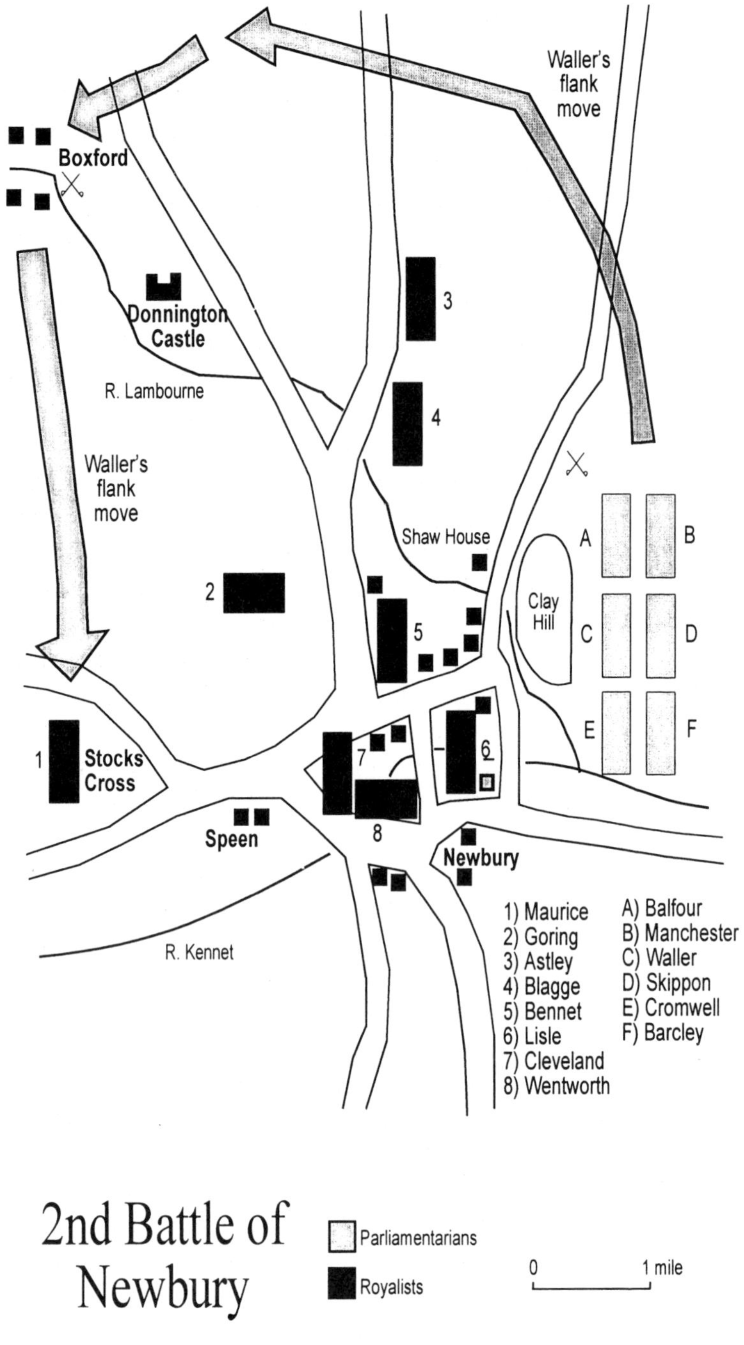

2nd Battle of Newbury

forces fanned out along the ridge west of Speen, with Skippon's infantry in the centre and cavalry on the flanks, they found that Maurice was ready and waiting.

But fighting had already roared into life at Shaw. Manchester's initial role was meant to be diversionary, a skirmishing tease launched in the early morning to hold the enemy's attention while Waller pounced on the Royalist rear. The sound of Skippon's guns behind the King's rear was to serve as a signal for greater effort, an attack with his entire strength as part of a concerted action by both wings of the Parliamentary party; a giant pincer that would then be set in motion. But, caught in a furious Royalist counter-attack, the Earl's strike that morning soon developed into something more, igniting almost spontaneously along the entire eastern front, and the report of Skippon's cannon was consequently never heard.

Waller enjoyed some early success. The regiments of the Earl of Essex, the men defeated at Lostwithiel, saw a sudden chance for revenge. A single word of encouragement was enough to send them hurtling towards the enemy trenches. An hour later they were in possession of Speen - and 8 guns snatched from them at Lostwithiel. Further advance, however, was impeded by the maze of hedges east of the village, and the Parliamentary steamroller was halted in its tracks.

Balfour's supporting cavalry advance was impressive by any standard. His men thundered across the open land that lay between Speen and Kennet, throwing aside the thinly spread ranks of Maurice's cavalry that lay in their path. The brigade of Thomas Wentworth, Earl of Cleveland, seconding the prince's men, fared no better, and their commander himself was captured. Only the firm stand of the Royalist third line, the Queen's regiment and the Lifeguard, held the Parliamentary advance and saved the King's rear from total collapse.

Adept minds in the Royalist councils saw a possible advantage in this apparently unfavourable position. For the Parliamentary army was now dangerously divided while the King's army remained intact.

Moreover, simultaneous Parliamentary hammering from two directions had merely served to make the Royalist army more compact. Its full weight could now be brought to bear on the weaker half of Westminster's army. And just beyond ,still waiting on the Lambourn's pastures, Goring's brigade remained unused - able and willing to punch where it was most needed.

Cromwell could have dealt with Goring's latent threat. Yet, instead of thundering into action on Waller's northern flank, he held his men back beyond the range of Donnington's guns. This uncharacteristic reluctance to fight has been explained away by his apologists: he was positioned upon unfavourable ground with intersecting hedges, and an advance would subject his men to withering fire from the castle's guns. Such excuses are hardly credible, for there were known to be only four demi-culverins in the castle - and these had a limited range and doubtful accuracy. Caught in the open, Cromwell's horsemen must have provided only a fleeting target, and would have soon become mixed with Goring's men on the flat meadows beside the river. When Cromwell did eventually lead his men to battle, Goring, supported by Sir Humphrey Bennet's regiment, easily blocked the advance.

Waller's cleverly forged weapon became blunted on the rock of stubborn enemy resistance. Thomas Blagge's musketeers, positioned north of Shaw House, had moved to Maurice's assistance. Against these stubborn and immovable men, Skippon's infantry could make no progress. The outcome of the day would probably be decided on the deeply rutted lawns to the east of Shaw House.

But here the Parliamentary assault was no sharper. The full attack was not launched until after 4 p.m., more than two hours after the western push had begun. Advancing in two columns, Manchester's men were greeted by a hail of musket and cannon fire from the lawns of the house and were soon driven back in confusion. Unable to chip at the King's solid ranks or find an alternative route to victory, Parliament's generals recalled their troops before the daylight faded.

So ended the second fight at Newbury, no more decisive than the first. Both sides had lost about 500 men, but had gained hardly a single strategic advantage to compensate. Men, drained of blood and souls for someone else's cause, had gone to meet their maker, their bodies discarded like casual litter in a country park. Others called out for their mothers, and weakening hands clutched at the damp earth that might soon become their graves. As in the earlier conflict, both sides remained hovering on the field, numbed by the day's activities into a state of vague uncertainty. The Royalist soldiers were the first to recover. Seeing little to be gained from remaining on a blood-stained field, they stole away under the blanket of the autumn night through the open gap between Shaw House and Donnington Castle.

The chance of ending the war stole away with them. If Manchester and his colleagues had deployed the army in a closed circle, this nocturnal bolt would never have been possible and the entire Royalist army would have been captured. The war would have been ended in one final and decisive stroke. Bad generalship and poor co-ordination were largely to blame.

18

'Without the noise of pistol'

NEWS of victory or disaster travelled more slowly than the men concerned. Newbury's tale failed to reach Hampshire's more distant parts until early November, days after the King and the Prince of Wales had been seen galloping through Marlborough at the head of just twenty men. Those who witnessed this strange event might have chosen to speculate; defeat of the King seemed the most plausible explanation.

But such theories were rapidly blown to bits. Charles's subsequent movements became far more purposeful and determined, hardly the actions of a man cowering in defeat. On November 1st, Winchester's Royalists rode into Petersfield, seizing several cartloads of clothing destined for Parliamentary backs. On the 12th Charles was reported to be marching west from Oxford at the head of an impressive show of strength, causing his enemy to guess at his exact intentions. '*Some are of an opinion that he hath an intent to fall on Malmesbury, but I cannot be so readily induced to believe it, this winter season is so very foul and heavy from Malborough to Malmesbury*', a London writer concluded on the 19th, just one of a number of speculative utterances that tried to make sense of the King's puzzling movements.

The garrisoning of strong points was one of his aims.

Throughout the nation, the fluid war of movement of the last twelve months, in which rival armies tramped vast distances in pusuit of over- ambitious goals, had congealed into a series of local struggles with a region's manor houses and castles as the building blocks of success- and garrison building had become fashionable. Able to weather all but the most ferocious of attacks, these garrisons could dominate the surrounding countryside and do more to win territory for their chosen cause than any half-day battle in a mud-strewn field. Highworth, Longford and Devizes in neighbouring Wiltshire were garrisoned during the coming weeks, and fortresses elsewhere were made increasingly impregnable.

'We see they intend to reduce the west into the state of the Netherlands', complained the Parliamentary Scout in December 1644 when the King's objectives had become abundantly clear, *'and have a garrison at every five miles, and not to fight so often in the open field'*. Parliament followed suit, using the timber from estates of Papists in Hampshire to strengthen the fortifications of Southampton and Portsmouth. And calls were made for Hampshire men to assist in the defences of Taunton, Lyme and Poole.

Basing, of course, was part of this formula of Royalist defence. In mid-November the King himself was reported to be marching to its relief. The Earl of Manchester waited at Aldermaston, ordered by the Councils of War to intercept any attempts at relief. On November 6th he received instructions to send the City Regiment to Basing House *'and any other units he could happily spare'*. The rest of the Parliamentary units, some of which had been too bloodied at Newbury to be active, were concentrated at Henley and Reading, available to campaign against the King in the Thames Valley if the need arose. The cavalry were stationed at Farnham, Maidenhead and Windsor, expected to assist the infantry or block the London road.

Somerset's Colonel William Strode and Wiltshire's veteran campaigner, Edmund Ludlow, brought their regiments to Basing on November 6th, both at the request of Colonel Norton himself.

'No man wished the King's army worse success',[1] Clarendon acidly speaks of Strode, recalling the political invective and military stance taken by the colonel during the early weeks of war in Somerset.

Royalists in the great house chose to venture out that day, capturing three sentries on the Basingstoke road under the cover of a swelling fog. Placing their own men in the lane instead, they awaited the challenge that was bound to come. Three more Parliamentarians were taken in the minutes that followed *'without the noise of pistol....a welcome to Stowde's* (Strode) *new come horse'.*[2] Desperate for food and supplies now that Gage's provisions had been consumed, Royalist foragers rode out that night to Piat's Hill, but returned empty-handed *'on account of the vigilance and numbers of the opposing cavalry.'*

Gage's supplies had, in fact, lasted only five weeks. The officers of the garrison survived now on just one meal a day, the soldiers on two- and the beer had completely gone. Men deserted to the enemy in consequence, carrying stories of hunger, thirst and the garrison's desire to surrender; one man even took his horse.

But the listeners were no keener to continue the siege than those within the house. Long nights, frequent fog, thoughts of home and family, and the dull repetition of events waged incessant war on even the steadiest of minds and men. Even Waller seemed to doubt the ability to press the siege: *'My horse have been in constant service ever since the first battle of Newbury both summer and winter. After the business of Alton and Arundel in the winter, and the battle of Cheriton, the House of Commons was pleased to promise £10,000 towards the recruiting of my horse, but I never received one penny. I have at the least 500 men on foot, and as many unserviceable horse'.*[3]

On the 9th, the desperate Cavaliers went out again to search for food, meeting only a dough-like response that completely fell to pieces on Piat's Hill. The raiding party took eighteen cows, six sheaves of corn and some barrels of ale that had been carelessly left

---

1 Clarendon Vol.111 Bk.8   2 Diary of the Siege   3 Waller W. 'Recollections'

outside an open barn.

King Charles seemed more enthusiastic about continuing than any of those who lay at night in the shattered house or on the frosty fields of Cowdray's Down. *'His heart was set upon the relief of Basing'*, Clarendon explains. *'He had a great mind to do it with his whole army, that thereby he might draw the enemy to a battle'.*[4] But Gage's earlier success shone like a beam of sunlight on the table in Marlborough where Charles and his councillors sat. *'Upon full debate'*, Clarendon continued, *'it was concluded that the safest way would be to do it by a strong party, thus 1000 horse should be drawn out....and Colonel Gage, who had so good a success before, was appointed to command the party'.*

On the 13th, Charles and his party retired to Hungerford, the chosen launching point for Gage's new expedition of relief. The following night, Gage and his party marched from the town, each man carrying match or munitions at his waist, a bag of corn on his saddle and the blessings of the King in his heart.

But the siege was already dying, killed, not by news of Gage's new approach, but by the wishes of Parliament itself. Sir William Waller and Oliver Cromwell were probably among those who made the decision to raise the siege *'for Colonel Norton....received a warrant from a chief commander in the army, to withdraw from Basing, which was to him a thing unexpected, but yet he obeyed'.*[5] Time, weather and enemy musket balls had reduced the besiegers' numbers from 2000 to no more than 700, and the capacity for further resistance had been drained away. At 8 a.m. on the 19th, (the 13th according to the Basing diarist), the wagons began to move away, most in the direction of Odiham, and the siege gun platforms were pulled to pieces. The Diary, with so much to say on the siege's more trivial events, tersely dismisses the collapse in just a few lines: *'The enemy wearied with lying 24 weeks, diseases, with the winter seizing them, his army wasted....fearing the forces of His Majesty now moving about Hungerford, raiseth his league...The Foot at*

---

4 Clarendon Vol. 111 Bk 8.   5 Godwin p.281

noon marched towards Odiham, the huts being fired, and some troops of horse being left to secure the rear'. Mercurius Aulicus was far more dismissive of Parliament's efforts, personally taunting Norton in an autumn issue: *'Norton himself has gone to Sir William and left the work to others, thinking it ill manners to attempt that for which his general was so handsomely basted'*. Basing House was to be frequently known thereafter as Basting House.

Colonel Gage, of course, rode on, unaware of the melting of the besiegers' lines, and reached the deserted park before night. Reining briefly on Chineham Down, he surveyed the smouldering ruins of the rain-soaked earthworks and the lines of trenches that had once been full of men. Now only hungry birds pecked in hope at the remnants of discarded rubbish that lay in piles on the trenchwork rims. And just beyond, the walls of the fractured house survived, a symbol of triumphant Royalism and more solid and enduring than the papery will of Parliament's colonels.

He remained, as before, for just three days, this time ruling over a nearby landscape that lay at peace. While resident there, Gage wrote a coded letter to Prince Rupert, highly critical of the garrison of Basing. And from Basing's open doors, his horsemen rode out each day, carrying warrants to the constables of the surrounding Hundreds. Basingstoke was visited first, ordered to contribute bacon, hay and malt *'to be conveyed as the warrants ordain and with no circumstances to be imposed instead'*. Odiham received similar demands, instructed to supply one hundred quarters of oats, sixty quarters of wheat, barley and malt and specified weights of cheese and bacon, all to be *'delivered by eleven of the clock'*.

They dined well at Basing that night, the flickering light from glassless windows seen only by the passing night-time traveller. *'I shall end all with these observations'*, the Diarist concludes. *'That seldom hath been a siege wherein the preservation of the place more immediately might be imputed to the hand of God...God that holdeth all things in His hand, appointing times and seasons, ordereth all that tends unto those ends he wills...Let no man therefore speak himself an instrument, only in giving thanks that God had made him so'*. God, however, would eventually change allegiance. In the autumn of the following year, Cromwell, backed by Heaven's angels, would break the house to dust.

In the meanwhile, Royalism would need to find the means to survive and somehow grow outwards from its fragile and isolated strong points. Parliament, by contrast, needed only to find the means to win - and embarrassments like Basing and Winchester could, for a while at least, be ignored.

It seemed that Charles was about to find the crusader for his cause. Lord Goring, the man with one hand, soon proved himself the lieutenant of the moment. Operating in West Somerset for much of the autumn, he was ordered during November to commence a march of liberty towards Sussex. Leaving his quarters at Bruton, he appeared in Wiltshire at the head of three thousand horse and dragoons, and called on the county's muted cavaliers to openly proclaim their loyalties. Many promptly did, and even the allegiance of Salisbury's and Andover's flimsier Roundheads began to wobble. On November 22nd Goring's cavalry reached Odiham, causing Samuel Jones at Farnham to plead for extra troops. Two days later he duelled with Royalist units in Crondall, testing his ability to resist in an exchange of musket balls in which the Parliamentarians were worsted. Less than one week later, Hampshire was awash with Royalists, nine thousand or more in sudden occupation of Odiham, Crondall and Basingstoke, according to the testimonies of reliable Sir Samuel Luke. Hampshire folk again groaned under double demand - obliged to pay taxes and contributions to the never satisfied raiders of both the warring sides.

In Goring's rear, however, Royalism in Somerset had become less secure and Parliament's supporters again grew bolder. Taunton, defended only by wooden fencings and besieged for weeks by Royalist forces, was relieved on December 14th. Cavalier influence in the county's other towns began to flow away. One of the war's most painful truths had now become evident: only the presence of

Cavalier generals could hold a region for the King.

Sir William Waller seems to have been powerless to stop Goring's spectacular advance. Ordered by Westminster to adopt several roles simultaneously, he succeeded in performing none. Ranging between Salisbury, Newbury and Farnham in an attempt to provide a defensive shield, he could merely respond like a barometer to the Royalist winter pressure.

It was to be Colonel Edmund Ludlow, Parliament's Wiltshire hero, and his officers who did most to stem this alien tide. Royalists under Sir Francis Cooke had recently fortified Salisbury's Cathedral Close, intending to use it as a base for excursions into Hampshire. In the first week of December, Cooke's men rode through Fordingbridge and Ringwood and almost to Southampton's gates, ultimately clashing with Hampshire Roundheads on the marshy ground near modern Millbrook. Ten Royalists were toppled in the unordered fight; the Royalist threat that had emerged from the fogs of the west was found to be no more substantial than the mist itself.

Ludlow, with little to do now that Basing's siege had drawn to an end, ordered his trusted officer, Henry Wansey, to bait the Royalists who sheltered within the walls of Salisbury's Close. With him on that day, the 8th, was Major Francis Dowett, at that time the most favoured of Ludlow's officers, but soon to become one of the war's most noted turncoats, and two hundred horse and dragoons.

Cooke's soldiers hastily shut the Close's gates, manning St. Anne's Gate in force and the houses that lay adjacent. Musket fire and the flames from burning timbers flushed them out - and Colonel Cooke with forty soldiers were led away in chains. The victors returned to Southampton, parading their captives like dancing bears in the streets of the Hampshire town.

Less than a month later, just when the sudden grip of winter turned all the rivers to ice, Ludlow made full use of the Cathedral close's solid facilities. Having returned from winter campaigning in Somerset, and probably intending to deal with the Royalist garrison at Longford Castle before crossing into Hampshire, he set about fortifying the cathedral's tall belfry. Anticipating an early visit from those who would be keen to oust him from his roost, he posted his men as sentries in the city's streets while most of his force rested beneath closely wrapped cloaks around the dying embers of evening braziers. Ordered to keep their horses bridled and ready for action at a moment's notice, they talked, no doubt, of tear-stained sweethearts and of the happier times that hopefully lay ahead.

Then came the sound of rapid hoof beat in Castle Street, menacingly amplified in the cold night air. Ludlow, with just six men, rode to investigate. Encountering the enemy squadrons in the market place, he galloped back to the Close to call his men to action.

The result was a running battle in the city's snow lined streets, a light affair by the standard of most of the war's skirmishes, but severe enough to be known thereafter as the Battle of Salisbury. Only eventual flight saved Ludlow's tiny force. In the purple light of a winter dawn, Edmund's men pulled back over Harnham Bridge, one of the soldiers with a Royalist sword still embedded in his arm, and sought the road to Fordingbridge. Ludlow, separated from his companions during these moments of hurried retreat, turned at bay in a frost bound field to face the baying hounds.

Here fell the last of the victims of Salisbury's small battle. A solitary Cavalier approached on called on Ludlow to surrender. A single ball from Edmund's carbine sent the man crashing to the ground - and Ludlow was free to leave. With only his horse for company, the Parliamentarian made his way to Southampton, '*a place infested with the stench of rebellion*'.

Apart from this town and stoutly held Portsmouth, only Farnham and Petersfield now remained in Parliament's hands, the latter occupied only briefly during early December in an attempt to give protection to Parliamentary soldiers and convoys of supplies that passed along the road from Portsmouth to Farnham. Crondall, Farnham's outpost, was hastily evacuated, Parliamentary soldiers leaving their saddles and cooking pots scattered in the churchyard.

Further west, the Marquis of Winchester was still replenishing his larders at the expense of those who had so little to give. Specifying his wants in the warrants carried by his soldiers to the constables of the Hundreds, he warned of the consequences of a failure to supply within the stated time, '*which if you fail to do, you must not expect any favour, but be left to the mercy of the soldiers, which will take your goods and destroy your houses'*. [6] Few failed to comply- and consequently Basing's larders filled again. One who resisted was tied to a hay cart and scalded with boiling oil. Another had his hair cropped and was then strapped to the back of a dead cow. Jones's Farnham men rode out as well, raiding the yards and hen houses of Hampshire's country folk with hardly a penny paid in compensation.

Winter generally was a time of inactivity, when numbed joints and freezing muscles sought out the comforts of a roaring fire and a refuge from the icy blasts. Little groups of soldiers of either side would sometimes ride the open roads, their slow languid pace the only sign of movement in a hoary landscape that had come to rest. With cloaks and hats pulled tightly around exposed faces that had become as white as the fields around, the men looked earnestly ahead and hardly a word was said.

Sometimes solitary riders went out, passing along the lanes at night or in the pre-dawn hours when their passage would be largely undetected. On December 14th a Royalist sympathiser, a man with no military experience and unknown to any of the enemy, was sent from Basing to Reading on a mission of espionage, ordered to find out the strength of the Parliamentary force that held the town. A brewer living near St. Mary's Church served as his accomplice while several others provided cover for the operation. In full expectation that the enemy weaknesses would be discovered and numbers calculated, a Royalist force of horse and foot from Oxford was to march towards the town during the night, scheduled to arrive outside Reading at about 2 a.m. on the 15th in the hope of surprising the guard and taking the town. The plan, however, failed. Spies and accomplices were arrested, their activities exposed, and the Royalist

---
6 Godwin p.287

plans laid bare. Subterfuge was no more successful than brazen aggression as a means of snatching strongpoints from the enemy.

In those days of winter quietness, both sides could give greater thought to how they might win the war and brief bouts of military activity took place. William Lenthall, Speaker of the Commons, was amongst those who urged the Committees of Hampshire, Surrey and Sussex to greater local action, arguing that torpor and poor strategy were largely to blame for failure to defeat the King. Orders from Westminster simultaneously went out to Parliament's lieutenants to raise extra finance from the counties that lay in their hands. With these orders went out instructions to re-equip and re-group the forces that had campaigned within Hampshire and the surrounding counties. Limited but decisive movements during the winter, therefore, swung advantage temporarily in Westminster's direction. Within days of this new initative, Parliament was again in control of Hampshire and Royalism receded. Sir Arthur Heselrige's regiment of horse was quartered at Petersfield in early January with detachments at Petworth and Midhurst, their mission being to police the South Downs and watch the Channel coast. Kentish regiments of infantry and horse were newly stationed at Alton, Alresford and Bishop's Waltham, some even taking temporary residence in Romsey and Stockbridge. Parliamentary horsemen watched at the gates of known Royalists, grazing their horses on the gentlemen's lawns and cooking supper in the suspects' parks. Visitors to the houses were observed, interrogated or turned away, and excuses were hatched to arrest the owners or seize their property. Even the most innocent, the country squire who had proclaimed for neither side and wished only to be left to his personal affairs, was questioned and robbed on the most tenuous of evidence during this period of rapidly reversing fortunes.

General Goring continued to be elusive, rarely threatening in force but always shadowing, appearing wherever Parliament's forces seemed weakest and least organised. On January 2nd, Christchurch was abandoned in a moment of panic when reports of the Cavalier's approach reached the garrison commander. With few defensive structures, the town was deemed to be too vulnerable. Soldiers, townsmen and *'those of the Puritan disposition'* crowded the boats that crossed to Hurst Castle, harassed by the first of the Royalist forces that reached the town just as the last of the vessels rowed out.

But Goring had no intention of remaining in the priory town and left within days; his withdrawal after so much effort was perhaps indicative of muddled strategy and a misted Cavalier sense of purpose. His sudden energetic movement, however, briefly swung the balance back in the Royalists' favour. Five days later Goring quartered at Romsey, probably intending to combine with Winchester men on some vague expedition to the east. Within twenty four hours he was in occupation of Petersfield and Petworth too - and in fruitful contact with the Royalists of Sussex. Sir Arthur Heselrige and his regiment seem to have melted away in the warm breath of the Royalist wind. Some contemporary reports place him further west at the time, others nearer Guildford. Only Samuel Jones and his steeled men of Farnham lay in Goring's way.

Parliament wobbled dangerously as a result, employing conflicting strategies in their attempt to stay the enemy advance. Sir Walter Erle at Poole and Sir Ralph Weldon at Weymouth were asked to make mischief in Goring's rear while Generals Waller, Cromwell and Massey were ordered west with most of the available horse in another bout of unstructured Parliamentary reasoning. Colonel Richard Whitehead, probably stationed in Sussex at this moment of crisis, was instructed to shield Portsmouth. No other Parliamentary force, however, was commanded to take up a position in Goring's way or block the path to London.

On January 9th 1645, Goring's forces occupied the town of Farnham, despite the presence of the Greencoats in the castle and the visible barrels of Parliamentary cannon that reached like gargoyles from the fortress walls. *'Why?'*, the Earl of Manchester was asked that day by the Commons when members heard the news, '*did not your forces that lay quartered on their friends near London, remove nearer to the enemy, according to former directions?*' [7]

On the 10th, Goring, probably with about 1000 soldiers in his ranks, left Farnham and headed south towards Portsmouth, attracted to his former haunts like a moth to a flaming candle. Portsbridge and Gosport seem to have been visited in the next two days, but the naval town itself, where Colonel Morris Jephson held command, was spared from Royalist aggression. '*Colonel Goring, his forces came down and plundered the town of Gosport*', Sir William Penn, at that time the captain of one of the smaller Parliamentary warships that lay in Portsmouth harbour, wrote in his account: '*...about six o'clock at night (Goring) fired some twenty four houses, and we, and the 'Swiftsure' and the ' Mary Rose' shot divers pieces of ordnance to them*'[8]. Those in Portsmouth who saw the flickering lines on Portsdown assumed that Goring would soon be knocking angrily at the town's closed gates.

On the 11th, however, he withdrew again, and the watery nature of the Royalist advance was revealed once more. Goring had neither the determination nor the means to pay his troops - and his lines of communication to Oxford, fuelled only by the impoverished Cavaliers of Basing and Winchester, were in danger of crumbling to nothing. Parliamentary colonels saw him for what he was, a vainglorious and blustering man who lived in a world of self-deception. Two days later, he was in full retreat westward, driving away the livestock of the men of Fareham and Titchfield, and personally supervising the hanging of a farmer who tried to stop the theft. He plundered Romsey on the way, '*not leaving a sheep or a hog*', his rearguard periodically brushing with the soldiers of Southampton and Colonel Whitehead's cruising troops.

Forty eight hours later, he viewed Christchurch again, the '*unfortified fisher town*' (Clarendon) that he had attacked less than a fortnight previously. - the Royalist crusade had clearly lost all its limited purpose. Major Philip Lower and his 200 men had returned,

---

7 Money W. 'Battle of Newbury'   8 'The Life of Sir William Penn' Vol. I, p. 104

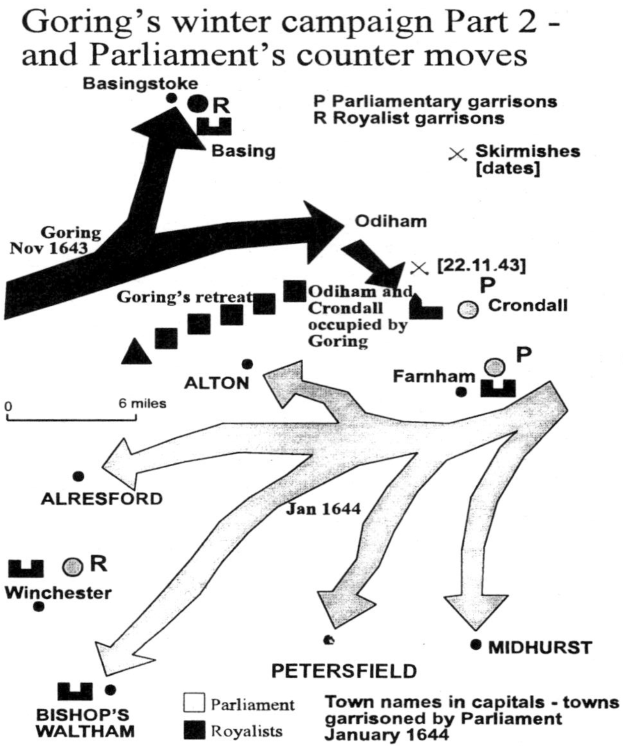

Goring's Winter Campaign Part 1

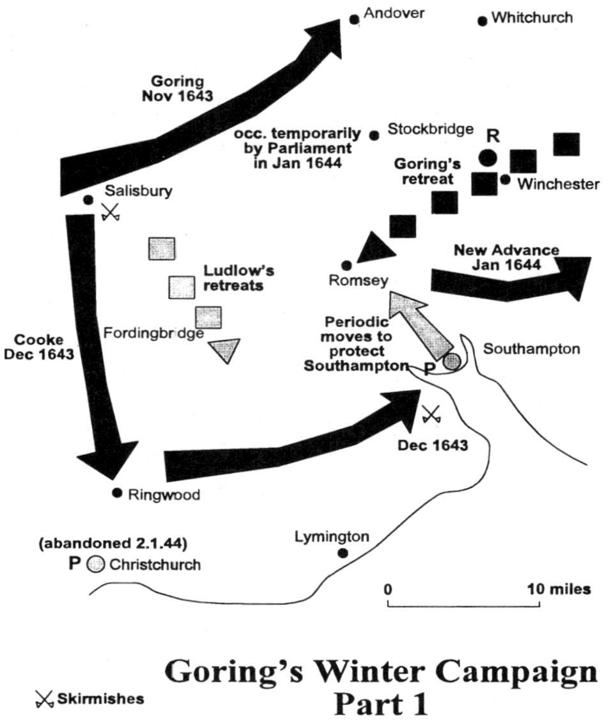

Goring's winter campaign Part 2 - and Parliament's counter moves

most of his command holding fast in the tiny castle that stood close to the priory's walls. An inhabitant of the town, bribed by the sight of Royalist gold, led the Cavaliers in, guiding them to a point from which they could most effectively storm the castle. Lower's men fought back this time, those positioned in the town drawing back gradually to join their colleagues in the church and castle. The treacherous guide was among the first to fall, pierced in the chest by a Roundhead musket ball; the promised reward for which he worked remained hanging from Goring's belt.

But the hopeful Cavalier was also to be deprived of his prize, thwarted by the unexpected stamina of Lower's men and the tiredness of his own dispirited men. Sudden bonfires on the western horizon were seen by the soldiers of both sides, and questioning minds paused for a moment to speculate what they might imply. Royalist and Parliamentarian interpreted the signs in a similar way: the men of Poole were coming to Christchurch's assistance.

For a moment the fighting intensified and musket balls blasted the exposed faces of the Cavaliers on the castle's lower slopes. Goring's men abandoned the effort soon afterwards - the sum of two weeks campaigning in Hampshire had secured nothing for the King and only a brief elevation of Goring's status in the minds of Charles and his courtiers. For, by now, Parliament had re-occupied Petersfield and Odiham while Parliamentary units had begun to harass the Royalist general's later movements.

Lord Goring next appears at Lymington, anxious to avoid the Parliamentary units that were searching for him in the shadowy expanses of the New Forest. Isle of Wight Roundheads under Ludlow, Parliament's hero of the Salisbury snows, were in pursuit too, crossing to the mainland and re-stocking Hurst Castle with men and supplies. Goring chose to avoid their challenge, hurrying up the valley of the Avon through Ringwood and Salisbury to an intended union with his king. Quartered in the Wiltshire villages of Whiteparish and Winterslow for almost a week, his horsemen *'committed the same horrid outrages and barbarities as they had done in Hampshire, without distinction of friends or foes; so that those parts, which before were well devoted to the King.....wished for the access of any forces to deliver them'.* [9]

Essex and Waller had hardly stirred and had done nothing to develop a strategy to block the activities of Lord Goring. Only the smaller fry, the regimental colonels, had been active in the field during those post-Christmas days when the Cavaliers had penetrated as far as the Surrey border. But the peer and commoner knew that they were about to become victims of the Self-Denying Ordinance, the political measure which would rob all members of Lords and Commons of their commissions in the armies. Unsure of their futures, both men had been like passive bystanders, and other men had been forced to deal with Goring instead.

Essex was at Alton with most of his cavalry and Waller waited at Farnham. But hardly a message passed between the two camps. On January 21st 1645, at a time when Lord George Goring was still hovering near Salisbury, the two men at last began to talk - and a belated joint move suddenly became possible.

In the meantime, Colonel Jephson took revenge on those inhabitants of Portsbridge who had assisted Goring during his recent visit. A miller, bribed by the Royalists to carry meal, was arrested and forced to sit on a heap of manure during his hurried trial. For sleeping with some of Goring's officers, three young girls were found guilty of every conceivable offence, their most heinous crime being to *'conceive vipers in their wombs for which they will need to be purged'.* Hot passions and unbridled fervour had taken the place of reasoning and quiet rhetoric and men had become the willing servants of wild demagogues and the cursing ministers of God. Believing that they fought on the side of the angels and those who bathed in Heaven's bright light, men chose to behave like devils.

Then came reports that French recruits were assembling at Brest, mercenaries purchased to fight for King Charles. Parliament's zealots portrayed them as far less than human, *'the miserable*

---

[9] Parliamentary Scout

excrement of Papist whores...vile and more perfidious than the Ottoman hordes', or *'profane and blasphemous, villainous, irish, French....and divers other nations as the world affords not the like'*. But poisonous rhetoric alone would not be enough; Parliament's field generals were ordered ' *at once to secure the arms and horses of those walloons and strangers, and to discharge them of the service'*.

Those in arms were accused of secular crimes as well. Acts of sacrilege against property were publicised in the news letters of the other side. The Parliamentarians were accused of stripping the lead from the roof of Basing church. Their offence was aggravated when, instead of confessing, they claimed that Lord Winchester's Cavaliers had committed the outrages themselves. '*My Lord Marquis'*, Parliament's Britannicus news sheet protested '*gave order to have the church unleaded to make consecrated bullets to shoot away the protestant religion'*. And every time that Parliamentary troopers stabled their horses at wayside farms, the Royalist propaganda machine broadcast the fact and spoke of outrageous crimes against the people.

Waller's inactivity at Farnham merely placed Hampshire in contention again. And Goring had apparently left troops behind in the county when he retired to the west. For, reports reached Southampton that Royalist troops, identified as Goring's men '*on account of a red-faced officer seen in their ranks and known to have earlier ridden at Lord George's side'* had attacked Parliamentary horsemen stationed at Crondall on January 27th. The Royalist horsemen appeared in the main streets of the little settlement before the Roundhead pickets could give warning. Fifty or more of Waller's men were stationed at Crondall, some in farmhouses that lay beyond the village's furthest limits - and any chance of a massed resistance became impossible. Men preferred instead to melt away when the enemy arrived, escaping through back doors of lodgings or in the guise of innocent non-belligerents. One hid in a hen house for an hour, causing the timid residents to scatter in fright. Some passing Royalist troopers chose to investigate. The man apparently escaped, but Basing's garrison dined on fresh poultry that night. Three or four Parliamentarians taken in the street pleaded for their lives; they were shot where they knelt. Many more were taken captive and were led in triumph through Basing's rebuilt gates. Crondall was set on fire -a crime against the people that Cavalier news sheets conveniently neglected to report. And they probably also chose not to identify the leader of the raid on Crondall, an Irish gentleman of noble birth and an unflinching Papist to boot.

Aldershot was also visited that day, a party of Cavaliers riding in noisily soon after dawn. About 40 Roundheads were billeted here. Still at rest in garret billets or hay-filled lofts, they were able to escape - and not a man was taken.

Worse still, the Royalist Sir Marmaduke Langdale had taken leave of Goring at Salisbury and ridden to Bishop's Waltham at the head of more than 1000 horse. Goring, presumably instructed by the King to rekindle the embers of Royalism in Hampshire, followed soon afterwards. He appeared initially at Andover and Stockbridge, causing Hampshire hearts to flutter anew. From here he moved towards Winchester, intent, it seemed, on another spontaneous raid towards London's softened under belly.

Westminster reacted nervously, ordering reinforcements that had not yet mobilised to immediately join Waller in the field. And their orders to Sir William were far too general, merely '*to go west towards the enemy*' and with no objective or target identified. Hampshire and Sussex troops took up position in Godalming, Petersfield and Alton while Ludlow, still without a full regiment at his back, was given command of unregimented troopers stationed at Odiham.

No-one, however, expected battle to be the outcome of this half-hearted winter manoeuvring. Both sides were merely re-structuring for the coming of Spring, when new regiments would be in the field and the days would be longer and warmer. For the Royalists, these fresh units would increasingly consist of Irishmen and mercenaries from the continent, men imported at cost to fight Charles's largely personal war. For Parliament, it would be the New Model Army, commanded by men of merit, Englishmen primarily, but with a Dutchman or two purchased by Parliament to fill the known deficiencies.

On February 4th 1645, Waller stirred at last, advancing from Farnham to Alton where most of Essex's cavalry had firmly bedded their roots. Here he received the arms and clothing for which he had been continuously asking. Six hundred pikes arrived on the 5th, carried in carts which had once been used for cheese. Supplies of bandoliers, stockings and shoes followed soon afterwards, but not the artillery on which success would probably depend. Goring and Langdale retired at once, pulling back towards Salisbury in another bout of seasonal teasing.

Southampton, however, would never feel at ease while their shadows lingered over the adjacent landscape. Lord George's troopers, aided by Basing's and Winchester's vigilant men, watched the county's roads like hawks, pouncing on Southampton's travelling merchants when the chance arose. *'Hants will never be scoured clean as long as that blaspheming wretch (* Goring) *remains there, with the collected filth of several countries, which the earth sure would vomit out, or take in, but that she is merciful to her native inhabitants'*, a Parliamentary journal spits out in a withering verbal assault on the Cavalier lord, likening him to a harpie which '*would steal from the table of God Himself'*.

But the harpie remained as elusive as previously, flitting from one vulnerable point to another, more like a butterfly than a man with a purpose. On February 13th he was reported to be at Weymouth, personally in command of the ranks of the Royalists who were worrying the seaside town. Two days later he was back in Wiltshire, quartering between Amesbury and Andover with most of his cavalry. Waller, however, was unable to move as quickly, dangerously slowed by a partial mutiny in his ranks which threatened to break up his poorly cemented army. For, amongst those who

'WITH OUT THE NOISE OF PISTOL'

now marched in his ranks were some of the Earl of Essex's previous command, men still infused with their previous commander's hostility towards Waller and his commanding officers. Refusing to march with him from Petersfield, they turned east instead, intending to return to their London homes. At Croydon, however, they were met by Westminster's messengers and warned of the likely consequences of their near-treasonable behaviour. Most returned to Waller's colours; a few were hanged instead and buried without honour beneath the spreading beech trees of Box Hill.

In slightly better spirit and with supplies on the way, Waller prepared to advance to Andover, hoping to catch the butterfly before it flew away. But word of his intentions travelled faster than his horsemen; Goring was forewarned of his enemy's approaching net. Withdrawing his forces from their Hampshire positions, he mustered again at Salisbury and awaited fresh orders from his King.

Parliamentary plans to simultaneously move against Winchester were thwarted too, the details of Waller's designs carried into the city by a trumpeter from the Roundhead army. Numerically, with 700 dragoons, 3400 horse and a large body of foot, Sir William should have had every chance of success. Newly equipped and armed at Westminster's request, the Parliamentarian was joined on February 27th 1645 by Oliver Cromwell, detached from Lord Manchester's inactive army. Making his debut in Hampshire's war, Cromwell met his new commander at Wickham to discuss the overdue destruction of the Cavalier garrison in Winchester castle. Three days later the two men jointly reviewed their available forces at Owlesbury, perhaps 2000 foot and 4000 horsemen and dragoons. Skirmishes took place during the following week at Twyford and Wickham, tense and bitter conflicts between Lord Ogle's men and Parliament's much fresher troops.

The affair at Marwell on March 2nd was the most notable of all. Marwell Hall, home of the Mildmay family, had been occupied by about 60 of Waller's men since the previous week, part of the scattered deployment that Cromwell and Waller had jointly planned.

Milder weather was encouraging Ogle's Royalists to venture further from their base. Two hundred of his men rode out that day, many still intoxicated after a night of ceaseless drinking. Informed of the proximity of the Roundheads in Marwell's Tudor hall, the inebriated Cavaliers set out to find new entertainment at Parliament's expense.

Fewer than half reached the house; many, still drinking as they rode, fell from their horses. Others lost their way. A single Parliamentary trooper challenged the survivors outside the house and was rewarded for his welcome with a musket ball through his arm. No semblance of strategy or reasoned thinking emerged from the muddled brawl that then followed in the grounds of the house. Ogle's soldiers swung wildly, swore loudly and fell heavily, disadvantaged by drink and poor leadership. Waller's soldiers, by contrast, used their carbines effectively and mainly kept beyond the range of Royalist swords and fists. Every Royalist capable of flight eventually turned and fled; those less capable were taken captive and punished for their insolence.

One week later, it was Andover's turn to host an event of far greater significance. On March 8th, Waller, still operating from Owlesbury, took 3000 horse and dragoons towards Andover, hoping to flush the last of Goring's men from Hampshire soil. Somewhere on the town's outskirts, they caught up with a party of horsemen, Royalists to the man, but clearly not part of Goring's command. Thirty were taken prisoner, among them Lord Henry Percy, a kinsman of the Earl of Northumberland, and several other men of quality. Waller, *'having at that time an inconvenient distemper'*, left the young peer in the custody of Cromwell. *'I desired Col. Cromwell to entertain him (Percy) with some civility'*, Waller explains in his 'Recollections', *'who did afterwards tell me, that amongst those whom he took with him...there was a youth of so fair a countenance that he doubted of his condition'*. Cromwell accordingly asked the young captive to sing - and the voice was that of a maiden!

Goring at last seemed to be about to leave the county's war, ordered by Charles to take command of the failing Royalist effort in Somerset and Devon. In his place, only Lord Ogle and the Marquis would remain on stage, but with neither the men nor the mobility to do much to assist the Oxford cause.

Lord Winchester was consequently forced to resort to baser methods of waging war. Tobias Beasley, a pewterer by trade, and now a servant in the Basing household, was sent to London as a spy, his mission being *'to there take note of divers matters'*. He was promised great rewards on his return and even the commendation of the King. But Tobias was to swing from a City rope instead, taken, it seems, in the course of his shadowy work by yet even more shadowy figures in Parliament's pay.

The time had also come at last for Waller to leave the military stage. In April the Self-Denying Ordinance was passed at last - and Essex, Manchester and Waller were among those who were flung aside. By a quirk of irrational reasoning, Oliver Cromwell, like Waller a Member of the House of Commons and therefore equally debarred from military command by this measure, was actually to survive and retain command of the New Model Horse. If he had not, the remaining course of the war and England's long-term future, might have been very different.

19

'That darling of the sectaries'

MILITARY defeat in Cornwall and muddled Roundhead thinking in the weeks since Newbury had prompted the autumn's violent debate and the eventual passing of this radical measure. But friction and differences of opinion had long been smouldering and defeat was merely a catalyst. Religious and political in origin, the dialogue that took place in both Lords and Commons had assumed an increasingly personal slant, and the real issues of the day had become submerged in bouts of mud slinging and character assassination.

At the very centre of this debilitating earthquake stood Oliver Cromwell, the member for Huntingdon, and a self-enlightened visionary. The religious argument was bound to be contentious. Episcopacy, the rule of bishops, had been undoubtedly overthrown, but Parliament's champions were divided about what to put in its place. Presbyterianism, the belief in an ordered but bishopless church hierarchy, held sway at Westminster and in the camps of Parliament's Scottish allies. An increasingly vocal minority, however, had begun to challenge this cosy arrangement, arguing for the autonomy of local congregations to conduct their own affairs without the constraints of a dictatorship from the centre. These Independents, led in the Commons by Henry Vane and Oliver St. John, were soon to discover that Cromwell would be their most persuasive and vociferous spokesman.

But Independency had political and military overtones as well as religious. In the autumn debates, issues of state and the conduct of war had become paramount. Cromwell and his associates looked for scapegoats on which to heap the responsibilities for defeat. Supreme amongst the chosen objects for ridicule was the Earl of Manchester, perhaps unjustifiably blamed for the debacle at Newbury. Whether responsible or not, he was personally targeted by the scornful Cromwell. In the heated debates on the floors of both Chambers, insults took the place of rhetoric - and passion was substituted for cool-headed reasoning. Unwisely perhaps, Cromwell added a social dimension, apparently declaring that: *'there never would be a good time in England till we had done with Lords'.* [1] This declaration of class warfare served only to inflame moods still further and cause the Lords to rally to Manchester's support.

The Scots, too, enlisted in the ranks of the Earl's supporters. Cromwell had long argued against the alliance with Scotland and had recently condemned proposals to invite the Scots to assist in taking Oxford. His articulate support for the Independents angered the Scottish Presbyterians who felt that, while Cromwell remained as a barrier, a uniform religion across the realm could never be applied. The Scots now began to angle for Cromwell's destruction, and elected Lawrence Crawford, major-general in Manchester's army, as their champion of debate. Slandering of Cromwell was about to become fashionable.

The Presbyterian scholar, Robert Baillie, fired the opening salvo: *'We must crave reason of that darling of the sectaries'*, he declared, *'and obtaining his removal from the army, which himself by his over rashness, has procured, to break the power of that potent faction'.*

---

[1] Carlyle T. 'Cromwell's Letters' XXII

This personal attack on Cromwell began at the very moment when the lower house started to debate the reasons for continuing military failures. '*The two Houses had taken notice of the bad success of their armies on several occasions, and at divers places, more especially of late at Donnington Castle, which was generally attributed to the ill conduct of certain eminent commanders of whom some were thought too fond of peace, and others over-desirous to spin out the war, and others engaged in such particular feuds, that there was little vigorous action to be expected*'[2]. Rushworth wrote in explanation of the autumn's political developments. On November 9th 1644, Cromwell pointed the blame at politicians: '*Members*', he exclaimed, '*of both houses had good places and commands, and by influence in Parliament or in the army, meant to keep them by lingering on the war*'.[3]

The solution was to remove those with vested political interests from exercising high command and to replace them with soldiers of proven skill. The latter bitter conflict between the politicians and the military would be moulded from the heated passions that were aroused.

That same day, Zouch Tate, the member for Nottingham, formally moved the Self-denying Ordinance. It called for the immediate resignation from their commands of all members of both houses. This measure would not only remove Essex, Manchester, Waller and Cromwell, but would similarly force the resignation of many of the regional Parliamentary leaders. The incompetent would be thrown out with the competent, after which it would be possible to restructure the high command of Parliament's armies on the basis of merit.

Support for the ordinance, however, was to be largely negative. Both sides, the pro and anti-Cromwell groups, felt able to back a measure which would deprive the other of military command. It passed the Commons with little opposition. But their Lordships were not so amenable. Seeing the proposal as nothing less than an

---

[2] Rushworth, Part IV, Vol.1, p.1   [3] Carlyle T. XXVI

attack on the Earls of Essex and Manchester, they refused to discuss it, sowing seeds of dissension at the very time when unity was most needed, and successfully delaying its approval until April 1645.

Re-organisation of the army came next. Success in battle required the forging of a sharper weapon - a professional fighting force capable of delivering victory. In December 1644 Cromwell had addressed the Commons: *'It is now time to speak, or for ever hold the tongue. The important occasion now is no less than to save a nation out of a bleeding, nay, almost dying condition...I do conceive that if the army be not put into another method and the war more rigorously prosecuted, the people can bear the war no longer, and will force you to a dishonourable peace'.*[4] Most present in the Commons chamber that day seemed to agree. On January 6th 1645, plans were laid for the creation of a new force of 22,000 men with Sir Thomas Fairfax as commander-in-chief, a position for which Sir Thomas himself questioned whether he was suitable: *'So... in the distemper of affairs, the army was New Modelled, and a new general was proposed....myself was nominated, though most unfit; and so far from desiring of it, that had not so great an authority commanded obedience.....But whether it was from a natural facility in me, that betrayed my modesty, or the powerful hand of GOD, which all things must obey, I was induced to receive the command'*[5]

But the New Model Army was the child of political and social motives as well as military. Determined to stamp out all remaining aristocratic influence in the army, the Commons decreed that its regiments were to be commanded by officers of calibre and sound judgement - and men of the right religious persuasion.

Yet it would be more than three months before the New Model's boots were heard on Hampshire's highways. By then the hedgerows would again be alive with colour and fresh growth while the sowing of summer crops would be nearly complete. Three years of warfare had failed to change the daily routine of rural life; an agenda dictated by the seasons and the need to survive. Starvation,

---

4 Carlyle T. XXVII   5 Fairfax MS. 36 Bodleian Library

cold and disease were the real enemies against which mankind was compelled to fight. These three knocked at the cottage door more frequently than the plundering soldier- and their demands were just as cruel. The contentious issues of the day, which fired the enthusiasms of the men of Westminster and Oxford, were of far less significance to these servants of the seasons than a sudden hailstorm or the arrival of another mouth to feed. Men, labouring in the field, seldom looked up when the soldiers passed by.

Yet, when the soldiers stopped, the fragile country lifestyle could be fragmented in seconds. Those visited would have only minutes in which to consider the safety of their property and their loved ones. The innocent of Hampshire were as vulnerable as the fox cubs of Spring, safe for most of the time from the huntsman's long reach, but subjected periodically to the savagery of the hounds.

The early Spring of 1645 seemed to be a time of distant rumblings. The war had temporarily receded from Hampshire, translated into largely irrelevant arguments in other parts of England. Cannon fire was seldom heard - and even the guns of Basing and Winchester slept without interruption. The soldiers of both garrisons, however, still rode out. Such sorties were as much strategic as attempts to gather food and supplies. Riding menacingly through the countryside was a form of visual propaganda, a way of reminding local people that God and Charles still ruled. Sorties also provided an opportunity to visit and punish those who might have offended the King. The constable of Somborne had his hands tied to a post by the Cavaliers of Winchester for some disrespectful comments that he seems to have made about his monarch. A puritanical speaker in Bishopstoke, ejected from his church after a sermon which incited unrest, was dragged by his feet from the village where he preached and left to die on a secluded track. With far less motive, Ogle's horsemen stole a cart and two hives from Micheldever men, demanding six times the estimated value of the contents for its return.

Parliament was no more discreet, equally failing to recognise that men's bodies and hearts could be won to Westminster's cause by more careful consideration of both purses and property. The excise had emerged as the second largest source of income, exceeded only by direct taxes on income and property. By the end of 1644 the excise on Hampshire trade was bringing in £500 monthly to Parliament's coffers and was still growing substantially. Frequently it was double levied. Merchants might be taxed on their raw materials and then obliged to pay again on the finished product. Periodically they would be plundered on route, their wagons held until duty was paid.

Displaced soldiers were partly responsible for these robberies on the open roads. The Earl of Essex's infantry, deprived of their commander and irritated by an arrears in pay, mutinied in Reading. Philip Skippon, now Major-General in the New Model Army, personally took up their cause, promising them full satisfaction in return for their continuing service.

Waller had been just as determined to eradicate lawlessness within his army and had a letter read out loud to every regiment: *'Whereas many abuses and violences are daily offered and practised upon countrymen, both in their dwelling and travelling on the road by soldiers in plundering their horses, cattle, sheep and other provisions from them, some of which intended for the market. It is this day ordered by the council of war that no soldiers upon any pretence whatsoever shall from henceforth plunder, seize or take away any of the goods, sheep, cattle, horse or horses, whether by exchanging or otherwise from any countryman or other traveller on the road, nor molest in their person or goods, any man or woman coming to or from the market without express order from the General or other superior officer having power thereunto, upon pain of death, without mercy'.*[6]

William Quincy, one of his quartermasters, chose to ignore this order and robbed a man near Alresford of his sword and six pounds. He then placed the blame on one of his subordinates, Nicholas Read, and the poor man was *'disgracefully cashiered, ...his*

---

6 The Courts Martial Papers of Sir William Waller's Army

sword broken over his head, never to bear arms again'. A few days later, a foot soldier was sentenced *'to have his tongue bore through with a red hot iron, for notorious swearing and blasphemy'*. The citizens of Kings Somborne were amongst the first to complain of their treatment, lodging a charge against Ogle's Cavaliers in March 1645 at a time when such complaints were still likely to be ignored. Contacting Parliamentarian and Royalist officials alike in clear impartiality, they asserted that the King's horse *'do much mischief in Somborne and Thorngate Hundreds....carrying off to Winchester divers honest goodly men'*. Ogle gave vague promises of redress and talked emptily of the King's justice, but materially did little to compensate the plaintiffs. Lord De La Warr, owner of Wherwell Abbey, petitioned the Lords at about the same time, claiming substantial damage to his woodland and pastures. Informed by their lordships during the course of his petition that his home had recently been earmarked by the New Model Army to accommodate a garrison, his only remark was that a garrison *'was likely to spoil the house and it would be of little advantage... by reason of the hills which adjoined it'*.

Oliver Cromwell seemed already to be conducting a one-man crusade, intent on carrying the banners of God and Parliament to the west, even before his new command was officially confirmed. On April 1st he appeared at Ringwood where Waller, despite his imminent loss of miltiary office, still held command. Well to his west, Goring and Royalism survived undamaged, and a Cavalier surge eastward from Devon still remained possible.

Yet, without orders from their London masters, Cromwell and Waller could do little. Eight days later both men were still in the Avon valley, awaiting the instructions that took so long to come. Forced into inactivity beside the Avon's waters, Waller wrote to London on the 9th in mild protest at London's failure to give directives: *'Send us with all speed such assistance to Salisbury as may enable us to keep the field and repel the enemy - at least to secure and countenance us so that we be not put to the shame and hazard of a retreat; which will lose the Parliament many friends in these parts, who will think themselves abandoned on our departure from them'.*[7]

Cromwell also shared in this unfolding pessimism. Uncharacteristically nervous at a time when the Royalist army was only a distant shadow, he wrote to Colonel Edward Whalley, one of the New Model's other burgeoning commanders, in the imperious style that would soon be so typical of his manner: '*I desire you to be with all my troops and Colonel Fiennes his troops also at Wilton at a rendezvous by break of day tomorrow morning, for we hear the enemy hath a design upon our quarters'.*[8]

Colonel Norton in Southampton expressed similar concern. With only a regiment of horse at his elbow and Edmund Ludlow at Odiham close enough to offer support, he asked for additional cavalry to be made available, reminding those petitioned that the garrisons of Basing and Winchester '*do range and rage about the country with all manner of intentions*'.

Growing Royalist aggression, however, forced him to take protective action before his letter ever reached its destination. Convinced that Ogle's Cavaliers had cast mischievous eyes on Southampton, he led six troops of horse to Romsey on the 14th April, intending to fortify the little town and '*stop the insolences of the garrison of Winchester*'. Half the men were detailed to commence the work of fortification while the rest rode north under a Major Stewart to Hursley to block the enemy's anticipated advance.

On the 15th, Hursley played its part in Hampshire's little war. Aware that Sir William Ogle himself was leading the Royalist force, perhaps 200 men, Stewart took up position near Winchester, probably at Oliver's Battery, attempting to hold his enemy at bay and so buy time for Norton to complete Romsey's defences.

Only brief hints exist of what happened next. Stewart, a reliable and forceful man, charged Ogle's unsuspecting lines, but achieved nothing more than a temporary dislocation of the Royalist ranks. The Roundheads then fell back to Hursley to await the arrival

---

7 Waller W. 'Experiences'

8 Sandford D. 'Studies & Illustrations of the Great Rebellion' p.618

of some of the men from Romsey and so offer a stronger defence.

But Norton failed to co-operate, and Stewart's small force was obliged to fight on its own again. Three times his men charged, breaking Ogle's defence with the speed of their sudden assault. The major, dashing forward at the head of his troops, was wounded in the thigh while his cornet was dishorsed. The Winchester Royalists disengaged first, leaving a dozen of their number in Parliament's hands or lying bleeding in the dirt. Norton and his troopers arrived an hour later and *'between Hursley and Winchester discovered the enemy's body, who sent out a forlorn hope to engage them'* [9].

Norton then speaks of unqualified success, rapid victory and eventual pursuit of the defeated as far as the walls of Winchester. But the gates had swung shut behind Ogle's discredited horsemen, and Norton's Roundheads were brought to a halt by the threatening muskets and cannons on the defending walls. For much of the evening, his entire regiment, 130 seasoned soldiers, drawn up beyond the range of Winchester's most powerful guns, could merely taunt the men of the city and boast of future times when Parliament's laws would be supreme.

Forty captives were taken that day, one-sixth of Ogle's garrison. Led in ropes through Hursley and Romsey, they were imprisoned in Southampton *'to sing another tune'*. And Norton's reputation as a saviour of Parliamentary souls soared as a result of his tiny victory. Weeks later, he was Governor of Portsmouth and consequently faced a much wider field of play.

Waller had, at last, lost his command. Returning to London on April 25th 1645, he resumed his political life in the House of Commons. Oliver Cromwell had left the county as well; curiously exempted from the requirements of the Self-denying Ordinance, he served as commander of the cavalry of the New Model Army. Successfully campaigning in Oxfordshire during the early weeks of Spring, he was apparently to cause the King to exclaim in torment. *Who will bring me this Cromwell, dead or alive?'*

---

9 Godwin p.304

In their absence, it was left to Norton to contain the spirited garrisons of Basing and Winchester. Unthreatened by Parliamentary harassment and the earlier pressure of besieging armies, these men had been able to dine like princes, parasitically draining the immediate neighbourhood of its lifeblood and means of self-survival. The soldiers of Basing in March 1645 consumed more than 1400 lbs. of mutton, more than 2000lbs of cheese and 20.000 lbs. of beef - almost a pound of meat per man each day. In addition, they drank liberally, each soldier consuming an average of fifteen pints of beer a week! few civilians or soldiers on the march could ever hope to dine like this, and garrison troops everywhere consequently fought hard to defend their posts and protect their bill of fare.

Yet relative peace and freedom from Parliamentary pressure caused Basing's men to search for other enemies instead. A Parliamentary news sheet provided the first hints on the 16th May of the dissension that now rocked the Marquis's well fed men. '*Royden (* Sir Marmaduke Rawdon) *is cast out from being Governor of Basing House...and the manner of his being put out, of the old will be true news to all that will be please to read it*' [10]. Rivalry between Protestants and Papists, men who had fought side by side in the service of the secular had parted company over affairs concerning Heaven.

'*Your petitioners*', the Humble Petition of His Majesty's Catholic Subjects of the Garrison of Basing House began.' *both during the time of the siege, which for some months was continued against this place, and since the raising thereof, hath had just cause to suspect divers persons of this garrison, for by reason of their different opinions from us, we do generally hold it more safe that this garrison, which hath been very serviceable to his Majesty, may consist of persons (both officers and soldiers) of one religion...*' [11]. The Catholics then went on to request the removal of all those who were not of the Papist faith, '*the fittest defendants and maintainers*

---

10 Parliamentary Scout   11 'Humble address of the loyal garrison of Basing' Hants Records Office

of a place of that strength and concernment'.

Charles heard their pleas - and Colonel Rawdon, the man who once professed that he would not surrender Basing, *'so long as a dog or a cat or rat did remain'*, was the immediate victim. He was relieved of his command of the house and received orders to join Goring on the Kennet.

The New Model Army was about to alter the colour and pace of this slow moving war. The nineteen regiments of horse which had served in the armies of Essex, Waller and Manchester were formed into twelve new regiments of the New Model cavalry, each officered by a colonel of unblemished merit. Veterans of Cheriton rode in their ranks: Arthur Heselrige's Lobsters formed the bulk of Colonel John Butler's 2nd Horse while Sir Michael Livesey's Kentish regiment lived on as the 5th under Sir Henry Ireton. Twelve infantry regiments, a total of more than 12,000 men, were similarly forged from the twenty existing units that had formed the three field armies present at Newbury. Six hundred of Waller's men would soon march out as the 12th regiment of Foot, led by Sir Ralph Weldon, a commander whom they all knew well. Essex and Manchester's armies both contributed about 3000 men apiece while impressment in towns and on village greens had brought forth the rest.

On 30th April 1645, this fledgeling army, cradled since its inception near London, left its hatching ground at Windsor and moved out to seek battle with the King. At its head rode Sir Thomas Fairfax, the *'rebels' new brutish general'*, the man chosen in January to command this fine army. *'The general was a person of as meek and humble carriage as ever I saw in great employment'*, a contemporary wrote in semi-praise of the sculptor of the victories in the north, *'but I have observed him at councils of war, that he hath said little, but hath ordered things expressly contrary to the judgement of all his council....I hath seen him so highly transported, that scarce anyone durst speak a word to him'.* [12]

---

12 Whitelocke B. 'Memorials Vol.11 p.20

Regiments of the New Model Army

Dragoons: 1 regiment of 10 companies
(1000 men under the command of John Okey)

Horse: 11 regiments, each of 6 troops (600 men in each regiment)		Foot: 12 regiments, each of 10 companies (1200 men in each regiment)	
Regt. No.	Commanding officer	Regt. No.	Commanding officer
1st	Sir Thomas Fairfax	1st	Sir Thomas Fairfax
2nd	John Butler	2nd	Richard Fortescue
3rd	Charles Fleetwood	3rd	Robert Hammond
4th	Richard Graves	4th	Edward Harley
5th	Henry Ireton	5th	Richard Ingoldsby
6th	Robert Pye	6th	Walter Lloyd
7th	Nathaniel Rich	7th	Edward Montagu
8th	Edward Rossiter	8th	John Pickering
9th	James Sheffield (Sheffeild)	9th	Thomas Rainsborough
10th	Cornelius Vermuyden	10th	Philip Skippon
11th	Edward Whalley	11th	Sir Hardress Waller
		12th	Sir Ralph Weldon

Trusting that professionalism and tight discipline would achieve what former forces had failed to obtain, he led seven of his new infantry regiments on 3rd May through Newbury into Hampshire, quartering for the night in Andover and the surrounding settlements. Messengers from London rode into town that night, with instructions to remain in the area *'till you receive further advertisement from us, which shall be very speedily'.*[13] The following day the army mustered for review in the fields near Middle Wallop to await the arrival of the cavalry and be informed of the consequences of indiscipline. *'And to the end that these laws and ordinances be made more public and known, as well to the officers as to the common soldiers,'* the official order began, *'every colonel and captain is to provide some of the books (* of regulations) *, and to cause them to be forthwith distinctly and audibly read in every*

---

13 Rushworth Part 1V, Vol.1, p.27

several regiment....that none may be ignorant of the laws and duties required by them'[14] Four men were singled out for execution, apparent leaders of a minor mutiny that had occurred in the days when the new army first formed. At their side during the hurried trial was a deserter, a local man who had been pressed into service against his will. He and one of the mutineers were condemned to hang from a wayside tree - as an example to all those soldiers present.

Less cautious than those in London who attempted even now to control his pace, he acted as a man who had no wish to be tamed. Initially ordered to rescue Taunton, he passed through Salisbury on the 5th and bivouacked at Sixpenny Handley on the 6th. By the evening of the following day, he was at Blandford, a journey of over eighty miles in just seven days. Here he received fresh orders from his Westminster superiors to split his tiring force, sending part of the army, *'provided it exceed not 6000 foot and 2500 horse'*, to secure the relief of Taunton while the larger remnant was to retrace its steps and tackle the Royalists near Oxford.

Three days later, another soldier swung from a rope at Romsey, condemned at a soldier's court to die for theft and murder. An entry in the register of Romsey Abbey records his hurried execution: *'a soldier, name unknown, hanged for murder when Sir Thomas Fairfax* (passed) *through'*.

On the 12th, the New Model Army reached Alresford, intentionally avoiding any contact with the enemy. *'I need not acquaint you with our hard march, hot weather and hard quarter, but in all our march we have not yet seen an enemy. We faced Winchester Castle as we came by, but no enemy appeared, nor any gun shot off against us'*[15] Fairfax reported in a letter to London. He reached Newbury on the 14th, twelve days after his energetic start -and not a single carbine or sword had been levelled at an enemy chest. From here the New Model Army crossed into Berkshire on a campaign that would result in eventual victory over the King at

---

14 Rushworth Part IV, Vol.1, p.27   15 Fairfax Correspondence Vol.1 p.234

'THAT DARLING OF THE SECTARIES'

Romsey Abbey, victim of desecration

Naseby.

Formation of the New Model Army and its absorption of Waller's soldiers, however, had not robbed Hampshire's Parliamentarians of their ability to fight. A strong force still held Farnham, Norton commanded at Portsmouth and Ludlow remained watchful at Odiham. Consulting periodically, the three men talked often of Basing House and of how they could bring the Marquis and his co-religionists to their knees. Odiham and Farnham men frequently rode out to view the house and park, sometimes capturing supplies of food that had been intended for Papist stomachs. On May 12th, a minor skirmish took place in Hackwood Park, just a mile from the village, during which two cartloads of hay were turned on their side.

London heard the Hampshire colonels' request for support. The three men were permitted to borrow money in order to clear the arrears on their soldiers' pay while the county's M.P.s were encouraged to introduce an ordinance into the Commons for permission to sell the estates of malignants and recusants *'and the timber that grew thereon.. 'It is but reason that incendiaries should have no wood left who strive to burn down the kingdom'.*[16]

Colonel Norton chose first to intervene in neighbouring Wiltshire's war, advancing against the Royalist garrison of Longford Castle, near Salisbury, on May 23rd. Feeling that subterfuge was their most effective ally, his soldiers claimed to be Royalists employed to levy taxes. The Cavalier commander and some of his officers came out, many without their shoes, and were promptly taken captive. Partly in recognition of his services that day at the side of Norton, a kinsman of Francis St. Barbe was appointed in July to fill the vacant post of Southampton governor.

Concern for the fate of Taunton, now under siege by Goring's army, diverted Parliamentary minds in London from thoughts of Basing and plans for a renewed siege of the Marquis's great house were consequently shelved. On June 7th the Hampshire committee

---

16 True Informer

received hasty orders from London to supply one hundred horse and a similar number of dragoons '*for the relief of Colonel Weldon and the brigade at Taunton*'. Norton, back in Portsmouth, took responsibility for meeting this request and personally supervised the arming of this expeditionary force. One of his most trusted officers and another of those who had served so well at Longford, Capt. Thomas Bettesworth, was placed in command and ordered to assemble his men at Romsey on June 13th.

Fairfax's soldiers were now following the King around the Midlands. Royalist strategy in the Spring of 1645 had faltered, and Charles lacked the muscle to deal simultaneously with the New Model Army and with the Covenanters in the north. But a Cavalier army under the Marquis of Montrose remained unbeaten in the Scottish Highlands while some northern towns still lay under Charles's control. At tense meetings in Oxford, Rupert had argued for an advance against the Scottish Covenanting army, claiming that defeat of the Scotsmen might restore the north to full Royalist control and even enable Montrose and his king to combine their remaining forces. Together the two men might work miracles. With the peer at his side, Charles could gather up the Royalist sympathisers of Northern England and then return south to meet the New Model on more favourable terms.

King Charles should have seen the folly of his nephew's suggestions. But, conscious that defeat was probably now just a matter of time, be began to bow to well-formulated rhetoric and listen to any proposals that might help to save his crown. On 7th May 1645, at the head of 11,000 men, he set out from Oxford on an uncertain expedition towards the north, provoking criticism in Royalist circles about the foolishness of abandoning his capital.

Fairfax and his Westminster masters took immediate advantage of the King's departure. By the 23rd, Oxford was under siege, while plans were forged to follow the King towards the north. Brief Royalist successes followed. The Roundhead investment of Chester was abandoned and on the 30th Rupert's men stormed

'THAT DARLING OF THE SECTARIES'

Leicester. The Prince's prediction seemed to be correct - and the King's dreams of eventual victory began to revive.

Indecision, however, in the days that followed gradually blunted the Cavalier drive. By June 7th, the King's army had withdrawn to Daventry, dulled by dissension in the commanding councils. On the 12th, the New Model, hurrying forward in energetic pursuit, clashed with the King's outposts on Borough Hill and a major confrontation seemed probable.

On the 14th, the Parliamentary forces drew up in force near Naseby, just miles from the King's positions. Charles had been wrong-footed and ensnared in the mud of a midlands field. A major engagement that day, however, could have been avoided. The King was still free to withdraw and might yet have chosen to pursue his path towards the north. But the fateful decision was made to stand and by 8 a.m. his army had deployed across Dust Hill, less than a mile from his opponent. At 9 a.m. the Royalist forces advanced. *'When I saw the enemy draw up and march in gallant order towards us'*, Cromwell later wrote, *'I could not but smile out to God in praises, in assurance of victory.'* [17]

By evening it was all over. Charles had watched the unravelling of his army during the day from the rear of his army's positions. At one point he had tried to interfere, preparing to personally lead the Life Guard in a charge against the enemy. But there was to be no Hollywood type ending with a hero king leading his men to a spectacular victory. Robert Dalzell, the Earl of Carnwarth, had laid his hand on the bridle of the monarch's horse and *'swearing two or three foul-mouthed Scots' oaths (for of that nation he was) said, " Will you go upon your death in an instant?"* [18]

Charles and his cause would never recover. More than half his army evaporated in the closing hours of that summer day and, with it, one hundred standards, two hundred carriages and the entire train of artillery. His nerve, too, lay shattered in the battlefield's

---

17 Walker, Sir E. 'Historical Discources'   18 op.cit

dust. He retired that night to Ashby-de-la-Zouch, a broken man with fragmented hopes. The deciding battle had at last been fought.

Fairfax and his army were now free to return to the south and test their swords against Goring's men and the few remaining garrisons of the area. Heading south-west to the relief of Taunton, he entered Wiltshire's upper corner on the 27th. Royalist soldiers who had taken possession of the church at Highworth were the first to feel the New Model's cutting edge. The garrison commander had constructed works around the church and placed a sizeable detachment of soldiers in the village to divert the enemy's attention. Positioning his cannon to face the church's west door, Fairfax sent an officer and a dozen men to demand the garrison's surrender. The Royalist commander at first refused. A volley of shot, however, brought him to his senses and *'he took down his bloody colours, and sounded a parley and yielded upon quarter'*. Cannon shot holes near the west door still remain visible. Fairfax's presence encouraged Parliament's southern colonels to once again blow the trumpets of war. Sussex and Surrey men mustered in strength and prepared to join Hampshire's soldiers in front of the walls of Basing. Col. Edward Massey, Governor of Gloucester *'where he had behaved actively and successfully'*, was ordered into Hampshire to assist, primarily to mould the assembling forces into a cohesive fighting unit that could break Lord Winchester's ability to resist.

On June 13th he arrived at Romsey with one thousand horsemen in his ranks. Southampton cavalry were ordered to join him in the abbey town on the 23rd, the prelude to a major muster the following day on fields beside the Avon. Amongst the Parliamentary officers who shared the comand was Col. Edward Popham of Littlecote, a man of *'a passionate and virulent temper of the Independent party'*,[19] and his brother Alexander. Several of the Jervoise family were also to ride in Parliament's ranks. Residents of Herriard, near Basing, they had suffered at the hands of Basing's Cavaliers. Sir Thomas Jervoise, the Whitchurch M.P., had already laid a substantial claim for damage.

---

[19] P. Scout

'THAT DARLING OF THE SECTARIES'

While waiting for his troops to assemble, Massey took the opportunity of baiting Ogle in Winchester, carrying of some of his lordship's penned sheep on the 19th and then personally taunting the Royalists from below the walls. On 26th June, at the head of more than two thousand horse, including more than three hundred who had once served in the ranks of the King, Massey left Romsey and rode west to join Fairfax on his Somerset campaign.

The war's 'third force' now emerged, igniting like a forest fire in the drying grasslands of summer. In the Spring of 1645, men of town and country rose in protest: plunder, double taxation and the demands of passing soldiers had become a cross too heavy to endure. Occurring simultaneously in all the neighbouring counties of the west, the risings of the 'Clubmen' were raucous, poorly co-ordinated and usually uninspiringly led.

And their goals would be far from lofty. Caring little for the politics and issues of the time or the passions that had forced men to go to war, the Clubmen had just one humble and unassuming aim: to be left in peace with their property intact. Assembling on the chalk downs near Petersfield with clubs and sickles in their hands, they petitioned both London and Oxford with a list of their grievances: '*We…..being too deeply touched with the apprehension and sense of our past and present suffering, received only by these civil and unnatural wars within the kingdom; and finding by sad experience….the true worship of almighty God and our religion are almost forgotten, and that our ancient laws and liberties are altogether swallowed up in the arbitrary power of the sword…...are unanimously resolved to join in petitioning his Majesty and both Houses of Parliament for a happy peace and accommodation for the present differences, without further effusion of Christian blood*'.[20]

But, prepared to shed their own blood in defence of their hallowed liberties, their threats became increasingly vocal. On their banners were inscribed clear warnings, aimed equally at the generals of both sides: '*If you offer to plunder or take our cattle,*
 Be assured we will bid you battle'.

20 Godwin

They were consequently regarded by both sides as allies of the enemy and possibly also of the Devil. '*They have not yet declared for the Parliament or the King,,* explained the True Informer. '*We fear they are of the worser party -they smell so strong of malignancy*'.[21]

Fairfax was just as unkind. In a letter to the Commons in July, he wrote: ' *They pretend only the defence of themselves from plunder, but not to side either with the King's forces or the Parliament's but to give free quarter to both. The heads of them all are so far as I can learn such as have been in actual service with the King's army or those that are known favourers of that party.....They meet with drums, flying colours; and for arms they have muskets...fowling pieces, pikes, halberts, great clubs and such like'*.[22]

In the weeks that followed their inception, the Clubmen were to grow bolder and more insistent, clashing indiscriminately with the patrols of Cavalier and Roundhead on village greens or on wayside tracks whenever the need arose. But, flourishing throughout the summer's golden days, they were to be as transitory as the season. Fading with the autumn leaves, the movement signified little more than the sighs of anguish of angered men. And it was never a mass movement: perhaps less than one in twenty heeded the call to the Clubmen's fluttering banners. Few were prepared to die for an unclear cause. No heroes were produced, no epitaphs were written. The Clubmen made little impression on the remaining weeks of a fading war.

Fairfax anyway had greater menaces to face. Goring remained active in the cause, his army growing like a tumour in the Somerset countryside. Only prompt surgery and an advance by the New Model Army could prevent the Cavalier army's further growth. On 30th June, after his seizure of Highworth, he moved west to Amesbury, intending to challenge Goring for control of the west. Here Sir Thomas hung a deserter from his army in another show of discipline

---

21 The True Informer   22 Fairfax Correspondence Vol.1 p.237

and called on the Clubmen to disarm. At Broad Chalke on 1st July, he was met by delegates of the Hampshire and Wiltshire Clubmen, who demanded that all the strongppoints of both counties should be placed in civilian hands. Cromwell, possibly the last to hear this outrageous demand, was the first to lose his temper. Referring to the Clubmen as *'poor silly creatures'*, he took all their leaders captive and so muted the voices that had spoken too loudly.

On 10th July, Goring was destroyed at Langport and the King's last dream was shattered. The victors now looked hungrily at Bridgwater, part of the vital thread that still linked Oxford and the far west. *'This town is of greater consequence, as we conceive, than any in the western parts'*, Fairfax wrote immediately after his success at Langport in open recognition of Bridgwater's strategic value. *'For, if we have it, we shall garrison in a line which will reach from Severn's mouth to the South Sea, and so divide Devonshire and Cornwall, where their chief force is driven. We intend presently, God willing, either to storm or block it up, that the rest of the army may be at liberty to go after Goring, or where there is most need'* [23]

Goring left England for ever, unable to serve his master further. *'As good an officer as ever served the King'*, a contemporary commented in generous praise, *'and the most dexterous in any sudden emergency as I have ever seen'*. [24] In the shadow of such defeat, the dreaming of further dreams would be pure folly, an act of self-deception that would merely delay the day of reckoning and compound the sins of the sinners. For the bald fact had at last become clear - Royalism in its traditional colours had been eclipsed and the dark shadows of an unsure age were already being cast across the realm of England.

---

23 Fairfax Correspondence Vol. 1 p.239   24 op. cit

20

'And the smoke of their torment shall ascend evermore'

THE Marquis of Winchester was amongst those who still chose to dream and fight on in a war which he could never hope to win. His men still sortied, raiding towns and villages almost as far away as the Sussex border. Yet he had been unable to stop the sequestrations - or the apostasy of the less strong-willed, the lukewarm Royalists of the county who increasingly approached the leaders of Parliament to seek forgiveness for their crimes. And he could never hope to halt unaided the growing Parliamentary pressure that brought enemy soldiers ever closer to his house. Detachments of Roundhead infantry now held the surrounding settlements as well as the larger towns: Upton Gray, Newnham, Greywell and Wootton St. Lawrence, and sported regularly on a dozen village greens. Every Royalist sortie was watched and reported to the commander at Farnham castle, but few were intercepted or held to account. Seen largely as irrelevant in the context of a dying war, the Royalist sorties were largely ignored and hardly merited retribution.

Some, however, brought on a more spirited reaction and minor skirmishes sometimes ensued. On 12th July, Parliamentarians returning with a laden cart were spotted on the road from Alton. Roundhead detachments from Farnham and Alton at once set out and clashed with the raiders in a field near Herriard. Reining for a moment to consolidate their ranks, they charged the Royalist party and scattered them with hardly a fight. The cart and fifteen horses were rounded up while a miller's son *'who swore like the Devil himself'* and eight others were led away to languish in Farnham's cells.

But more Royalists were abroad that day, a party of one hundred horse from Winchester's garrison on a mission whose purposes lie unrecorded. Bentley Green, the venue for Waller's review nearly two years previously, now hosted a clash in which the Royalists were quickly routed. Retiring to Basing instead of Winchester because Alton men lay across their path, the Winchester men were hit again, this time by the Parliamentary infantry based at Upton Gray and a Cavalier captain received two shots in the chest.

Soon the Marquis would be denied the freedom to send his parties out. Few Cavaliers dared ride the roads of Hampshire and even the stream of sorties from Basing and Winchester began to dry up. Parliamentary patrols were everywhere, intercepting travellers, merchants and all those who were suspected of *'being abroad for the King'*. Those with a legitimate cause might apply for a pass and so travel in relative safety. On 4th August the Countess of Southampton was granted the right to return from Oxford to visit her aged mother at Titchfield. She was permitted to take a coach and ten servants, but to return to Oxford within thirty days. *'The Lords have commanded us to acquaint you'*, the official pass stated, *'that they have granted a pass for the Countess of Southampton with her two young children, with a coach, waggon, and a competent number of her ordinary servants and horses, to go from Oxford to Titchfield... it being the desire of the old Countess Dowager of Southampton to see them'*.[1]

---

1 Commons Journals Vol.4 p.229

News of the fall of Bridgwater on 27th July and the subsequent availability of the New Model Army to assist in the capture of Basing enabled the Commons to take stock of the resources at their disposal. Fifteen hundred horse and dragoons serving the county committees of Kent and Sussex were ordered to Fairfax's side to help in any campaign that might soon unfold. John Lisle, Winchester's MP, and active politically since the war's start, succeeded in pushing through a measure which allocated £5000 from the Exchequer *to be employed for the reducing of Winchester, Donnington and Basing'*. Convoys of ammunition wagons were already on the road from London to Portsmouth, protected by dragoons based at Guildford and Petersfield. One hundred men rode with each convoy, every man paid eighteen shillings weekly for his duties, and the warehouses of Portsmouth swiftly filled with the necessary paraphernalia of war.

Parliament's patrols on the roads were fully paid, but those that drove the carts were frequently deprived of their promised rewards. Some had been faithful throughout the summer, manning the convoys that streamed out from London with supplies for the men who fought in the fields. By late August, they were in vocal protest and the ranks of the Clubmen grew dangerously. A sudden payment dampened their anger and the build-up of supplies at Portsmouth resumed again.

The fresh siege of Basing, however, commenced before Parliament's resources were fully prepared and while the New Model Army was still far to the west. Choosing to play down the potential role of Fairfax's forces in the intended reduction of the Marquis's home, Colonel John Dalbier, previously Quartermaster-General in the Earl of Essex's army and an engineer of some experience, proposed that purely local forces should be involved at Basing. On 20th August he drew up in Basing Park at the head of eight hundred horse and foot, apparently having offered to forfeit his pay until he had secured the house's surrender.

By the 23rd, he was in full possession of the church and

village and his cannon were positioned close by. But, with too few men and guns to take the house by storm, he searched for more subtle and less expensive means to force the defenders out. Chemical warfare was his favoured way: brimstone and arsenic poured on dampened hay and set alight around the house and a *'dependence upon the wind to do its poisonous work'*.

Heavy rains, however, soaked the powder of his waiting guns and the Marquis, *'used to the strong breath of old priests and Jesuits'*, seemed impervious to the smell of soaking straw and the heavy smoke that drifted through the house. The labour of digging began outside the house instead, the start of an intricate pattern of well planned trenches to add to those built earlier which still scarred the landscape.

Throughout early September the trenches grew. Dalbier did his best to maintain the reputation for the military and engineering skill in which he was held. Employing *'many good engineers and pioneers, such as use to dig coal pits'* to construct his ambitious works, he was able to write confidently to Westminster on September 17th that he hoped *'to give a satisfactory account within a few days of that business'*. But the forces assembling to help him in this task were growing less rapidly, slowed by the lethargy of the county committees and the failure of those who were in charge. *'Hants and Sussex have failed of their men, and the business is like to fall to naught'*, a contemporary complained in reference particularly to the torpor of the Hampshire committee who had so far sent only two men to aid Dalbier at Basing. The London armourers were more energetic, supplying grenades and guns for use in Hampshire; a supply of scaling ladders was already in transit.

Further murmurings of the Clubmen now threatened to interrupt Parliament's daily planning. Gathering at Rowkeshill on the Sussex border in an area under Parliament's control, their activities seemed likely to benefit the King. The Hampshire, Surrey and Sussex committees met in joint session to review the danger and ordered Morley and Norton to lance the menacing boil. *'A party is assigned to pacify them... if... they draw trouble upon themselves, let them thank themselves'*, A despatch from Petersfield reported.

Norton rode out from Bishop's Waltham at the head of horse and foot on September 15th. Troops from Col. Fleetwood's regiment of the New Model Army, now again on Hampshire soil, joined him near Twyford and on the 17th Clubmen and soldiers faced each other at Fisher's Pond near Colden Common. Norton, restrained by his orders to deal gently with the outraged men, attempted to persuade them to lay down their weapons and return to their homes and fields. Hotter passions, however, prevailed and a one-sided fight ensued. Some of the Clubmen were sadly killed, others unhorsed, and several were taken captive. *'There were only two towns that resisted us (Bishops Waltham and Petersfield) which were very ill affected and it pleased God to separate from the rest before they gave us occasion to fall on them: I believe we took from them above 500 arms, their colours and drums....it is evident by the heads of them that they intended mischief and I am persuaded it is the last and most devilish plot that the enemies of God and good men have left them'.*[2] Norton himself reported on the day's brief event. *'This day I hear worthy and religious Colonel Norton, with the Committee of Parliament, have given warrant to apprehend all the principal gentlemen of the Clubmen to prevent further mischief... ...which made their neighbours in Sussex to shrink in their heads, and we hear most of them are departed to their own homes'*, the Kingdom's Weekly Intelligencer reported the following week.

With almost equal bitterness against his own political and financial masters, Norton complained of the consequences of the failure to pay the troops under his command: *'Truly I have not a penny to pay them on Monday seven night and if I am not supplied by the Excise men I am sure they will mutiny here for I am confident there is not a more disorderly soldiery in England'.*

Dalbier attempted to use his chemical weapon again at Basing - and the smell of sulphur still hung on the air when the

---

[2] 'Norton's Report on the Clubmen' Historical Manuscripts Report page 163

besieging soldiers assembled for their morning act of worship on Sunday, September 21st. The text had been carefully chosen to justify the actions of the previous days: '*And the smoke of their torment shall ascend evermore and they shall have no rest day or night which worship the beast and his image*'.[3]

On Monday Dalbier, whose bombardment had started two weeks previously, '*shot in some granadoes, some of which are believed to have done execution*'. One apparently killed the Countess's waiting maid and another burned quietly for two hours before being extinguished. But he was a man obsessed by awareness that greater men than he would soon be responsible for operations against the house. Cromwell and a brigade of the New Model Army reached Andover on 20th September, intending first to reduce Winchester before entrenching in Basing's great park. He consequently worked feverishly to snatch some of the glory while it was still available to share, ordering his batteries to concentrate their fire against the New House, possibly the weakest point in the defences.

On 22nd September, his guns wreaked particular havoc, destroying one of the towers of the Old House in which had apparently been deposited '*a bushel of Scots twopences, which flew about their ears*'. The Weekly Account, generally reliable in its reporting of events, almost crows with delight: '*Monday and Tuesday last (22nd and 23rd) Colonel Dalbier played with the cannon very fierce upon the new House, and after many shots against the midst of the house, which loosened the bricks and made a long crack in the wall, he made another shot or two at the top of the house which brought down the high turret, the fall whereof so shook that part of the house.....that the outmost wall fell down at once, in so much that our men could see bedding and other goods fall out of the house into the court*'[4] That awful destruction caused the Marquis to claim that '*Dalbier is a greater trouble to him than ever any was that ever came against the house*'.

On Sunday, 28th September, Cromwell and his brigade

---

3 Revelations XlV v.14   4 The Weekly Account -(reprinted in J. Adair's 'They Saw It Happen')

'AND THE SMOKE OF THEIR TORMENT SHALL ASCEND EVERMORE'

Winchester Castle in the 17th century

East Front

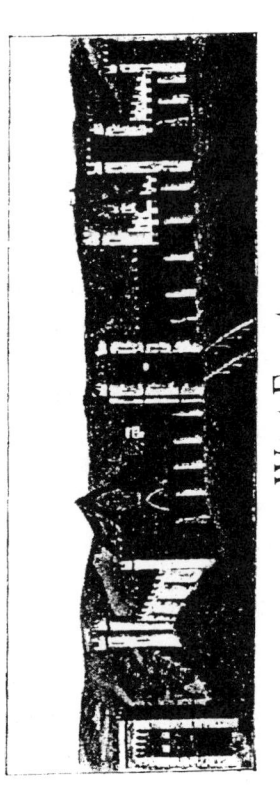

West Front

From an engraving by J. Cave

reached Winchester, causing Parliamentary news sheets to quiver with excitement and speculate on the date of both Basing's and the city castle's fall. The Parliamentary Scout, acidly eloquent in its desire for revenge, considered the collapse of Royalism to be imminent and gloated unkindly over the suffering that inevitably faced Basing's long- resisting Papists.*'They all Papists in that garrison, and if there were purgatory upon Earth, the Papists do find it and feel it there, for, besides the thick and perpetual darkness which the wet and soaking straw doth make, the burning of brimstone and arsenic and other dismal ingredients doth infinitely annoy the besieged, which makes them so to gnash their teeth for indignation.....On every side desolation dwells about them'.*

Winchester's Royalists were to be spared such extended suffering. On the evening of the 28th, Cromwell drew up outside the city and wrote immediately to William Longland, the Mayor, demanding admission for his forces. *'I come not to this city but with a full resolution to save it and the occupants from ruin. I have commanded the soldiers upon pain of death that no wrong be done.....only I expect you to give me entry into the city, without necessitating me to force my way, which if I do, then it will not be in my power to save you or it.......I expect your answer within half an hour'*[5]

Longland replied as promptly as he could, unwilling to anger Cromwell and so cause unnecessary destruction to the city's fabric. Thanking the Parliamentary general for his concern for Winchester's safety, he explained his limited role in the city's government.*'The delivery up of the city is not in my power, it being under the command of the Right Noble, the Lord Ogle, who have the military government thereof'.*[6] Clearly sensing, however, that the balance of strength lay in Parliament's favour, he offered to work on the noble lord and persuade him of the merits of prompt surrender. But Ogle's Royalism had made him inflexible and he would have found it impossible to bend to Cromwell's call. The thought of kneeling shamed at Oxford

---

5 Bailey C. 'Archives of Winchester' page 148   6 Godwin page 334

might also have strengthened him in his clear defiance. He tacitly chose instead to withdraw into the castle and slam the gate.

The bishop, choosing to join the lord within the fortress, might have been influenced by more spiritual concerns: the scorn of God and his fellow clerics. For, it is clear that Cromwell, no lover of bishops but still able to show respect for the Cloth, had written to the prelate on October 1st, offering him free passage and a pass from the city before the bombardment began. Curle, however, refused and so threw in his lot with the secular arm.

On Monday, September 29th, Parliament's forces, firing the Itchen bridge and gate, entered the city from east and west. Few defenders, it seems, were prepared to quarrel with the Roundhead muscle. Muskets might have briefly appeared at windows or house top gables and shouts of contempt heard. Yet there are no records of unnecessary heroism or blood spilling in the streets - only the pithy statement of a contemporary account: *'Here was found short dispute......but the enemy was driven off'*, the report merely explains, leaving men's imaginations to embroider the event. Ogle, Bishop Curle and 400 men had taken refuge inside the castle and, hoisting a red flag of defiance, would fight from there. The Roundhead lines probably ran from St. Clements church, used as a guardhouse during the siege, down South Gate Street and then west towards St. James's church. Turning north towards present day Clifton Terrace, the cordon then swept east past the West Gate to enclose the castle completely.

Placing his battery on high ground west of the city,* Cromwell himself describes what happened next: *'I summoned the castle; was denied; whereupon we fell to prepare batteries, which we could not perfect (some of our guns being out of order) until Friday following. Our battery was six guns, which being finished, after firing one round, I sent in a second summons for a treaty, which they refused. Whereupon we went on with our work, and*

---

*Reputedly at the site known as Oliver's Battery, but this is too far from the city to have served as an effective site for artillery

made a breach in the wall near the Black Tower; which, after about 200 shot, we thought stormable; and purposed on Monday morning to attempt it'.[7]

Cromwell's forces at the taking of Winchester

Horse:	Col. Fleetwood's regt. (3rd) 4 troops
	Col. Sheffield's regt. (9th) 6 troops
	Col. Vermuyden's regt. (10th) 4-6 troops
	Col. Norton's regt. (not part of New Model)
	Total: 2000 troops
Foot:	Col. Montague's regt. (7th) 8 troops
	Col. Pickering's regt. (8th) ? troops
	Col. Waller's regt. (11th) 7 troops

Note: Some sources, notably the 'Perfect Passages', make no reference to the presence of the 10th Horse at Winchester.

Ogle briefly pulled down his red flag of resistance on the 4th, the first full day of bombardment, realising that his chances of holding out had slimmed. But, fuelled by false rumours that a relieving party was about to arrive and rescue him from Parliament's grip, he hoisted the banner again, placing 50 men under a Major Clarke to guard the breach. The party was, in fact, a Parliamentary convoy carrying supplies for the besieging army. Sir William Waller, now reduced to the role of a civilian and political observer of military affairs, accompanied the train and would witness the coming pulverisation of the castle which was his by right of marriage.

Sunday, October 5th, was eventful, both sides posturing as though their fates would depend on what happened that day. '*The Lord's Day we spent in preaching and prayer*', Hugh Peters, Cromwell's chaplain, relates, choosing to disregard the heavy bombardment that rained all day on Ogle's head. '*Our forces began*

---

[7] Carlyle T. 'Cromwell's Letters' Vol.1 p.220

The Siege of Winchester
October 1645

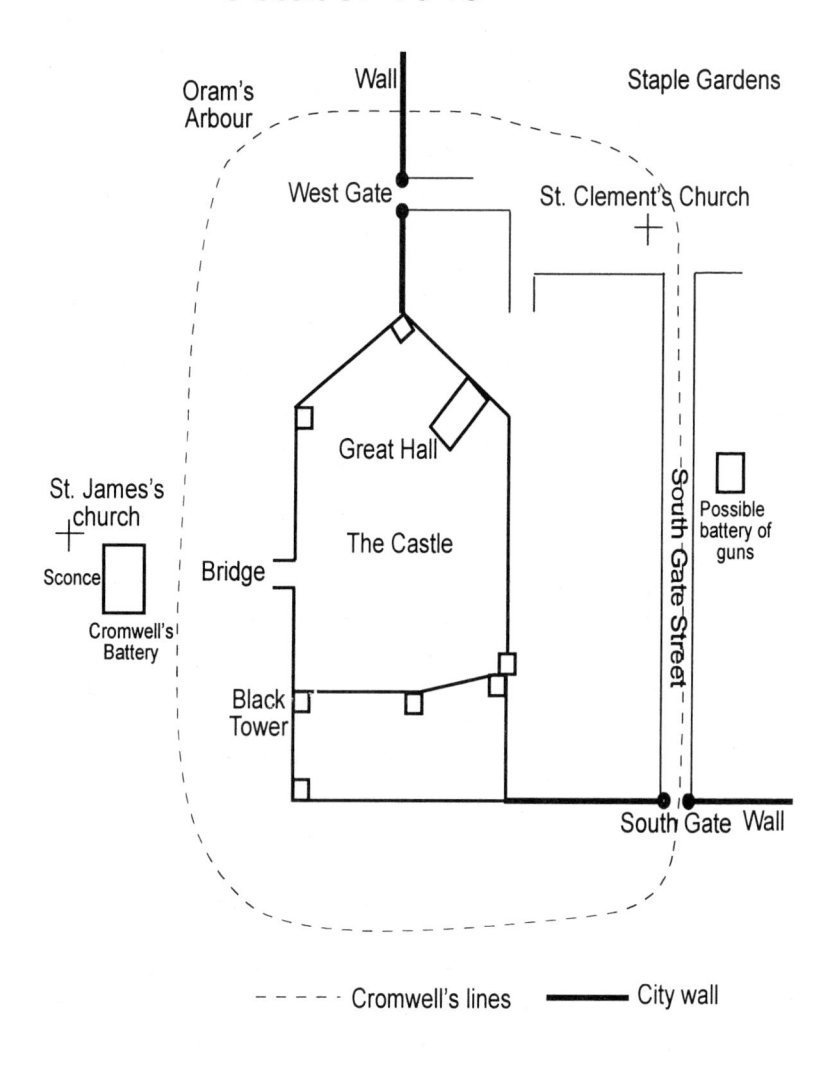

to play with the cannon, and played six continually, one after another, as fast as they could charge and discharge, and made 200 cannon shots in one day against the castle',[8] relates a more descriptive account of military activities. The Royalists, however, were just as active, spilling into the city in a quest for revenge against Roundhead soldiers and townspeople alike. *'The chiefest street of the town the enemy played upon, in which street my quarters being, I have that cause to bless God for my preservation'*, mused Peters, convinced that he fought on the side of the angels. And there are references of a Royalist sortie towards the guns and a letter of complaint from Ogle about Parliament's tactics.

A third summons was sent to Lord Ogle on the evening of the 5th soon after a grenade had landed in the castle's great hall and another had felled the pinnacle on which Ogle's red flag had flown. News had just reached Cromell of Lady Ogle's death at nearby Michelmarsh, an event that should surely have persuaded her husband to soften his tone of defiance. But the proud, unbending lord still wore a mental armour of steel and remained as immune to Cromwell's new demand as he seemed unmoved by his lady's death. And he was equally impervious to his garrison's calls for surrender amidst the sounds of falling masonry: *'O, for God's sake, grant a parley; articles, articles. O, let us have articles'*, they cried, their calls drowned out by the continuous boom of Parliament's six guns. But the breach was now wide enough for thirty men or more to enter abreast, and Winchester's Royalism was clearly disintegrating as fast as the castle's walls. *'Indeed, the guns played so fast and the business was so well followed that we could hear them, and they perceiving what a straight they were in, and how the house began to tumble upon their heads, thought that we should presently enter, and that they should all be killed'*.[9]

At 10 p.m. that night, according to Cromwell's own account, Ogle at last bent to realism and the plight of his men, requesting a parley and the discussion of purely honourable terms. *'Sir'*, he wrote

---

8 Peters H. 'The full and last relation of all things concerning Basing House with divers other passages'

9 Sprigge J. 'Anglia Rediea' page 130

'AND THE SMOKE OF THEIR TORMENT SHALL ASCEND EVERMORE'

to Cromwell, '*I have thought fit to desire a treaty whereby we might pitch up some means, both for the effecting of that* (the avoidance of further bloodshed) *and the preservation of this place. And that I may receive your letter with all convenience, I desire that neither officer nor soldier of your party may come off their guards, and I shall take the like course with mine*'. [10]

Negotiations started almost immediately. Colonel Robert Hammond, commander of the 3rd regiment of foot, represented Parliament in the nocturnal talks. Colonel Sir Humphrey Bennet and Sir Edward Ford, the Sussex Cavalier, spoke for Ogle and the King. Lights flickered throughout the night, the giant shadows of the serious minded men cast grotesquely across the courtyard*. When dawn arrived, the lights were extinguished but the talking went on; earnest, hard-faced men with their individual futures and reputations at stake. The guns of both sides remained muted and the flag still flew. Like singers awaiting the final chorus call in a drawn out opera, Parliament's soldiers rested in silence. Some played dice, others conversed, and an occasional cannon ball was loosed against the fortress to remind the garrison that a speedy decision was required.

It came in mid- morning. Ogle had been reduced virtually to the rank of beggar, obliged to accept whatever scraps were offered. But Cromwell was prepared to be generous, his virtually dictated terms enabling Lord Ogle to remain clothed with honour. The defeated commander was to '*deliver up the castle of Winchester with all its arms, ordnance, ammunition, provisions, and all functions of war whatsoever, without any embezzlement, waste or spoil*'. [11] at 3 p.m. on Monday, 6th October. He and his officers would be free to depart to Oxford, swords at their sides and their colours flying, and with one hundred of his soldiers as his personal guard. The rest were to lay down their weapons and return to their homes, having promised never again to take up arms on behalf of a discredited King.

---

10 Rushworth Part IV Vol.1 p.91   11 Op. Cit.

* There is a belief that a negotiation took place at 24 St. Thomas Street

'AND THE SMOKE OF THEIR TORMENT SHALL ASCEND EVERMORE'

The Marquis of Winchester
(reproduced with the kind permission of Mr. Alan Turton)

John Pawlet Marqueffe of Winche
ſter Earle of Wiltſhire and Lord St
John of Bafing.

Ceremoniously, Ogle emerged, mounted on his horse, as proud as any peacock in a country park. Reining briefly at the gateway, he acknowledged the victors and then rode off to seek reconciliation with his monarch. Parliament's soldiers would escort him as far as Tichborne; a letter of safe conduct signed by Cromwell himself would suffice to protect the lord along the road from that point.

Bishop Curle, however, was faced with a different fate, condemned by his refusal to accept Cromwell's earlier offer of free passage. The cleric had, in fact, soon regretted his decision to stay at Ogle's side. On the 2nd, he had sent a message to Cromwell accepting the offer that had been so graciously made. *'The Bishop was so far awakened in his judgement by the thundering of the cannon that he sent a message to Lieut-Gen. Cromwell to this effect, 'That the Bishop was sorry that he had not accepted of Lieut- Gen. Cromwell's former proffer, and being better advised, did now desire the benefit thereof'* [12] The Parliamentarian, however, chose not to honour his original offer and so informed the clerical gentleman that he would now be subjected to the same terms and treatment as the rest of those who had elected to resist.

Lord Ogle was just one of a stream of garrison commanders who had failed their King. But he was to suffer less heavily than most and was exonerated from blame by the councils of the King. His critics, convinced by inspection of the fortress and stories of its near impregnability, were less forgiving, even Lord Clarendon commenting on the ease with which it was taken. Sir Francis Wortley, writing his hackneyed verse a generation later, contrasts the stance taken by Ogle with that of the Marquis at Basing - and the latter, whose final defence of Basing was far more heroic, comes off far more favourably:

> *'The first and Chief a Marquess is,*
> *Long with the State did wrestle,*

---

[12] Peters

'AND THE SMOKE OF THEIR TORMENT SHALL ASCEND EVERMORE'

> *Had Ogle done as much as he,*
> *They'd spoyled Will Waller's Castle.*
> *Ogle had wealth and title got,*
> *So lay'd down his commission.*
> *The noble Marquess would not yield,*
> *But scorned all base conditions'.* [13]

Hugh Peters, passing into the castle with the victors, was impressed with the stoutness of the defences and so lends his weight to those that believe that Ogle's surrender was premature: '......*for when we had entered by our breach we had six distinct works and a drawbridge to pass through, so that it was doubtless a very strong piece, very well victualled.....and by the judgement of knowing and experienced soldiers, they had made it the strongest* (fortress) *in England'* [14]

List of provisions found in the castle at its surrender (Source:Rushworth)

Seven pieces of ordnance
Seventeen barrels of powder
Two thousand weight of musket bullet
Eight hundred weight of match
Thirty eight hogheads of beef and pork
Fifteen thousand weight of cheese
Eight hundred pounds of butter
One hundred and forty quarters of wheat and meal
Three hogheads of French wine
Ten quarters of salt
Twenty bushels of oatmeal
Seventy dozen of candles
Thirty load of wood
Forty quarters of charcoal
Thirty bushels of sea coal
Fourteen sheep
Four quarters of fresh beef
Seven thousand weight of biscuit
One hundred and twelve hogheads of strong beer

---

13 Printed in Baigent J. and Millard J. 'History of the Ancient Town and Manor of Basingstoke' p. 422

14 Peters H. 'The Fall and Last Relation of All Things Concerning Basing House with divers other Passages'

According to Peters, Lord Ogle and his men drank heavily before quitting the castle, intending to leave only empty casks for Cromwell's men. But of far greater significance to this scathing Puritan accompanying the army were the *'divers crucifixes and Popish pictures'* left by the departing Royalists.

Cromwell, of course, might have reflected differently, crediting God for the victory over bricks and stones. He had lost just fourteen men, a clear sign of Providence's supporting hand. Writing to Fairfax on the day after his victory, he placed credit where he believed it to be due: *'Sir, this is the addition of another mercy. You see God is not weary in doing you good. I confess, Sir, His favour to you is visible, where He comes by His power upon the hearts of your enemies, making them quit places of strength to you, as when He gives courage to your soldiers to attempt hard things. His goodness in this is much to be acknowledged; for the castle was well manned with six hundred and eighty horse and foot......It's very likely it would have cost much blood to have gained it by storm'.*[15] The general paid five shillings to each of the soldiers present at the castle's capture.

Bishop Curle was not amongst those who took the road to Oxford. Instead he sought protection within the city, asking Parliament's Lieutenant-General for an escort to his lodgings and a guard to protect him there *'lest the common soldiers should use violence to him and his Chaplain who were in their long gowns and cassocks'.*[16] Plundering inevitably followed that day, perpetrated by the free spirited and vengeful men of Cromwell's army against those weighed down by defeat and often with little more than the shirts on their backs. At King's Worthy, one of Ogle's officers was stripped of his clothes and several men were deprived of their boots. But punishment of the culprits followed swiftly, meted out by God's fair-minded general as soon as he heard of this crime on the move. *'I cannot but observe a remarkable piece of justice to the enemy, for some injustice they had sustained at their marching forth of*

---

15 Rushworth Vol. 1 Part 4 p. 91-92   16 Sprigge J. 'Anglia Rediviva' p.144

Winchester, by plunder, contrary to the articles, which was done by some troopers', reports Sprigge in full commendation of Oliver's action. *'Who, being apprehended, were afterwards tried by a council of war, and condemned to die; and after cast lots for their lives (being six of them), he whose lot it was to die was brought to the place of execution, where with a demonstration of great penitence he suffered death for his offence, which exemplary justice made a good impression upon the soldiery. The other five were sent with a convoy to Oxford.....to be delivered over as prisoners'.*[17] Sir Thomas Glemham, Oxford's governor, was equally impressed by this show of Cromwellian justice and sent them back *'with an acknowledgement of the Lieut. General's nobleness'.*

The secular and ecclesiastical were to suffer equally in Winchester. During another bout of Parliamentary licentiousness, a small part of the city was consumed in flames. A Peter Chamberlain, living next door to the castle, apparently lost his home ; an army of rats was seen scurrying from his cellar. The castle and Wolvesey Palace were punished too, slighted by order of Cromwell himself with little regard for the laws of ownership. And the proscribing of the city's Royalists was to begin in earnest.

News of the city's fall reached the defenders of Basing House two days later and, like Dalbier's cannons that bombarded daily, served to undermine the core of the resistance. Men periodically left at night, seeking anonymity in the world outside. One, caught by a Roundhead patrol, offered candles as a bribe for his freedom.

Cromwell sent 800 men to assist Dalbier after Winchester's surrender was sealed, possibly intending himself to march first against Wiltshire's Longford castle and then join Fairfax again in further cleansing operations wherever the need arose. Wagers were placed in London on which of the two local Royalist nests would be emptied first. The vituperative press grew louder in its comments about the Marquis and his followers, describing the house as *'the habitation of devilish men and the sink of English abomination'*. In

---

17 Op. Cit.

the first ten days of October, additional supplies of ammunition were sent to Dalbier, and the convoys on the roads from Reading and Windsor became more numerous, causing the London press to become more speculative in their interpretation of what might happen next. *'Basing is now closed up'*, states the 'City Scout' on the 9th, even before Cromwell's plans to move against Basing were known to the world. *'Lieut. General Cromwell makes his batteries, and hopes to put the Lord Marquis into the same posture that Bishop Curle was in at Winchester, and within a few days you will hear that the house is as broken as the citizens that are in it'*. Two days later, however, in slightly less sanguine mood, it pays tribute at last to the bravery of the defenders: *'They within (are) as resolute to stand it out to the last man, they are notable marksmen, and with their long pieces can take a man at half head, as one would kill a sparrow'*.

Leaving a garrrison in Winchester under the command of Lieut. Col. Philip Lower, the hero of Christchurch's defence, he set out on the 7th to Alresford, the first leg of his short journey to Basing Park. On the morning of the 8th, his battalions were seen from the Marquis's windows, and another mental wall of resistance must surely have fallen. *'The next morning, about eight, our forlorn hope came into Basingstoke'*, reports Mercurius Verdicus, *'…… and drawing all our forces into a body in the field betwixt Hackwood Park and Basingstoke, three regiments of foot and two of horse were sent through the town, and drew up on the hill by the highway that leadeth to Andover. The rest of our forces kept on the other side of the river, and drew up towards the House by the Park, and Dalbier remained on the other side, where he had placed his battery next to Basing town'*.

Most of the artillery, including five large mortars, were positioned to the south-east, complementing Dalbier's overworked guns near the church. Seven thousand men were soon in readiness for assault or investment, tuned to respond to whatever strategy Cromwell might consider to be most appropriate. But, unlike the more impulsive heart that beat in Waller's chest at the earlier siege, Cromwell chose to survey the crumbled walls of Basing House, looking for the point that would be most likely to allow his soldiers in. Captain Richard Deane, Comptroller of the Ordnance and later an admiral of some repute, was at his side, the two men as methodical as chess players on a public stage.

On the 10th, the mortars opened fire, destroying the lady's private chamber. But the mortars were soon silenced, and a summons for surrender was delivered on the following day. Some in the house undoubtedly counselled surrender, citing Ogle's honourable capitulation at Winchester and the honourable terms which he received as evidence of Cromwell's generosity. The Papists, however, are said to have argued otherwise, for *'knowing how ill it would go with them if the place were taken, do persuade the defendants to persevere in their obstinacy, telling them that it is meritorious and that if they die in the defence of that place they shall be numbered in the catalogue of martyrs'*.[18] Cromwell's demands were consequently refused, the Royalist reply accompanied, no doubt, by a flourish of fine words and gestures of undying defiance.

And so detailed plans for storming were formulated, Dalbier's command continuing to man the siege lines next to the Grange where his men were now fully entrenched. Colonel Pickering's regiment stood on his left, facing the New House where a breach had already formed. Hardress Waller's and Montague's regiments held the south with the regiment of Colonel Edward Hartopp * possibly protecting the artillery to the south east of the house.

On Sunday, October 12th, Parliament's God-fearing regiments paraded for worship, clustered in the open air to secure their alliance with Heaven. While Peters fired up their spirits with words chosen carefully to fall like seeds on fertile soil, the house

---

* Not officially part of Cromwell's brigade and probably attached to Dalbier's force

18 Peters H and &Carlyle T. p.225 and Sprigge J. p.137

stood like a disconnected backdrop, an irreverent witness of Parliament at prayer. Despite the months of siege and unkind bombardment, much of the building's former dignity remained - as one contemporary suggests: *'The Old House had stood two or three hundred years, a nest of idolatry, the New House surpassing that, in beauty and stateliness, and either of them fit to make an emperor's court. The rooms before the storm, in both Houses, were all completely furnished; provisions for some years rather than months, 400 quarters of wheat, bacon, divers rooms full, containing hundreds of flitches, cheese proportionable, with oatmeal, beef, pork; beer divers cellars full, and that very good.....In truth, the House stood in its full pride, and the enemy was persuaded that it would be the last piece of ground that would be taken by the Parliament, because they had so often foiled our forces which had formerly appeared before'* [19] For the Marquis, the house was as inviolable as his own body, something private, personal and to be defended until the last drop of his blood was drained. The guns resumed that afternoon, the batteries to north and south seeming to compete in their punishment of the house.

October 13th was shrouded in fog and even the lingering majesty of the buildings was lost in the clinging mist. Prisoners were swapped that morning, twenty or so defenders brought to the peer's doors and exchanged for Parliamentary troopers who had been held within. Cromwell remained in his quarters for most of that day, consulting with those that knew the configurations and weaknesses of Basing House, and planning the mechanisms of assault.

A party of the Marquis's men, however, chose to make a sudden sortie, using the cover of the fog to conceal their movements. Whether they intended to escape or merely bring mischief to the besieging troops remains unclear, but the trouble subsequently caused is well-recorded in ink. For Colonel Hammond, visiting the scene with one of his officers, had ridden out too, apparently to review the cavalry first and then go on to consult with Cromwell.

---

[19] Adair J. 'They saw it happen'

Enemy met enemy in the fog strewn lane, Hammond apparently mistaking the Cavalier horsemen for Parliamentary troopers, and he and his companion were soon inside the marquis's gaol. Cromwell wrote to the peer that night, warning the latter *'that if any wrong or violence were offered these men, the best in the house should not obtain quarter'.* [20] Released a day later when the house was stormed, he made no complaint about his treatment as Lord Paulet's forced guest, losing *'neither the rings on his fingers, nor the clothes on his back'*. He was later to serve as the King's jailer at Carisbrooke Castle.

Oliver sat in prayer that night, the eve of the intended storming of Loyalty House. The Royalist guards also kept their vigil, patrolling roof and courtyard as they had done for weeks gone past. Beyond, the campfires of four enemy regiments glowed, their flames dulled by the fog that continued to persist. Sometimes the sound of singing drifted forward to the cavalier ears, the well-known words of favourite psalms delivered in onerous, almost mechanical tones from Parliament's soldiers who should have been at rest. By contrast, the Marquis and his household slept soundly in their beds, possibly unaware of what the coming day would bring. For many, it would be the last sleep of their lives.

Cromwell's colonels knew their designated roles and the appointed time of the intended storm. Some slept intermittently, tensed by anticipation of possible death on the field of battle. The last of the campfires faded, the singing stopped too, and the usual silence of an autumn night was allowed to invade the scene.

At 6 a.m. on the 14th, four cannon fired, the signal for the storming to commence, surprising the guard on duty in the house, some of whom were apparently playing cards. Colonel Pickering's soldiers were probably the first to move, swarming through the yawning breach in the outer wall in numbers too great for the defenders to halt. The Royalists stood their ground, small numbers at each breach trying to stem the enemy flow. *'The dispute was long and sharp. The enemy for aught I can learn, desired no quarter, and I believe*

---

20 True Informer

'AND THE SMOKE OF THEIR TORMENT SHALL ASCEND EVERMORE'

This is believed to be a copy of a rare etching by W. Hollar

that they had but little offered them. They were most of them Papists, therefore our muskets and our swords did show but little compassion and this house being at length subdued did now satisfy for her treason and rebellion by the blood of her defenders'[21], another of the news sheets of the time reports in pithy testimony of the overrunning of the outermost walls. Retreating Cavaliers blew up some barrels of gunpowder in the courtyard and threw grenades from the windows, every man desperate to stave off the hour of Parliament's final retribution. Colonel Hammond was somewhere within, witnessing the futility of this pathetic attempt at self-defence.

Only minutes later, the New House was in Parliament's hands. The Royalists, reluctant to fight in the open courtyard between the two buildings, were retreating again, dragging wounded comrades and looking nervously back at the building in which they had so perilously lived for several months. For just a brief moment, the New House seemed at peace, savagely broken but still alive, like a man who has successfully overcome a ravaging disease. Then the red-coated hordes emerged, flooding out from doors and windows -an unstoppable tide that engulfed every Royalist who tarried too long. Beyond was the gateway to the Old House, part of the fortress's inner defences, and now the narrow funnel through which the defenders would be forced to pass. This gateway seems to have escaped the attack: robust and formidable, and with loose blocks of timber stretched across its entrance, it was considered impregnable. A small wooden bridge seemed to offer a greater chance of success and it was upon this structure that the Roundhead force was concentrated. Some of the Marquis's men stood to aim their weapons at approaching Parliamentary hearts and others threw the last of their grenades, but still Pickering's men swept on. Sudden flames, however, forced them back: timbers and planks on the bridge itself had been hurriedly set alight in a final effort to save the citadel for King and Pope.

Black ensigns appeared at the windows above, visible tokens

---

21 Kingdom's Weekly Post

'AND THE SMOKE OF THEIR TORMENT SHALL ASCEND EVERMORE'

Position of the wooden gateway to the Old House

of defiance that served at least to hearten those who sheltered within. And a few Royalists stood on the bridge behind the smoke and flames, swords drawn, choosing to be listed amongst the martyrs for the cause and earning the admiration of the journals of the time: *'And then the besieged showed incredible boldness, for although they knew that it was impossible for them to subsist, yet they fought it out to the last, and disputed every entry and passage with the edge of the sword, being all resolved to die, and as any of them fell their second, with infinite boldness, adventured to revenge their fellows' death'.*[22]

Colonels Montagu and Waller had been just as active, storming from the south when the guns gave the signal. Here the strong walls of the Old House had not been breached and a moat lay across the soldiers' path. Like waves on a wild headland, the Parliamentarians came on, 3000 or more against the citadel's outer walls on which stood a single 18 pounder cannon and a handful of grim-faced men.

Two hours later, the storm had abated and the Marquis's colours had gone. No longer individuals with fears and personalities of their own, the attackers had become an impersonal machine with a motive power entirely of its own. The walls had been reached, scaling ladders had been put in place, and the mass had climbed, *'beating the enemy from a whole culverin, and from that work, which having done, they drew their ladders after them, and got over another work, and the house wall before they could enter...we have had little loss; many of the enemy our men put to the sword, and some officers of quality, most of the rest we have prisoners, amongst which the Marquis and Sir Robert Peake'*, Cromwell records, remembering, of course to thank a higher being for the day's soon won victory: *'God exceedingly abounds in His goodness to us, and will not be weary until righteousness and peace meet, and that He hath brought forth a glorious work for the happiness of this poor kingdom'.* [23]

---

22 Kingdom's Weekly Post   23 Carlyle T. Vol.1 p.223-225

The storming of Basing House

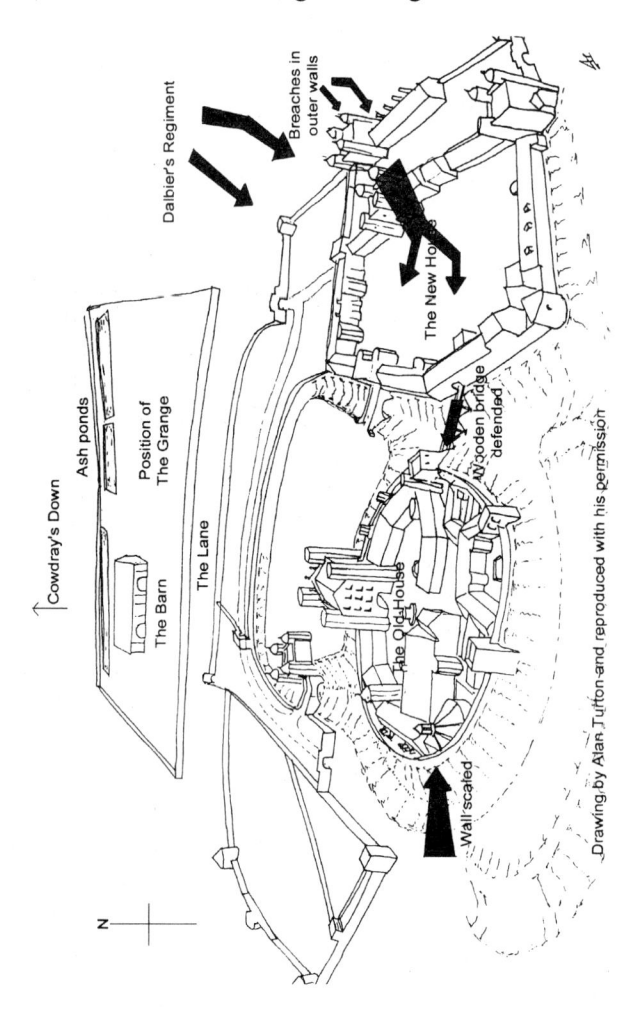

Drawing by Alan Turton and reproduced with his permission

Labels: Breaches in outer walls; Dalbier's Regiment; The New House; Wooden bridge defended; Cowdray's Down; Ash ponds; Position of The Grange; The Barn; The Lane; The Old House; Wall scaled

It was barely eight o'clock and the autumn dews were only just lifting. The rust brown trees in the parkland, companions of the house in times of peace as well as war, refused now to be part of the agitated scene, remaining stubbornly detached when the retribution began. Inside the house the killing went on, much in cold blood during a fit of religious frenzy. For these were quaking Papists, as vile as the cockroaches that crossed the cellar floors and undeserving of any mercy that might be offered by Roundhead swords. Two majors met their deaths while trying to escape, both shot on sight by the righteous Colonel Thomas Harrison, self-appointed punisher of papally tainted souls: one was the fearless Major Cuffand, *'a man of great account amongst them....*(both) *slain by the hands of that godly and gallant gentleman'*.

The lower ranks of soldier stole freely and killed as well. *'Some soldiers were eager to plunder, otherwise there had hardly any in the place 'scapt with life. The soldiers or others that were in the house, seeing our men come, to save their lives would bring them to chambers where there was a good store of riches; others minded not booty, but fell upon them and killed many'.*[24] The numbers slaughtered during the twelve hours of plunder possibly exceeded the number killed during the actual fighting, and classification between the two groups would be impossible. *'We know not how to give a just account of the number of persons that were within. For we have not quite three hundred prisoners, and it maybe have found a hundred slain,....whose bodies, some being covered with rubbish, came not at once to our view'*, Sprigge states in his matter of fact style. His next statement is more fanciful and might have been added as an attempt to boost his readership amongst contemporaries: *'Amongst those that we saw slain, one of their officers lying on the ground, seeming so exceedingly tall, was measured, and from his great toe to his crown was 9 feet in length'*. The skeleton of a tall man was recently unearthed in the garden of

---

24 Sprigge p. 137

the Old House; his spirit still apparently haunts the spot where he fell.

The Marquis survived the ordeal. Relying on Colonel Hammond's protection during the hours of fighting, he chose to conceal himself in an oven when the ransacking commenced. He was ceremoniously unclothed and taken away to overnight lodgings in the old 'Bell' inn in Basingstoke, concealed in a common soldier's clothing. Sir Robert Peake, Basing's military governor, lived on as well, purchasing his life by offering the key to his room where his money bag was found. Inigo Jones, architect, the favourite of kings and the *'contriver of scenes for the Queen's dancing barn'*, was amongst the prisoners. Now aged 72, he had been sent by the King to serve as engineer to the garrison. Deprived of his clothes during the afternoon's plunder, he was carried away in a blanket after an hour of ridicule and torment. And Robinson, the peer's fool, was slain *'as he was acting and turning like a player'*.[25]

Far more hated and consequently the greatest prize of all was Dr. Griffith, the rector of a London church and a man already proscribed by Parliament for *'the stirring and fomenting of seditious divisions and mutinies in the City of London'*. Wounded during the early minutes of fighting, he was now under armed guard in a Basing cellar. One of his three daughters lost her life on his behalf. Choosing unwisely to upbraid his captors for their harsh treatment of the elderly cleric, she provoked an instant reprisal and her head was almost sliced in two. Her naked body was found in a passage, only the second female known to have been killed in a year of fighting at Basing House.

By nightfall, Loyalty House was consumed in flames and several unfortunate men were burned to death. *'Riding to the house on Tuesday night'*, continues Peters, *'we heard divers crying in vaults for quarter, but our men could neither come to them, nor they to us'*. Probably not started deliberately, it effectively completed what the ransackers had begun, leaving nothing but bare walls and

---

25 Mercurius Veridicus

chimneys. Yet, by then, everything worth taking was already in the troopers' hands. Conservative estimates suggest that the tapestries, jewellery, furniture and plate taken from the buildings before fire consumed the shell were valued at £200,000 in contemporary prices. The countess's wardrobe was ransacked and household trophies taken, every man gaining something at the Marquis's expense. And the food - 300 flitches of bacon, 400 quarters of wheat, 200 barrels of salted beef and 4000 pounds of cheese, were auctioned in to the country folk who arrived in the evening to watch the flames.

List of articles taken at the surrender of Basing House

Ten pieces of ordnance	A great many crucifixes and Popish pictures
Twenty barrels of gunpowder	One thousand chests, trunks and boxes
Nine colours	Four hundred quarters of corn
Two thousand arms	Two hundred barrels of beef
Two hundred horses	Three hundred flitches of bacon
Three hundred slain and burned	Four thousand lbs. of cheese
One hundred and eighty prisoners	Plate worth £5000
Twenty gentlewomen	The Marquess's cabinet and jewels
One gentlewoman slain	Sir Robert Peake's plate worth £500
Six priests slain	The Marquess's bed and furniture Cost £1300
Four priests taken prisoner	£300 gold taken in one hole by one soldier
£8000 worth of beads, clothes and other goods	One cabinet of jewels burned
	Sir Robert Peake's box of jewels, rings and bracelets
Many firkins of butter	A box of brass graven plates of Sir Robert Peake
Much bullet and match	One hundred rich gowns and Petticoats
All their ammunition taken,	A great quantity of wine
Bags and baggage	Many hogsheads of beer

Source: Mercurius Veridicus No.25

'The soldiers sold the wheat to country people, which they held up at good rates a while. After that they sold the household stuff......and the country loaded away many carts, and continued a

great while fetching out all manner of household stuff, till they had fetched out all the stools, chairs and other lumber, all which they sold to the country people by piecemeal.......And the last work of all was the lead, and by Thursday morning they had hardly left one gutter upon the house'. Amongst the weapons seized from the hands of the fallen and captured were 600 muskets and swords, 10 cannon, 100 horses, 500 bandoliers - and musket balls in profusion!

At the very moment when the doors and timbers collapsed in flame and the fire became brighter against the evening sky, two messengers reached Westminster with news of the day's great happenings. Leaving their sweat covered horses in the hands of grooms, they strode confidently into the Chamber in the knowledge that their reports would be well received. The assembled M.P.s listened intently to their account, early disbelief dissipated by the firm assurances of two men who had witnessed all. *'God hath delivered'*, one of the members was heard to say and all gave thanks to the Almighty for *'His great mercies and manifest blessings'*.

Peters and Hammond arrived the following day, ceremoniously placing the Marquis's personal banner at the foot of the Speaker's chair. And for two long hours, they listened to Peters' detailed account and his public acknowledgement of God's great help, *'which his fingers, eyes and nostrils helped his tongue to dispatch'*. In Oxford on the same night the same news was brought to the ears of the King. There were those at his side who now considered that the cause was finally and irretrievably lost.

21

'A knavish committee of clowns'

'*THIS is now the twentieth garrison that hath been taken this summer by the army.....and men do now talk of likely peace*', Sprigge writes during the sunny aftermath of Basing's fall. But the final victory had not yet been secured and Royalism still lived. Like a disease in remission, it could burst forth again or be carried inwards from far away on the backs of an invading army. In Devon and Cornwall, it almost flourished, nurtured by a strong regional identity and the charisma of local leaders.

It still survived in South Wiltshire too. Yet Longford Castle had given no trouble and caused no offence, and might have been safely ignored. But Cromwell was anxious to see its destruction, planning to appear before Longford's walls as soon as he had flushed Royalism from the walls and chambers of Basing House. Receiving orders to assist in the capture of Donnington Castle, he wrote to Fairfax about his preference for dealing first with Longford Castle.'*I hope the work will not be long. If it should, I will rather leave a small part of the foot (if horse will not be sufficient to take it in) than be deterred from obeying such commands as I shall receive*'.[1] At

---

1 Fairfax Correspondence

dawn on October 15th, while Basing still smouldered, Cromwell's brigades moved on, reaching the Wallop villages that night after a march of nearly twenty miles.

Colonel Bartholomew Pell's Royalist garrison is described as villainous, even by those most sympathetic to the cause. Lord Coleraine, the castle's owner, had long since moved into his steward's house in nearby Britford, leaving Pell to adapt the castle to the needs of defence. Rose trees and ancient vines had been savagely pulled up and the gardens desecrated to make room for outworks and earthen banks. Stands of ancient woodland had vanished too, and the almost continuous sound of axes at work had prompted Lord Coleraine, watching the vandalism from his place of exile, to protest in fury to both Pell and the King.

Then on October 16th, just as the park's few remaining trees turned gold, Cromwell's soldiers had arrived, filing almost ceremoniously through the parkland's gates and taking up their positions on the higher land to the castle's north. For almost eighteen months, the garrison had been waiting for this moment, aware that the unstoppable Roundhead wave sweeping from the north and east would eventually engulf them as well. Slamming shut the castle's doors, they prepared to face the flood, determined to remain afloat for as long as God might give them strength.

On the 18th, castle and garrison passed quietly into Parliament's hands with hardly a shot fired in anger. One, however, had barely missed Cromwell. Fired from a southern window, the ball killed an officer at Oliver's side. Providence, or Satan, had plucked the Roundhead commander from the jaws of death.

The house was cruelly punished for its non-resistance. The Rev. H. Pelate, Lord Coleraine's personal chaplain, has left a jaundiced account of what subsequently happened: '....*quickly repossessed by viler devils than formerly haunted. For instead of soldiers of fortune, and some honest Cavaliers, there was put in by order of Parliament a knavish committee of clowns, who first pillaged the house of whatsoever the former guests had left or could be torn from doors or walls or windows'* [2]

News of the surrender travelled rapidly, sending a thrill of finality throughout the south. *'There was now no garrison in the way between Exeter and London',* wrote Sprigge in even greater optimism than before, *'to intercept the pasage so that a single man might travel without fear of the enemy'.*[3] Yet, unlike Basing, the building survived. Cromwell, presiding over the complete collapse of Royalism in Hampshire and Wiltshire, could afford to be generous.

But his influence still hovered over the smoking ruins of the house which he had so recently destroyed. *'I humbly offer unto you to have this place utterly slighted',* he had written in a letter to the Speaker of the Commons. *'It will ask about 800 men to manage it; it is no frontier; the country is poor about it; the place exceeding ruined by our battering of mortar pieces, and a fire which fell upon the place since our taking it'.*[4] Within days of his suggestions, the Commons were acting on his suggestions and overseeing Basing's final destruction. *'Whoever will come for brick or stone shall freely have the same for his pains',* one of their orders states.

In a further bout of politically motivated vandalism, he advocated dissolution of the castle at Farnham and the removal of its garrison to Newbury, arguing that the castle served little purpose in a landscape of rapidly disintegrating Royalism. *'If you please to take the garrison at Farnham, some out of Chichester, and a good part of the foot under Dalbier, and to make a strong quarter at Newbury with three or four troops of horse, I dare be confident it would not only be a curb to Donnington, but a security and frontier to all these parts - Newbury lies upon the river Kennet and will prevent any incursion from Donnington, Wallingford and Farringdon into these parts...And I believe the gentlemen of Sussex and Hampshire will with more cheerfulness contribute to maintain a garrison on the frontier than in their bowels.'*

All three of the Royalist strong points named in his letter

---

2 The Longford MSS. Private Collection   3 Sprigge J. 'Anglia Rediviva' p.156

4 Commons Journal Vol.IV p.229

flew the King's colours until the following year, only succumbing to pressure when the King lost heart. Swept back across the neighbouring borders into Berkshire and Oxfordshire, Royalism was like dirt discarded outside a door, trodden underfoot and possibly of little danger to Hampshire's coming affairs. But a sudden favourable wind might blow it back, and the county's leaders consequently responded to Westminster's still continuing calls for help. On October 18th, only days after Basing had been consumed in flame, Thomas Bettesworth, the county's High Sheriff, was given orders to raise fresh horsemen and funds, and join with the New Model Army in any action against Donnington that might be planned. And in a bid for an even greater hold on Hampshire, Colonel Jephson, the soldier M.P., was commissioned to raise a new regiment of Hampshire men to support the New Model Army in its final campaigns in the west.

The army and Cromwell, however, were soon well to the west, intent on dealing with the still living Royalism that remained defiant beyond the Exe and Tamar. Forced therefore to develop the skills of self-protection and guard the county against an irruption of the enemy, a force of 500 horse and 200 foot assembled at Basingstoke and called for active support from throughout the county. From Basingstoke they marched out to form part of the swelling garrison at Newbury. Garrisons still manned the coastal towns of Portsmouth and Southampton while detachments of troops took up residence in Lymington, Petersfield and Odiham to administer the new laws that would now prevail.

Yet the victory newly won by the sword and musket was already in doubt, threatened by increasing disharmony within the camps of the victors that might yet leave King Charles on his throne. Since late summer Parliament and its Scottish allies had sung in noisy discord, each distrustful of the long-term aims of the other. Presbyterians and Independents clashed constantly in the Commons, the latter calling for a post-war religious settlement that jarred with the sentiments of English Presbyterians and Scottish Covenanters.

Baillie, the Scottish general, constantly dug at the rift, and the military alliance between the two nations seemed likely to become an immediate victim of religious disagreement. *'Our greatest trouble for the time is from the Erastians of the House of Commons....they give to the ecclesiastical courts so little power that the Assembly, finding their petitions not granted, are in great doubt whether to set up anything...The only means to obtain this and all else we desire is our recruited army about Newark'.* Baillie wrote in dismay during the autumn quarrels. Alarmed by such utterances and open threats to use Scotsmen's muscles to impose a settlement to the Kingdom's religious strife, English Presbyterians increasingly made common cause with Edinburgh's religious leaders, and the arguments within the Commons consequently grew yet stronger.

Quarrels amongst the King's enemies were buttressed by secular issues too. On September 23rd 1645, the Scots had been asked to assist in the siege of Newark, one of a handful of Nottinghamshire strong points that still lay undeniably in the monarch's hands. £1400 a week was to be paid to Leven and his infantry, enough, it was hoped, to keep the Scotsmen healthily active in the allied cause. But previous promises had seldom been kept, and the Scottish commissioners had little confidence in Parliament's new commitment. Westminster's frequent complaints about the Scottish soldiers' conduct on their march through northern England and the Commons' virtual dictation of the terms on which the Edinburgh army should operate served only to embitter the language of diplomacy and widen the gulf between the King's two enemies.

Charles and his advisers, usually inept at the subtle arts of negotiation, cleverly exploited the situation and attempted to harvest the political fruits that consequently landed on his path. In October, Henry Rich, the Earl of Holland and the King's ambassador, controversially proposed that the King should seek refuge with the Scottish army. Covert intrigue followed, carried on by the King's more shadowy counsellors in a back stage drama that did Charles no credit. Documents captured at Sherburn in Yorkshire on October 15th revealed to the Roundheads the purpose and direction of the negotiations with the Scots and other parties, a series of opaque dialogues that had gone on since the summer. Written by George, Lord Digby, the King's Secretary of State, one of the letters referred to discussions with the Prince of Orange for the use of Dutch ships, approaches to the King of Denmark and the purchase of Irish Catholic muscle. Most alarmingly, it provided tangible evidence of the recent approaches made to the Scottish commissioners: *'We are'*, Digby had written, *'in hourly expectation of an answer from the Scots' army and we have cause to hope well of that negotiation'.*[5] On October 17th, these clandestine negotiations achieved their first solid results: a paper from the Scottish commissioners in which they asked the King to accept a religious settlement in both kingdoms according to the patterns of Presbyterian thinking. The coming months would witness further complicated diplomacy, bilateral talks between King and Parliament, Scots and Parliament, and even an approach by the Independents to open their own dialogue with the King himself.

    Revelation of the messy situation which threatened to erode the power of Parliament's sword to dictate the terms of peace served to stir those who commanded Parliament's armies into greater energy to secure total submission of the King's surviving armies. Three months of intensive effort would eventually cause Charles's house of cards to collapse beyond repair. Hereford and Chester, the gateways to Wales and major centres of Royalism throughout the war, fell to Parliament's blasts during the winter, and a galaxy of more minor garrisons capitulated at much the same time. Isolated points still held out until the Spring: Raglan in South Wales, Newark on the River Trent, Worcester on the Severn and Oxford, the King's chosen capital, all strongly garrisoned but individually powerless to stop the one way tide. And in Devon and Cornwall the King's standard still flew, stoutly impervious to the waves of reality that everywhere else had washed away the fortunes of his family.

    The Parliamentarians of Hampshire remained active too,

---

5 'Lord's Journals' Book VII page 366

policing the county's roads and villages with the enthusiasm of young boys at play. Vessels in the Solent were still watched and Roundhead patrols in the Avon valley searched the carts and packhorses that travelled into the county from the west. But for most of the county's people, a semblance of peace had already returned and the routines of pre-war life would gradually re-emerge. The values of those earlier times, however, would take longer to reappear. Mistrust, suspicion and religious bigotry had become too firmly embedded in men's minds, forcing each man to take on the clothes of self-protection and search for a personal formula for survival.

Periodically, the peace would be interrupted and the noisy clatter of Parliamentary hooves would be heard on the rutted tracks. Desertions from the New Model Army were not infrequent, and the County Committee was instructed to be vigilant and arrest all those who had unilaterally departed from the ranks. Just days before Christmas, a patrol arrested several deserters found in Andover, flogging one as an example to his fellows before escorting them back to their regiments serving further to the west. One, taken in Hursley on the day of his wedding, was treated more generously. Permitted two days leave to consummate the marriage, he was later paraded in Winchester and forced to wear a badge of cowardice to atone for his crime.

Moreover, relative peace would come at a price. In January 1646, Westminster's commissioners assessed the county at £3,400 monthly, the burden of payment falling largely on those who had been forced to pay before. At about the same time, Westminster imposed an excise on beer. The students of Winchester College howled in protest, petitioning the Commons for exemption from its demands. Nicholas Love, a Hampshire man serving as an official in London, did his best to intercede with the politicians on the college's behalf: *'We....intend upon the first opportunity, when the House is in a fit temper for it, to put in.....for the exemption, in which you shall perceive the readiness of your servants to do all faithful service for that foundation'.*

Existing religious practices, too, would be shattered by the Parliamentary hammer or forced into the mould that suited the victor's image. The new Directory was imposed on village priest and town alike, replacing the traditional Book of Prayer. '*The said book of Common Prayer should not remain or be from thenceforth used in any church, chapel and place of public worship....and that the Directory for Public Worship in the said recited ordinance set forth, should be from thenceforth used pursued and observed*',[6] the Commons regulation in August 1645 had ruled. Those who might choose to object were driven from their parish roosts and forced to join the more fragile life of the dispossessed. Hampshire's lanes were full of the victims of a drawn out war: the widows of the fallen, the maimed, the itinerant - and now the martyrs of a vanquished church.

The documents of dean and chapter were erased as well, symbolically destroyed in the passions of the day. '*All my ledger register books were taken away, the records, charters, deeds, writings and muniments lost, the foundation of the church cancelled, the common seal taken away, and divers of the writings and charts burnt, divers thrown into the river, divers large parchments they made kites withal to fly into the air*',[7] Mr. Chase, the Chapter clerk at Winchester cathedral complained early in 1646* - and the last of the surplices were consigned to bonfires. Men critical of the absolutism of Charles and his church, had already imposed a system equally as narrow.

The property of the churchmen would be taken too, disposed of by the State and with little concern for the rights of the former owners. One of the first orders passed by the Hampshire committee in the quieter days after the fall of Basing transferred temporary ownership of houses in the Winchester Close to John Woodman, newly appointed Solicitor for Sequestration in the county, who '*shall have the house, late in possession of Henry Foyle, delinquent, during pleasure, for laying up and preserving sequestered goods of Papists*

---

6 Kirby T. 'Annals of Winchester College' p.334   7 Cathedral Documents p.75

* Possibly October 1645 during the time of the great siege

and delinquents'.[8] A later Act of Westminster conferred greater rights to ownership of confiscated property on those who served the winning cause *'by virtue of a commission.......grounded upon an Act of the Commons of England assembled in Parliament.....for the abolishings of Deans and Chapters, Canons, Prebends and other officers and titles belonging to any Cathedral or Collegiate church or chapel within England and Wales'.*

Punishment of the secular and the seizure of property paralleled this state-run destruction of the fabric of the established church. The machinery that would be used to administer this chastisement of the defeated had already been constructed. In March 1643, a Commons Ordinance had decreed that all who assisted the King politically were to be charged with 'delinquency' and their property confiscated by the committee of the county in which their estates were situated. Common men were sitting in judgement of their betters and the social order had now been completely upturned. In a touch of human softness, the new rulers of the state agreed to set aside a proportion of the fine for the benefit of the delinquent's spouse and children. In August, the principle of compounding with delinquents was established, enabling prisoners to pay for their crimes by a payment to the state. By September, a committee was appointed to sit in the Goldsmiths Hall in London, charged to find ways of raising money to meet the demands of the Scots. The Committee for Compounding, administering the scheme nationally, had sat since then in almost daily session compiling a list of those who had sinned. The first of the list, presented to the Commons later that year, contained 3197 names, more than 90 of whom were Hampshire men, headed, of course, by the sinful Marquis of Winchester.

In September 1644, faced by the need to raise £15,000 monthly to finance the operation of the New Model Army, the committee was empowered to treat with any delinquent who might choose to compromise. Each compounder was merely to obtain a

---

8 Cathedral Documents p.77

statement from his county commissioners confirming the value of his estate and he could then effectively purchase his liberty and possibly his property as well by payment of part of its value.

The less offensive Royalists were the first to compound, those who had sat out the war in passive inactivity or timorous opposition to Parliament's demands. An unwise action or suspicious action might have been enough to place them on the list of the proscribed - and only early penitence would save them from the victors' wrath. On October 6th 1645, during the mood of optimism that followed from Parliament's late victories, Westminster extended a forgiving hand. All those who submitted by December 1st and agreed to accept the Covenant would be allowed to compound on highly favourable terms, forfeiting half the value of their estates, '*to be taken and employed for the payment of the public debts and damages to the kingdom'.* Sir William Kingsmill of Sidmonton was typical of those who took advantage of this early Parliamentary concession. Having inadvertently fallen into the slough of suspicion, he was summoned to London in November 1645 and unhesitatingly obeyed in order to protest his innocence. The committee '*hearing from well affected gentlemen that he was forced to undertake action for the king, that his personal estate between both armies is ruined, restored him to his lands on payment of just £500.'* [9] He claimed in his petition that '*he had never deserted Parliament, but always held correspondence with the chiefest gentlemen of Hants.'* Richard Shallett of West Harting in Sussex, was another of those named for disloyalty, accused in December 1645 of being '*one of the chief ringleaders and formenters of the mutinies and unlawful assemblies of the Clubmen of Hampshire'.* He was fined £50 for his error. Daniel Roberts, a butcher of Basingstoke, whose only offence was to sell meat to Cavalier soldiers, was also summoned. Equally contrite, he agreed to sign a simple confession and apologise for his misdemeanour. '*Your petitioner therefore humbly prayeth, being heartily sorry for these offences, that he may be admitted to a*

---

9 Godwin page 367

favourable composition and receive the benefit of the mercy offered to others'. And an elderly man was also hauled before the county commissioners for giving enemy soldiers the direction to Odiham. No record of his punishment survives.

The Marquis of Winchester's punishment, however, is well recorded. Taken to London on October 19th, he and Sir Robert Peake were 'lodged' in the Swan Inn in the Strand while the captors discussed their fate. The following day, the Lords pronounced, demanding the peer's immediate appearance in the House '*to acknowledge his offence committed against this House, he being taken in arms at Basing House, and then, this House will take into consideration how to dispose of him further*'.

They chose to lodge Paulet in the Tower while his estates were alienated and parcelled out to lesser men. One of those who benefited was Oliver Cromwell himself, awarded by a Parliamentary ordinance with the manors of Abbotstone and Itchen Stoke. But the peer was to outlive his Roundhead rival and would appear again in lordly robes and kneel at the new king's feet.

Sir Robert was imprisoned in less eminent surroundings, satirised in the days following in a particularly caustic pamphlet. '*With an intention to weaken the King's most excellent irreligious army, he did betray into the hands of the rebellious enemy the lives of many of his Catholic subjects, who very like hath neither been at prayer nor confession these seven years*'. The writer then goes on to playfully condemn all the men in Peake's control: '*They never plundered any man of more than he had, robbed nobody but friends and foes; were never drunk but when they could get strong liquor.....they were ever ready to sally upon the least occasion, when the enemy was farthest off, and, to speak the truth, I think they would never have yielded had they been sure that the garrison would never have been stormed*'. [10] Sixty other serving officers of Basing were held in custody in the capital. Two Popish priests, Edward Cole and William Morgan, swung publicly from the gallows.

---

10 'A Looking Glass for the Popish Garrison as held forth in the life and death of Basing House'

Like the Marquis, Peake was to live and breathe in another reign, resuming his work as a print seller and engraver.

Military developments in the early days of 1646 were to bring the King's supporters to their knees far more quickly than any posturing and threats from Parliament. On February 16th, Hopton's western army was destroyed beyond reform at Torrington in Devon, and Royalism became an outcast beyond the Tamar. Cut off from Oxford by miles of solid Parliamentary territory, this secluded outpost of the King's empire could not hope to last for long. *'The best you can hope for in the west is a reprieve'*, wrote Culpeper, one of the King's advisers, in a letter to a friend. *'The Scottish treaty is the only way left to save the crown and the kingdom...this is no age for miracles, and considering the King's condition is such, less than a miracle cannot save him without a treaty'.*

In early March the shattered fragments of Royalist armies and garrisons were glued together by Sir Jacob Astley, the King's most reliable general, and assembled at Bridgnorth on the Severn. But this rebirth of Royalist hopes was broken almost as soon as it formed: on the 21st Astley's force, 3000 strong, stood for a last ditch action at Stow-on-the Wold, but proved as transitory as gossamer on a dewy morning. *'Here certainly was a more than ordinary hand of God'*, wrote a commentator of passing events, *' which could not pass by without observance, being the last battle fought in England'.*

But he was not in a position to foretell events to come. Astley, now a captive, was to prove more successful at foreseeing the future. Seated on a drum in the presence of his captors, he quietly remarked: *'Gentlemen, you may now sit down and play, for you have done all your work, if you fall not out amongst yourselves'*[11]

The unity in the victors' ranks would rapidly become unravelled during the weeks to come. But for now, Parliament's political minds and military muscle remained firmly wedded, and the build-up of forces around Oxford continued. In place of the earlier see-saw of fortunes, the war's progress was just one way, an

---

11 Rushworth Vol.VI page 140

accelerating and probably irreversible path to rebel victory. On April 27th 1646, at 3 a.m. in the morning, Charles left Oxford, disguised as a servant and with hair trimmed for the occasion, hoping to achieve an honourable accommodation with the Scots. Reaching Southwell in Nottinghamshire where the Scottish generals resided, the fallen monarch sought salvation in the terms that he had recently proposed.

Within hours, however, he was a virtual prisoner; the earlier negotiations with the Scottish commissioners were held with little regard. For the Scotsmen were aware of the man's deviousness and were consequently little inclined to accept his royal word. And, at that very moment, Royalism was still holding court well to the south. Princess Elizabeth was staying at Wilton House, apparently oblivious of her father's fate. Around her gathered a few of the South's Cavaliers, like colourless moths near a fading light. Days later, the truth caught up, and the young princess and her entourage were gone, hurrying to the south-west and an eventual boat to France.

Few of Hampshire's Royalists were in that throng. The defeated began to knock more loudly at the compounding committee's door, reduced to the level of beggars within a social realm that had once been theirs to direct. The bond between tenant and landlord had been the cement of the pre-war structure of life. Now it seemed that Cavalier landlords would be dispossessed and thoughtful men began to fear the consequences: '*Men no longer know their masters',* lamented a contemporary pamphlet, ' *and we must fall apart'.* Sir John Oglander, at home in the Isle of Wight during the twilight weeks of the war, was more eloquent, grieving for the social order that had now been swept away. '*From AD1641 till AD 1646, in our unnatural way, no man understanding the true grounds of it, most of the ancient gentry were either extinct or undone. The King's side were almost all gentlemen, and, of the Parliament's few...Death, plunder, sales and sequestration sent them to another world or beggar's bush...I verily believe that, in the quarrel of the Two Roses, there were never half as many gentlemen slain, and so many base men, by the other's loss and slaughter, made gentlemen'.*[12] And all around lay an injured countryside, bleeding from the cuts of four years of war. Fields lay untilled for want of horses and men, wives wept for fallen husbands and children for their fathers.

Thomas Wriothesley, 4th Earl of Southampton, was the first of the dignitaries to compound. In September 1646, he was fined £6466 for his crimes - one tenth of the value of his estates. Sir William Ogle followed soon afterwards. With smaller estates to his name, his fine amounted to just £240.

Parliament used some of the proceeds to repair the harm caused by the bitter years of struggle. A stream of supplicants had already come forward, seeking redress in the courts for damage to property or compensation for their injuries. Thomas Hollinshed of Stockbridge received £20 for damage to his barn caused by passing Roundhead troopers while Sarah Dunbridge of Meon obtained £10 for loss of stock. Others were less successful: William Ayrton, wounded in Parliament's service, appealed in vain. County records speak of his attempt: *'He has altogether lost the use of his left hand and is thereby disabied to do any work and feed himself and his three children'.* John Rogers, apprenticed in 1642 to a weaver, also claimed for his loss of livelihood. Impressed into the King's army in 1644, he *'having no affection that way got himself off and went onto ye Parliament army and there served until May 1645 after which he repaired to his master and tendered his service.'* The weaver, impoverished by the demands of war, refused to take the young man back and successfully defended his stance before the Bench. Widows, too, asked for financial assistance. An Andover woman whose husband had been killed at Newbury, passionately pleaded her case. Living in poverty since her spouse's death, she had recently been *'plundered by the adverse party of what little she had, and was now like to perish for want of food and to be turned out of door naked'.* She received nothing for her efforts.

Westminster had earlier legislated to bring succour to those

---

12 'The Commonplace Book of Sir John Oglander' p.109

who had suffered in Parliament's cause, placing responsibility on the parish in which the victims had previously resided. *'Whereas divers well-affected persons have gone forth in the army raised by the Parliament .....and, in fight, have received divers wounds and maims in their bodies, whereby they are disabled to relieve themselves by their usual labour, and divers others have lost their lives in the said service,....the Commons assembled....do hereby ordain, that in every parish within the kingdom, wherein any such person, either now maimed or slain,did last inhabit before their going forth to the aforesaid service, shall raise a competent stock of money, by way of assessment, upon the inhabitants of the said several parishes, for the relief of the said maimed soldiers, and the widows and fatherless children of the said slain persons'* [13]. But, passed in March 1643, at a time when legislation was generally disregarded and the sound of muskets and cannons were the only voices that were heeded, few parishes had done much to succour their war torn inhabitants.

  The men of Jephson's new regiment were probably amongst those responsible for much of the more recent terrorism in Hampshire's countryside. Angered by the arrears in their pay, they took compensation at the expense of innocents and Parliamentary officials alike. Gabriel Floyd, an officer's servant, was robbed of his boots by Jephson's men. When his master complained and asked for justice, he was visited at his house and deprived of his linen. Countrymen returning from Collingbourne Fair in January 1646 were lined up in a field and their clothes taken. The county committee wrote immediately to William Lenthall, Speaker of the Commons, and demanded *'payment for God's soldiers and justice for God's miserable servants'*. A sum of £1746 15s 8d was promptly awarded to the colonel's restless troopers, money taken from those Hampshire delinquents who had chosen to compound.

  Parliament's servicemen, past and present, were now to be protected against the rule of law. In a series of measures passed by

---

[13] Commons Journals Vol.11 p.989

the Commons in Spring 1646, all those who had committed acts of barbarism or violence whilst on Parliamentary duties were indemnified against claims for damages and placed beyond the reach of legal retribution. *'For as much as in the times of this late war and public distraction'*, the Commons ordinance declared, *'there have been many injuries done to private persons, and other offences committed by private persons bearing arms in the service of the Parliament; the Lords and Commons in Parliament assembled, taking into their consideration, that it is expedient that the injuries and offences aforesaid be pardoned, and put in oblivion...Do therefore ordain....that all persons who have committed any offences, trespasses, injuries or other misdemeanours whatsoever during such time as they have been employed in arms, by or for the service of the Parliament, be, is, and are hereby discharged and pardoned of the same'.*[14] With a simple stroke of the pen and only very limited debate, Parliament circumvented the nation's established laws and ushered in a state of tyranny no better than that imposed by the Stuart Kings.

The two houses simultaneously took action against the spiritually tainted; those labelled as 'recusants', were to be treated far more harshly. Amongst these were the Papists, men so vile that not even money could wash their souls clean of the crimes that they had committed. Men found guilty of delinquency could atone for past sins and might one day again sit in the halls of the favoured. But the devilish lapdogs of Rome, *'abominations in the sight of God'*, could expect no such mercy and would be condemned to *'roast in hell for the impurity of their deeds'*. In the summer of 1646, Parliament formally identified the names of the totally unpardonable. *`All Papists and Popish Recusants, who have been, now are or shall be actually in arms, or voluntarily assisting against the Parliament or Estates of either kingdom'*. Just fourteen names appear on the national list. Lord John Paulet, Marquis of Winchester, again appears at the very top.

---

14 Rushworth Part IV Vol.1 p.519

The constitutional struggle was now largely political and the clash of armies was heard only in those few places where the King's standard still flew. Charles, ambivalent, misguided or merely unwise, had been negotiating concurrently with both his enemies, a posture subsequently exposed in a letter to Lord Digby in which he wrote: *'Not without hope that I shall be able so to draw either the Presbyterians or the Independents to side with me, for extirpating one another that I shall really be King again'.*

News of the King's departure from Oxford unnerved Parliament's military commanders. Unaware of the monarch's destination or intentions, army and politicians worked in unison to limit the possible consequences of Charles's flight An edict was issued, forbidding anyone, on pain of death, from physically assisting the King. Parliamentary forces appeared in strength at Lymington and took up residence outside the gates of the monarch's known supporters. In those days of early summer, England became a military state, one of the earliest of the modern world, and people spoke in cautious whispers and reacted nervously at the approach of strangers.

Charles's escape from Oxford did more to break the alliance between the Scots and Parliament than any amount of intentional intrigue could ever hope to achieve. Covenanters and Westminster were to wrangle bitterly over custody of the King, the latter even sending General Poyntz to watch and shadow the Scottish army. On 24th June 1646 Oxford surrendered to the New Model Army, a symbolic end to the war which send Rupert and Maurice scuttling off to the Continent while other less prominent Cavaliers went to ground in country shires. The Scots withdrew to Newcastle, taking their regal prisoner with them, and stubbornly stood their ground in England's northern territories.

Charles exploited every growing dissension, negotiating for his soul, life and the tarnished crown upon his head. On 23rd July 1646 Parliament laid out formal peace proposals, sending 9 commissioners to Newcastle to talk to the King. Abandonment of

Episcopacy remained their central demand and the morass in which the talks were condemned to flounder. Loudon, Chancellor of Scotland, present at the meetings, reminded Charles that the *'consequences of his answer to the propositions were so great, that on it depended the ruin of his crown and kingdoms'*. Stubborn and unbending in principle and practice, Charles Stuart stood firm and the Parliamentary commissioners withdrew; the story of their failure was to travel south more quickly than they.

Six months later, on 30th January 1647, Parliament purchased the King from the Scots for £200,000, the money carried north to Newcastle in 36 well-laden carts. The air of distrust between the two allies was almost as tangible and chilling as the winter fog and likely to be just as difficult to disperse. With little outward ceremony, Charles was handed over to the commissioners from Westminster - hardly a word was exchanged, greeting given or deference paid to the man who had once sat upon the English throne. Tight-lipped and wrapped closely against the cold, the men appointed by the winning side to take custody of the defeated King merely acknowledged their charge and prepared for the journey south. Behind them they left a war of recrimination and bitter accusation that soon spread south almost to London itself. For everywhere the pamphlets shouted in condemnation that the mercenary minded Scotsmen had sold their King and their principles for cash.

During his journey to semi-captivity at Holdenby House in Northamptonshire, Charles acquired some of the trappings of saintliness with which he was to be fully endowed in the years after his death. People tried to touch his garments as he passed, hoping to be cured of ailments and disabilities....and some even claimed that they were miraculously cured ! Near Nottingham, he was met by Sir Thomas Fairfax, the Parliamentary general who had done so much to bring this haughty monarch to his knees. *'The General is a man of honour'*, Charles said to one of his guardians, *'He has been faithful to his trust, and kept his word with me'*.[15]

---

15 Gardiner S.R. 'History of the Great Civil War' Vol.III p.212

'A KNAVISH COMMITTEE OF CLOWNS'

The named delinquents of Hampshire

William Ashburnham of Andover
Dr. Ayry
Sir John Arundel of Owlesbury
Sir Thomas Badd of Andover
Samuel Barrack of Andover
Richard Bevis of Hound
William Beacham of Andover
Richard Braxton of Winchester
Thomas Brook of Andover
Richard Broome of Andover
John Brown of Soke
Benjamin Bufford of Hursley
Thomas Butcher of Bishopstoke
Ferdinando Bye of Winchester
Lord Capel
Alexander Churcher of Hursley
Sir Henry Clarke of Avington
John Colson of Winchester
Widow Complin of Boyatt
Roger Coreham of Andover
Jasper Cornelius of Nursling
Lord Cottington
Thomas Cradock of Andover
John Crane of Euston
Henry Crapp of Morestead
Robert Cully of Twyford
Widow Dastin of Owlesbury
Henry Day of Hursley
Richard Dennet of Winchester
Giles Dowse of Andover
Pearce Edgecombe of Andover
Richard Edgecombe of Andover
William Fisher of Soke
Sir Gerard Fleetwood
Henry Foyell of Andover
Sir Edward Ford of Bishopstoke
John Ford of Botley
Dowse Fuller of Sparsholt

John Jones of Andover
Henry Kelsey of Weyhill
Thomas Kercher of Hursley
Edward Knowles of Hursley
Lady Katherine Knowles of Nursling
William Lacy of Kimpton
Thomas Lan of Hursley
John Lane of Boyatt
Richard Lawson of Hursley
Sir James Linkhorn of Boyatt
Ald. Longland of Winchester
Lord Lumley
Sir Spencer Lucy of Andover
William Mathew of Boyatt
Lord May of Bentley
John Mill of Bury
Thomas Mills of Andover
Thomas Mill of Nursling
John Miller of Wallop
William Mowday of Owlesbury
Sir Gerald Musgrave
Sir Edward Nicholas of Andover
Sir Edward Norton of Testwood
Sir Richard Norton of Testwood
Richard Noyse of Andover
John Nutier of Boyatt
John Onwins of Euston
Sir William Ogle
Paulet, Lord Henry
Sir James Phillipps of Andover
George **Philpot of Compton**
Henry Philpot of Andover
Thomas Philpot of Andover
Villiers Philpott of Horton
Sir William Portman of **Andover**
Sir Edward Richards of Marwell
Thomas **Sadler**
William say of **Twyford**

405

Richard Goddard of Andover
Ann Godwin of Twyford
Peter Gilliams
Dr. Green, Rector of Avington
William Gwater of Hill
Thomas Hadley of Hursley
John Harfield of Winchester
Antony Hide of Hursley
John Jones of Andover
Henry Kelsey of Weyhill
Thomas Kercher of Hursley
Edward Knowles of Hursley
Lady Katherine Knowles of Nursling
William Lacy of Kimpton
Thomas Lan of Hursley
John lane of Boyatt
Richard Lawson of Hursley
Sir James Linkhorn of Boyatt
Ald. Longland of Winchester
Lord Lumley
Sir Spencer Lucy of Andover

John Seviour of Winchester
Joshua Silvester of Tichborne
Bartholomew Smith of Soke
Joshua Silvester of Tichborne
Thomas South of Winchester
Southampton, Earl of
Richard Stubbington of Bishopstoke
William Swaine of Andover
Sir Benjamin Tichborne
Sir Richard Tichborne
Robert Tucker of Twyford
Ambrose Wait of Tything
John Weborne of Boyatt
Swithin Wells of Eastleigh
Widow Wells of Eastleigh
Thomas Willis of Andover
Winchester, Marquis of
Thomas Wyatt of Exton

At Holdenby Charles was to enjoy partial liberty, free to ride with the hounds and play bowls on the sunlit lawn. And here he was to continue his games of compromise and subterfuge, attempting all the time to widen the gap that had opened between Parliament and the Scots over the matter of religion.

But the parallel gulf between Parliament and army was growing far faster, and in this the King played virtually no part. Presbyterians and Independents in the Commons were at each other's throats, kindling a dispute that was far more vehement and potentially disruptive than any quarrel with the Scots. Uncontainable within the walls of Westminster Hall, the argument spilled out into the camps of the army where the Independents now held sway. Irritation over arrears of pay merely made the soldiers even angrier and brought the discontented regiments threateningly close to London. And in tactless disregard for already ruffled military feathers, the

Houses declared that no-one who refused the Covenant or failed to subscribe to Presbyterian thinking should hold an army commission.

Independents and Army reacted immediately, and the seeds of a new war were carelessly sown. Regiments of the New Model Army encamped at Saffron Walden while the Independents in the Commons howled in protest. Every utterance of politician or army officer seemed designed to incite - and cooler, wiser heads appeared to have vanished from the world. Charles, excluded from the political and religious stage on which he had once so pompously strutted, seemed content to observe events and intrigue when the chance arose.

Members of the Lords played their destructive part as well. Sensing that the Army might take possession of the monarch and employ him as a valuable weight in their likely arguments with the politicians, the peers ordered his removal from Holdenby to Oatlands, just to the west of London. The soldiers, however, were just as perceptive and their agents reached Holdenby's doors first. On June 2nd 1647, Cornet Joyce 'spirited' Charles from the house and escorted him to Newmarket, where part of the New Model Army had placed its roots.

Over-reaction by Westminster followed, a series of clumsy pronouncements matched by equally injudicious responses from the Army. A political order for the arrest of Cromwell was an empty but harmful gesture, impossible to procure but fatal in its consequences.

Parliament's declared intention to reduce the army's numbers caused the New Model's officers to issue the Solemn Engagement, a refusal to disband until its growing grievances had been redressed and full liberty of conscience secured. By the autumn of 1647, the rift had become a chasm and was clearly impossible to breach. Less than one year later, swords were again unsheathed and pikes taken down from their places of rest.

In the meantime, the Isle of Wight played host to the fallen king. Held by the Army in semi-captivity since August, Charles made his escape in November, choosing to place himself in the hands of Colonel Robert Hammond, Governor of the Island since September and still only 26 years old. The pens of historians have promoted various reasons for the choice of venue and guardian, some suggesting that Cromwell himself might have deliberately engineered the escape to remove Charles from the punitive reach of Army militants and place him instead in the hands of an officer on whom he could rely. Hammond himself stated the reasons in a speech to the island's gentry: *'He (Charles) informs me necessity brought him hither and there were a sort of people near Hampton Court, from whence he came, that ....were resolved to murder him...and therefore so privately he was forced to come away and so to thrust himself on this island'* [16.]

The King spent a night or two at Titchfield House before crossing the Solent on November 13th. That same day, Hammond, still unaware of the new responsibility which monarch and fate had decided to place on his shoulders, set out from Carisbrooke to Newport to address a meeting of islanders. Somewhere on the road, he received the news from two gentlemen that Charles Stuart was about to disembark. *'O, Gentlemen'*, he was heard to exclaim. *'You have undone me by bringing the King into the island, if at least you have brought him; and if you have not, pray let him not come'.*[17]

The unhappy monarch spent the night of the 13th at the 'Plume of Feathers' in Cowes, his arrival a poorly guarded secret that quickly became public. *'I could do nothing but sigh and weep for two nights and a day. And the reason for my grief was that I verily believed he could not come into a worse place'.* Oglander wrote in his notebook. A woman on the road to Carisbrooke offered the King a freshly picked rose while others, greeting him like Christ riding into Jerusalem, laid branches at his feet.

Constitutional monarchy might have been established during those dismal days of captivity at Carisbrooke. Two days after taking up his quarters in the castle, he drafted proposals for peace with Parliament, the most conciliatory terms offered so far and well within

---

16 The Commonplace Book of Sir J.Oglander p.114   17 Op. Cit.

the boundaries of what moderates at Westminster would be likely to accept. On Christmas Eve, the Earl of Denbigh arrived to present the Houses' response: total and unconditional submission to Westminster's hardening demands. But a third player arrived next day, commissioners from Scotland still nurturing a hope for accord. On Christmas Day, in the castle's great chamber, the second war effectively began: in return for a Scottish invasion of England, Charles, the deposed, would recognise the Covenant and implement Presbyterianism in his kingdom for at least three years. Encased in lead and buried in an island garden, the written agreement seems never to have crossed the Solent. Three days later, Charles handed Denbigh his final, blunt rejection of Parliament's demands, confident of Scottish support: '*His Majesty cannot imagine how to give such an answer to what is now proposed, as thereby to promise himself his great end, a Perfect Peace. And when his Majesty further considers, how impossible it is (in the condition he now stands) to fulfil the desire of his two Houses; since the only ancient and known ways of passing laws, are either by his Majesty's Personal Assent in the House of Peers, or by commission under the Great Seal of England. He cannot but wonder at such failings in the manner of address, which is now made unto him*'.[18] In January 1648 Parliament at last resolved to finally break off negotiations with the King and his journey to the scaffold had begun.

He might still, however, have re-secured his throne. At the head of the Scots and Irish, and with continental mercenaries and Papists in his ranks, Charles the Divine could have swept to victory, overturning Presbyterianism, the Covenant and the dangerous tendencies towards liberty of the subject. But first he would need to reach those more distant lands from his close confinement on a south coast island and pass through territories that lay in enemy hands.

Escape from Carisbrooke proved impossible, as coming events soon showed. But Charles the dreamer remained Charles the

---

18 'His Majesty's Most Gracious Answer to the Bills and Propositions presented to him' Hants. Records Office 15M84 23/5

'A KNAVISH COMMITTEE OF CLOWNS'

Carisbrooke Castle
(Reproduced with kind permission of Isle of Wight Records Office)

schemer, the forger of plans and always receptive to other people's suggestions. Accounts of his near escape are legion, some factual, some embroidered, full of heroes and dark plotting, and the subject matter of fanciful novels. A laundress called Mary, who placed messages under carpets, willing accomplices in the stables and kitchens, and a man called Henry Firebrace all feature in the plots to extricate the King. On 20th March 1648 Charles made his first attempt. Two months later, on 28th May, he tried again, this time descending by rope to the castle courtyard. But Hammond was doing his job too well and his men held the gates securely. Hammond and his prisoner had apparently met almost daily, conversing on the green or in the governor's chamber - cordially at first and with degree of mutual respect. But the King had become *'much discontented with Hammond and said it would be wisdom in him to use him better, for one day he might be beholden to him or his son for help. Hammond replied, 'you are grown very high since you came into the Island'. Whereupon the King said, 'Then it is my shoemaker's fault; and looking on the soles of his shoes, said he found himself no higher than before'.*[19]

News of the defeat of the Scots at Preston on 17th August 1648 brought Charles down to size and sealed his eventual fate and even he, always somehow seeing light in the darkness of the future, was forced to concede that nothing promising now lay ahead.

On 6th September he was taken to new lodgings in the grammar school in Newport. He and his enemies met in an earnest but fruitless round of discussions, but few observers expected success. He had conceded to most of Parliament's demands, giving ground on all but the thorny issue of Presbyterianism. But if the politicians still had some hope for an eventual agreement, the military leaders had lost all patience. On November 16th the officers in council talked seriously of trial for high treason, describing the King as *'the capital and grand author of all our troubles'*. On 29th November he was formally arrested and taken to Hurst Castle, where he

---

[19] The Commonplace Book of Sir J. Oglander p.128

remained until December 10th, destined for the final journey of his life and an appointment with the executioner's axe. Arriving in Winchester on the 10th he was greeted by the Mayor and aldermen and presented with the Mace, *'as though he were King in all but name'*. Spending just one night in the security of the castle he continued his unhappy journey to Windsor.

Captain Robert Burley, the faithful officer who had masterminded the King's failed escape from the island, died first. Tried in the Great Hall of Winchester Castle on 22nd January 1648, he was condemned *'to be drawn from his prison to the place of execution; as being unworthy to tread anymore upon his Mother Earth, backward, with his head downward, for that he had been retrograde to dutiful courses; hanged by the neck between heaven and earth, as not deserving the enjoyment of either'*.

On 30th January 1649, Charles was executed in London for even greater crimes against the state. *'The blow I saw given'*, wrote an eye witness to the sad event, *'and can truly say, with a sad heart, at the instant whereof I remember well, there was such a groan by the thousands then present as I never heard before and desire I may never hear again'*.[20]

His death would not end the recriminations or the internecine bitterness. This had become too deep rooted in the Englishman's psyche -and a myriad of different political and religious views would come welling to the surface. A facade of unity and military dictatorship was eventually imposed over the tortured nation, ushering in a period of rule that was no more benign or generous to man's aspirations than the worst excesses of Charles Stuart. The 'martyred' King should be allowed the final words. Written in his hours of captivity at Carisbrooke, his poem reveals a personal loss of hope for his own future and perhaps hints at his belief that he was about to serve as the Redeemer for his people:

> *'Great Monarch of the World, from whose power springs*
> *The potency and power of Kings,*

---

20 Letters and Diaries of P.Henry p.12

'A KNAVISH COMMITTEE OF CLOWNS'

Record the royal woe my suffering brings,
But, Sacred Saviour, with Thy words I woo
Thee to forgive, and not be bitter to
Such as Thou know'st do not know what they do'.[21]

The legacy: Perhaps as much as 15% of Hampshire's land changed hands in the years following the war. New landlords, those who had chosen the winning side or had the means to buy, moved in, seeing the rolling acres as the source of profit and new status. Different masters for a while prevailed, but the dull monotony of rural routine, never really halted by the war's demands, continued as it had for years gone by. Maidens still courted on village greens and the slow economy of rustic life droned on, like an unstoppable engine with unalterable parts. A decade later, when fortunes were reversed and Kings restored, much of this land would revert to its former owners, and lordly ways would be known again.

Other surface scars of war were just as quick to mend: weathervanes on spires, felled by passing troopers, were replaced, and grapeshot holes in doors and walls softened with the passing of time. But the deeper scars on hearts and minds took far longer to fade. Three hundred or more of Hampshire's folk probably died in battle, and as many more were maimed or mutilated. For the families of the unfortunate, life might never resume its pre-war pattern, and vagrancy or poverty would be the end result. Yet seen in the context of the county's thousands, they would be a mere drop, reminders of the age just past and a burden on the parish rates. The war, with all its nightmare reality and shattered limbs, was to be as transitory as the passing seasons.

Faded scars remain today: the pock-marked and ivy clad walls of houses and churches where men had fought and watched, countless inns and taverns in which Cromwell was reputed to have slept and the road side sign from which mutinous soldiers are reported to have been hanged. And some of those who watched and

---

21 'Letters Archaelogical and Historical Collected by E. Boucher James' Vol. II page 195

fought still remain, recorded in stories that have passed down through succeeding generations. In Andover's Union Street a headless cavalier sometimes appears. Those unfortunate enough to be pointed at with his sword are destined to die. And at Wolversdene a grief-stricken girl still sobs audibly. The daughter of a strict Roundhead, she had fallen in love with a young Cavalier quartered nearby. Their clandestine romance was nurtured in the hours of darkness: moonlit walks and lovers' pledges of eternal fidelity. One night she was followed by her suspicious father and the young soldier was killed in the consequent dispute. Unconsolable, the girl threw herself from an upstairs window---and her soul has never found rest nor comfort. At Coombe Manor another young Cavalier had hung inside a chimney by his fingertips while New Model soldiers searched the building. Spotted by a vigilant soldier on the rooftop, the fugitive's fingers were chopped off. A bloodstain on the hearth where he died usually re-appears as soon as it is washed away.

Countless other stories are told: men galloping through the night, their horses lathered in sweat and the animals' eyes glowing white in the darkness, men with a sense of purpose travelling along Hampshire roads and with hats pulled low. Other accounts tell of shadowy images outside wayside inns or at village crossroads, some with carbines in their hands, some in shrouds, all replaying the last hours of their earthly life.

Amongst the living, the war sometimes retains an indelible place. Long-standing rivalry between the villages of Upper and Lower Clatford have only recently faded. The former had declared for Westminster, the latter for the King. Men throughout the nation still champion the cause of a martyred king and mention of Cromwell might cause these champions to curse. And several thousand men, women and children frequently go out to re-enact the battles, sieges and skirmishes of those dreadful years. For all of these, the war still goes on.

INDEX

Note: a few places and personalities appear on almost every page and consequently the references are too numerous to be listed. These are: Basing; King Charles 1; Farnham; Col. Richard Norton; Lord Paulet, Marquis of Winchester, Portsmouth, the city of Winchester and William Waller

Only places and personalities directly involved in the Hampshire war or events of national significance are included.

A

Abingdon 247, 260, 284, 287, 294, 300
Abbotstone 397
Adwell 252
Aldbourne, Battle of 121-122
Aldermaston 287, 289, 295, 315
Aldershot 96, 102, 195
Alton 97-99(1st Battle of), 142,145, 159,163, 167, 172, 173, 175, 176, 177 179, 178-185 (2nd Battle of), 186, 188, 209, 232, 248, 267, 316, 323, 328, 330-31, 357
Amesbury 165, 331, 354
Andover 8,12, 13, 16, 25, 27, 34, 83, 92, 96, 103, 131, 142, 145,163, 208, 235-37, 254, 256, 266, 286, 290, 301-04, 319, 330-33, 346, 361 374, 393, 400, 414
Appleyard, Col. Sir Matthew 219, 220, 222
Apsley, Col. Allen 166, 219
Apsley, Col. Edward 173, 174
Arundel 88,89,159, 173-74, 187-88, 190-92, 194-96, 209, 316
Arundel, Earl of (Thomas Mowbray) 88
Arundel, Sir John 405
Archer, Elias 143, 145, 150, 164, 177, 180, 211, 231
Alresford 8, 148, 163, 172-73, 208, 213, 214, 218, 231, 323, 340, 347, 374
Ashburnham, William 405
Astley, Sir Bernard 219
Astley, Sir Jacob 162,166, 172-73, 195, 306, 398

Aston, Sir Arthur 68, 102, 283
Aston, Sir Thomas 128

B

Badd, Thomas 405
Bagshot 247-8
Baillie, Robert 336, 391
Balfour, Sir William 175, 208, 210, 213-14, 221, 226, 233, 236, 237, 306,311
Ballard, Thomas 65
Bampfield, Col. Edward 173-74, 187-88, 191, 194
Barrack, Samuel 405
Barrington, Sir John 22
Bard, Sir Henry 110, 219, 224
Basing House **see note at top**
Basingstoke 3, 12-13, 71, 102, 138,148,162-63, 171, 248, 252, 254, 286, 292, 302-04, 318, 374, 384, 390, 396
Beacham, William 405
Beaulieu 3
Beasley, Tobias 334
Belasyse, Col. John 188
Bennet, Sir Humphrey 141, 158, 173, 187, 219, 227, 312, 368
Bentley 357
Berkeley, Sir John 132, 166, 171
Bettesworth, Capt. Thomas 107, 138, 275, 350, 390
Bevis, Richard 405
Birch, Col. John 180 184, 229, 231
Bishop, Sir Edward 195

415

Bishopstoke 339
Bishops Waltham 83, 93 204, 208, 239, **240**, 323, 330, 360
Blandford
Blagge, Sir Thomas 312
Bolles, Col. John 163, 166, 175, 177, 180, 184
Boteler, Sir William 188, 219
Bowerman, Thomas 262
Bowerman, William 262
Botley 239
Boys, Sir John 256
Braxton, Richard 405
Brading 55
Bramdean 208, 224, 226-227
Bramley 248
Bramshill House 5
Breamore House 5
Brentford, Battle of 67-68
Brentford, Earl of (Patrick Ruthven) 217, 224
Brereton, Sir William 201
Brett, Jerome 53-56, 59
Bristol 95-96, 112, 119, 302
Broad Chalke 355
Brook, Thomas 405
Brown, John 405
Browne, Col. Richard (or Brown) 77, 79, 88, 203, 210, 234, 243, 287, 294-96
Brundon 176
Bucke, Brutus 58
Bufford, Benjamin 405
Bulkeley, John 24, 138
Bulkeley, Joseph 262
Butcher, Thomas 405
Buncle, Lt. Col. 290
Burrell, Co. Robert 118
Burghfield 296
Burley, John 58
Burley, Capt. Robert 412
Bushell, Capt. Browne 43, 48, 59, 63
Butler, Col. John 345-46
Button, John 27, 138, 262
Bye, Fernando 405
Byron, Sir John 125-28
Byron, Sir Nicholas 127
Byron, Sir Thomas 166
Burrell, Col. Robert 118

C

Calshot castle 71, 103, 135
Campion, Sir Henry 27, 138
Capel, Lord 405
Carrick, William 138
Carne, Col. Thomas 136-37, 262, 301
Carnwarth, Earl of (Robert Dalzell) 351
Carr, Col. James 178, 218, 228-29, 303
Carey, St. Maj. 100
Carey, Col. Edward 80
Carey, Col. Horatio 166, 193
Carey, Col. Lucius, Viscount Falkland 25-26, 127
Carisbrooke castle 24, 54-55, 58-59, 408-9, **410**, 412
Carnarvon, Earl of (Robert Dormer) 103, 125
Carrick, William 138
Catherington 210
Challoner, Capt. 47-48
Chandeler, Thomas 138
CharlesI **see note at top**
'Charles' 43, 59, 70
Chase 374
Cheriton, Battle of 197, 215, **216**, 217-233, 241, 303, 316, 345
Chilton Candover 148
Chineham
Chichester 7, 43, 85-89, 93, 99, 142, 159, 172-73, 192-93, 210, 389
Chittey, Henry 85-86
Churcher, Alexander 405
Christchurch 7, 24, 26-27, 237, 323, 325, 327, 374
Clarke, Sir Henry 405
Clarke, Sir William (or Clerke) 219
Clarendon, Earl of (Sir Edward Hyde) 19, 21, 23, 25-26, 37, 52-53, 105-06, 227, 303, 316-17, 370
Clerke, Thomas 138
Cleveland, Earl of (Thomas Wentworth) 311
Clinson, Capt. 153, 157
Clubmen 353-55, 358, 359-60
Colden Common 360
Cole, Edward 397
Coleraine, Lord 388

Collingbourne 401
Collins, William 138
Colson, John 405
Cooke, Edward 214
Cooke, Sir Francis 219, 320
Coreham, Roger 405
Cornelius Jasper 202, 405
Cottington, Lord 405
Cotton family 192
Courtney, Sir William 219
Covert, Sir John 166
Cowdray House 159, 172, 188
Cowes 24, 54-56, 58-59, 135, 408
Craddock, Thomas 405
Crane, John 405
Crapp, Henry 405
Crawford, Lord Ludovic Lindsay 90,113, 132-33, 142, 145, 153, 166, 173, 175-76, 185, 193
Crawford, Lawrence 300, 336
Cresswell, Thomas 138
Crisp, Sir Nicholas 219
Crondall 73, 145 **146**, 168, 319, 321, 329, 330
Cropredy Bridge 261-64, 273, 283
Cromwell, Oliver 304-06, 312, 317, 319, 324, 332-38, 341-43, 355, 361, 363-5, 367-8, 370, 373-7, 381, 387-9, 390, 397, 407-8
Cuffaud, Capt. (or Cuffaud) 274, 278 383
Cully, Robert 405
Curle, Walter, Bishop of Winchester 239, 364, 370, 372, 374

D

Dalbier, John 214, 358-61, 373-75, 382, 389
Davies, Matthew 24, 26
Day, Henry 405
Deane, Capt. Richard 375
De la Warr family 341
Denbigh, Earl of (Basil Feilding) 409
Denham, Sir John 75
Dennet, Richard 405
Dering, Sir Edward 166
Devizes 105
Digby, Lord George 392, 403
Dillington, Robert 54-55

Dingley, Sir John 54
Doddington, Edward 138
Doddington, John 138
Doddington, William
Donnington Castle 256, 299, 300, 302, 306, 308-09, 312-13, 337, 387, 389-90
Douse, Thomas 138
Dowett, Francis 320
Dowse, Giles 405

E

East Meon (see Meon)
Eaton, Robert 86
Edgecombe, Pearce 405
Edgecombe, Richard 405
Edgehill, Battle of 64-66, 73, 78, 122
Edmundsen, Henry 92
Edwards, Richard 24
Elliott, John 138
Erle, Sir Walter 113, 324
Essex, Earl of (Robert Devereux) 35, 64-65, 68, 88, 99, 102-03, 112, 116, 121, 123, 125-26, 137, 175, 186, 202, 206, 246-47, 272-73, 275, 286, 301-02, 304-06, 311, 328, 331, 334, 337-38, 340, 345, 358
Evans, Capt. Thomas 138, 207
Evelin, Arthur 138
Exton, Edward 26,27, 138

F

Fareham 83, 96, 208, 325
Farnham **see note above**
Fairfax, Sir Thomas 338, 345-47, 350, 352-55, 358, 372-3, 387, 404
Fielden, John 138
Fielding, Col. Richard (or Feilding) 232
Fiennes, Celia 9
Fiennes, Capt. Nathaniel 81, 112, 342
Firebrace, Henry 411
Fisher, William 405
Fleetwood, Col. Charles 346, 360, 365
Fleetwood, Col. Dutton 219
Fleetwood, Sir Gerard 405
Fleury, Capt. Raoul 231
Fishers Pond 360
Ford, Sir Edward 86-87, 90-91, 166, 172-

74, 195, 219, 368, 405
Fordingbridge 113-14, 320-21
Fortescue, Col. Richard 346
Forth, Lord 219, 222, 224, 228, 233
Four Marks Hill 147
Foyle, (or Foyell) Henry 394, 405
Fuller, Dowse 405

G

Gage, Col. Henry 284-85, 287, 289, **291**, 292-96, 305, 316-18
Gate, Thomas 138
Gerard, Lord Charles 125, 131, 145, 166, 174
Gerard, Sir Gilbert 125
Gloucester, siege of 119-21
Glemham, Sir Thomas 373
Goddard, Edward 138
Goddard, Richard 405
Gollop, George 26, 27, 138
Gosport 43, 45, 47, 325
Grandison, Lord (William Villiers) 34, 71, 77-78, 80
Granville, Sir Richard 248
Graves, Col. Richard 346
Grenville, Sir Bevil 105
Greywell 109-110, 248, 356
Griffin, Col. Arthur 166
Grove Place 3
Grove, William 138
Goodwin, Sir Arthur 77
Goring, Lord George 22, 23, 24, 26, 34, 36, 37, 39-40, 42-45, 47-48, 50, 52-55, 86, 306, 308, 311-12, 319, 323-31,333, 345, 349, 352, 354-55
Guildford 97, 99, 169, 324, 358
Guy, Richard
Gwater, William 405

H

Hackwood Park 305, 349
Hadley, Thomas 405
Hall, John 135
Hammond, Col. Robert 346, 368, 376-7, 379, 384, 386, 408, 411
Hampden, John 35

Hamilton, Sir James 166
Hanbury, Thomas 138
Harby, William 59
Harley, Col. Edward 222, 226, 229, 231, 236, 239, 346
Harrington, Sir James 243, 306
Harris, John 73
Harrison, Col. Thomas 383
Hartop, Col. Edward 375
Harward, Robert 138
Harting, West 174, 187
Haslemere 188
Havant 38, 87-88, 193
Haywards Heath, skirmish at 87
Henrietta Maria ,Queen 37, 114, 162
'Henrietta Maria', pinnace 37, 43, 202, 204
Herriard 352, 357
Heselrige, Sir Arthur 77, 88, 91, 99, 118, 144, 147-48, 168, 177-78, 180, 186, 214, 221, 224, 226, 228-29, 236, 241, 246-47, 261-62, 305, 323-24, 345
Herbert, Philip (see Pembroke, Earl of)
Hertford, Marquis of 62, 104, 139, 141, 166, 219-220
Heveningham ,William 27
Heyman, Sir Henry 188
Highworth, siege of 352, 354
Hinton Ampner 3, 192, 215, 218, 224, 228
Holborne, John 125, 127
Holles, Denzil 67
Hook 169
Hooke, John 138
Hooper, Edward 138
Hopton, Sir Ralph **see note above**
Hopton, Col. Edward 222
Hopton, Lady 236
Hounsdown, skirmish at 31
Howard, Col. Thomas 219
Hungerford 317
Hursley 106, 114 (1st skirmish), 191, 266, 342-43 (2nd skirmish), 393
Hurst Castle 58, 103, 135, 324, 327, 411
Hutchinson, Lucy 17
Hurry, John (or Urry) 38, 77, 80, 88

418

I

Iford 237
Ingoldsby, Col. Richard 346
Ireton, Sir Henry 345-46
Itchen Stoke 397

J

Jeffreys, Edward 268, 282, 285, 289
Jermyn, Lord Henry 37
Jephson, Col. Morris 325, 328, 390, 401
Jephson, William 25,27, 138
Jervoise family 5, 352
Jervoise, Sir Richard 25,27, 138
Jervoise, Sir Thomas 25,27, 64, 72, 96, 107, 137-38, 294, 352
Jones, Elias 114
Jones, Inigo 384
Jones, John 405
Jones, Col. Samuel 144, 163, 178, 214, 249-50, 252, 319, 322, 324

K

Kelsey, Henry 405
Kemp, John 138
Kercher, Thomas 405
King, Henry, Bishop of Chichester 91
Kingsclere 103, 162
Kingsmill, Sir William 390
Kings Somborne 266, 339, 341
Kings Worthy 372
Kitwell, John 138
Knollys, Sir Francis 3
Knowles, Edward 405
Knowles, Katherine 405

L

Lacy, William 405
Lan, Thomas 405
Lane, John 405
Langdale, Sir Marmaduke 330-31
Lansdown Battle of 104-05, 118
Langport, Battle of 355
Laud, William, Archbishop of 13

Lawson, Richard 405
Layton, Sir Ellis 195
Legge, Maj. Robert 220
Leigh, Sir John 27, 54, 137, 262
Leighton, Lt. Col. Walter 218, 222
Lenthall, William 323, 401
Leven, Earl of (Alexander Leslie) 200-01, 391
Lewknor, Christopher 85, 90
Lewis, Sir William 27, 63, 93, 138
Lindsey, Col. Andrew 219
Linkhorn, Sir James 405
Littlecote House 352
Lisle Family 5
Lisle, Sir George 217, 219, 221
Lisle, John 25,27, 63, 137-38, 259, 262, 358
Lisle, Lord Philip 27
Lisle, Sir William 262
Livesey, Sir Michael 89, 169, 190, 214, 226, 261, 345
Lloyd, Col. Walter 346
Long Sutton 163
Longford Castle, siege of 320, 349, 373, 387
Longland, William 363
Lostwithiel, surrender at 282-3, 311
Love, Nicholas 138, 393
Love, Richard 138
Lower, Maj. Philip 325, 327, 374
Lucy, Sir Spencer 405
Ludlow, Edmund 286, 315, 320-21, 327, 342, 349
Luke, Sir Samuel 142, 319
Lumley, Lord 405
Lyme, siege of 112, 247, 261, 272, 315
Lymington 9, 27, 114, 327, 390

M

Major, Richard 24,33, 138
Malmesbury 102
Malshanger House 3
Manchester, Earl of (Edward Montague) 206, 284, 286, 299, 300, 302, 304, 306, 308-9, 312, 324, 332, 334, 336-8, 345
Marlborough 75,79, 201, 236, 243, 314, 317

Marding 174
Marston Moor, Battle of 263-64
Marshall's Elm, skirmish at 62
Marwell, skirmish at 332-3
Mason, Robert 202
Mason, Thomas 138
Massey, Col. Edward 119, 121, 324, 352-3
Mathew, William 405
May, Lord 405
Maynard, William 262
Maurice, Prince 61, 106, 112, 166, 219, 246-47, 306, 308, 311-2, 403
Meldrum, John 65, 214
Meon, East 210, 211, **212**, 214, 400
Meon Valley 93
Meon, West 211
Merrick, Sir John 38, 42
Meux, Bartholomew 262
Meux, John 24, 26, 54
Michelmarsh 367
Micheldever 339
Middleton, Col. John 77, 126, 214
Middle Wallop 286, 346
Midhurst 159, 167, 172, 188, 209, 213, 323
Mildmay family 332
Mill, John 405
Mills, Thomas 405
Millbrook 115, 320
Miller, John 405
Minstead 83
Mowday, William 405
Montague, Col. Edward 346
Montrose, Marquis of (James Graham) 260, 350
Morgan, William 397
More, Richard 138
Morley, Col. Herbert 86, 89, 91, 93, 117, 144, 165, 190, 196, 252, 254, 259-60, 263-64, 269, 273, 277-79, 281, 290, 295, 359
Mottisfont 3, 24
Murford, Maj. Peter 71, 114-15, 137, 139, 141, 186-87, 202
Musgrave, Sir Gerald 405
Mynn, Col. Charles 191

N

Naseby, Battle of 349, 351-2
Newbury and battles of 25, 77, 119, 122-130 (1st Battle), 138, 208, 236, 256, 284, 295, 299, 300, 304, 306, 308, 313, 315, 320, 335-6, 345-7 (2nd Battle) 389-90, 400
Newcastle, Marquis of 200
Netley 3, 71, 139, 141
Newnham 356
Newport 25, 26, 27, 54-56, 59-60, 135, 301, 411
Newton 24, 26
Neville, Col. Richard 219, 231, 235
Nicholas, Sir Edward 158, 300, 405
Northampton, Earl of (James Compton) 304
Norton family 5, 24, 405
Norton, Lady 116
Norton, Sir Gregory 137, 262
Norton, Col. Richard **see note above**
Nottingham, standard raised at 44, 58, 61, 85
Noyse, Richard 405
Nursling 115, 204
Nuttier, John 405

O

Odiham 93, 96, 142, 163, 167, 169-171, 195, 203, 205, 208, 239-41, **242**, 248-49, 250, 252, 255, 258, 317, 319, 327, 330, 342, 349, 390
Oglander, Sir John 23, 54-56, 83, 135-36, 399, 408
Ogle, Sir William 22, 24-26, 77-78, 80, 99, 108, 131-32, 142, 208, 210, 235, 265, 268, 289-90, 332-4, 339, 341-3, 353, 363-7, 370-2, 375, 400, 405
Oliver's Battery 196, 342
Onslow (or Onslowe), Sir Richard 252, 254, 259-60, 263, 270, 285, 294
Onwins, John 405
Oram, Capt. 278
Owlesbury 332-3

P

Padworth 295
Paget, James 3
Pangbourne 296
Paulet family 114, 166, 219
Paulet, Edward 248
Paulet, Henry 109-110, 117, 405
Paulet, Lord John (see Marquis of Winchester)
Peake, Sir Robert 109-110, 155,157, 165-66, 294, 381, 384-5, 397-8
Percy, Lord Henry 333
Pelate, Rev. H. 338
Pell, Col. Bartholomew 388
Penn, Sir William 325
Pembroke, Earl of (Philip Herbert) 27-28, 33, 53-54, 63, 87, 301
Percy, Lord Henry 147, 162, 166
Peters, Rev. Hugh 365, 366, 371-2, 375, 386
Petersfield 8,12, 24, 26-7, 83, 96, 159, 163, 172-74, 190, 203, 210, 215, 304, 314, 321, 324, 327, 330, 332, 353, 358, 360, 390
Petsworth 167, 203, 209-10, 323-4
Phillipps, Sir James 405
Philpot, George 405
Philpot, George 405
Philpot, Thomas 405
Philpot, Villiers 405
Pickering, Col. John 346, 365, 375, 377, 379
Pierce, (or Peirce) Col. Edmond 29
Pirbright 167
Pitman, Capt. John 107,138
Poole, siege of 62, 112-14, 132-35, 147, 315, 324
Popham, Alexander 286, 352
Popham, Edward 104, 352
Portland, Earl of (Jerome Weston) 22, 23, 52-3
Portsbridge 37, 39, 43, 325, 328
Portsdown 37, 39, 304, 325
Portman, Sir William 405
Portsmouth see note above
Porstsea 37, 39, 43, 93, 116
Potley, Col. Andrew 148, 178, 214, 218, 262

Powick bridge, skirmish at 64
Potynger John 73
Poyntz, Sedenham 403
Preston, Battle of 411
Preston Candover 233
Pye, Col. Robert 346

Q

Quincy, William 340

R

Rainsborough, Col. Thomas 346
Rainsford, Henry 25
Ramsey, Sir James 67-8, 87
Rawdon, Sir Marmaduke 110, 149, 155, 157, 165-66, 249, 252, 279, 344-5
Read, Moses 54-5, 59
Read, Nicholas 340
Reading 68, 102, 162, 195, 235, 247, 254, 284, 287, 295, 299, 306, 315, 322, 340
Redbridge 190
Rich, Henry, Earl of Holland 391
Rich, Col. Nathaniel 346
Rich, Robert see Earl of Warwick
Richards, Sir Edward 405
Riggs, Ralph 138
Ringwood 113-4, 237, 320, 327, 341
Rivers, Francis 138
Roberts, Lt. Col. Nicholas 89
Robinson, Nathaniel 115
Romsey 8, 13, 34, 101, 107, 110, 115, 138, 141, 163, 173, 186-87, 201-02, 204, 207, 210, 235, 238, 323-5, 342-3, 347, **348**, 350, 352, 353
Rossiter, Col. Edward 346
Roundway Down, Battle of 106, 118, 141, 209, 232
Rowkeshill 359
Rupert, Prince 61, 67, 97, 101, 122-23, 125, 127, 158, 174, 190, 195, 201, 263, 300, 302, 318, 403
Rushworth, John 336, 371

S

Sadler, Thomas 405
Say, William 405
Salisbury 101, 135, 145, 246, 256, 286, 299, 300-02, 319-21, 327-8, 331-2, 341, 349
Sandown Castle 58
Sandys family 3, 24, 158
Seale, Peter 69-71, 96
Seviour, John 405
Seymour, William (see Marquis of Hertford)
Sheffield, Col. James 346, 365
Shelley, Henry 219
Sherfield 252
Silvester, Joshua 406
Sixpenny Handley 347
Skippon, Philip 88, 123, 126, 128, 282, 304, 306, 311-12, 340, 346
Slingsby, Col. Walter 211, 219, 226-27
Smith, Bartholomew 406
Smith, (or Smyth) Sir John 20, 78, 217, 219, 227
Southampton 10-11, 13, 27, 30, 45, 69, 70-71, 75, 92-93, 96, 107, 112, 114-15, 117, 135, 138, 139, 141-42, 187, 190-91, 202, 239, 243, 246-47, 263, 265, 277, 299, 301, 390
Southampton, Earl of (Thomas Wriothesley) 3, 21, 32, 138-39, 141, 400, 406
Southampton, Countess of 357
Southsea Castle 47, 48, **49**, 50, 103
Southwick 38, 208
Speed, John 10
Spencer, Col. Richard 166
Sprigge, Joshua 373, 387, 389
Springate, Sir William 144, 190, 196
St. Barbe, Francis 24, 33, 107, 110, 115, 127, 138
St. John, Oliver 336
Stapeley, Col. Anthony 91
Stapleton, Sir Philip 122-27, 138
Stawell family 3
Stawell, Sir Edward 3, 166, 170, 192, 213, 219, 227
Stewart, Maj. 107
Stockbridge 1, 25, 27, 34, 83, 92, 138, 236, 238, 323, 330, 400
Stoke Charity 235
Stoneham 115

Stourton family 83
Stow-on-the-Wold, Battle of 398
Stratton, Battle of 104
Strode, William 315-6
Stuart, Lord John 206, 219, 229
Stubbington, Richard 406
Stukeley family 215
Sutton common 215
Swanley, Capt. Richard 43, 55, 58-9, 63, 70-1, 87
Swaine, William 406
Swainston 135
Sydenham, Capt. Francis 132-3

T

Talbot, Sir Gilbert 219
Tate, Zouch 337
Thompson, Col. George 214, 261
Thorney Island 87
Tichborne 209, 211, 231
Tichborne family 24, 203
Tichborne, Sir Benjamin 24, 406
Tichborne, Sir Henry 24
Tichborne, Sir Richard 131, 406
Titchborne, Sir Robert 24
Tisted, West 24
Titchfield 3, 325, 357, 408
Torrington, Battle of 398
Treyford 210-11
Trusell, John
Thatcham 295, 306
Tucker, Robert 406
Tull, James 138
Tulse, Henry 24
Turner, Col. Richard 118, 148
Turney, Capt. Humphrey 55-6
Turnham Green, near-action at 67-8
Twyford 187, 332, 360 skirmish at 203

U

Upton Gray 356-7
Uvedale, Sir William 24, 26
Upham 87

V

Vane, Henry 336
Vandruske, Col. Jonas 118, 147, 170, 214, 261
Vaughan, Sir George 166, 219
Vavasour, Sir Charles 219
Vavasour, Sir William 175
Vermuyden, Col. Cornelius 346, 365
Verney, Sir Edmund 19-20
Vernon, Henry
Vicars, John 18, 39, 44, 48, 52, 79, 89, 91
Villiers, William, Lord Grandison
Vyne, the 3, 158

W

Wait, Ambrose 406
Waldegrave, Sir Edward 219
Waller, Col. Hardress 346, 365, 375, 381
Waller, Sir William **see note above**
Wallop, Sir Henry 25-26 ,27
Wallop, Robert 25, 27, 64, 107, 138
Wallop, see Middle Wallop
Wansey, Henry 320
Warblington House 192-94
Wardour Castle, sieges of 108
Warnborough, skirmish at 249-51
Warnford 163, 211
Warwick, Earl of (Robert Rich) 42, 135, 138, 202
Wavell, Thomas 262
Webb, Col. William 284, 290
Weborne, John 406
Weldon, Sir Ralph 144, 206, 214, 248, 262, 324-5, 345-6, 350
Wells, Swithin 406
Wentworth, Thomas (Earl of Cleveland) 39-40, 45, 311
West family, de la Warr
Westbourne 191
West Meon, see Meon
Weston, Jerome, see Portland, Earl of
Weston, Nicholas 22, 23, 36, 52, 54, 59
Weyhill 12
Weymys, Lt. Col. James 231, 261
Whalley, Col. Edward 342, 346
Wherwell 3, 78 (skirmish at), 131, 196, 236, 341

Whitchurch 8, 25, 27, 142, 304
Whitehead, Sir Richard 25, 27, 33, 63, 70, 114-5, 138, 277-8, 286, 324-5
Wickham 239, 332
Wight, Isle of 52-3, 57, 60, 63, 83, 135-7, 262, 299, 327, 407
Willis, Thomas 406
Wilmot, Lord 125, 190
Wilton 108, 237, 399
Winchester **see note above**
Winchester, Marquis of (Lord John Paulet) **see note above**
Wilson, Alexander 138
Wither, William 138
Woodman, John 394
Worldom, East and West 145
Woulger, William 138
Wolversdene 414
Wolvesey Palace 373
Worsley, Sir Henry 27, 137-8, 262
Wortley, Sir Francis 370
Wriothesley, Thomas, (see Southampton, Earl of)
Wyatt, Thomas 406

Y

Yarmouth castle 24, 27, 58

Z

Zouche, Lord 5